Suddenly

George F. Will

Suddenly

The American Idea Abroad and At Home 1986–1990

THE FREE PRESS
A Division of Macmillan, Inc.
NEW YORK

Collier Macmillan Canada
TORONTO

Maxwell Macmillan International
NEW YORK   OXFORD   SINGAPORE   SYDNEY

The Free Press
A Division of Macmillan, Inc.
866 Third Avenue, New York, N.Y. 10022

Collier Macmillan Canada, Inc.
1200 Eglinton Avenue East
Suite 200
Don Mills, Ontario M3C 3N1

Printed in the United States of America

printing number

1   2   3   4   5   6   7   8   9   10

Library of Congress Cataloging-in-Publication Data

Will, George F.
    Suddenly : the American idea abroad and at home 1986–1990 / George
F. Will.
      p. cm.
    Includes index.
    ISBN 0–02–934435–2
    1. United States—Politics and government—1981-1989. 2. United
States—Politics and government—1989– 3. World
politics—1985–1995. 4. United States—Civilization—1970–
5. Democracy—History—20th century. I. Title.
E876.W56 1990
973.928—dc20

90–3851
CIP

To the Memory of
HENRY M. JACKSON

Suddenly freedom prevailed.
But only because freedom's friends,
such as Scoop Jackson,
waged the long twilight struggle.

Contents

Introduction   xiii

1. OVERTURE   1

Making History and Orphans   3
1789's Echo in Iron   5
They Are the Children   7
Ideological Storms   9
Tearing the Social Threads   11
Hobbes in Chicago   13
Agitprop in New York   15
Subsidized Shocking of the Bourgeoisie   17
"If You Must Sleep With More Than One Partner . . ."
  Must?   19
The Triumph of Pharmacology   21
A Professional's Sense of Responsibility   23
Wilding: Evil in the Park   25
"Tragedy" As an Entitlement   27
"Merely" a Nurse   29
"Throw Deep"   31
1986: A Typical 1986   33
1987: "Keep Honking, I'm Reloading"   36
1988: Year of Oat Bran and Ozone   38
1989: History Clears Its Throat   41
The 1980s: The Suicide of Socialism, and Other
  Pleasures   43

2. THE CURTAIN COMES DOWN   47

Europe's Second Reformation   49
Gorbachev, Meet Jefferson   52

The American Idea in Tiananmen Square   53
A Dark Theory Slain by Luminous Facts   55
Death of a Pensioner   57
Science and the Primitives   59
Irina's Choice   61
Beneath Lenin's Glare   63
Jokes As Tiny Revolutions   65
Gorbachev and the "1946 Rules"   68
The Sickening Soviet Reality   70
Marx's Nationalities Problem   72
Lithuania and South Carolina   74
Capitalism's Modern Times   77
Bonapartism in Poland   79
The Man Who Is Not Paganini   81
"Communism"? Never Heard of It   83
What "Community" of Nations?   85
New School Ties   87
New Truths About the Wired World   89
Totalitarianism Falls to the Suction Effect   91
Germany: From Spiked Helmets to Soft Caps   93
Germany: Seeing the Solution As a Problem   95
The Quadrille of Nations   97
"Wir Sind Wieder Da"   99
Are Germans Always Dangerous?   101
Realism in Machiavelli Country   103
Inventing Europe   105
Margaret Thatcher: A Nation's Nanny   107
Prime Minister of the Wrong Country   109
British Socialism Comes Down in the World   112
Romanticizing the Missile Crisis   114
Good News Makes Some Liberals Morose   116
John Foster Dulles: Re-moralizer   118
Maxwell Taylor: From Hot War to Cold   120
American Power: Machiavellian and Moral   122
Remembrance of Another War Worth Winning   124
Treblinka's Unquiet Earth   126
Sowing Seeds of Democracy   128
Woodrow Wilson's Hour Comes 'Round   130

The Good Neighbor Policy in Panama   132
The Revision of Reputations   134
A Tale of Two Julys   136

3. AMERICAN GOVERNANCE: GOING THROUGH
THE MOTIONS   139

Ronald Reagan: The Captain Who Calmed the Sea   141
George Bush's Rightmindedness   150
George the Good, If He Does Say So Himself   152
Government As an Ethics-Free Zone   155
The Bush Presidency's Hollow Center   157
Conservatives Making Big Government Cheap   158
The Pastel President   161
America's Weak Commitment to Progressive Taxation   163
Abandoning the Income Tax, Absentmindedly   165
Dr. Moynihan Suggests Surgery   167
To the Boca Raton Station   169
Listen to the Bridges   171
Hamiltonian Conservatism and "Internal Improvements"   173
The Basin Runneth Over   175
Dayton's Mundane Machines and Your Taxes   177
Playing With Guns   179
The Weathervane of the Western World   181
Slow-Motion Death in Miami   183
Desperate Euphoria in the Ghetto   185
Mothers Who Don't Know How   187
Where Bayonets Are Beside the Point   189
Fighting Drugs: Blame America First   191
A Gang Banger Goes to Jail, Briefly   193
Hooked on Legalization   196
Life Becomes More Regressive: The Case of Drugs   198
The Pleasures of a Killjoy   200
The Trauma in Trauma Care   202
"Life Is Priceless" Is Useful Nonsense   204
The Flag, the First Amendment and the President's
    Viscera   206
Crime Wave in the Locker Room   208
Too Bad Rousseau Was Not an Eskimo   210

Allan Bloom in the Bazaar of Culture   212
Professors Playing Politics   214
Don't Worry: Half of All College Seniors Have Heard
    of Moby Dick   216
The Politics of Cheating the Children   218
A School for Families   220
Mayor Daley, Act II   222
New York, New York, It's a Declining Town   224
Houston Hits the Comeback Trail   226
Lyndon and the Liberal   228
Mario Cuomo's Sparring Spirit   230
Democrats Learn a New Language   232
A Law to Send Lawmakers Home?   235
In the Grip of Gambling   237
"Realism" by the Polls   239
Bush's Year One: The Echoing Emptiness   241
Less About the Man in the Kremlin, More About the
    Boy in the Bronx   243

4. THE MINIATURIZATION OF AMERICAN
POLITICS   247

Surely He Didn't Say That! (Yes, He Did)   249
Two Cheers for Iowa   251
The Rhythm Method of Politics   253
Lincoln-Douglas Without Either   255
Oh, Go Bowling, Both of You   257
Boomerology, With Fries   259
Jesse Jackson's Verbal Meringue   261
What Democrats Won't Say   263
Competence Liberalism or Compassion Liberalism:
    It's Still Liberalism   265
The Contraction of the Presidency   267
Dan Quayle's Ideological Lint   269
Quayle the Candidate: Not "The Candidate"   271
So Much Cash, So Few Ideas   273
The Pollution of Politics   275
Honey, We Shrunk the Issues   278
Sound-Bite Debates   280

The Final Debate (Thank God!) 282
The Political Echo of Ecophobia 284
An Argument About Class, Waiting to Be Made 286
Mike, *What . . . do . . . you . . . mean?* 288
The (Best I Can Do) Case for Dukakis 290
The 5,000 Reasons for Voting for Bush 292
Another Muddy Message 294
The Democrats Get Started on Losing the 1992 Election 296

5. RIGHTS . . . AND WRONGS 299

"Informative and Persuasive" Panhandling 301
The "Right" to Live on Sidewalks 303
Theocracy in Pittsburgh 305
Chemistry and Punishment 307
Capital Punishment: Cruel and Unusual Because
    Infrequent? 309
The Abortion Issue: Back From Litigation to Legislation 311
Abortion: There Are Splittable Differences 313
Abolition and Abortion: Reasoning Lincoln's Way 315
Baby M in the Legal Thicket 317
Censorship the Liberals' Way 319
The Liberals' Racism 322
Rolling Back the Racial Spoils System 324
The Supreme Court Defers to Democracy 326
Punishing Deviation: The Case of an Uppity Black 328
Race As an Intellectual Credential 330

THE BORK CONTROVERSY 333

The Groups Jerk Joe Biden's Leash 335
The Whale and the Anchovies 337
No Due Process in the Confirmation Process 339
Could Justices Black, Harlan and Frankfurter Be
    Confirmed Today? 341
Extremism in Pursuit of Bork Is, Apparently, No Vice 344
The Compassion Industry Against Bork 346
The Bork Nomination 348
The *Post* and Moral Exhibitionism 351

Dear George . . .   353
Senators Say the Darndest Things   354
The Tempting of America   356

6. CODA   359

Why Are We Here? Accidents Do Happen   361
Science and Sensibility   362
In Defense of the Messy Desk   364
The Rolling Stones: A Revolt Turned Into a Style   366
Stephen King: The Horror, the Horror   368
Nubile Feet? Yes, and It Was a Dark and Stormy Night   370
The Enjoyment of Joseph Alsop   372
Sidney Hook, an Honest Man   374
Washington Unrefined   376
The Bouillabaisse of Bookselling   378
Take Me Out to a Night Game   380
Therapeutic Rudeness and Other Signs of Decline   382
Enraging News About Anger   384
Measuring Out Our Lives in Coffee Spoons   386
Ms. Popcorn Detects Cocooning   388
Ambush Advertising and Other Attention-Getting Ideas   390
Spenser Becomes (Say It Ain't So!) Sensitive   392
Tom Wolfe's Lasting News   394
"Play Bail!"   396
"I Was Raised But I Never Grew Up"   398
Only—Only!—The Pleasure of Words   400
Father and Hot Air   402
Modernity Arrived by Bicycle   404
Winston, the User-Friendly Cat   406
Jon's Friend Angel   408

Acknowledgments   411
Index   413

Introduction

Proper conservatives, having a pessimistic bent, go through life hoping to be (and philosophically poised to be) pleasantly surprised. The twentieth century has served up such surprises sparingly. But as the century turned the corner into its tenth decade, such surprises suddenly became plentiful. Abroad, at least. At home, there were fewer reasons for congratulations.

Events invariably are in the saddle, riding journalists. In the period covered by the work in this volume, events gave to this journalist's work two themes, one inspiriting, the other dispiriting. First, the good news.

An argument that has convulsed the politics of this century, and enlivened intellectual life for longer than that, is now over. On one side were those who argued that justice required society to be run from above, from the center, by the commands of a cadre claiming privileged insight into the inexorable, inevitable unfolding dynamic of history. On the other side—the American side, it is fair to call it—were those who argued that justice demands wide dispersal of decision making, broad scope for the private pursuit of happiness as individuals envision it, a pursuit protected and facilitated by government deriving its powers from the consent of the governed.

Of course this latter idea is not America's alone. Parts of it had a distinguished pedigree before America's Founders, who knew they stood on the shoulders of giants, gave it philosophical clarity and institutional life. Still, America has become the most vivid exemplar of the idea in action. It has been thrilling to see the power of that idea as it has been embraced abroad. However, it has been dismaying to watch the American idea debased at home.

In the late 1980s, in the Soviet Union and its satellites, history exuberantly took a hop, skip and jump and the world was suddenly better. The prospect for freedom became brighter than at any time in the memory of anyone now living. Here is one way to gauge the pace and scope of change. There have been large literate publics—newspaper reading publics in many nations—for perhaps a century and a half. Never, until the autumn of 1989, was there a period when, day after day, for many months, newspapers carried headlines that would have been unbelievable six months earlier. In the span of a few months the phrase "bourgeoisie republic" was transformed from an epithet into an aspiration. Who predicted things like this? No one.

Prophecy is an optional folly. For one proud practitioner, it was fatal. Girdana Cardana (1501–76), a mathematician of distinction, also was famous throughout Europe as an astrologer, in which capacity he constructed a horoscope predicting the date of his own death. When the fateful day dawned and found him feeling fine, he could not bear to have his "science" falsified. So he killed himself. Fortunately, we who practice period journalism are not required by the code of our craft to live or die by predictions.

In a collection of columns I published in 1983, a section on Cold War subjects was titled "The War Against the Totalitarians, 1939–   ." Fortunately, nothing lasts, certainly not regimes purporting to have deciphered History. All wars must end, even cold wars. The Cold War had many false dawns, so at first when the concrete seemed to be cracking in the Soviet bloc, skepticism was in order. Then with stunning swiftness the disaffection of the populations within the Soviet sphere reached a critical mass—an amount sufficient to cause a collapse of confidence, and nerve, in the governing class. The drama of communism's demise is not yet played out. The Chinese, Cuban and a few other regimes have set their flinty faces against the future. But communism as a creed, and as a historical movement, is as dead as a doornail.

History has not come to an end, and history means dangers. But the likelihood of a major war, meaning a conflict between the great powers, is less now than ever before in my lifetime (which began six months before Pearl Harbor). The game of nations never ends, but the sudden revision of the rules of that game has been a news story unlike any we are apt to see again. Rarely if ever can it have been as much fun to be a journalist as it has been in recent years. There has been a roaring cataract of momentous news, much of it good news.

Now, it sometimes seems that "good news" is a journalistic oxymoron. An axiom of the journalist's trade is: "We do not report planes that land safely." There is a tendency, and it is understandable, to think that what matters, journalistically, is what goes wrong. There is not time to dwell on the rest. However, the big story of the last few years has been a spate of safe political landings.

Safe, that is, so far, and relatively speaking. All political outcomes are "so far." All situations (and institutions, and regimes) are transitional. That is why, in a sense, there never really is a suitable occasion to use the journalistic notation "30," which denotes the end of a story. All political journalism is part of a running story, always.

On the home front, the story of the American idea in this period has been less triumphal. An American's political ear has been hearing an odd symphony: trumpets abroad and piccolos at home. Abroad, public life has resounded with the great categories of political philosophy. Justice, liberty, equality, legitimacy, representation, constitutionalism, legality—these topics have been the currency of common conversation.

At home, there has been a flight from the rigors of governance and from the grandeur of politics.

Now, I, who in my youth was a professor of political philosophy, found exhilarating the spectacle of "the world as a seminar." But I know better now. A healthy, happy nation should not, at least for long, resemble a seminar. Only in unhappy nations are the most fundamental questions constantly debated. The fledgling democracies of the formerly communist world will not have come through to safety—or to as much safety as politics ever permits—until their domestic arguments are considerably *less* interesting than they recently have been. Still, those arguments have been exhilarating to watch, particularly because American politics has been so thoroughly miniaturized.

The receding of the threat that defined the Cold War releases American energies and resources for other purposes. But there is scant purposefulness. Why? Sometimes exhaustion is the explanation for what democracies do or fail to do. After the 60 strenuous years from the stock market crash (October 29, 1929) to the fall of the Berlin Wall (November 9, 1989), Americans may be weary. They are in no mood to stiffen their sinews and summon up their blood. Too bad. There is work—home work—to be done.

It is almost as though all the nation's reserves of discipline were invested in international challenges, leaving nothing for domestic affairs. Exhibit A is the federal budget deficit. American government has become institutionalized indiscipline, permitting, indeed encouraging the nation to consume its seed corn. There has been a concomitant vulgarization of election campaigns and other political practices. And there has been a trivialization of the language of rights, constitutional and others. As for civic responsibilities, the subject does not arise. There is a comprehensive failure—no, worse, a cold-eyed refusal—to take care for the future. In short, there is a continuing dereliction of the duty of stewardship.

The pursuit of "fairness" has become a particularly unlovely and unedifying frenzy. Perfect fairness is a will-o'-the-wisp, the pursuit of which produces short tempers, long arguments, intense litigiousness, bad law, abused institutions and diminished social comity. And, there has been much unfairness in fights waged in the name of fairness. A particularly clear example was the battle over the confirmation of Justice Robert Bork.

This volume contains a record of my participation in that argument, including my response to a *Washington Post* editorial (reprinted here) concerning my arguments. I have included this record for two reasons. First, readers may enjoy examining a columnist's part in a single controversy from beginning to end. Second, the Bork episode was extraordinarily important, because of the jurisprudential issues involved and the style of political argument employed. Great questions of constitutional governance were at issue. And the way they were treated was portentous. We have sunk to a tawdry ferocity in public discourse. That sinking is apparent in methods of campaigning that are discussed in this volume.

The perennial drama of democratic governance in America arises from the turbulent individualism of this economically capitalist and politically and culturally pluralist society. Individual rights do not lack for advocates. What often is lacking is the will, or skill to balance them against the rights of the community, which carries within it the future. Such balancing is a test of a democracy's maturity.

There is a dismal smallness to much of American politics today, even—especially—when the subject is the large one of ethics. But some small things are pure pleasures, such as children and their cats and dogs and other preoccupations. Our children are the most important reasons why we care about politics and governance. And they represent the claims of the private, the personal sphere of life, which public affairs are supposed to serve. So from time to time I write about children and other subjects that do not often appear "above the fold," or even below it, on the front pages of newspapers. Children in their wonderful everydayness may not be news but they are life, and that is a suitable subject for journalism, now and again.

PART 1

Overture

Making History and Orphans

Was Napoleon poisoned? I certainly hope so. A heartening new book, *The Murder of Napoleon*, says arsenic, not cancer, killed that dreadful Corsican. Not soon enough: by then he was in exile, fat as a pastry, long past careering around Europe making history and orphans. But today it is salutary, because instructive, to recall this vulgarian who prefigured the worst of modern politics.

He was the first modern tyrant, an absolutist without hereditary pretenses, an upstart compensating with brutality and cynicism for his lack of legitimacy, grounding his power in manipulation of the masses. He was (to borrow a Disraeli phrase) a self-made man who worshiped his creator. But he would refer to Louis XVI as "my uncle."

Like Hitler, who was not German, and Stalin, who was not Russian, Napoleon, who was not French, was a complete outsider, outside all restraints grounded in principles or affections. He had a megalomaniac's estimate of the importance of his undertakings. When planning to invade England he said: "Eight hours of night in favorable weather would decide the fate of the universe."

He had what we now recognize as the totalitarian's thirst for revising as well as making history: one of the most famous of his melodramatic orders-of-the-day ("Soldiers, you are naked, ill-fed . . .") was written 20 years later on Saint Helena. He combined a philistine's sense of culture and a martinet's reverence for the state: "People complain that we have no literature nowadays. That is the fault of the Minister for Home Affairs."

Believing that "the people must have a religion and that religion must be in the hands of the government," he pioneered a modern industry—the manufacture of ersatz religions for political purposes. His birthday (August 15, a black-crepe day in sensible households) became the Feast of Saint Napoleon. But he felt he had been born too late, that Alexander the Great had had more fun:

". . . after he [Alexander] had conquered Asia and been proclaimed to the peoples as the son of Jupiter, the whole of the East believed it. . . . If I declared myself today the son of the eternal Father . . . there is no fishwife who would not hiss at me."

Correlli Barnett, a biographer of Napoleon, is what a biographer should be, "a conscientious enemy." He says Napoleon was "perhaps the earliest example of that phenomenon of the emerging mass society, the superstar." His career aggravated the tendency of 19th-century romanticism to celebrate "great men," the "geniuses" who are "artists of history-making." Romantic painters loved mountainscapes and despoiled many by painting Napoleon into the foreground, struggling through the Alps, like Hannibal.

Napoleon believed that in order to have good soldiers, a nation must always be at war. He gave France good soldiers—and good roads. Like Hitler with the autobahns, Napoleon adored roads for moving armies. He wanted 14 highways radiating from Paris toward any conquest his heart might desire. But highways can carry traffic two ways, and in May and June, 1940, France's roads were enjoyed by troops from Germany— a nation which Napoleon helped make into a modern state by reforming its administration and inflaming its nationalism.

In the 18th century—"the age of reason"—better furnaces for iron-making resulted in better artillery, which conquered what until then had been the key to war—the fortress. Napoleon rose like a rocket as an artillery officer who understood how to use artillery when reasoning with a restive populace.

A century later, another Frenchman enamored of artillery (Marshal Foch) said: "Artillery conquers the ground, infantry occupies it." At dawn of the first day of the third battle of Ypres, British and French artillery fired 107,000 tons of shells and metal. 'Twould have been bliss that dawn to be alive for Napoleon, who boasted that he cared "little for the lives of a million men." He used conscription—"the nation in arms"— to make war bigger: 539,000 fought at Leipzig in 1813.

Barnett calls Napoleon "Byron-in-field-boots," the eternal fidget who turned Descartes's "I think, therefore I am" into "I order everybody about, therefore I am." He was the sociopath in politics, utterly without softening values, celebrating bureaucracy for others but willfulness for himself: "I am having three heads cut off here every day and carried around Cairo. . . ."

The only lasting good he did was inadvertent: he excited Beethoven to compose *Eroica*. At least Beethoven dedicated it to Napoleon tempo-rarily. Beethoven then had better, second thoughts and changed the dedication. Thus did one of Europe's vilest lives intersect with one of Europe's noblest.

May 30, 1982

1789's Echo in Iron

Denouncing the French Revolution is indeed like preaching a sermon to an earthquake, so in this Bicentennial moment let us let bygones be bygones. Instead, let us now praise the most pleasing result of the Revolution, something built for the Centennial—the Eiffel Tower. It really reflects the Industrial Revolution, but in life one thing leads to another and the Industrial Revolution owed much to the breaking of restraints—social structures, intellectual habits—by the political Revolution.

Revolutions are like boulders hurled into ponds. Ripples radiate for centuries. Unintended consequences often matter most. The Revolution's most important result was Napoleon, whose most important result (as France learned in 1871, and again in 1914, and again in 1940) was the invention of Germany. Revolutionary radicalism provoked conservatism's finest proclamation, Burke's *Reflections*. And the Revolution's centennial echo, in the form of the Tower, itself echoes clearly 100 years on. Deciphered, it makes an age intelligible. Ours.

The Tower has been called the Notre Dame of the Left Bank, cathedral of an alternative faith. It bestrides the Champ de Mars, formerly parade ground of the Ecole Militaire where cadet Bonaparte studied war. The Tower expressed the *belle époque's* confidence that mankind's remaining problems were material and solvable by technology—by applied reason rather than swords. The Tower was the centerpiece of the 1889 Exposition Universelle, which had the partly conservative purpose of turning Centennial thoughts from the fratricidal politics of the past, toward the scientific future. It was one of those 19th-century carnivals of machines expressing capitalism's confidence and throbbing vigor. In Europe this meant the triumph of the upstart, entrepreneurial urban bourgeoisie over landed wealth. The Tower, writes art critic Robert Hughes, soared above ownership of land and "occupied unowned and previously useless space, the sky itself."

Gustave Eiffel was not an architect; he was an engineer, working with an industrial material, iron. The Tower is a work of art by a nonartist, democratic art, to be viewed not just by the museum-visiting minority but by the multitudes. By literally everybody, so completely does it dominate the vista. It uses height to produce democratic intimacy, showing the swarm of common life. In 1889 the Tower surpassed the Washington Monument (homage in stone to the maker of the successful 18th-century revolution) as world's tallest structure. It remained that for four decades, until the Chrysler Building. The Tower anticipated sky-scrapers, those assertions of heroic materialism, and it soars over Paris because the city was built before the coming of structural steel, when the height of buildings was limited by the load-bearing strength of stone. (The curse of Manhattan, its suffocating density, is the result of too many buildings made possible by the two things that made the Tower possible, structural steel and the elevator.)

The Tower, writes Hughes, was the master image, the great metaphor of radically accelerating change, gathering "all the meanings of modernity together." The Tower and the Brooklyn Bridge were the century's consciousness-changing constructions, conquering horizontal and vertical distance. The Tower even shaped art. It altered, in the most artistically susceptible city, what Hughes calls "the cultural conditions of seeing." More spectacular than the sight of the Tower from the ground was the view of the ground from the Tower. The highest that people (other than a few balloonists) had been was Notre Dame's gargoyle gallery. People lived their entire lives within 40 feet of the ground. Then came the Tower and "a new type of landscape began to seep into popular awareness. It was based on frontality and pattern, rather than on perspective recession and depth." It influenced modern art generally.

As an emblem of machine-age capitalism, when engineers were Masters of the Universe, the Tower was a huge sculpture of Hope. Machines then held no menace for the middle class, which felt itself suddenly at the wheel of the world. Mass production from standardized parts (girders, rivets: the Tower) would be matched by peaceful politics for the masses, with nations shedding antique differences and animosities. But a baby born in 1889 was just 25 when he learned in Flanders to think of the noun "machine" as part of a compound noun: machine gun. There is a stunning photograph of Hitler alone at dawn during the few hours he spent in Paris. The Tower soars behind him, expressing faith in the inevitability of progress through the fusion of science and industry. In the foreground stands the refutation. He, too, was born in 1889.

Still, the Tower, standing midway between the Revolution and us, stands for a great truth: What is dangerous in politics can be creative elsewhere. In politics, an extravagant idea of the possible leads to extremism, then terror and tyranny, as in the 1790s. Napoleon was the Revolution on horseback. One of his ministers said, "He never could see where the possible left off." Hence the retreat from Moscow, the defeat at Waterloo, a legacy of corpses and orphans. But a century ago a sense of limitless possibility was both cause and effect of unleashed creativity in culture: Freud, Edison, Marconi, Einstein, Pasteur, Ford, the Impressionists, the phonograph, the movie camera. The era brought what

Hughes calls "the greatest alteration of man's view of the universe since Isaac Newton." Eiffel's Tower insisted: The future is as open as the sky.

Many of Paris's leading lights denounced the new Tower as proof of "faltering French good taste." The writer de Maupassant said he often lunched at a restaurant in the Tower because that was the only place in Paris where he did not have to see it. What is the *use* of it? asked intellectuals, who often are the last to understand. It was an act of splendid audacity, not least because, in the climate of capitalist practicality, it fashioned a romantic statement from utterly utilitarian material. The fact that the Tower was at first ridiculed has made it forever after a force encouraging the French to be receptive of the new. In France when something daring is reviled, defenders says: "Just like the Tower!" In America, we say, "They all laughed at Rockefeller Center; now they're fighting to get in."

July 17, 1989

They Are the Children

Witness America's zest for short-term crusades and cost-free weekend idealisms, as in Earth Day II. (It deserves Roman numerals, like a Super Bowl.)

A few years ago, when rock stars and politicians and many others marched off to do battle with injustice, they sang an anthem announcing that they are the world, they are the children. The latter certainly is true. Children are us.

"What are we going to do on Earth Day, Daddy?" asks a nine-year-old girl of my acquaintance. If she has been rigorously conscripted and is marching in lockstep with all of America's children (if she is not, it is an Earth Day II oversight), she will busy herself badgering her father about (these are the thoughts of Chairman Hayes—Denis Hayes, chairman of Earth Day II) "what kind of light bulbs do we use, do we have a flow-restricter on our shower head, are we having an appropriate diet, is our car the most efficient vehicle that meets our needs?"

Great. Egged on (or so Hayes hopes) by her teachers, this daughter-as-commissar is going to pioneer new dimensions of pre-teen obnoxiousness. Does Hayes know what an environmental disaster a nine-year-old is? The subject of her diet is not for the squeamish, she has never turned off a light, her complaint about my cars is that the van does not have a VCR and, as for showers, don't get me started.

MTV is currently inoculating America's young with (among many other things) the emphatic, if vague, injunction to "save the planet" (as Hard Rock Cafe sweatshirts also enjoin). This week the rest of the media have joined the serried ranks.

America now has saturation journalism, CNN forever, one network or another from before dawn until after midnight, all-news radio, and radio call-in shows, which are broadcasting's equivalent of letters to the editor. Saturation journalism is like a shark, unsleeping and insatiably ravenous for new subjects to devour.

When the media all jump feet first, on cue, into the coordinated manipulation of public opinion, as with this week of environmental "concern," they are doing something rather different from just covering the news. And one result is the reduction of complex issues to a pudding of trendy simplifications and synthetic anxiety and indignation.

Naturally, human progress puts stress on nature. The mission of modernity is to expand the dominion of humanity by shrinking the rule of necessity. However, the hidden agenda of some environmentalists is to expand the dominion of some people's political will over others.

The current surge of environmentalism coincides with the thawing of the Cold War in a way that puts an exclamation mark at the end of a decade of electoral routs for the traditional agenda of the left. That agenda evolves over time but has one constant: the expansion of state direction over society, and the expansion of control of the regulating state by a clerisy claiming privileged insights into the unfolding future.

Hence the hatred—not too strong a word—by some environmentalists for the automobile, that symbol and servant of the individual discretion for the masses. There is no more direct route to the regulation of the masses than restrictions on consumption, especially of energy and transportation. Thus the slogan of some European conservatives: The green tree has red roots.

This is not to say that any particular environmental argument is sublimated politics, or otherwise pernicious or misguided. It is to say that some skepticism is in order when the media fall into line behind a political line, such as: "The environment" (a noun that denotes rather a lot) is in critical condition and getting worse.

To govern is to choose, usually on the basis of inadequate information, partly because of the pressure of events. Earth Day II will gin up pressure (evanescent, thankfully) for choices where information is especially problematic—in environmental sciences. Regarding a range of subjects from climatic change to global warming (they are not the same subject) to the dangers of asbestos, there is on today's fast-rolling political bandwagon a high ratio of certitude to certainty.

Democrats hoping to ride the environmental wave into the White

House should understand that it is an issue perfect for the brush-and-dash politics of the Bush Administration. As with education, transportation, deficit reduction and other matters, the policy—style, really—is right-minded gestures, ringing rhetoric and pep talks, then a quick change of subject before the tacky matter of costs comes up.

Bushism is feel-good politics, adding self-satisfaction to the material comfort of the comfortable. It is highly popular and applicable to any issue. It feeds the media and makes for pleasant weekends of unexacting moralism. We are the children.

April 19, 1990

Ideological Storms

CHEVY CHASE VILLAGE, MD.—Picking my way warily past coagulated traffic (no street was passable), through fallen branches and power lines, clambering over the trunks of large trees that had snapped like twigs, past crushed cars and shattered houses, with devastation all around, I thought with sickening certainty: The Will Children did this. What excuse will they offer for breaking an entire suburb?

My second thought about the freak storm that visited unprecedented destruction on the old houses and older trees of this community was: It must have been something I wrote. Self-absorption is second nature to writers, as Stephen Leacock understood: "When I state that my lectures were followed almost immediately by the union of South Africa, the banana riots in Trinidad and the Turco-Italian war, I think readers can form some opinion of their importance."

My third thought was, as Washington thoughts will be, political: This never happened when Reagan was president. Then, darkly: Perhaps this happened *because* Reagan was president.

This highly ideological storm had what the Supreme Court calls a "disparate impact." It blasted the affluent with uncanny discrimination. The storm seemed guided by exit polls, its fury falling on upper-middle-class enclaves. It came amid renewed Republican talk about cutting the capital-gains tax. Please stop such talk until we are sure the storm was not negative feedback from God concerning recent political victories by the rich.

The battered neighborhoods are ones in which you cannot fling a brick without conking a lawyer, so you cannot have trees tossed about without threats of litigation being tossed, too. Unfortunately (for lawyers) the law is sensible about wind-tossed trees: They are "acts of God."

It may reveal the real standing of religion in the modern age that we see His hand only in such calamities. Novelist Peter De Vries puts this prayer on the lips of a minister whose flock is suffering from a flood: "Let us hope that a kind Providence will put a speedy end to the acts of God under which we have been laboring." Or, as Virginia Woolf wrote in a letter: "I read the book of Job last night—I don't think God comes well out of it."

The Will children relished seeing the social fabric shredded. All children find chaos congenial. Any unruliness, even by nature, advances the child's program of subverting authority. I struck a blow for the *ancien régime* when I delivered a crushing rejoinder to their gloating. Note, I said austerely, that the spaghetti of wires entangled in branches in the backyard includes the wire that delivers all that is dear to you—cable television, meaning the Baltimore Orioles and MTV.

Incredulity is indeed the first step toward philosophy and the Will children became philosophical, in their several fashions. The sons said that without electricity they could not be expected to do their summer reading. The daughter said how jolly it is to read by candlelight. The father philosophized that perhaps boys' virtues can be real without being visible.

These days Washington is philosophizing about planet Earth. Washington is in another cycle of environmentalism, which is half common sense and half sensitivity grandstanding. Environmentalism is rich in late-'80s language about "caring" and "nurturing." We in Chevy Chase Village, digging out the stumps of what once were stately trees, think the environment itself could be a bit more caring.

Flying trees and flopping power lines are dangerous. So are suburbanites dangerous—to themselves—when they get it into their heads to play Paul Bunyan. A lot of men who for years have not operated anything more menacing than a word processor headed for hardware stores to buy axes and chain saws, thereby putting at risk their own limbs.

Another risk inherent in a natural disaster such as a storm is forced sociability. It is the mandatory bonhomie of the lifeboat. Neighbors who had lived in peace suddenly got to know one another better. No good can come of that.

Liberals, being sentimentalists, love that sort of thing. But British playwright Alan Bennett understands the crucial difference:

POLLY: He's a Socialist, but he doesn't like people.
BRIAN: Nor do I much.
POLLY: You're a conservative. You don't have to.

The storm forced sociability upon the community, but time will heal the resulting wounds. Still, society cannot stand too much of that. The storm is another ominous omen that the winds are no longer blowing the conservatives' way.

June 22, 1989

Tearing the Social Threads

San Francisco's geography is histrionic—its fogs can be as spectacular as the vistas they obscure—and its geology is downright dangerous. On Tuesday (October 17) that geology taught the nation three lessons. They concern the predictability of some surprises, the sovereignty of nature and the web of dependencies that define civic life.

The earth's shell is composed of numerous plates from 45 to 95 miles thick, slowly migrating. North America—The United Plates of America, as a geologist calls it—is united only for now. This "collage of wandering fragments" (geologists are phrasemakers) may disperse to form new aggregations in a few hundred million years.

Meanwhile, California straddles two plates, one moving south, the other north. No good can come of this. Sudden slippages between plates produce quakes, and not only in the West.

Quakes around New Year, 1811–12, near New Madrid, Missouri, reached perhaps 8.8 on today's Richter scale. They reversed the flow of the Mississippi, altered its course, caused waves in the Earth several feet high and rang church bells in Boston. Last November, a 6.0 quake hit rural Quebec. In 1983, a 6.5 quake shattered Coalinga, California. The scale is logarithmic: San Francisco's 1906 quake (8.3) was 90 times more powerful than Coalinga's and less powerful than Alaska's 1964 quake (8.4).

There are between 2,500 and 10,000 measurable tremors during a normal day on this fidgety planet. (Instruments can measure ground movements the size of an oxygen molecule.) Big quakes are rare. They also are certainties.

Earth sciences predicted the 1980 eruption of Mount St. Helens and six months ago *Science* magazine examined evidence that "dangerous quakes are closing in on the San Francisco area." A 1976 quake in China killed 400,000, but in 1975 the evacuation of a Chinese city in response to a correct prediction saved an estimated 100,000 lives. As a predictive science, seismology is still developing, but it suggests that a big quake is highly likely in eastern America within 30 years.

Tuesday's quake should concentrate minds. One-tenth of all Americans live in California. One-quarter of the semiconductor industry is in one county near the San Andreas fault. About 47,000 Americans die each year in motor vehicle accidents, the equivalent of a major plane crash every day. An 8-strength quake—smaller than 1906, larger than 1989—could kill that many in 15 minutes. Only 60 people died when Charleston, South Carolina, shook for eight minutes in 1886, but people then did not live in high-rise structures over natural gas lines and downwind from chemical plants.

An earthquake once shook the Western mind. It struck Lisbon on All Saints' Day, 1755, killing thousands in churches and thousands more who, fleeing to the seashore, were drowned by a tidal wave. It was as though nature were muttering "Oh, really? Says who?" in response to mankind's expanding sense of mastery. The quake was an exclamation point inserted arbitrarily into the Age of Reason, raising doubts about the beneficence of the universe and God's enthusiasm for the Enlightenment.

In this secular age, when the phrase "acts of God" denotes only disasters, we still can learn lessons from them. One of the striking vignettes from television coverage of the aftermath of San Francisco's quake was a policeman exhorting citizens to "go home and prepare for 72 hours without services." Perhaps no electricity, no gas, no running water for three days. Of course mankind lived for millennia without any of those. Today, however, our well-being depends on a network of many systems too easily taken for granted.

The words *civic, civil, citizen* have a common root. They originally pertained to residents of cities. It is in these complex creations—cities—that we see the truth of the phrase "social fabric." Any community, but especially a modern city, is a rich weave of diverse threads. The strength of each thread is derived from its relation to the rest. All the threads can snap or unravel when the fabric is ripped by jagged events. San Francisco's fabric has been strained but not torn.

From any catastrophe some good can come. It is no bad thing to be reminded—the world relentlessly sees to this—of the fragility of all social arrangements. Americans, for whom individualism is instinctive, need periodic reminders that their individual pursuits of happiness are utterly dependent upon the functioning of civic, collective community institutions—government—and upon habits of civility of the sort San Franciscans showed in their crisis. An earthquake is a tough teacher but it tells the truth.

October 22, 1989

Hobbes in Chicago

CHICAGO—The police cruiser crawls, like a cockroach across worn linoleum, through the concrete and grassless dirt of an urban lunarscape called Cabrini Green. It is a public housing project on the Near North Side, not far from the posh shops of Michigan Avenue's "Magnificent Mile" and cheek by jowl with some gentrified yuppydom.

This cluster of high-rise and half-abandoned buildings is a dispiriting beat for the two police officers who give their passenger a laconic lecture on their experiences as part of the half-hearted pretense of government in the project. They describe which gangs control which buildings, which weapons are used in the sporadic firefights that erupt between building-fortresses, how many foolhardy people have been hit by snipers while trying to cross the free-fire zone between buildings.

Public housing, particularly in high-rise configurations, usually is a concentration of pathologies. During today's drug plague, public housing has become a recrudescence of the worst of the American frontier— Dodge City without a marshal.

So, you modern-day Jeffersonians, you who think that government is best that governs least: Welcome to your world. It is Hobbes's world, where life is always poor, nasty and brutish and often is short. Public housing here is anarchy tempered by juvenocracy—power wielded by adolescents.

Cabrini Green will eventually be eradicated by the most powerful and revered social force, the real estate market. Developers are salivating for these 70 or so acres near good shopping. The concentrated pathologies will be shuffled away, perhaps even dispersed. But they will be recon-centrated daily in the public schools.

In a series of hammer-blow reports, the *Chicago Tribune* has docu-mented its characterization of this city's school system as "institutional-ized child neglect." The bureaucracy and teacher's union are culprits. However, the reports rightly stress that two-thirds of the students live in poverty and come to school from environments of deprivation that would defeat the best intentions of even the best school system.

One high school provides day care for the children of its students, 90 percent of whom come from public housing. At another school, a 14-year-old girl is in her third pregnancy. "Another student," the *Tribune* re-ports, "sleeps with five other children on three piled-up mattresses in an unheated apartment. During the winter the boy often came to school smelling of urine because it was too cold for the smaller kids to get up and go to the bathroom at night." A teacher asks, "How can you learn when people tell you you smell of piss, and you do?"

Some sixth-graders, never having used rulers, do not know how many inches are in a foot. Some eight-year-olds from homes without books tear pages from schoolbooks to use as toilet paper. Some children come to kindergarten not toilet trained. There are first-graders who have not learned numbers or colors. "A teacher," says a teacher, "cannot take mom and dad's place. What am I going to accomplish when mom doesn't take the time to pick up a can of peas and say, 'Green! Round! Peas!'?"

This panorama of pain, waste and the perpetuation of squalor and violence is a chilling example of rebarbarization. It is the eruption of primitivism in the midst of urbanity. Let us have no more abstract arguments about the relative importance of nature and nurture in the formation of individuals. Look around here, and in all other cities, and you will see the consequences of the abandonment of nurturing.

In Anne Tyler's novel *Breathing Lessons,* a woman attending classes to prepare for natural childbirth exclaims, "Breathing lessons—really. Don't they reckon I must know how to breathe by now?" To which a wise woman responds, "I remember leaving the hospital with Jesse and thinking, 'Wait. Are they going to let me just walk off with him? I don't know beans about babies.' "

She continues: "You're given all those lessons for the unimportant things—piano-playing, typing. . . . But how about parenthood? . . . Before you can drive a car you need a state-approved course of instruction, but driving a car is nothing, nothing, compared to . . . raising up a new human being."

In any city in any age, a walk among the underclass is apt to be a walk on the wild side, with glimpses of deeply moving bravery, tenacity and heroism in nurturing. However, the drug epidemic and the disintegration of families under the pounding of today's urban poverty is giving us a glimpse of how much social regression can occur in a modern society.

What is called the "cycle" of poverty is actually a downward spiral. The spiral tightens, gaining speed, because so few people live in Cabrini Green and similar places who give, or learn, lessons in the important things.

March 30, 1989

Agitprop in New York

A document, just come to light, decries the "intellectual and educational oppression that has characterized the culture and institutions of the United States" where school curricula reflect "deep-seated pathologies of racial hatred" and impose "ego starvation" on all but the elite whose "arrogant perspective" produces "intellect-victimization" and "cultural oppression" and "invisibility" and "marginality" and "dehumanization" and "genocide."

American education, it says, "deliberately" leads students to disrespect people who are different. There is an American educational "policy" of destroying "the positive aspects and attitudes" of blacks, victims of "white supremacy" and "white nationalism." America's "policy" of "sacrificing higher ideals on the alter [sic] of materialism" is grounded in the Constitution, "a seriously flawed document" good primarily for "articulating and aggregating the interests of the rich and powerful."

Praise of the Constitution is, according to this document, "vulgar and revolting" because the social system has "heaped undeserved rewards on a segment of the population while oppressing the majority."

Now, where do you suppose this crude agitprop comes from? Some ransacked East German propaganda office? An old Stalinist text from Hungary or Czechoslovakia? No, from the New York state education department. It is a report recommending curriculum changes for public schools.

Welcome to the world of adversarial pedagogy. Lumpen leftism with its clanging jargon ("Eurocentric conceptualization and modality") has gone to earth in the education system.

New York's proposed reforms for correcting "underrepresentation" of certain government-approved minorities in curricula are nothing if not thorough: While "mathematics and science do not lend themselves" to "multicultural treatment," no topic is "culture-free" and by "omitting cultural references" from science and mathematics materials, "a subtle message is given that all science and mathematics originated within European culture."

No nit is too small to be picked: The term "Mexican War" is ethnocentric, inferior to "American-Mexican War." All this is part of the great growth industry of victimology. The stated aim of the reforms is curricula reflecting "the pluralistic nature of our society." The real aim is to enforce the resentments that are packed into this assertion: "European culture has no inherent claim to superiority."

The document is affirmative action run amok, an ethnic spoils system within the school system, an intellectual quota system under which all cultures are declared of equal moral worth and of equal importance in the making of America. This is said to be necessary to serve the goal of prompting students' "emotional health" and "ability to empathize" and "positive self-esteem" (which is the best kind of self-esteem).

Nothing can be done about the fact that Locke, Montesquieu and other DWEMs (today's academic acronym-as-epithet: dead white European males) were important and African, Latin and Asian philosophers were not, as sources of the American Revolution. And of this century's civil-rights revolution: Martin Luther King's namesake was a DWEM. But New York's reformers solve the "problem" of the indisputable centrality of our European heritage by declaring that heritage, on balance, vicious (racist, exploitive, imperialist, etc.).

Certainly, education should do justice to the full range and richness of America's cultural heritage. However, justice begins with truth, and the fundamental truth is that the ideas and institutions that undergird our commonality—our organic life as one body politic—come from Europe. In what matters most—the political philosophy that makes us a nation "dedicated to a proposition"—our country is a branch of European civilization.

It is perverse: Attempts to politicize America's curricula by purging "Eurocentrism" are occurring when America is more than ever the beckoning model for scores of millions of Europeans who, emerging from tyranny, rightly see America as a fulfillment of European civilization. Gorbachev understands and fears this. Historian Fritz Stern detects in Gorbachev's phrase "the common house of Europe" an anti-American ring that Gorbachev made explicit in these words about the "threat" hovering over "European culture":

"The threat emanates from an onslaught of 'mass culture' from across the Atlantic. . . . A deep, profoundly intelligent European culture is retreating to the background before the primitive revelry of violence and pornography and the flood of cheap feelings and low thoughts."

The attempt to define American culture in terms of its worst manifestations is the standard enterprise of anti-Americans, and is as tendentious as defining Europe in terms of communism and fascism. America's founders were steeped in, implemented and improved European ideas. In this century, as Stern says, "Americans understood the unity of European culture in many ways much better than the fratricidal Europeans themselves."

And during much of the 1930s and until 1945, America was the refuge—the second house—for some of the most luminous carriers of European culture. After the war, it was an American idea—the Marshall Plan—that helped resuscitate Europe's social vitality.

"Eurocentricity" is right, in American curricula and consciousness, because it accords with the facts of our history, and we—and Europe—are fortunate for that. The political and moral legacy of Europe has made the most happy and admirable nations. Saying that may be indelicate, but it has the merit of being true and the truth should be the core of any curriculum.

December 17, 1989

Subsidized Shocking of the Bourgeoisie

Senator Pat Moynihan (D–N.Y.) sent a two-sentence note attached to his statement opposing the legislation that would forbid the National Endowment for the Arts (NEA) from supporting art that is "obscene or indecent" or is hostile to almost any individual or group for almost any reason. Moynihan's note said: "The '20s are coming on fast? I *knew* we would regret the end of Cold War."

Perhaps that is it. Détente has relieved us from seriousness. We have returned to "normalcy" and do not remember how to act sensibly.

The legislation moved by Senator Jesse Helms (R–N.C.) is a foolish reaction to two photographic exhibits supported by institutions receiving NEA funds, exhibits that included photos of sadomasochistic practices and a crucifix in a jar of urine. The amendment is a recipe for timidity, paralysis and, of course, litigation. But many of the arguments—or the hysteria and arrogance serving as arguments—against the amendment are intellectually incoherent, indeed anti-intellectual.

Opponents of the amendment say government is obligated to support art and equally obligated not to think about what art is, or is good for. They argue that government support for the arts serves the public interest, but that government cannot express an interest in the kind of art that is supported.

The argument for subsidizing the arts must be communitarian, not severely individualistic. It must be that it serves some social good, not just that it gives pleasure to individuals (artists, certainly, and perhaps viewers). Were that the argument, there would be as strong an argument—stronger on strictly democratic grounds—for subsidizing bowling or poker.

Artists who say art has a public purpose say that purpose can include discomforting the comfortable. Shocking the bourgeoisie is fun and, arguably, good for one and all, but it is cheeky of artists to say the bourgeoisie is obligated to subsidize the shocking. America's bourgeoisie has a remarkable record of generously subsidizing the ridiculing, despising and subversion of itself. If you doubt that, examine a public university's liberal-arts curriculum.

Another problem for the NEA is art that eschews all purpose, art that is not shocking but baffling to the common viewer. What of the post-minimalist artist who exhibited a pig in a cage? The artist who draped a curtain across a Colorado valley? The "environmental artist" whose "kinetic sculpture" was a bucket of fireworks atop the Brooklyn Bridge? The police called that a bomb.

A milestone in the liberation of art from the law was the 1928 court ruling that Brancusi's *Bird in Space*—a graceful shaft symbolizing flight, but not resembling a bird—was sculpture and therefore not subject to import duties. Customs agents would not be defining art.

But artists welcomed government into their world in the form of NEA subsidies. Subsidies require reasoning about public purposes. Yet some artists deny that art has any such purpose.

Abstract art and its degenerate progeny were once celebrated as "democratic" because purged of "academicism" and immediately "accessible" to "understanding" by everyone. But this was the egalitarianism of nihilism, art equally understood by everyone because it had no meaning. Having no content, it was immune to the charge of elitism. But the people don't like it, preferring art depicting the human condition and passions about it.

The artist Robert Rauschenberg, wanting no restrictions on his entitlements and no critical standards to inhibit his fun, says: "It is extremely important that art be unjustifiable." But government expenditures must be justified. Some years ago someone asked the NEA to support this work of art: He would dribble ink from Haley, Idaho, to Cody, Wyoming, birthplaces of Ezra Pound and Jackson Pollock respectively. The NEA refused. It must have had a reason.

If art has no improving power or purpose, it has no claim on the interest of government. So advocates of government support for the arts must say that art serves society. There is a long American tradition of support on the grounds that the arts elevate the public mind by bringing it into contact with beauty, and even ameliorate social pathologies. But if the power of art is profound, it need not be benign. And the policy of public subsidies must distinguish between art that serves an elevating purpose and that that does not.

The Helms amendment should be quietly killed. However, alarmists relishing the fun of faking great fear about the impending end of civilization say the ruckus over the amendment will have a "chilling effect" on the NEA. If that means the NEA may think more often about the public interest in the visual arts, then: good.

If, as some artists say, no one can say what art is (or, hence, what the adjective "fine" means as a modifier), then art becomes a classification that does not classify. Then the NEA should be the NEE—National Endowment for Everything. It will need a bigger budget.

August 3, 1989

"If You Must Sleep With More Than One Partner . . ." Must?

Television, a wit says, allows you to be entertained in your home by people you would not have in your home. Soon some of that entertainment will be sponsored by commercials you might prefer not to see from your sofa, commercials for condoms. Some of them may be sponsoring programs concerning condoms. Recently on *St. Elsewhere* an unmarried pregnant woman said she should have had her lover "condomized." Another noun has given birth to a verb. *Valerie* has a son who has a condom. *Cagney and Lacey, Kate and Allie, The Facts of Life* and other shows have at least sideswiped the subject of teenage contraception. As Fred Allen said, "Imitation is the sincerest form of television."

In 1952 the television code forbade advertisement of "intimately personal products which are generally regarded as unsuitable conversational topics in mixed social groups." Mixed where? Mobile? Manhattan? Does place make a difference anymore? Many newspapers and magazines have carried condom ads. One ad features a worried woman saying: "I enjoy sex, but I'm not ready to die for it." For *Newsweek* that ad was made more delicate: "I'll do a lot for love, but I'm not ready to die for it." America's newspaper of record (*The Sporting News*) carries an ad that shouts: "Test your condom. Right here. Right now." It contains a questionnaire about spermicides, testing for strength and "a lubricant" for greater sensitivity. AIDS is not mentioned. That is a preview of coming television commercials.

Today's condom commercials tiptoe into living rooms. A young man says he goes out with "nice girls" but "some pretty terrible things are happening to some really nice people." A young woman says, "You might know someone pretty well. But do you really know him?" Another young woman says, "I never thought having an intimate relationship would be a matter of life and death, but because of AIDS, I'm afraid." I'm afraid I do not believe AIDS is much more than a pretext for the sudden condomization of television. And to the limited extent that AIDS is the real reason, feminists have a just grievance.

American females are, on average, sexually active at 16. Every year about 1 million adolescents become pregnant. About 400,000 have abortions. Half of those who give birth are not yet 18. Planned Parenthood acidly, and rightly, notes that there are about 20,000 sexual scenes on television each year; yet no one gets pregnant. This relentless presentation of sex-without-consequences is almost certainly one reason the government spends $17 billion a year on care for unwed mothers. However, so long as the problem with sex was "just" pregnancy, condoms were not advertised. Now that men also are at risk (AIDS), condoms are advertised.

But what are condom commercials doing? Telling people that condoms exist? Try to find an unaware 13-year-old. Certainly anyone aware of AIDS is aware of condoms, which are displayed as conspicuously as toothpaste in drugstores. Advertising is supposed to make money for the advertiser. Most advertising aims to do something other than alert the public to a product of which the public is unaware. Beer commercials are not supposed to make you thirsty, or get you to buy beer rather than a Buick or root beer. Beer commercials try to get you to buy Miller rather than Bud. Once the public is used to condom commercials—a matter of months—condom advertising will be a straight fight for market share. It is a market worth more than $300 million a year, with Americans buying 80,000 condoms a day.

The first television station to run condom commercials is in San Francisco, which has a large AIDS problem. One of the next stations is in Indianapolis. *Et tu*, Indiana? You bet. Forty years ago a quiet Indiana zoology professor was completing research that shattered America's sexual innocence that rested on reticence. Mrs. Kinsey said of her husband, Alfred, "I hardly see him at night since he took up sex." What he found out about sexual activity was that there was lots of it going on. For example, there were 450,000 acts of fornication in Indiana, every week. Oh! Indiana!

Oh! Everywhere else! Kinsey's army of investigators found that 85 percent of married males had had sexual intercourse before marriage; 50 percent of husbands had committed adultery; by the age of 40, 26 percent of wives had committed adultery. Want to know how many orgasms the average unmarried male was having weekly in the late 1940s? How many the average groom had experienced before his wedding? As Casey Stengel used to say, you could look it up. Kinsey wrote it down. And the world was turning upside down.

In *The Glory and the Dream*, historian William Manchester recalls that when in 1948 Norman Mailer published *The Naked and the Dead* he had to invent a three-letter word ("fug") to substitute for the four-letter word that soldiers used. In 1949 *The New York Times* revised or rejected 1,456 advertisements. Lingerie described as "naughty but nice" became "Paris inspired—but so nice." A nightclub's boast "50 of the hottest girls this side of hell" was transformed to "50 of the most alluring maidens"—maidens, yet—"this side of paradise." Manchester says, "Curves were painted out of models in girdle displays, giving them an eerie, unisex appearance and raising the question of why they needed foundation garments at all."

Today's condom commercials may not be harmful, but neither are they merely a response to an epidemic. Too much delicacy about contraception and disease can be harmful. But a certain delicacy about intimate things does not need to be defended; it is inherently good. And "candor" about sex can be capitulation, suggesting that being "sexually active" is as much a matter of moral indifference as jogging. A British condom commercial says, "If you must sleep with more than one partner . . ." Must?

However, attitudinal change has its own dynamic and, regarding sex, the dynamic has been nothing if not, well, dynamic. In the 1940s a major oil company sent employees to visit gas stations to check on service and cleanliness of rest rooms. One visitor, a woman, was startled to find a condom-dispensing machine in the ladies' restroom. She told the operator of the station that the machine was inappropriate and must go. He said: Nothing doing. I get $100 a week from that machine—and there has never been a condom in it.

We've all come a long way, baby.

February 16, 1987

The Triumph of Pharmacology

Sport is play, but play has a serious side. Competition can be elevating for participants and spectators. Thus the integrity of sport is a civic concern. And it is important to say precisely why what Ben Johnson did was wrong.

Runners at the highest levels of competition comprise a small community. They know all that is possible regarding enhancement of performance. And they know what is permissible. Johnson used steroids surreptitiously and in defiance of clear rules that are constantly reiterated. However, Johnson and many others involved in the intense pursuit of competitive edge may not really understand the reasons for the rules he broke.

Legs have 40 percent of the body's muscle mass. Steroids build muscle mass as well as hasten healing. Johnson's legs exploded him to victory by a margin of 13/100ths of a second. Did steroids make the difference? Hard to say. What has to be said is why using substances constitutes cheating.

When judging a performance-enhancing technique or technology, the crucial criterion is: Does it improve performance without devaluing it? Begin by considering precisely the value drained away by cheating, then decide if use of steroids constitutes cheating.

Bartlett Giamatti, the designated metaphysician of American sport, flexed his mental muscles regarding disciplinary action against a pitcher who was caught using sandpaper to scuff balls, thereby giving pitches more pronounced movements.

Giamatti noted that most disciplinary cases involve impulsive violence, which is less morally grave than cheating. Such acts of violence, although intolerable, spring from the nature of physical contests between aggressive competitors. Such violence is a reprehensible extension of the physical exertion that is integral to the contest. Rules try to contain, not expunge, violent effort.

But cheating derives not from excessive, impulsive zeal in the heat of competition. Rather it is a cold, covert attempt to alter conditions of competition. As Giamatti put it, cheating has no organic origin in the act of playing and cheating devalues any contest designed to declare a winner among participants playing under identical rules and conditions. Toward cheating, the proper policy is zero tolerance.

Now, advances in training and sports medicine (medicine broadly defined, which reaches beyond prevention or treatment of injuries) make problematic the idea, central to sport, of competitors competing on an even footing. Nowadays there can be significant inequalities regarding techniques of training and nutrition.

Intensity in training should be rewarded with success in competition. But intense training should involve enhancing one's powers by methods (e.g., weight training) or materials (eat your spinach) that enhance the body's normal functioning. It is one thing to take vitamins, another thing to take a drug that facilitates abnormal growth (or makes a competitor abnormally aggressive).

An athlete steps over the line separating legitimate from illegitimate preparation for competition when he seeks advantage from radical intrusions into his body. A radical intrusion is one that does not enhance normal functioning but rather causes the body to behave abnormally. Illegitimate interventions cause an athlete to perform not unusually well—every athlete's aim—but unnaturally well.

Steroids are dangerous to the user's health. Even if an athlete is willing to run the risk, his competitors should not have to run it in order to compete. That is a sufficient reason for proscribing them. But even if steroids and other performance-enhancing drugs were risk-free, there would still be sufficient reasons for cleansing sport of them.

Drugs that make sport exotic make it less exemplary. Sport becomes less of a shared activity. It becomes less a drama of people performing well than a spectacle of bodies chemically propelled.

Athletes who seek a competitive edge through chemical advantage do not just overvalue winning; they misunderstand why winning is properly valued. It is properly valued as the reward for, and evidence of, praiseworthy attributes. They include the lonely submission to an exacting training regimen, and the mental mastery of pressure, pain and exhaustion.

In short, sport is valued not only because it builds character but because it puts on display, and crowns with glory, for the elevation of spectators as well as participants, attributes we associate with good character. Good character, not good chemistry.

A society's recreation is charged with moral significance. Sport would be debased, and with it a society that takes sport seriously, if sport did not strictly forbid things that blur the distinction between the triumph of character and the triumph of pharmacology.

October 2, 1988

A Professional's Sense of Responsibility

TORONTO—Concision and simplicity can be elements of eloquence, as Jamie Quirk showed when he said, "I'm a professional catcher." Those words in context revealed one reason why it is right for grown-ups to play, and care about, baseball games.

With one out in the eighth inning of their 160th game, the Baltimore Orioles were leading the Toronto Blue Jays 1–0 and were five outs from tying them for first place in the American League East. But a Blue Jay runner was on third. The Orioles' pitcher was a rookie who has, as baseball people say, a knee-buckling curve. Quirk called for a curve low and away. It was too much of both. It went in the dirt, bounced to the screen, the runner scored. The Blue Jays won in the eleventh.

The official scorer called it a wild pitch. Quirk called it a passed ball: "A major-league catcher has to block that ball. . . . I should have blocked it. . . . I'm a professor catcher." Maybe he should have, maybe not. Two things are certain. One is that America would be immeasurably improved if more Americans—teachers, workers, journalists, everyone—had Quirk's exacting standards of craftsmanship and accountability. The other is that Quirk, who will be 35 this month, did a manly thing in trying to block blame from reaching a 22-year-old pitcher.

In the hours before D-Day, General Eisenhower drafted a statement to be issued if the invasion failed. First he wrote: "Our landings in the Cherbourg-Havre area have failed to gain a satisfactory foothold and the troops have been withdrawn." But then he struck the last six words and wrote instead: ". . . and I have withdrawn the troops." By replacing the passive tense with the first-person pronoun, Eisenhower stepped up to the pitch: He took responsibility. Quirk was like Ike.

Quirk is, in baseball's evocative language, a journeyman. His travels took him to the Royals, Cardinals, White Sox, Indians, Royals again, Athletics and Yankees before he arrived in Baltimore in midseason, in time to vivify the axiom that sport reveals as well as builds character. He may not be back in Baltimore next year, but he is a nice emblem of this year.

After beginning the 1988 season with a record 21 consecutive losses and going on to lose 107, the 1989 Orioles relied heavily on hungry rookies and some veterans who had been given up on by other teams. (Quirk had been released nine times.) The 1989 Orioles, who were in the hunt until the last weekend of the season, are called "overachievers." Meaning what? They achieved more than they were "supposed" to? Who are these supposers who lay down the law about other people's limits?

Baseball teams often reflect their cities. The Cubs have the edgy insecurity of The Second City. The Mets and Yankees are pure New York: chaos leavened by recriminations. Baltimore is just a nice town built around basics—a harbor, some manufacturing. The Orioles rebuilt around baseball's basics, speed and defense.

Frank Robinson—Hall-of-Famer, 1989 Manager of the Year (surely) and all-star aphorist—says: "Speed comes to the ballpark very day. The three-run home run does not." Speed serves defense, which improves pitching: Pitchers become aggressive, putting the ball in the strike zone, counting on fleet fielders to catch it.

Defense is baseball's underappreciated (by fans, not baseball people) dimension. Players spend more time with leather on their hands than with wood in their hands. The 1989 Orioles were the second team in history to have fewer than 90 errors. Their fielding percentage (.98602) was the best ever.

"When you've been around seven or eight years," said Cal Ripken, the shortstop, during this his eighth season, "you might think twice about making a diving catch on gravel and sliding into the wall. But at this stage of our young players' development, they don't think about it."

Ripken is not exactly Methuselah. He will be 29 on Opening Day,

1990. This is awfully far away. Today, baseball, the sport that combines, better than any other, team play and personal accountability, is coming to its autumn crescendo, beyond which stretches. . .

Jonathan Yardley says there are only two seasons, baseball season and The Void. When, toward the end of this season, George Bush was asked who he thought would win the American League East, he said, "I've given up on the Rangers." Good thinking. The Rangers are in the AL West.

Mr. President, read Baltimore's lips: The 1990 AL East champions open at home, 40 miles from your front porch, April 2, the end of The Void.

October 5, 1989

Wilding: Evil in the Park

NEW YORK—"There seem," says a professor described as a specialist in adolescent behavior, "to have been some socioeconomic factors involved." Ah.

Here is what those "factors" were "involved" in.

More than 30 boys, most under 16, went "wilding." In their rampage, they raped and battered nearly to death a 28-year-old jogger in Central Park near Harlem. They hit her with a pipe, hacked her skull and thighs with a knife, pounded her face with a brick, bound her hands beneath her chin with her bloody sweatshirt, which also served as a gag. Seven or more boys raped her. (One boy says he "only played with the lady's legs" and another says he only felt her breasts and held her down while others raped her.)

Her larynx may have been crushed. She lay undiscovered for nearly four hours, losing three-quarters of her blood. The puddle she lay in hastened hypothermia and her temperature fell to 80.

Various experts say they know why this happened. Alienation, anomie, boredom, rage—raging boredom?—peer pressure, inequality, status anxieties, television, advertising.

The professor who says "there seem to have been some socioeconomic factors involved" elaborates: "The media, especially television, is constantly advertising these various things that are necessary to define yourself, to be an acceptable person, and the joggers may represent a level of socioeconomic attainment that the media has convinced everybody is necessary to be an acceptable person. So, to that extent, such people become a target." Ah.

Who is the victim? Well, yes, of course, the woman. But her identity, even her reality, disappears as she recedes into a category: high attainers. The boys, too, are victims. They were provoked by high attainers and disoriented by media-imposed criteria of acceptable personhood.

We have here another triumph of the social science of victimology. Its specialty is the universalization of victimhood, the dispersal of responsibility into a fog of "socioeconomic factors."

"On the other hand," says the professor, "that doesn't explain why they would attack a homeless person." A homeless person was one of the "wilding" pack's eight victims before they caught the woman.

The fact that *The New York Times* considers the professor an illuminating source is itself illuminating. It reveals the rhetoric that elite liberal institutions find convincing and comforting when confronted by horror.

Another theorist is heard from: "One doesn't have to excuse sociopathic behavior to notice the contrast of visible, great wealth and massive poverty." Verily, nail your political agenda to every passing tragedy: The "lesson" here is to "do something" about the "underclass." First, of course, a task force.

Never mind the fact that most of the attackers come from comfortable middle- or working-class homes. Four live in a building with a doorman.

Another theorist speaks of the boys' "unfocused rage." The frequent references to the attackers' "rage" are fascinating because there is not a scintilla of evidence of rage. Actually, one of the boys blurted out the reason they did it. The reason he gave is theoretically unsatisfying, politically unuseful and philosophically unsettling, so he will not be heard: "It was something to do. It was fun."

Newspaper reports have repeatedly referred to the "wilding" attacks as "motiveless." But fun is a motive. Policemen, with their knack of the language of unvarnished fact, refer to "wildings"—packs of boys looting stores and inflicting random beatings—as a "pastime." Pastimes are adopted for fun.

In earlier, simpler—or were they?—days, descriptions of an episode like the one in Central Park would have begun with a judgment that today is never reached at all: The attackers did what they did because they are evil.

Today people respond: " 'Evil'? Such a primitive notion—not at all useful as an explanation." But that response is not real sophistication, it is a form of flinching. It is a failure of nerve. A vanishing moral vocabulary is being replaced by academic rubbish collected reflexively by "serious" newspapers. They serve up a rich sauce of sociological cant that coats reality, making it unrecognizable.

We have lost the ability to speak the language of emphatic judgment.

As James Q. Wilson says, "Our habits of the heart have been subverted by the ambitions of the mind."

The ambition of the modern mind is to spare itself a chilling sight, that of the cold blank stare of personal evil. The modern program is squeamishness dressed up as sophistication. Its aim is to make the reality of evil disappear behind a rhetorical gauze of learned garbage.

Until relatively recently in most societies, people who did what the "wilding" boys did would have been punished swiftly and with terrible severity.

Punishment in this case will be interminably delayed and ludicrously light. The boys know that; that is one reason they were singing rap songs in their jail cells.

A society that flinches from the fact of evil will flinch from the act of punishment. It should not wonder why it does not feel safe.

April 30, 1989

"Tragedy" As an Entitlement

New York's miraculous Cardinal O'Connor—turning water into wine is a miracle; so is turning religion into applesauce—visited the victim of the Central Park gang rape. Then "as I reflected on it," he says, he decided to visit the accused rapists in jail. "I didn't want to be seeming to single anyone out."

Recently the *Washington Post* reported that 16 years ago a man who until this week was Speaker Jim Wright's (D–Tx.) principal aide, and who in 1973 was a store manager, led a young woman customer into a storeroom, smashed her skull five times with a hammer, stabbed her repeatedly, slit her throat, left her for dead, then went to a movie. She survived. He was sentenced to 15 years in a Virginia prison but served less than 27 months in county jail, then joined Wright, the father-in-law of his brother.

The attacker said the reason he "just blew my cool for a second" was that he was under stress. And a psychiatrist reported that the attacker believed that he had "reacted in a way in which any man would perhaps react under similar circumstances" of pressure.

Representative Steny Hoyer (D–Md.) is, like Cardinal O'Connor, too evenhanded to single out anyone. Calling the *Post* story "stale news," Hoyer says: "There was a tragedy on both sides. The tragedy has now been compounded."

Hoyer's histrionic rhetoric, assigning "tragedy" promiscuously, is the sixth hammer blow. His inanity is the ultimate indignity, condemning the woman forever to close confinement with her attacker in the embrace of a cold abstraction: She and he are casualties for a "tragedy."

The word "tragedy" is just one of those puffy dumplings of words that tumble together in jumbles of blather when politicians, confronted by an event and a microphone, turn on their spigots of sententiousness. The mind of the Congressman, who sees tragedy distributed "on both sides," is like the mind of the Cardinal, who is too scrupulous to "single out" the victim from the victimizers.

Someone who speaks facilely of tragedy on all sides really sees it on none. The concept of tragedy presupposes a moral order that Hoyer's use of the word denies. If there is tragedy on both sides—the woman whose body was slashed and smashed, the man whose "cool" was "blown"—then life is too random, too absurd to support the idea of human dignity inherent in tragedy. Then people are creatures of accidents, formed by impersonal forces and moved by impulses that could cause "any man" to act the same way.

The social atmosphere is heavily dosed with such assumptions. They are carried in the rhetoric of the Cardinal and the Congressman: the reflexive rhetoric of perfunctory compassion.

Conspicuous consumption has been supplanted by a new vulgarity—conspicuous compassion (Allan Bloom's phrase). It is flaunted by people too exquisitely evenhanded to "single out" the raped from the rapists. It is the moral ostentation of people so delicately sensitive that they will not discriminate, in the ascription of tragedy, between the wielder of the hammer and the one whose skull was hammered.

This egalitarian compassion—everyone gets a share—is a result of modern man's liberating moral transaction: The right to judge has been exchanged for immunity from judgment. Even the worst acts are said to arise from causes that are both trivial ("cool" is "blown" for "a second") and irresistible ("any man" might act the same way).

Unlimited tolerance in the form of indiscriminate compassion is supposed to yield "nihilism with a happy ending" (Bloom, again). But the real result is the re-animalization of man, a moral anarchy that is the inevitable consequence of intellectual incoherence.

If there is nothing that can be called human nature, if there are only random results of varied socializations, then there is no natural right. The great enterprise of philosophy—presenting a coherent view of nature and the way of living in it that is right for man—is dead.

So universities might as well practice "democracy of the disciplines" with curricula in constant flux. If there are no real truths, only shifting sands of cultural norms, there can be no texts that deserve to be called classics because they teach real truths.

It is an age in which children are taught not to discover the good but to manufacture "values," not so they can lead the noble life but so they can devise pleasant "life-styles." It is an age in which the aim of life is not autonomy in the sense of the regulation of life by real standards but, rather, "authenticity" in following strong feelings. It is an age of egalitarian distribution of esteem as well as compassion.

In such an age, indiscriminateness is a moral imperative. In such an age, there will be clerics who, as a sign of tender sensibility, will not "single out" the brutalized from the brutes. And there will be lawmakers who insist that the dignity of tragedy is an entitlement to be distributed democratically, one portion per voter.

May 14, 1989

"Merely" a Nurse

Lytton Strachey dipped his pen in the acid of his malice in order to etch word sketches of *Eminent Victorians.* However, one of his subjects proved impervious to his considerable powers of disparagement. She was Florence Nightingale, the founder of nursing as a modern profession. Strachey, unable to suppress an emotion strange to him—admiration— wrote that in the filth and carnage of the Crimean War she was "a rock in the angry ocean." She profoundly influenced hospital construction and management and nurses' education. Amazing, said Strachey, for someone who was "merely a nurse."

Well. A nurse is a remarkable social artifact, and there are not nearly enough nurses, in part because of backward attitudes packed into phrases like "merely a nurse." Today's nursing shortage is not just another crisis *de jour.* By the end of this century—in just 12 years—the demand for nurses will be double the supply. Fourteen percent of hospitals in large urban areas and 9 percent in small urban areas are delaying admissions because of the shortage. The shortage has strange aspects. More nurses are needed because Americans are healthy longer. And although we have more nurses than ever—about 2 million—more are needed because people are sicker when admitted to hospitals.

The advance of medicine and public health accelerated in the late 19th century with improved control of infectious diseases. Then the 20th century's characterizing phenomenon—war—brought progress in surgery and trauma control. Next came rapid strides in diagnosis and pharmacology. Today, and partly as a result of these advances, the most pressing medical problem is care for the chronically ill. This usually requires intense application of nursing skills. And because demography is destiny, we know that the need will intensify. The number of Americans 85 or older is rising six times as fast as the rest of the population.

Important basic needs of the chronically ill are emotional and social. But the intense specialization and technological emphasis of modern medicine have diminished the ability and willingness of doctors—once upon a time they were esteemed for their "bedside manner"—to satisfy such needs. The American ideal of a doctor—kindly, caring, reassuring Dr. Welby—was, says Lucille Joel, essentially a nurse. She is one. She also is a Rutgers professor and a forceful advocate of the proposition that nursing should be accorded the dignity of a profession parallel to that of doctors.

The crux of today's deteriorating physician-nurse relations is that many physicians cannot understand, or will not accept, that nurses can, should and want to do more than carry out doctors' orders. Nurses should be regarded by physicians more as complementary and less as subordinate professionals. Physicians are an episodic presence in the life of a patient. Nurses control the environment of healing. Assisting the rehabilitation of a stroke victim or monitoring and coping with chronic disease is essentially a nurse's, not a physician's function. A nurse—a mere nurse—superintends complex technologies, dispenses information and health education and strives for a holistic understanding of patients' needs, which include empathy.

For various reasons, ranging from AIDS (in New York City AIDS patients occupy about 5 percent of all hospital beds) to the use of toxic substances in treatments, nursing is still a dangerous profession. It also is increasingly demanding, physically and emotionally. Most people in hospitals are hurting and frightened and their families are in distress. This is increasingly true because, for cost-containment reasons, hospitals are increasingly reluctant to admit people unless they are quite ill. More and more patients are older and sicker and require more nursing. There is an 86 percent higher ratio of nurses to patients than 12 years ago. Then there were 58 per 100 patients, now there are 91 (spread over three shifts).

Patients progress quicker when they can get ample assistance in walking, eating and other elemental matters when they need it. Because of the nursing shortage many patients either take longer to heal or are discharged feeling more unwell than they would if given needed nursing. Furthermore, cost-cutting hospitals are trimming the staff (ward clerks, secretaries, transport and laboratory aides) that supports nurses, who now do extra duties. Nurses are paying a price for their reputation for versatility and dependability.

The nursing profession has a supply-side tradition of generating a high flow of highly motivated nurses and not worrying about retention. However, the emancipation of women, opening careers to talents, has enlarged women's choices while making nursing, a female-dominated profession (only 3 percent are male), less attractive to young women. There are, Joel believes, severe limits to the ability to attract male nurses, partly because of the difference between the sensibilities required for nursing and those produced by the socialization of men.

Nurses' salaries are low, starting, on average, at $21,000, and the ceiling can be hit in less than seven years. Many 20-year nurses make less than $30,000. An attorney in private practice can reasonably hope to increase his or her salary more than 200 percent in a career. A nurse can expect an increase of less than 40 percent. Add to monetary deprivation the denial of the psychological income of status, respect and intellectual growth and you have a recipe for a shortage.

Nightingale set a tone of brisk practicality for the nursing profession when she noted dryly that whatever else can be said of hospitals, this must be said: They should not spread disease. They should not be dangerous places, but they are becoming more so because of society's neglectfulness regarding nurses. Such neglect can have consequences for you, mortal reader. "If we live long enough, something wears out. I don't care how much oatmeal you eat," says Joel, viewing the columnist's breakfast with as much distaste as he does. The nursing profession must be nurtured with financial and emotional support. Otherwise, someday when you are in a hospital and are in pain or other need you will ring for a nurse and she will not come as soon, or be as attentive, as you and she would wish. And the chances are, aging reader, that the day will come when you will ring.

May 23, 1988

"Throw Deep"

After hearing scientific arguments for, and budgetary complaints about, the proposed $4.4 billion atom smasher, President Reagan swerved the discussion into an anecdote. He recalled Jack London's personal credo:

I would rather be ashes than dust,
I would rather my spark should burn out in a brilliant blaze,
Than it should be stifled in dry rot.
I would rather be a superb meteor,
With every atom of me in magnificent glow,
Than a sleepy and permanent planet.

Then Reagan said that London's credo was once read to Ken Stabler, the pro quarterback, who was asked what it meant. Stabler said: "Throw deep." Stabler was right. So was Reagan in endorsing the Superconducting Super Collider (SSC). Now the future of elementary particle physics is in the hands of Congress.

Congress willing, the SSC will be a tunnel in a circle with a 52-mile circumference. Atom smashers are, in effect, gigantic microscopes for peering into the heart of matter. In the SSC, counterrotating beams of protons, each beam traveling at nearly the speed of light, will be steered by magnets into collisions. Only a few of these protons will collide, producing a shower of other subatomic particles. The characteristics of the resultant particles will be measured, often in intervals of billionths of seconds.

In order to probe into nature's smallest simplicities, progressively more gigantic and complex devices must employ progressively higher energy. The higher the energy, the finer the scale of investigation. In this century, we have progressed downward in scale, from atoms to nuclei to protons and neutrons and electrons, then to quarks and leptons, which seem—so far—to be the elemental constituents of matter.

The more energy is contained in the space where particles collide, the better the chance the energy will be transformed into new forms of matter. Fermilab, a particle accelerator in Batavia, Illinois, can create collisons yielding 2 trillion electron volts. The SSC will yield 40 trillion.

The collisions in the SSC should replicate energy and temperature conditions in the first fraction of a second at the creation of the universe. This should yield knowledge about the four known basic forces of nature: gravity, electromagnetism, the weak nuclear force responsible for certain radiation decays and the strong nuclear force that binds atomic nuclei. And perhaps the SSC will yield evidence about the Grand Unified Theory, the theory that the four forces form a single unified force.

Fundamental science such as high-energy physics inevitably has large economic and, more important, cultural effects, including effects on mankind's moral sensibility. And the SSC, the largest and costliest experimental device ever, will have a profound effect on science.

When Congress comes to consider approval of the SSC, it should bear in mind that many of America's foremost scientists were born elsewhere and came here to be on the moving frontiers of science. The sociology of scientific enterprise is complex, but this is clear: The momentum generated by synergism among scientists, spanning generations, can be quickly dissipated. It can be forfeited by government negligence and philistine parsimony in scientific investment.

The first cyclotron was at Berkeley in 1930. It was five inches in diameter. Until recently, America clearly led the world in high-energy physics research. In this decade, Europe has secured the lead, with the Soviet Union rising rapidly. The SSC will make America's particle physicists preeminent in the competition to understand the ultimate constituents of matter and the forces that bind those constituents to form the universe.

Roy Schwitters, Harvard physicist, says: "High-energy physics is the ultimate extension of man's curiosity about what things are made of and how they work." Such physics is increasingly interwoven with cosmology because of the "big bang" theory of the origin of the universe.

Approximately 15 billion years ago, when the universe was a nanosecond old, hitherto unapproachably high temperatures decomposed matter into its most primitive constituents. As the universe cooled, matter resulted. Understanding the nature of these constituents and processes is essential to understanding the history of the universe since creation.

Given the grandeur of this intellectual undertaking, it is demeaning to justify the SSC in terms of economic benefits. Suffice it to say there will be benefits and we cannot now know what they will be.

Who in the 1860s thought the synthesis of electricity and magnetism, and discovery of the laws of electromagnetic waves, would produce today's communication technologies? Who in the 1920s could imagine that quantum mechanics would produce the semiconductor industry? Applications of the two intellectual revolutions of the 20th century—quantum theory and relativity—account for a significant portion of today's gross national product.

When Reagan ended the meeting by saying, "Throw deep," thereby signaling his support for the SSC, James Miller, head of the Office of Management and Budget, said: "You're going to make a lot of physicists ecstatic." Reagan replied, "That's probably fair, because I made two physics teachers in high school very miserable." Reagan likes to say, "You ain't seen nothing yet." The human race has never seen a project of any sort as ambitious as the SSC. But, then, the human race is designed to "throw deep."

February 15, 1987

1986: A Typical 1986

Long ago when the earth was young and the Cleveland Browns and Cincinnati Bengals were preparing to play each other for only the second time ever, one of the coaches predicted: "It will be a typical Browns-Bengals game." In the same analytic spirit let us say that 1986 was pretty much what we have come to expect from 1986s.

Halley's comet, as is its wont, wandered by and departed hastily, doubtless convinced that every 76 years is enough exposure to earth, where no one thought there were too few Elvis impersonators at the celebration of Miss Liberty's face-lift. Bureaucracy and complacency combined to kill the seven *Challenger* astronauts. The Chernobyl accident caused a French newspaper to say, "Communists make electricity the way they make war—without worrying too much about victims and by eliminating observers." Explorers examined another relic of technological hubris, the *Titanic*. Nature turned nasty in Cameroon when volcanic gases spewed from beneath a lake and killed 1,700.

All God's chillun got shoes or can get them in Mrs. Marcos's closet, which is large enough to house Mr. and Mrs. Duvalier, itinerant non-laborers. American moralists-at-a-safe-distance got tough with South Africa by throwing lots of blacks out of work. This was the result of disinvestment, which served its chief purpose, namely to make the moralists feel good. File under "paradise postponed": one day in May millions of people held hands and yet poverty remains. The most effective antipoverty program in generations came packaged as tax reform, which removed millions of the poor from the tax rolls. Wall Street recoiled in horror from the scandal of people getting rich by insider trading rather than the sweat of their brows. Edward Kennedy announced that William Rehnquist was morally unsatisfactory.

On November 4, not one of the GOP's grander days, Democrats captured the Senate and a Beirut newspaper broke a story—too absurd to credit—about U.S. arms sales to Iran. Everyone who should have known about this policy said they did not, calling to mind the occasion when a boxer landed a punch after a round ended and the TV announcer explained, "It's hard to hear the bell up there. There's a tremendous amount of smoke here in the Boston Garden." A six-year spell of national ebullience was dead as mutton. For the third of eight Christmases Iran was too much on America's mind. Amazingly, Donald Regan had even worse moments than his jaunty riposte to persons favoring sanctions against gold- and diamond-producing South Africa: "Are the women of America prepared to give up their jewelry?" Americans worried about their government's rationality but adorned their cars with yellow signs announcing "Baby on Board," presumably to dissuade people who otherwise would decide to crash into them.

The Reagan years have been years for calling bluffs. First, the public that had been complaining about big government had its bluff called when Reagan pushed for domestic spending cuts and the public decided it did not really want them. This year in Iceland, arms-control zealots got their bluffs called. Reagan and Gorbachev Ping-Ponged radical proposals—scrap ballistic missiles, scrap all nuclear arms—and suddenly people began to have second thoughts, almost kindly thoughts, about the structure of deterrence that has kept the peace. Even arms controllers flinched at the thought of the costs—conscription, money—of deterring Soviet conventional forces with conventional forces.

A summit in Iceland (Gorbachev loves Iceland: few Jews and other disturbers of the peace) was Gorbachev's reward for releasing the hostage Daniloff. Gorbachev was released from his promise that the summit after Geneva would be in the United States, where Anatoly Shcharansky would rally 400,000 Jews, one for each refusenik. Released in Berlin by KGB agents who ordered him to walk directly toward waiting Western officials, Shcharansky defiantly zigzagged to freedom. Castro's 60th birthday was spoiled by the book of the year, *Against All Hope,* by Armando Valladares, Cuba's Solzhenitsyn. Austria, most of whose Jews were murdered by a man born in that country, elected as president a man with a dark Nazi past, thereby pioneering this phenomenon: anti-Semitism without Jews.

Two superb athletes (Len Bias, Don Rogers), each a man-child with more money than maturity, killed themselves with cocaine. In the 1940s a survey listed the top seven discipline problems in public schools: talking, chewing gum, making noise, running in the halls, getting out of turn in line, wearing improper clothes, not putting paper in wastebaskets. A 1980s survey lists these top seven: drug abuse, alcohol abuse, pregnancy, suicide, rape, robbery, assault. (Arson, gang warfare and venereal disease are also-rans.) In 1986 AIDS made sex scary. An announcement of a Wednesday program at an Edinburgh church read: "1:10–1:35 P.M.— Lunchtime Service. God thought of sex first. Coffee and sandwiches afterward." The most mysterious woman of the year was a Pennsylvanian named Helga. In the department of things we would rather not know, thank you, a computer analysis of the Mona Lisa suggested that the portrait is not of an unknown model but of Leonardo himself, in drag.

Death, as it must to all, came to musicians representing strikingly different generations—Benny Goodman, 77, and just hours before 1986 began, Ricky Nelson, 45. Stalin's henchman Molotov, 96, died old and in bed, a privilege he helped to deny to millions. Exactly 50 years after becoming the focus of world attention, the Duchess of Windsor died in lonely seclusion in Paris. Cary Grant, 82, died not in a posh drawing room but in Iowa, which just goes to show. And Heaven will have its hands full with Lady Diana Cooper, dead at 93, the beauty and eccentric who once said: "I do think servants should not be ill. We have quite enough illness ourselves without them adding to the symptoms."

Baseball's Tom Gorman was buried in his umpiring uniform with a ball-and-strike indicator in his hand, the count reading three balls, two strikes. Baseball also lost Bill Veeck, who could remember when the

Chicago Cubs were "mostly drunks off the field and craftsmen on it." In 1986 the Cubs did not win the World Series. They have not won it since 1908, two years before Tolstoy died. Regarding the Cubs and the series, 1987 will be a typical 1987.

January 5, 1987

1987: "Keep Honking, I'm Reloading"

To paraphrase a country-music poet, if 1987 were a fish, you'd throw it back in. Fawn Hall's boss (as Oliver North will be remembered) testified about having had this "neat idea," something about taking Khomeini to the cleaners. Donald Regan hung up on Nancy Reagan, who was accused of having a mind of her own. Conservatives correctly warned that if Howard Baker became chief of staff, the Soviet flag would soon fly from Washington lampposts. Reagan declared the Cold War over, Gorbachev declared the Soviet human-rights record spotless, the Soviet rape of Afghanistan entered its ninth year.The trial of Klaus Barbie and the death of Rudolph Hess were faint echoes of another war. The Navy did what navies do, projecting American power, and the USS *Stark* showed that high-tech weapons can be rendered negligible by low-caliber officers.

Margaret Thatcher won a third election, beating someone who spoke like Joe Biden. Patricia Schroeder said it's my party and I'll cry if I want to. Gary Hart challenged reporters to follow him around but warned that they would be bored. In December he said his lies, misjudgments and general strangeness are irrelevant to his quest for control of nuclear weapons. Lincoln, call your office: Hart says he is as qualified to be president as anyone who has ever sought the office. Give Aristotle the news: Hart wants his epitaph to read, "He educated the people." Donald Trump, landlord and statesman, announced himself put out that politicians cannot solve problems that he would not put up with for one minute. The Beastie Boys (no, not the Iran-contra gang) had their 15 minutes of fame, and George Bush made a determined bid for Iowa's debutante vote.

Spam, Superman and the Golden Gate Bridge turned 50, and on the Constitution's 200th birthday scientists surmised that George III's loopiness was caused by his passion for lemonade and sauerkraut, both made in lead-glazed pottery. In the Central African Republic a man identified as the former cook for the former emperor Bokassa testified that he had served the emperor a human body stuffed with rice and flamed in gin.

For breakfast. Back in civilization, on California freeways pistol-packing drivers gave rise to a bumper sticker: "Keep honking, I'm reloading." Thirty-two hundred tons of Long Island garbage traveled 6,000 miles in 155 days to a Brooklyn incinerator.

The unpleasantness on Wall Street produced a satisfying surge of *schadenfreude* about Yuppies getting their comeuppances. Insider trader Ivan Boesky was sentenced to go inside, and a worried capitalist handed Harvard $30 million to fund ethics instruction at the Business School. The donor says: "I believe ethics pays—that it's smart to be ethical." Galvanized by the deficit crisis, Congress required pizzas containing artificial cheese to be so labeled. That supposedly will stimulate consumption of the real stuff, thereby saving a few million in cheese subsidies next year. In England, the Islington city council fine-tuned justice: the Gay and Lesbian Committee was renamed the Lesbian and Gay Committee. Galvanized by the AIDS crisis, Reno radio station KONE distributed 5,000 condoms imprinted with the station's logo. Apostolic asceticism is chic, but Oral Roberts got an ultimatum from God: raise a whopping sum by March or I'll kill you. God then stayed the execution. Stay tuned. Jim ("God wants his people to go first class") and Tammy Bakker learned that there will be no more $9,000 shipments of truffles from Brussels for PTL bashes.

Planned Parenthood, one of the voices of moderation denouncing Robert Bork's "extremism," said that if Bork were confirmed it might take a constitutional amendment to make contraceptives available. Various similar groups, claiming to adore the Supreme Court as a guardian against passionate majorities, turned Bork's confirmation process into the first national plebiscite on a nominee. New Jersey said Baby M's natural mother would not be her actual mother.

Victor Hugo was boffo on Broadway. The publishing surprise of the year was Allan Bloom's mind-opening *The Closing of the American Mind.* Two terrific novels, *Presumed Innocent* and *The Bonfire of the Vanities*, dealt with professionals falling into the toils of the criminal-justice system. Michael Deaver was convicted of perjury and Washington was shocked—shocked!—by his influence peddling. Garrison Keillor moved from Minnesota to Manhattan, where small-town gentleness is as scarce as Powdermilk Biscuits.

SMU learned that there is learning without football, Michael Jordan demonstrated that the law of gravity does not apply to all equally, and Sugar Ray Leonard showed how elegant mayhem can be. A Dodger executive showed that he lacked "the necessities" for talking sensibly about the role of blacks in baseball 40 years after Jackie Robinson was a rookie. Was the ball juiced or was the pitching poor? There were a record 4,458 home runs—about 1.5 million feet of homers or three Mark Mc-

Gwire homers laid end to end. A Kansas City relief pitcher, asked if the problem with his shoulder might be mental, said, "How could it be mental? I don't have a college education." Yogi Berra, the syndicated movie critic, confused Glenn Close, the actress, with Glen Cove, a suburb.

Death, as it must to all, came to the American woman of the century, Clare Boothe Luce. It also came to one of America's great artists, Fred Astaire, and a great merchandiser, Andy Warhol. Danny Kaye was what a wise Walter Mitty would want to be—extraordinarily talented, life-affirming and kind. Babe Herman was one of three Brooklyn Dodger runners who arrived at the same base. Ralph Waldo Taylor, dead at 105, was the last of the soldiers who charged up San Juan Hill.

NASA switched on a computer capable of 1.72 billion computations a second, and a Citicorp report said that good information is as important today as it was when carrier pigeons brought "the news that Nelson had triumphed at Waterloo." The English language is another year older and the worse for wear, with a supermarket chain (no, not the one advertising "semiboneless ham") announcing that it is open "24 hours a day" and urging customers to "check local stores for exact hours." Someone should send those folks, and this year, to the camp that describes itself as offering "individual attention to the minimal exceptional."

January 4, 1988

1988: Year of Oat Bran and Ozone

Mankind, a small flame in a strong wind, had a stimulating year in which nature got our attention. It demonstrated imperious indifference to our pretense of mastery over all we survey. It also demonstrated some consequences of our inadequate stewardship of the planet.

More than 25 million were homeless when a monsoon put 80 percent of Bangladesh under water. Hurricane Gilbert had the lowest barometric pressure (26.13) ever recorded in the Western Hemisphere. In Armenia the earth's movable crust brought additional suffering to one of the earth's most long-suffering peoples. In high summer an American headline revealed that journalism had stalked Truth to its lair: "Heat Wave Blamed for Record Temperatures." When in 1863 Vicksburg fell to Union forces, Lincoln wrote (presidents really used to write like this): "The Father of Waters again goes unvexed to the sea." The drought of 1988 almost caused the Mississippi to trickle to New Orleans.

The warming of the planet became a political as well as scientific preoccupation. The sky is not falling but the ozone is thinning ominously in spots. Forests are the earth's lungs. Senator Al Gore says they are being destroyed at a rate of one football field a second—a Tennessee every year. *Life* magazine says that in 1988 Brazilian settlers set aflame a Nebraska-size area of the Amazon rain forest. By winter nature was proving more resilient than many had feared when forest fires ravaged Yellowstone. Fifty miles of East Coast beaches were closed because of medical waste washing ashore. All right, save the whales, but give us a break: no more media extravaganzas to save them three at a time from nature's natural harshness. One of the three whales probably died beneath the ice before the other two made it out to a rendezvous with the sharks and whalers in the Pacific.

Cholesterol-conscious Americans gorged themselves on oat bran on the assumption that eating like that will lengthen life, or at least make life seem long. A professor of medicine, next to whom I do not want to sit, suggested fighting cholesterol by eating a strong raw onion each day or drinking the equivalent in onion juice. The No. 9 killer of children between the ages of one and four and the No. 7 killer of people 15 to 24 was AIDS.

Make a better mousetrap and the world will beat a path to your door, but why bother? Leveraged buyouts are more lucrative and less work. With just $15 million of their own and $25 million borrowed, some investors bought RJR Nabisco. It may be dismantled. That's the way the Oreo cookie crumbles. E.T., phone home, your accountant says you have sold 15 million videocassettes. David Packard gave $2 billion to charities. Donald Trump played with his yacht, the one with a chamois ceiling, a disco, an onyx shower, a solid gold sink. In the Sudan 250,000 starved.

The State Department wrote cue cards for the U.N.'s favorite terrorist, thereby advancing peace in our time. Golly, why hadn't anyone thought of that before? Iraq, which might have had nuclear weapons by now if Israel had not decided otherwise, used poison gas. The Soviet Union promised to end its fraternal socialist solidarity in Afghanistan. Gorbachev promised a cut of 4 percent of the Soviet armed forces, which have been increased 6 percent in the last two years and 25 percent in the last six years. Benazir Bhutto, 35, became the first woman to lead an Islamic nation. Do you still doubt Jeane Kirkpatrick's distinction between authoritarian and totalitarian regimes? One of the former, in Chile, lost a referendum on its continuation.

Congresspersons who recoiled in horror from aiding the contras (it is naughty to interfere in the "internal affairs" of the Sandinista Stalinists) cheered the U.S. attempt to overthrow the government of Panama. Noriega, bidden to go, declined to do so. He finds U.S. power resistible.

Do those who killed aid to the contras see any connection? An influential tome (Paul Kennedy's *The Rise and Fall of the Great Powers*), much praised and occasionally even read by semi-isolationists, suggested that America is suffering from "imperial overstretch." Sandinistas and Noriega rejoice that America's real problem is understretch, the atrophy of underused muscle.

Nature (human) imitated art (Tom Wolfe's novel *The Bonfire of the Vanities*) in New York's Tawana Brawley fraud. The name of the lead charlatan, the Reverend Sharpton, even sounded like Wolfe's Reverend Bacon. Geraldo Rivera's nose met the cutting edge of trash television. Jimmy Swaggart asked for forgiveness and a new television show. Steroids propelled sprinter Ben Johnson into disgrace. Arizona's Evan Mecham became the first governor impeached since 1929. Wedtech, supposedly a Republican and executive branch scandal, produced a conviction and an indictment of Democratic congressmen.

Gary Hart announced that he was as qualified to be president as "anyone in the past 200 years." Jesse Jackson said that Hitler had been "an ally of the United States" and the next morning the media were up in arms about . . . Dan Quayle's military record. George ("Read my lips: Be kinder and gentler or I'll break your kneecaps") Bush beat whatwashisname. By December Bush's appointees had *The New York Times* purring about his "healthy preference for nonideological, practical people." Ah, so the election was about competence, not ideology, after all.

Irving Berlin turned 100. George Burns, 92, wrote a best seller, a love letter to Gracie. Pistol Pete Maravich fired his last shot at 40. Kim Philby, the traitor, died at 76, 50 years too late. Bart Giamatti got Pete Rose's approval as baseball commissioner: "He's an intellectual from Yale, but he's very intelligent." The Chicago Cubs, in the 80th year of their rebuilding effort (they last won the World Series in 1908), discovered electricity. The Baltimore Orioles started 0–21 and finished 23½ games out—out of sixth place, that is. Then they were sold for $70 million, $58 million more than they were sold for nine years ago. Billy Martin's fifth—dare we hope final?—term as Yankees manager ended.

At the end of another December—the month before the month before spring training starts—the wind blows and the flame flickers and we feel for mankind respect for its endurance, sympathy because it faces another year so soon after the last one, and foreboding because next year is the year before the year before the year before the Iowa caucuses.

January 2, 1989

1989: History Clears Its Throat

Having survived Hurricane Hugo in his home state of South Carolina, Marvin Craig, brother of Roger, the San Francisco Giants manager, settled into his seat in Candlestick Park to enjoy the World Series. It was that kind of year. Eventful.

Voyager 2 discovered 1,500-mph winds on Neptune, but even more impressive winds blew down the Berlin wall. History seemed self-consciously tidy. The bicentennial of the French Revolution occurred in the year in which Europe at last had a revolution—an October Revolution, no less—worth having. It came on the 50th anniversary of the outbreak of the war that sucked Soviet power into Central Europe. Czechoslovakia's Communist regime denounced the coming of pluralism in Hungary as "a coup d'état by parliamentary means." A blink later the Czechoslovakian town of Gottwaldov named for Klement Gottwald, leader of the 1948 Stalinist coup, reclaimed its old name, Zlin. *Sic transit* just about everything. Empress Zita, 96, last empress of Austria-Hungary, died 70 years after her empire did, and in the year of the death of the (one more time!) evil empire that eventually filled the void left in Central Europe by the fall of thrones. As communism was dying, so was Communist Dolores Ibarruri, 93, "La Pasionaria" of the Spanish Civil War, famous for her cry *"No pasarán"*—"They shall not pass." (They— Franco's forces—passed.)

Six months after China's gerontocracy sent tanks against bicycles and a makeshift Statue of Liberty, President Bush's emissaries were in Beijing commiserating with the killers about the "negative forces" in America and China who are impeding "cooperation." In October a coup failed in Panama, perhaps for want of U.S. support, but Bush derided critics who he said wanted him to "unleash the full military and go in and 'get Noriega' . . . that's not the way I plan to conduct the military or foreign affairs of this country."

A Congress that produced the $300 billion (so far) savings and loan scandal judged John Tower unfit for a cabinet office. To many in Congress the scandalous part of the HUD scandal was private influence peddlers dipping into programs that Congress considers its private pork. Then there was Jim Wright. Perhaps he will write a book. Congress and Bush did act with lightning speed to stop the epidemic of flag-burning. (If you want to confuse Bush, desecrate a flag by riddling it with fire from your trusty assault rifle.) Congress beat a pell-mell retreat when the self-sufficient elderly rebelled against attempts to inflict upon them a welfare-state kindness (catastrophic health insurance) they did not want. Congress did have the stamina to stay the course and take the heat and take a pay raise.

One year after Michael Dukakis promised (threatened?) to do to America what he has done to Massachusetts, his state has the nation's worst bond rating. The Supreme Court put the abortion issue part of the way back where it belongs, in the arena of political argument, to the intense distress of politicians, not least those who had opposed the court taking custody of the issue 16 years earlier. A coven of Rhode Island witches won tax-exempt status as a religious group. Laundrygate ended when, in the District of Columbia, the (no kidding) Coalition Against Discriminatory Dry Cleaning got cleaners to quit charging more to launder a woman's shirt than a man's.

Leona Helmsley's deducted girdle and Malcolm Forbes's birthday bash gave money a bad name—not that anyone started avoiding the stuff. Japan said: "I'll take Manhattan," or at least the most famous site in the center of it, and a morsel of Hollywood, too. Remember when New York called itself Fun City? A white woman was nearly killed when blacks went "wilding" in Central Park. A black teenager was killed when whites behaved as execrably in Bensonhurst. However, it was a year for high-achieving blacks. The two most frequently seen celebrities in television commercials were black athletes—Bo Jackson and Michael Jordan. The two hottest talk-show hosts were black (Oprah, Arsenio). The nation's top soldier and the mayor-elect of the largest city were blacks. The capital of the Confederacy was awaiting the nation's first black governor. Suddenly the question of whether Jesse Jackson would run for mayor of Washington did not seem so interesting.

In a year in which so much history was made, a survey showed that 42 percent of college seniors—*seniors*—did not know in which half-century the Civil War occurred. However, history happens, understood or not: At the outbreak of World War I a porter in London's Waterloo Station declared, "I shall volunteer like my grandfather, who a hundred years ago was among those who defeated Napoleon on this very spot."

Oil from northern Alaska stained southern Alaska, a harbinger of a 1990s preoccupation with the environmental costs of modern life. If you are going to ship billions of barrels of oil on water, every once in a while millions will spill. Two Chilean grapes with tiny traces of cyanide, and an anonymous telephone call, set off panic about food hazards. Americans ate enough peanut butter to make more than 8 billion ordinary-size sandwiches, and were told that decaffeinated coffee might raise their cholesterol levels.

Salman Rushdie, one of those leftists who love the Third World—from a safe distance; he lives in Britain—brought out the literary critic that slept in the late Ayatollah Khomeini, scourge of modernity. Speaking of which (modernity): By the end of the year 60 percent of America's households had VCRs, 99 percent of them with their clocks flashing "12:00." Millions of Americans drove a herd of cattle to Montana with "Lonesome Dove." NBC aired a steamy serial about the shattering effect of The Other Woman on a placid family. It was called the "Today" show.

Three elegant artists died—Vladimir Horowitz, Laurence Olivier and Sugar Ray Robinson. In a faint echo of baseball's worst gambling problem, Bibb Falk, who replaced Shoeless Joe Jackson in the White Sox outfield when Joe was banned, died at 90. In a year in which almost anything seemed possible, the Cubs came close to winning the pennant. Instead, they broke the record (they set it in 1988) for the most consecutive years without winning. Not since 1945, the year the Iron Curtain descended.

January 1, 1990

The 1980s: The Suicide of Socialism, and Other Pleasures

What a difference 3,653 days can make. But, then, this decade got a running jump into itself.

Abroad, it began June 2, 1979, when the "Polish Pope" returned to Poland. The vicar of an ancient faith kindled the secular passion of nationalism, lighting the fuse that would detonate all the revolutions of 1989.

Intellectually, the decade's great development was the death of the socialist idea. The old argument, made by intellectuals, that intellectuals should plan economic life in accordance with equalitarian notions of "fairness," and two flaws: Intellectuals did not know how, and the masses did not want it.

Institutionally, socialism committed suicide, and not just in the East bloc. In France, a socialist president embarked upon a predictable program of "planning" and redistribution, with predictable, disastrous results. In Spain, too, a socialist government wound up embracing the market and pruning government ownership and subventions. Even Britain's invincibly ignorant Labor Party found the wilderness conducive to rethinking.

In 1981, the world's three largest figures—Reagan, Sadat and the Pope—were shot, the Pope by a Bulgarian-backed agent of "the Evil Empire." By calling it that, Reagan, who did more than anyone to end the Cold War, was accused of "taking us back" to the Cold War. In a sense, he did. To end the Cold War, the détente mentality first had to end.

The hinge on which the decade turned was 1983. Reagan used the phrase "Evil Empire" in March, 1983. Two weeks later, he proposed the Strategic Defense Initiative (SDI), the devastating challenge to the Soviet Union to compete in an arena—the most advanced science—that depends on the fecundity of freedom. Elections in 1983 in Britain and, more problematic, in Germany defeated the Soviet attempt, using Western "peace movements" to stop NATO's Intermediate Nuclear Forces (INF) deployment.

In America, the 1980s began June 6, 1978, when Californians passed Proposition 13, the beginning of the revolt of the middle class. So in Eastern Europe and the western United States, the two revolutionary (meaning, transforming) forces of the 19th century were still going strong: nationalism and the bourgeoisie.

At the beginning of the decade, rational people—that is, pessimists—feared that inflation was the systemic and perhaps fatal disease of democracy. It no longer seems to be, because it radicalizes, and drives to the right, the middle class. Reagan's tax cuts shrank the government's revenue base and shifted to the right, perhaps for a generation, the nation's political agenda.

The two most interesting democratic governments, Reagan's and Thatcher's, were highly ideological about economics at a moment when economic theories seemed to have lost their predictive uses. America's national debt doubled in five years, the stock market in 1987 dropped 508 points in a day, but inflation declined and expansion continued.

The chord struck by two books, Tom Wolfe's novel *Bonfire of the Vanities* and Allan Bloom's *The Closing of the American Mind*, indicated that a vague sense of—dare we say it!—malaise survived from the 1970s among a significant minority of Americans.

For the mass of Americans, a suitable symbol of the decade was the remote-control wand for VCRs and cable-equipped television. The American grazed in private in a vast field of frivolous choices, actively choosing which pictorial stimuli passively to absorb. For much of the rest of the world, the next decade will not allow the luxury, such as it is, of passivity.

Although the 1990s are supposed to feature the blurring of particularities (Europe '92), these years may see sharpened distinctions, including new sovereign nations—three in the Baltics, six or so from what has been Yugoslavia. The end of *perestroika* (such as it was; it barely began in the

1980s) and *glasnost* may arrive abruptly in suppression of national aspirations in the Ukraine and other captive nations within the Soviet Union.

The Soviet Union—dismembered or not—will be eclipsed by Germany, reunited whether or not others wish it. The most intriguing question about reunification has not been imagined by most people, but it has been by Geoffrey Wheatcroft of the London *Sunday Telegraph*. There are, he notes, not two but three German states, the Federal Republic, the People's Republic—and Austria.

In 1945, the Allies chose to regard Austria as liberated rather than conquered. But, says Wheatcroft, the Austrian republic is essentially artificial. It was created "in spiteful fashion" by the victors after the war against the Kaiser, when the Austrians were the only people formerly ruled by the Hapsburgs who were deliberately denied self-determination. They would have joined the rest of Germany if they could have.

Perestroika was the foreign word given widest currency in the 1980s. In the 1990s the word could be *Anschluss*, and Germany could extend from the Baltic almost to the Adriatic.

December 31, 1989

PART 2

The Curtain
Comes Down

Europe's Second Reformation

Snapshots of modern history in the making often are blurry pictures of crowds in which faces are indistinct. Let us focus on two young Germans who acted alone and are part of the complex pedigree of the crowds that have trampled the Berlin Wall. Peter Fechter. Martin Luther.

On August 17, 1962, one year and four days after the first rudimentary Wall was put in place in the dead of night, Fechter, 18, was shot while trying to scale it near Checkpoint Charlie. He died slowly, while communist police refused to give assistance. Fechter, whose blood puddled at the base of the Wall, was a mason. He would have been 45 this year. Most of the young East Germans who last week perched like songbirds on the Wall were not born when he died. But they are his echoes, reverberations of his refusal to have his life circumscribed by concrete and communism.

When, as last week, history is being made in a big way, it seems to consist of jolting discontinuities. But history is the history of the mind, and great events invariably are beads on a thin, strong thread of ideas. Today's turmoil, in Germany and elsewhere, is in part a legacy of Luther.

History is bubbling in an old familiar kettle. It is just 60 miles from Berlin to Wittenberg, where the 34-year-old Luther nailed his 95 theses to the church door. Four years later at the Diet of Worms he spoke seven words that define the modern frame of mind: *"Hier stehe ich. Ich kann nicht anders."* ("Here I stand. I can do no other.") The primary idea of the Reformation was the primacy of individual conscience. It has been the high-octane fuel of all subsequent history.

Today history is marching to the cadences of an American president. Not the 41st president, but the 3rd, who spoke also through the 16th. The ideas and rhetoric reverberating through the middle of the Old World come from the New World, from Jefferson and Lincoln. They are still the most resonant expositors of the moral foundations of popular sovereignty. Of course American material as well as moral force has prevailed. In the 40 years since Soviet behavior provoked a reluctant America to stop disarming, defense (computed in today's dollars) has cost $10.4 trillion, approximately twice today's annual GNP. It has been history's biggest bargain. It held the line while Jefferson's ideas sowed their wholesome disorder.

There is an intellectual line connecting Wittenberg and Worms with Philadelphia, 1776, and Gettysburg, 1863. Luther, frightened by the forces he had unleashed, favored rendering too much to Caesar. But by his defense of the emancipation of private judgment he put Caesar permanently on the defensive. The most dangerous counterreformation against the impulse Luther let loose in modern life was not the one immediately launched from Rome. Rather, it came precisely 400 years after Wittenberg when communism came to Russia, imposed by a party claiming a monopoly on the understanding of history. Soon there was another totalitarianism triumphant in Berlin. This one tried to resubmerge the individual into tribalism. Since 1933 the eastern part of Berlin had known no respite; it has been under the heel of first one and then the other of these ideological assaults on individualism.

In 1989 history's fast-forward button has been punched hard, but no Luther, no contemporary intellectual leader did it. The breathtaking acceleration of events is a long pent-up reaction to socialism's impoverishment of every facet of life, from commerce to literature. However, one individual was the spark that lit the short fuse that led to this year's explosions. He lives 300 miles from Wittenberg. Europe's First Reformation was announced by banging on a church door. The Second Reformation began amid the heavy metal sounds of a shipyard, at Gdansk (once the German city of Danzig). There worked an electrician named Lech Walesa.

And there is sublime symmetry in the fact that Berlin has become the symbol and summation of communism's failure. The Wall has been communism's starkest confession of moral bankruptcy. And in Berlin, 47 years before the Wall went up, communism suffered a shock from which it never recovered. In August 1914, when the Western world slid into the abyss from which it may at last be climbing, communism's central conceit was shattered. Germany, with its industrial proletariat, was then, according to Marxist analysis, the nation most ripe for a communist revolution. Orthodox Marxists knew, simply *knew* that the workers of the world would unite because they had no fatherland. Workers supposedly had only the class interests of the oppressed and would respond to any international crisis with transnational solidarity. But within hours after the outbreak of war, Germany's socialist deputies in the Reichstag (meeting a few hundred yards from where the Wall now slices past the Brandenberg Gate) voted for war credits to finance the fatherland's war—the war that communists considered self-evidently a squabble among imperialists.

Today Gorbachev watches almost helplessly as the Soviet Union is riven by national, ethnic, religious, linguistic and cultural differences—all those things that Marx knew, simply *knew* had lost their saliency. The Evil Empire (those who took such strong exception to that characterization have fallen silent; it's about time) is going the way of the Ottoman and Austro-Hungarian empires. Czechoslovakia—a dagger pointed at a continent of supermarkets—cannot for long resist the tides lapping around it. Soon those tides may surge south and engulf even Europe's most brackish backwaters, Bulgaria and Romania. (Albania should be compelled to remain communist, as a museum.)

So we may end the century as we began it, worried about Germany and the Balkans. We shall see. One thing is certain: we have never seen a year like 1989. Only the Reformation is remotely comparable to today's gale-force intellectual winds and loud cracking of institutional foundations. No year, even in the 16th century, ever swept so many people or such complex societies into a vortex of change. Nineteen eighty-nine has been the most startling, interesting, promising and consequential year, ever.

November 20, 1989

Gorbachev, Meet Jefferson

At the United Nations Mikhail Gorbachev said, impertinently: "Two great revolutions, the French Revolution of 1789 and the Russian Revolution of 1917, exerted a powerful impact on the very nature of history . . . those two revolutions shaped the way of thinking that is still prevalent . . ." *Two* great revolutions? Trust a historicist to miss one of the largest lessons of history. It is that the American Revolution unleashed the most potent force surging through the last two centuries. The force is the passion for freedom grounded in respect for rights. And the American Revolution contained the principle that is indispensable for political legitimacy—something that the Soviet regime has not achieved in seven decades—in a nation as diverse as the Soviet Union.

At the United Nations Gorbachev spoke, as Marxists are wont to do, of "the laws of social development." But the social ground is shaking beneath his feet for reasons that refute (redundantly) Marx. The earthquake shaking the foundations of the Soviet state is, in part, a reverberation of the French Revolution. That revolution presaged many odious aspects of modern politics. These include the ideological intoxication of intellectuals, the mobilization of the masses by ersatz religions and liturgies, and the concentration of the modern state's power in a single overbearing, overreaching, hyperkinetic person. Lenin's precursor was Napoleon, who ushered in the age of mass effects. It is clear why the likes of Gorbachev like the French Revolution. But it implanted in European history an idea convulsing the Soviet Union, the idea of a culturally distinct people attaining fulfillment in a revived nation. Revival is the idea animating the recrudescence of the problem that Soviet ideologists gingerly refer to as "the nationalities question."

Ethnic assertion, not class struggle, is the prevalent kind of conflict, worldwide. Marxism says that should not happen. That is a pseudoscientific, not a normative "should." With characteristic forcefulness and falsity, Marx forecast that because of the primacy of economic factors, all preindustrial attributes—religion, ethnicity, culture—would lose their importance as influences on social development. However, from Ulster to Beirut to Tehran, in Afghanistan and throughout Africa, in Eastern Europe from Catholic Poland to the non-nation of Yugoslavia and especially in the Soviet Union, disparate events prove a common point—the durability of ancient attributes.

The Soviet Union is an aggregation of unreconciled groups hammered and held together by force and the iron hoops of bureaucracy. What the Soviet Union utterly lacks is what the American Revolution made possible—the consensual association of culturally diverse peoples. The philosophic core of the American Revolution—the revolution that fails to make the grade as "great" in Gorbachev's blinkered eyes—made America, as Lincoln said, a nation dedicated to a "proposition." It is that all persons are created equal in the right to freedom. Jefferson's message, not Robespierre's or Marx's, is the one that reverberates today. Lincoln's political vocabulary, not Lenin's, expresses the aspirations that are growing like grass in the slowly widening fissures in the foundations of oppressive states.

The Soviet Union, too, has always asserted that it is founded on propositions with universal validity. People unfamiliar with the intellectual pedigree of a Leninist think Gorbachev's talk about "universal human values" expresses a fundamental rupture with the Soviet regime's orthodoxy. Not true. That Orthodoxy claims universal validity as a science. The premise of the Leninist state is that Marxism is convincing to all minds unclouded by ignorance, but such minds belong to a minority. This "vanguard" is concentrated in the Communist Party which, having a monopoly on the understanding of "the laws of social development," deserves a monopoly on power.

However, the dry, brittle husk of Marxism is a comprehensively falsified prophecy. It has lost whatever power it once had to serve as a source of a unity transcending ethnic and cultural diversities. No nation can be dedicated to a proposition drawn from Marx. Actually, the communist claim to universality—"Workers of the world unite!"—never really recovered from August, 1914, when socialists in the German Reichstag, representing the workers of Europe's most industrialized nation, voted for credits to finance the war. The transnational solidarity of the working class was a fiction; the workers had fatherlands after all. The particularities of life—the ethnic, religious, cultural affinities that are the glue of most nations—prevailed.

Often there is an unlovely facet of ethnic assertion. Animosity is a common characteristic of it. Ethnic hatred is so prevalent it must be pleasurable. Indeed, hatred has been called "the longest pleasure." The definition of politics as the systematic arrangement of hatreds is too cynical, but hatreds are durable. They are passed down the generations more intact than religions, or at least more intact than religions teaching mercy and forgiveness.

Around the fraying rim of the Soviet empire, from Estonia to Armenia, captive nations and groups are seething because Moscow has made a dark art of politics as defined by Paul Valéry—"the art of preventing people from meddling in their own affairs." In Prague in 1968 that definition became a bitter joke: "Czechoslovakia is the world's most neutral nation—it doesn't even interfere in its own affairs." In 1988, from Stettin in the Baltic to Trieste in the Adriatic, nationalism is the pulse of politics among people with a quickened sense of "their own."

Nationalism is blamed for this century's wars, but nationalism need not mean militarism. And the nation-state has been the laboratory of liberty. Furthermore, nationalism is an indigenous pluralism in the Soviet sphere, so it should be delicately nurtured by friends of freedom. This nationalism is not without dangers. There have been two world wars. Both world wars began in Eastern Europe. The worst, the first, began in what is—for the moment—Yugoslavia. That region was then known as the Balkans which, it was said, produced more history than could be consumed locally. Look for exports of history as the region comes to a boil. Americans are part of this drama because the fire comes from the glowing embers of the first and the greatest of the three—count them, Mr. Gorbachev—great revolutions.

December 19, 1988

The American Idea in Tiananmen Square

The year 1989—bicentennial of the French Revolution and ratification of the U.S. Constitution, the codification of the American Revolution— may be commemorated in 2089. That year may be the centennial of a regime-toppling echo of Occidental revolutions in the Orient.

Chinese protesters speak Jefferson's, Lincoln's and Thoreau's words, and have built a small replica of the Statue of Liberty, underscoring the relative sterility of the French Revolution as a source of vocabulary and symbols. (Robespierre's rhetoric? A replica of a guillotine? Please, no.) America is still the fuse that ignites the world, by 18th-century moral ideas and 20th-century material example.

But Western analogies are perilous. One reason for skepticism about the transforming power of China's protests is the memory of Paris, 1968. Remember Daniel Cohn-Bendit, the sandbox Lenin of the student "revolution"? That bubble arose from the boredom and vanity of privileged, badly educated and overpraised students who believed democracy should mean juvenocracy. It offered feckless prattle about the "oppressive tolerance" of the West's open societies; then the bubble burst, leaving no institutional traces.

In China, the oppression occasioning the protests is real. That, paradoxically, enlarges the chances for change. But the chances are limited precisely because the stakes are so large.

China's protesters have studied America's civil-rights movement. Here again, differences, not similarities, are most instructive. And they are not encouraging.

That movement was essentially conservative, in this sense: Just as the American Revolution was a conservative claim of ancient liberties, the civil-rights movement criticized American society for not living up to its professed values. Once segregation was stigmatized as contradictory of America's public philosophy, it was doomed.

The civil-rights movement challenged the performance, not the fundamental legitimacy, of America's political arrangements. China's protesters, although polite and aspiring to prudence, cannot help but be radical, striking at the roots of the regime.

The protesters' moral and material desires are inextricably entwined. They want freedom and progress; they understand that the latter presupposes the former. But both, then, presuppose the overthrow of the core institution of a communist society, the party.

A Communist Party exists for two reasons, one ostensibly elevated, the other obviously mundane. The elevated purpose is to administer a monopoly of interpretation—of morals, art, the unfolding of history, everything. The party's mundane purpose is to serve as a substitute for a price mechanism, administering the allocation of wealth and opportunity and energies by fiat rather than economic rationality.

Furthermore, a Communist party administering an economy is holding a wolf by the ears. Letting go is dangerous because all prices having been subsidized, freedom's first fruit is inflation.

While watching China, remember Panama. Noriega knows something: Brutality works. Not always and never forever, but often long enough for the brute's purposes. Fifteen months ago, Ambassador Juan Sosa, the mild man who pretends to represent Panama, but not Noriega, in Washington, was asked how Panama's opposition could prevail when all force is on the other side. Sosa replied: "The force of reason is on our side, and we can win with that." Abundant pages of history, not least of China, refute that sweet liberal theory of life.

It is too soon to say if China's public has done what Panama's has not—if it has generated a critical mass of insurgency. The survival of all nonconsensual governments depends on inertia. The totalitarian enterprise has been to produce inertia by atomizing the masses, allowing no independent intermediary institutions between individuals and the state.

But the result of that is social enervation. And if enough people surge into enough streets for long enough, even if for no precisely defined purpose, the regime is reduced to impotence and hence is demoralized.

Will China's protesters produce a Madison—a constitutionalist, a codifier of liberty—before there emerges a Napoleon whose riposte to philosophy is artillery? Probably not. But a 20th-century Chinese thinker said when asked the significance of the French Revolution, "Too soon to tell."

Looking back on 1989 from, say, 2005, as Wordsworth looked back on 1789 from 1805, many Chinese, young no more, will surely think, "Bliss was it in that dawn to be alive,/But to be young was very heaven!" However, many may then feel as Wordsworth did about the long gone "hour of universal ferment" when "the soil of common life" was "too hot to tread upon." They may say as he did, "Now do I feel how I have been deceived."

May 25, 1989

A Dark Theory Slain by Luminous Facts

These are the most momentous months in mankind's history. This is so not merely because of the scale of events shaking regimes from the Danube to the China Sea, but also because of the clarity with which great ideas are clashing and historical controversies are being resolved.

Imagine, said Orwell, a boot in your face—forever. His nightmare is the totalitarians' dream, the terrifying promise of permanence. What died in Tiananmen Square was the totalitarian pretense, the claim to have broken history, and all human spontaneity, to the saddle of a party's political will.

To sense the stakes of today's turbulences, go back 33 years. But first go back 2,500 years. Political philosophy began with Plato, who sought ways to prevent cycles of civic virtue from decaying into tyranny. His comprehensive prescriptions concerned education, poetry, rhetoric.

Modernity has meant preoccupation with history as linear, not cyclical. History is a narrative infused with the drama of the possibility of progress.

The last two centuries have given birth to various historicisms—doctrines purporting to decipher laws of historical development. Theories claim to explain the course of history in terms of vast impersonal forces. These theories stipulate that history is a series of inevitabilities independent of individuals' political wills and choices.

The totalitarian impulse arises from historicism. It arises from the claim that a particular party has a monopoly on understanding and has a right to unbridled administration of insight, however brutal that might be for those who contest its monopoly of interpretation.

Paradoxically, in the 20th century, when history has accelerated giddily, the great political invention, totalitarianism, has promised regimes that would perpetrate themselves—forever. The world has been haunted by the specter of permanence, the permanent boot in the face.

In 1951, Hannah Arendt, a refugee from Hitler's Europe, published a stunning treatise, *The Origins of Totalitarianism*. Her deeply troubling thesis was that ideological intoxication, combined with modern instruments of social control, might make totalitarianism an unassailable tyranny, immune to all dynamics of change from within.

Terrorism—the end of legality; random violence—is but one totalitarian instrument. Another is gray bureaucracy controlling all cultural institutions. Totalitarianism aims at the conscription of the citizen's consciousness—state ownership not merely of industries but of minds. So totalitarianism requires control of the flow of information. It requires the central scripting of all public argument—which means no real argument in public.

Intermediary institutions standing between the individual and the state—schools, churches, clubs, labor unions, even families—must be pulverized or permeated by the state. The totalitarian aim is the atomization of society into a dust of individuals. This dust is to be blown around by gusts of ideology emitted by the tutelary party.

The totalitarian enterprise is the extirpation of all autonomous institutions and hence of autonomous impulses in society. Instead of Marx's withering away of the state, there would be the withering away of society through the unlimited penetration of life by the state—by politics.

In 1956, in the streets of Budapest, Arendt's profoundly pessimistic theory was slain by a luminous fact. For 12 days, Hungary flung its unconquered consciousness in the face of the totalitarian state. There was no civil war because the nation was not divided: Ideological indoctrination had left the public utterly unmarked.

In Budapest, as in Tiananmen Square, tanks prevailed, but Arendt rejoiced in the refutation of her hypothesis. In an epilogue to the 1958 edition of her book, she wrote:

"The voices from Eastern Europe, speaking so plainly and simply of freedom and truth, sounded like an ultimate affirmation that human nature is unchangeable, that nihilism will be futile, that even in the absence of all teaching and in the presence of overwhelming indoctrination, a yearning for freedom and truth will rise out of man's heart and mind forever."

A striking fact about Tiananmen Square is that there was no single acknowledged leader there. Note a stirring similarity. A Hungarian professor speaking 33 years ago: "It was unique in history that the Hungarian Revolution had no leaders. It was not organized, it was not centrally directed. The will for freedom was the moving force in every action."

What made Tiananmen Square terrifying to the totalitarians was precisely what made it insubstantial in the face of force but will make it triumphant in time: no leaders, just unconscripted spirits.

A watching world marveled at the bravery, politeness and good will of the protesters, but wrongly spoke of their moderation. The watching world, like the protesters themselves, did not understand the inherent, irreducible radicalism of their categorical challenge to the totalitarian pretense. The regime understood.

June 8, 1989

Death of a Pensioner

The Soviet foreign ministry, with an austere proletarian tone, said merely that "the pensioner" had died. Vyacheslav Molotov, dead at 96, never received notice commensurate with his involvement in large matters.

Perhaps part of his problem was his unprepossessing appearance. Churchill wrote of "his cannonball head, black mustache and comprehending eyes, his slab face." Molotov edited *Pravda* before organizing the first Bolshevik committee in Petrograd during the 1917 February Revolution, yet Trotsky called him "mediocrity incarnate." Trotsky, however, died 46 years before Molotov, in Mexican exile, with an ice axe lodged in his skull by the long arm of Stalin, whose right hand was Molotov.

Lenin disparaged Molotov as "the best file clerk" in Russia. However, Russia's files bulge with interesting documents. For the vanguard of the proletariat—the leaders of the Communist party—building socialism does not involve heavy lifting, but, my, the paperwork.

In *The Great Terror*, Robert Conquest describes how Stalin and Molotov would arrive at their offices and find in their in-trays a list of 40 or so names compiled by Yezhov, an enforcer.

> Comrade Stalin:
> I am sending for your approval four lists of people to be tried by the Military Collegium:
> List No. 1 (general)
> List No. 2 (former military personnel)
> List No. 3 (former personnel of the NKVD)
> List No. 4 (wives of enemies of the people)
> I request sanction to convict all in the first degree.
>
> —Yezhov

The lists would go into out-trays, with this notation: "Approved—J. Stalin, V. Molotov."

These lists of a few dozen victims were part of retail killing in a country, and a century, characterized by wholesale killing. However, Molotov and Stalin did not usually deal in small numbers. Although there have been many mass murderers with more flourish, few have been more prolific than the methodical Molotov.

Robert Conquest's *The Harvest of Sorrow* is a new history of "the biggest unreported story of this century," the "terror-famine" engineered by Stalin in crushing the kulaks, a term denoting peasants prosperous enough to be considered "class enemies." The famine killed 7 million people, more than half of them children, in the Ukraine in 1932 and 1933. More than 15 million people—more than were killed in the First World War—were killed by the brutal collectivization of agriculture which the famine was intended to accelerate.

Conquest notes that while official documents at the time spoke decorously of "limiting" the kulaks (a semantic evasion that anticipated the Nazis' "final solution"), Stalin and Molotov, plain speakers, preferred the word "liquidate." This was years before Hitler embarked on his genocide that claimed fewer victims. Here, too, Molotov was a pioneer whose achievements as Stalin's servant have not yet received due notice.

Molotov would chair meetings of committees that included men whose death warrants he had already signed—"dead men talking," in Conquest's phrase. But once he did rebel, in his fashion, against the purge of a person close to him. When, in 1948, the Politburo, doing Stalin's bidding, voted to purge and imprison Molotov's wife, Molotov did not join the vote. He abstained.

(She was a live wire. Before she was imprisoned, a senior military officer recalled being greeted by her at a reception: "Ah, Sasha, whatever's this? Why haven't you been arrested yet?" She was at that time head of the cosmetics industry, a post she obtained when the man above her was sent to a slave-labor camp.)

Molotov's name is on the agreement—the Molotov-Ribbentrop non-aggression pact—that lit the fuse of the Second World War. Ribbentrop was hanged at Nuremberg 39 years before Molotov died. Justice falls unevenly on winning and losing camps.

Of the regimes that were once allied with Hitler, only the Soviet regime survives with institutional and ideological continuity. Molotov was a suitable symbol of the durability of the regime he helped create. When the 27-year-old Molotov plunged into the revolutionary turmoil, Russia was so prostrate and anarchic that a rabble could seize it. When he died, a 20th-century success story, the state he helped launch as the center of what historians Mikhail Heller and Aleksandr Nekrich in their new book *Utopia in Power* call "the last world empire. From Cuba to Vietnam, from Czechoslovakia to Angola, the sun never sets on the zone of Soviet control."

Molotov must have felt ill-used when, in 1962, Khrushchev, the Stalinist "de-Stalinizer," expelled Molotov from the party. Ingratitude is never pretty. Khrushchev's path to glory ran through the Ukraine, where he helped Stalin and Molotov suffocate that captive nation.

But filial piety is always nice, and recently the new, different, open, reforming, modernizing Kremlin leaders have rectified that injustice. Two years ago Molotov was readmitted to the party. Also, party records were falsified to show uninterrupted membership, a suitable tribute from that regime to a founding father.

November 16, 1986

Science and Primitives

It is a paradox of modern politics that two of the most intellectually primitive regimes have considered themselves servants of science. In 1934, Rudolf Hess said: "National Socialism is nothing but applied biology." The Soviet regime applies "scientific socialism," within which psychiatry has a special place, as Dr. Anatoly Koryagin can testify.

Koryagin, 48, recently was released to the West from a prison camp where he served six years of a 14-year sentence for the usual offense, "anti-Soviet activities," which included getting out to the West an article about Soviet abuses of psychiatry. Such abuses are as old as the Soviet regime. Historian Paul Johnson notes that in 1919 the Moscow Revolutionary Tribunal sentenced an anticommunist leader to treatment in a sanatorium. In the 1930s, the secret police built a 400-bed penal hospital (two words perversely joined in communist societies) on the grounds of a mental hospital. In the 1940s, the leading Soviet research institution for criminal psychology had a department of "political" cases.

Koryagin says that since 1977 the number of psychiatric "hospitals" where dissidents are imprisoned with the criminally insane has grown from 11 to 16. And *glasnost* has not involved the release of any dissident from a psychiatric "hospital."

The 1939 Nazi-Soviet pact truly was a joining of kindred spirits. Neal Ascherson, in the *New York Review of Books,* says German doctors were dazzled to discover that, under Hitler, medicine was "the central intellectual resource of the New Order." Doctors practiced "biological soldiering," perfecting the race by killing the unfit and using them for "research" to benefit the master race. And in the Soviet Union, psychiatry, a less-settled science than biology, has been conscripted by the regime.

Since Freud postulated that the self is a fractious committee—the ego, id and libido—there has been "scientific" doubt about the importance of reason in the individual's life. Freud, a semimaterialist, believed in the body and "consciousness," a passive ghost in the machine. His intimation was that civilization is a misfortune because neuroses result from maladjustments to the unyielding reality of modern society.

But Marxists believe anything will yield to their "science," backed by force. They fancy themselves architects of societies so well-designed that they can not be sources of discontent. As Khrushchev said in *Pravda* in 1959 about people "who might start calling for opposition" to communism: "Clearly the mental state of such people is not normal."

Psychiatry, with its expanding arsenal of drugs, can be abused as a brutal instrument of social control. And the official Soviet premise, that only the psychologically disabled could fail to love socialism, enlists psychiatry as a rationalization for the regime.

In the West, neurological discoveries and pharmacological sophistication are confirming this much of a materialist thesis: Mental illness often is biologically based, as in brain chemistry. This of course does not confirm or even support the Soviet premise that mental disorders of Soviet citizens must be biologically based because Soviet society is too advanced to be a source of suffering for Homo Sovieticus, the new Soviet man manufactured for communism. However, what is known about the biological basis of mental disorders is distressingly useful to totalitarians who believe there is no intractable tension between human nature and society because both are infinitely malleable under the forceful application of this or that science.

Technically speaking (scientific socialists love speaking technically), the Soviet Union is, 70 years after the Revolution, still in the Glorious Transition Period. The transition to pure communism is not over because the state has not quite withered away. But Soviet society is close enough to scientific perfection that mental disorders, including persistent dissent, must be biologically based and hence treatable with drugs, at least theoretically.

A perennial question about the Soviet regime is: Does it believe and act on its ideological inanities? A reasonable conclusion is that the regime's mind is a strange alloy of cynicism and sincerity. Koryagin stresses the cynicism, and cites a telling detail about the confinement of dissidents in psychiatric hospitals: Whereas people who are really mentally ill are confined until cured, dissidents have been given fixed sentences.

And the regime has elastic standards regarding deviant behavior. When Koryagin's nine-year-old son received a severe concussion when he was beaten (as all members of the family were at various times in the street), a court held that the beating was a "natural" expression of public feeling against an anti-Soviet family. Such is the sphere of spontaneity in Soviet society.

May 21, 1987

Irina's Choice

The brunch menu at one of Washington's posh hotels reminds Irina Ratushinskaya of the story of the donkey who, placed midway between two feed bags, starved to death from indecision. Not long ago, mealtime choice was not a problem for Ratushinskaya, whose lunch was spoiled cabbage floating in salty water. Supper was an unclean fish in salty water.

Four years ago she was 29, and received the harshest sentence a woman political prisioner has received since the Stalin era: seven years' hard labor in a camp for "especially dangerous state criminals." Her principal crime was writing poetry.

She describes her poetry as unpolitical, but nothing is considered unpolitical by a totalitarian regime. Furthermore, her poetry expresses a religious sensibility, for which she credits the regime. Just as boring

Sunday schools have produced unbelievers, the reaction of eight-year-old Irina to antireligious propaganda in school was: God matters.

Poetry and human-rights activism led first to six months of interrogation in the KGB's Kiev prison, used for Gestapo interrogations after the Soviet-Nazi pact fell apart and Kiev was in German hands. She was transported to the labor camp in a windowless cargo car—another echo of Soviet-Nazi affinities. When Ratushinskaya confronted the provocations of camp authorities, this woman with the mild surface displayed a porcupine personality, bristling with spiky resistance.

She does not speak as though—she does not seem to feel that—the choices that brought her to the Gulag, and then to torture and the edge of death, were choices. Her moral metabolism made the choices as natural as breaths. Because of her spiritedness, camp authorities shaved her head. When she fasted to protest mistreatment of others, she was handcuffed and force-fed by six men. Knocked unconscious in the struggle, she had liquids poured down her throat.

Swollen from the salty diet, she spent much time in icy punishment cells where at times she was fed only every other day. Yet she used matchsticks to carve poems into soap bars, memorized them, then washed them away:

> We live stubbornly—
> like a small beast who's gnawed off his paw
> to get out of a trap on three—
> we've mastered that science
> And with brave smile—
> that way the wounds are bandaged tighter—. . .

She could share her poems, as she did with her two guards, who asked her to recite an example of her criminal deeds. They were struck by this glimpse of beauty and intelligence in their barren world, but had no paper. So one guard transcribed the poem on the other guard's undershirt.

Ratushinskaya has large brown eyes that do not blink often; they have seen much. Her matter-of-factness about her pilgrimage through fire makes an untested Westerner feel as flimsy as papier-mâché. Isolated, tortured, harassed, starved, exhausted, frozen, she could at any time have won release by signing an acknowledgment of "guilt." She never considered that. Instead, she fought the enforced senselessness—of camp life, the petty regulations and duties by which the authorities seek to break spirits and flatten personalities.

Because of the gentleness of life in good societies, we can live long lives and never need to be as brave as she was daily, instinctively. In her prison poems, her voice was at times almost jaunty:

Well, we'll live
as the soul directs,
not asking for other bread.
And I will get myself a tame mouse
while having a dog is impossible . . .
He and I will invent a land
where there are neither cats nor camps . . .
We'll make a home behind any bars,
beyond any February—spring . . .
We'll raise a dog anyway,
but in better times.

Those who believe that the release of Ratushinskaya and a few others like her means much better times for her country should hear her contrary opinion. She knows that she is out only because she is a poet, and that thousands of others languish because they have no comparable hold on the world's imagination. That is why she can not yet know the ease she imagined in prison, the contentment of being able to say, "We'll unsaddle the day—to graze."

She was released from prison the day before the Iceland summit, as a party favor for the West, a sign of Soviet interest in new agreements. So ended the saga that began when the KGB raided her flat and seized books they described as "ideologically dangerous." The books included a volume of international agreements to which the Soviet Union has subscribed.

May 14, 1987

Beneath Lenin's Glare

Watching a new thought pass through a Marxist gathering is, said H. G. Wells, like watching a breeze blow across a field of ripe corn: The breeze passes and the serried ranks of minds return to their original position. Wells never saw the likes of Aleksandr Obolensky and Lenoid Sukhov.

Obolensky will someday be the answer to a trivia question, but today he is not trivial: He is the first person publicly to challenge a supreme Soviet leader in an election. At the new Congress of People's Deputies, he offered himself as an alternative candidate to Gorbachev for president.

"I understand," he said with nice understatement, "that I have a very slim chance. I want in our history an example of something resembling alternative elections. This is what my voters wanted and what I promised them."

He does not yet quite have the hang of it. In a democracy, making promises is enough; keeping them is foolhardy. Anyway, only one-third of the delegates would vote even to include his name with Gorbachev's on the ballot (which Gorbachev won 2,123 to 87).

However, Obolensky's antic spiritedness was dazzling in light of this: The debate occurred in the shadow of one of those huge, overbearing Soviet statues designed to diminish individuals—a monstrous gleaming likeness of Lenin, glaring into the future.

The statue represents an intractable problem. All the symbols and icons are antithetical to pluralism. None is more so than Lenin, the mummified corpse at the center of the state.

The referents of American political argument are Washington, Jefferson, Lincoln—all of them embodiments of democratic consensus. The omnipresent visual and ideological referent in the Soviet Union is the father of totalitarianism.

Lenin lived in the clean, well-lit prison of one idea: "scientific socialism." His remorseless savagery flowed from it and from the lesson he chose to learn from the European left's greatest trauma, the suppression of the Paris Commune in 1871. The communards were, Lenin said, guilty of "excessive magnanimity. . . . [The Commune] should have exterminated its enemies."

By exterminate, Lenin meant exterminate. Having supplanted the idea of individual guilt with class guilt, he set about killing categories of people and thus became a Founding Father of genocide.

Soviet political vocabulary, including symbols and heroes, is utterly antidemocratic. There are few indigenous cultural resources for democrats to draw upon. Thus it is breathtaking to read the words of Leonid Sukhov, a deputy identified as "a driver from Kharkov." His words were spoken beneath Lenin's glare and to Gorbachev:

"I compare you not to Lenin or Stalin, but to the great Napoleon, who, fearing neither bullets nor death, led the nation to victory, but owing to his sycophants and his wife, transformed the republic into an empire. You can put me to death, but I fear this path."

Dwell upon that last sentence. Democracy is trying to sprout in stony soil indeed. Death-on-a-whim has been so central to the political culture that it is part of the syntax of public discourse. But once such discourse is public in the sense of political, everything changes, or perhaps has changed.

Note that Sukhov's statement is movingly European, making its point with reference to one of the continent's great shared experiences, Napoleon. The reference says: History did not begin in 1917. Then, we seceded from European civilization; what was done can be undone.

The hall in which the Congress meets is a more promising venue for the incubation of lasting liberalization than Tiananmen Square could ever be. Tiananmen Square is no place to give structure to yearnings. The Congress's hall is the scene of reform from above. This is, necessarily, reform on a short leash; it can be jerked around, even choked. But mass protests from below, as in Beijing, invariably face the reluctance of elites to liquidate themselves and usually founder on the task of institutionalizing an impulse in the open air.

In Beijing, brave words of defiance were hurled at power. In the Moscow Congress, words have been addressed to power which submitted to be addressed in a setting of rules and respect.

Obolensky's and, even more, Sukhov's words are more momentous than Gorbachev's arms proposals. Those proposals are consistent with modernization and rationalization of Soviet armed forces, irrespective of any changes in Soviet global goals. Besides, policy changes can be changed back.

But dramatic political words cannot be called back. They reverberate. Doing so, they change the the public's most important sense, the sense of the possible. And that change can in time change the goals of the state.

June 5, 1989

Jokes As Tiny Revolutions

Russia is no longer a riddle wrapped in an enigma. It is an open book, a book of jokes. *What is 150 yards along and eats potatoes? A Moscow queue waiting to buy meat.* There is an unlimited supply. Not of meat, but of jokes about trying to buy meat. *A boy asks, "What will communism be like when perfected?" His father replies, "Everyone will have what he needs." The boy asks, "But what if there is a shortage of meat?" The father replies, "There will be a sign in the butcher shop saying, 'No one needs meat today.'*

The 20th century has been a lot of laughs, in one small and hardly redeeming sense: It has provoked much political humor. Above the roar of war and through the gray smog of tyranny has come the sound of laughter, sometimes bitter, sometimes defiant, always telling a truth. George Orwell called political jokes "tiny revolutions." Under tyranny, humor is a form of coping, of forbidden intimacy. As Freud said, in joking there are three participants—the teller, the listener and the target. In

1985 two witty scholars, Steven Lukes of Oxford and Itzhak Galnoor of Hebrew University in Jerusalem, published a collection of political jokes, *No Laughing Matter.* Read today (and sometimes amended to include new names) the jokes are a comprehensive guide to today's encompassing crisis of communism.

Socialism is the synthesis of the stages of mankind's development. From prehistory it takes the method. From antiquity, slavery. From feudalism, serfdom. From capitalism, exploitation. From socialism, the name. The once shimmering ideal of socialism now stands for exploitation, even of "fraternal" nations at the empire's fraying edge. *Deng Xiaoping tells Gorbachev that three demands must be met before relations can improve. First, China wants 100 million tons of coal. "Agreed," says Gorbachev. And 20 new ships. "Done," says Gorbachev. And a million bicycles. "Impossible," says Gorbachev, "the Poles don't make bicycles."*

Because communism's boast of material productivity has proved hollow, communism's confidence has collapsed. Therefore it can no longer produce even its characteristic product, ideology. *A Soviet theoretician is asked to explain styles of painting. "Expressionism," he says, "is painting what you feel. Impressionism is painting what you see." But, he is asked, what is socialist realism? "That," he says, "is painting what you hear."* Communism's captive subjects have always heard relentless mendacity from the party, but the party's clanging certitudes were a source of security, something to conform to. But today the "vanguard of the proletariat" is just another ruling class, too cynical to sustain its philosophic and "scientific" pretense. *Khrushchev says to Zhou Enlai, "The difference between the Soviet Union and China is that I rose to power from the peasant class, whereas you came from the privileged Mandarin class. Zhou replies,"True. But there is this similarity. Each of us is a traitor to his class."*

Communism's core value, equality, is achieved only in deprivation. *"After the revolution everyone will have strawberries and cream." "But I don't like strawberries and cream." "After the revolution you will like strawberries and cream."* Such an optimistic joke. The actual uniformity is scarcity. *A Soviet visitor to Budapest says to his Hungarian host, "You must have terrible shortages." The astonished Hungarian asks why he thinks so. The Soviet visitor replies, "Because you have no queues."* After four years of foreign-policy pirouetting and domestic promising, what has Gorbachev achieved? Living conditions have declined. Cuba is a wholly owned subsidiary of the Soviet Union, yet sugar is rationed in the Soviet Union. *Gorbachev addresses his nation: "When I came to power the economy stood on the edge of an abyss. I am proud to say that since then we have taken a bold step forward."*

The *Economist* reports: "Mr. Gorbachev's policies seem to be bringing the Soviet people to their knees. There is a growing sense of panic as fewer and fewer goods find their way to the shops and inflation continues to rise." There is panic buying of salt and matches. Meat, butter, soap and washing power are rationed—when there is any to ration. *A Muscovite asks her butcher for beef and is told there is none. She asks for chicken. None. Lamb? None. Pork? None. Veal? None. The shopper leaves and the butcher exclaims to his assistant, "What a terrific memory!"*

The memory of Soviet men runneth not to when times were, by even the most unexacting standards, good, let alone lush. But what should worry Gorbachev is that people remember that times were better before him. The Soviet elite, sobered by the example of China, sees that *glasnost* makes possible the expression of discontents that *perestroika* does nothing to diminish. Gorbachev the traditionalist has done the traditional. He has blamed his predecessors. Now what? *A new manager of a collective farm finds two letters from his predecessor, with instructions to open the first when difficulties begin. When the farm fails to meet its quotas, the manager opens the first letter, which says: "Blame me." He does. It buys some time. But the farm fails again and he comes under fresh criticism, so he opens the second letter. It says: "Prepare two letters."*

The extravagant promise and terrible menace of totalitarianism was permanence. The fear was that new instruments of power (broadcasting, bureaucracy and others) used with new thoroughness and ruthlessness would mean that totalitarianism is forever. It might not be productive, it might be backward, but it would last. Now, however, we know that stasis is not an option in the modern world. The Soviet Union is still theoretically, which is to say officially, in "the glorious transition" to communism. *(What is the transition stage between capitalism and communism? Alcoholism.)* But by now it is clear that there is no future in The Future. Even communists know that "the road ahead" is a dead end. So the glorious—or least unsatisfactory—transition would be from the Soviet Union to Russia. Can it change from a mistake on the march, into a nation?

A census official questions an elderly citizen of Leningrad: "Where were you born?" "St. Petersburg." "Where were you educated?" "Petrograd." "Where do you live?" "Leningrad." "Where will you die?" "St. Petersburg."

Could be. No Joke.

June 5, 1989

Gorbachev and the "1946 Rules"

A quarter of a century ago a listener addressed a question to a Soviet radio program: "You say the West is teetering on the edge of a precipice. You also say that the Soviet Union is determined to overtake the West. So my question is . . . ." Today the question is: Will Gorbachev remain at the wheel as the Soviet jalopy lurches over the precipice?

This is a typically unusual month in the crisis of regimes involving 1.5 billion people from Beijing to Berlin. A wit muses, "Khrushchev threatened to bury us, but not under an army of converts." Actually, they are not converts. The masses making their dashes—some figuratively, some literally—for freedom never believed the rubbish their regimes espoused. A Russian philosopher once said that the trouble with socialism is that it deifies the proletariat but has no respect for work. Today, a bitter Soviet jest is that the trouble with the Soviet system is that the people pretend to work and the government pretends to pay them. A Soviet economist says the Soviet Union "exploits its work force more than any other industrial nation," paying only 37 percent of GNP in salaries, about half the rate in Western nations. The moral pretense of communism was to end exploitation, as defined by Marx's labor theory of value: all value is created by labor but capitalists siphon off surplus value. China's government siphons with forced "saving": Some workers are given government bonds in lieu of 25 percent of their wages.

In a millennium of Russian history there is no precedent for the social energy that democracy nurtures and economic dynamism requires. Serfdom was abolished just 128 years ago and totalitarianism was imposed just 56 years later. The Soviet Union is suffering not only from institutional sclerosis but also from prolonged debasement of its human resources. One result is pervasive maliciousness, as suggested in this story. God grants one wish each to an Italian, an Englishman, a Frenchman and a Russian. The Italian says, "I want Italians to be world's finest singers." The Englishman says, "I want Englishmen to be world's finest horsemen." The Frenchman says, "I want Frenchwomen to be world's most beautiful." The Russian says, "I want my neighbor Ivan's mare to drop dead." In civil disorders throughout the Soviet Union, mobs attack cooperatives which produce private profits for individual strivers.

Most Americans believe that Gorbachev (as President Carter's secretary of state said of Brezhnev) "shares our dreams and aspirations." But Gorbachev became a reformer for managerial, not moral reasons. He became a reformer not because he considered the existing system evil but because he knew it was unproductive. For Gorbachev, freedom has only instrumental value. He values it for unleashing critics of his critics and for facilitating productivity. It was said that Gladstone valued the people's prosperity only as a source of taxation. Gorbachev values freedom only as a source of new economic dynamism to sustain the old military agenda. Gorbachev was a protégé of Andropov, the KGB chief before the KGB put on a smiling face. Gorbachev began where Andropov left off, denouncing alcohol, laxity and his predecessors.

The pedigree of Gorbachev's *perestroika* goes back to Marshal Ogarkov, the foremost Soviet soldier at the dawn of this decade. He launched an insistent campaign for reform because he was alarmed by the inability of the Soviet economy to produce the innovations in electronics needed by a modern military. Edward Luttwak writes that Ogarkov's alarm became acute on June 10, 1982, when, in a few hours over Lebanon, Israel's air force used electronic advantages to master Soviet antiaircraft missiles and shoot down at least 85 of Syria's Soviet-supplied MIGs. Next, in 1983, came Reagan's Strategic Defense Initiative, a shattering challenge to the Soviet Union to compete technologically. As a result, says Luttwak, Ogarkov, not Gorbachev, shattered Soviet complacency.

Luttwak places this story squarely in the context of continuing Soviet implacability. In 1946, with the war-ravaged nation starving in hovels, with acute shortages of every elemental necessity—food, clothing, shelter, medicine—the Kremlin gave top priority to military production. Gorbachev, having acknowledged that all previous Soviet defense spending figures were lies, has supplied his own fabrication. Luttwak says "the implacability of 1989 differs only slightly from that of 1946." In a nation where the regime admits shortages of 1,000 of the 1,200 items that comprise the basic Soviet "basket of consumer goods," in a nation with intestinal parasites in a major metropolitan water supply, where hospital patients must bribe attendants to get bandages and bedpans; in this shambles, says Luttwak, "the 1946 rules are still in effect."

Until those rules change, the United States has an interest in seeing the Soviet crisis deepen. We are witnessing what Leo Labedz calls "competitive decadence": What is decaying quicker, communism or the will to contain it? Soviet military power certainly is not withering away. The Committee on the Present Danger has just released a new assessment of the U.S.-Soviet military balance, concluding that "Soviet military growth remains politically sacrosanct" and "in most important respects the United States is worse off entering the decade of the 1990s than it was entering the decade of the 1980s." The Soviet military is getting qualitative upgrading to compensate for the quantitative reductions that are the centerpiece of Gorbachev's détente campaign that is fueling disarmament, moral and military, in the West.

However, neither Russian nor Soviet history has predisposed that nation to feel about any leader the sort of sentimentality and euphoria the West feels about Gorbachev. His country values him the way he values freedom: only instrumentally. He is valuable only if things get better. Things are getting worse. He is pleasing neither the top nor the bottom of Soviet society, neither the entrenched *nomenklatura* nor the disgusted shoppers. Gorbachev is attempting to cure the inefficiencies of tyranny with carefully calibrated rations of freedom. This has been compared to ordering a nation to make a gradual transition from driving on the left side of the road to driving on the right. And there is a precipice dead ahead.

September 25, 1989

The Sickening Soviet Reality

The Soviet regime has kept a promise. It promised to build a society unlike any seen before, and has done so: it is the first industrial nation to sink toward preindustrial levels of public health. In the 1970s life expectancy for Soviet males declined as much as four years. The Soviet Union is the first industrialized society to achieve such a decline during peacetime, and in the 1970s was the only nation of any sort with such a decline, except Cambodia, where vigorous communists killed almost 25 percent of the population, about half of what the Black Death did to Europe's population in the 14th century.

The Kremlin has been releasing a dribble of political prisoners as part of a campaign to seem more morally civilized. This underscores the desperate poverty of communism today, the bankruptcy of its traditional boast that it wants to be measured against capitalism by material achievements. Thirty years ago many Westerners assumed that communism could compete as a system for creating prosperity. Eleanor Roosevelt spoke of free people not being tempted "to accept the material benefits afforded by communism as a substitute for freedom." It was considered axiomatic that communism offered "material benefits."

The Soviet ruling class, like the Mafia, combines disreputable lives with a craving for respect. It hates being told that its country is a Third World country with first-world weapons. However, Nick Eberstadt of Harvard's Center for Population Studies and the American Enterprise Institute says: "There is not a single country in all of Europe . . . in which lives are so short, or babies' death rates so high—not even impoverished, half-civilized Albania. Measured by the health of its people, the Soviet Union is no longer a developed nation." In the mid-1970s, when the Soviet Union still dared to release comprehensive data on health levels, its infant-mortality rate was about that of Panama, the Dominican Republic, Chile; its life expectancy was that of Costa Rica, Malaysia, Sri Lanka. The health levels in those nations are rising; Soviet health levels have declined. Eberstadt says that if trends continue, the Soviet Union's health levels will soon be surpassed by most of Latin America and East Asia.

Unlike any noncommunist industrialized society, the Soviet Union has, since the 1960s, devoted a declining fraction of its GNP to health care. The regime has a ravenous military sector and an investment-poor industrial sector. One way to economize is to starve the health sector. The Marxist labor theory of value, and communist reverence for heavy industry, produces disparagement of the service sector.

Fifteen years ago the average rate of pay for doctors was below the average rate for blue-collar factory workers. (Official pay, that is. Doctors also barter services on the black market. Western feminists have hailed the Soviet Union, where so many doctors are women. But there medicine is considered "women's work" and hence paid poorly.) The regime is committed to full employment, so wheelchairs are used sparingly: Stretchers employ two people. It is said that as recently as this decade one of Moscow's main cardiac clinics was on the fifth floor of a building with no elevator. That was imaginative: Anyone who could make it to the clinic did not need the clinic.

Liquor has been the Kremlin's "liquid policeman." Drunkenness is preferable to dissent. As of 1980 the Soviet consumption of hard distilled spirits was the highest in the world, three times that of Western Europe. Some is homemade. Made wrong, it causes blindness and madness. The Soviet Union has one-tenth as many vehicles as the United States yet has about as many vehicular homicides, a result of drunken driving. Machinery operated by drunken workers causes many accidental deaths. A Soviet Army medical journal recently saw fit to advise surgeons not to drink heavily the day before or the day of an operation. The Soviet Union has 80 to 90 times more deaths by alcohol poisoning than the United States. Poisoning often takes a while—and so do Soviet ambulances. In the late 1970s a study of family budgets in the Baltic republics indicated that the average household spent more on liquor than on clothes. That was especially remarkable considering that in the Soviet command-economy clothes prices are set high because everyone must buy clothes. The high price is a kind of tax.

A study of Leningrad—a privileged city—in the early 1970s indicated that 6 percent of all children up to the age of seven suffered symptoms of malnutrition, meaning disabilities such as rickets. The reported incidence of such easily controllable diseases as measles, mumps and typhoid fever is more than 20 times higher in the Soviet Union than in the United States. Some Soviet republics have health levels comparable to areas of India.

Communist worship of industrialism has unleashed pollution that helps account for the 6 percent annual increase in birth defects. Abortion—10 million to 16 million a year; two to three times more than live births—is the primary means of birth control. This, and the general collapse of public health, suggests to Eberstadt a "virulent strain of anomie" running rampant in the Soviet Union. A Soviet citizen may agree with the bag lady played by Lily Tomlin: "I made some studies, and reality is the leading cause of stress among those in touch with it. I can take it in small doses, but as a life-style I found it too confining."

The statistics above are based on Soviet sources. In keeping with Lenin's notion that in communist societies statistics are meant to serve ends other than scholarship, communist regimes often cook numbers to make things seem better than they are. In the late 1960s, after much hoopla about sugar harvests of 10 million tons, Castro said he had inflated the figures so as not to give comfort to enemies of the revolution. Cuba may recently have falsified infant-mortality data. Eberstadt says this conclusion is reached using Occam's razor: The conclusion cannot be proved, but it is the simplest explanation of Cuban statistical incongruities. Papers captured in Grenada included requests for help from Cuba and Nicaragua with falsification of Grenada's economic data. Regarding communist "information," remember what Tomlin's bag lady says regarding almost everything: "No matter how cynical you become, it's never enough to keep up."

January 19, 1987

Marx's Nationalities Problem

There goes the neighborhood. "Show me a country without nationalist problems," says Mikhail Gorbachev in Yugoslavia, "and I will move there right away."

The renewed simmering of what the Soviet regime has always referred to gingerly as "the nationalities question" could be seen recently in satellite photos of huge demonstrations. The demonstrators were Armenians asserting national complaints against a neighboring Soviet republic concerning a territorial dispute. Any manifestation of nationalism is an ominously sputtering fuse in the Soviet Union, an empire built on the subservience of about 130 nations and nationalities to Russia and a fallacy.

As the 21st century approaches, events in the Soviet Union underscore that regime's continuing adherence to a 19th-century pseudoscience. The regime cannot cope politically with the nationalisms of its captive nations because Marxism cannot accommodate nationalism, conceptually.

The stubborn assertion of nationalisms, after seven decades of suppression, is a refutation, albeit redundant, of Marx's core contention: economic determinism. Marx's belief in the sovereignty of economic forces over ethnicity and other cultural factors is just another failed prophecy from "scientific socialism."

Because Marxism is so boastful about its predictive powers, Marxists have regularly suffered emotional traumas as events have refuted it. No trauma was worse than that of August 1914 when Reichstag deputies representing working-class parties, supposedly the most "progressive" in Europe, voted credits to finance Germany's war effort. This nationalist behavior stunned those who believed that, as Marx had said in *The Communist Manifesto*, "the proletariat has no fatherland."

When Stalin, who was Lenin's commissar for nationalities, said "Marxism replaces any kind of nationalism," he was echoing Lenin (socialism "abolishes" and "merges" nations), who correctly represented Marx: "There is not a single Marxist who, without making a total break with the foundations of Marxism and socialism, could deny that the interests of socialism are above the interests of the right of nations to self-determination." Marx had said in the *Manifesto* that the acids of international capitalism would dissolve "every trace of national character."

The recent wave of nationalist assertions in the Soviet Union began in the Baltic states (which were swallowed by the Soviet Union after the other great 20th-century trauma for Marxists, the Hitler-Stalin pact). But the "nationalities problem" has always troubled the Soviet regime, which initially tried "indigenization," staffing local adminstrations with local people. But the logic of "democratic centralism" was the ascendancy everywhere of the center, meaning Moscow and Russians.

Soon Russians will be less than today's 51 percent of the Soviet population. Weigh that fact against the Soviet tradition whereby a poet who wrote "Love the vast sweep of Ukraine immemorial" was castigated for depicting "the Ukraine as standing alone." Worse, he was silent about how the Ukraine achieved socialist fulfillment under "Leninist-Stalinist leadership" and "the beloved elder brother, the Great Russian people."

Nationalism became a good thing when it was time to play Hitler, and a bad thing when Hungarian nationalism became a problem in 1956. But the persistence of nationalism is an intellectual problem for Marxism, and therefore threatens the regime.

The regime lurching toward the 20th century rests uneasily on a 19th-century act of bravado, a manifestation of that century's belief in the permanent ascendancy of science over mere culture. Specifically the regime rests on Marx's claim to have decoded history. From his claim to have discovered iron laws of social development flows the Communist Party's claim to possess a monopoly of insight. On that the entire tyranny rests.

In a stupendous triumph of ideology over evidence, Marxists must deny what everywhere—from Tehran to Belfast, from Beirut to Africa—is obvious: Religious and other ethnic conflicts, far from losing their saliency, are as prevalent and as powerful as ever.

So where should Gorbachev move to? Not Yugoslavia, which is another ersatz nation coupled together from small nations. Not Belgium or Canada or perhaps even France, where there are Breton separatists. Or Britain, where there are Welsh and Scottish nationalists.

No doubt there are some homogenous nations such as Demark that are too small to provide scope for "nationalist problems." But the nation most immune to such problems is a big one with more pluralism than any other, the United States.

Unlike the Soviet Union, which requires the imposition from above of a preposterous "science," the United States is freely "dedicated to a proposition" that is, as the nation's founders said, "self-evident" to unclouded minds. The immigrants who made this nation shed many nationalities and acquired a new one by the simple act of assenting to the proposition that all persons are created equal. American pluralism poses many problems, but never "nationalist problems."

So here comes Gorbachev. There goes the neighborhood.

March 27, 1988

Lithuania and South Carolina

Why is it right for Lithuania to do what South Carolina was wrong to try to do? Is Lithuania's case for secession significantly stronger than the cases of many other Soviet "republics"? Why would it be wrong for the dictator Gorbachev to do what Lincoln did—use force to save a union?

American arguments supporting secession as constitutional were not frivolous but fell far short of sufficiency. Secessionists argued that sovereignty is indivisible; that it was retained by the several states that made the union; that powers delegated to the federal government could be withdrawn. The case against the legitimacy of secession was that the Constitution mentions no such right or process; federal sovereignty is asserted by the existence of federal powers immune from state interference and by the supremacy clause (federal law is the supreme law of the land). Also *states* were not parties to any compact. They did not make the Constitution. The Preamble begins, "We the *people* of the United States [emphasis added, by Lincoln and the Army of the Potomac] . . . do ordain and establish this Constitution . . ." It was freely ratified to replace a mere league of states (under the Articles of Confederation) by a sovereign national government.

Another theme was struck in 1863 at the dedication of a cemetery. There Lincoln said a new *nation*—not a mere union of states—had been brought forth fourscore and seven years earlier, before the Constitution, in 1776, by the Declaration of Independence that, in asserting inalienable rights, made a *nation* dedicated to a proposition.

History is not a seminar, so the argument about secession was settled by the sword. But the contrast between Lithuania's arguments now and South Carolina's then is striking, beginning with the fact that Carolinians wanted secession to preserve slavery, whereas Lithuanians want secession to escape it. The Baltic states came to their current condition by a particularly odious diplomatic event, the Nazi-Soviet pact of August 1939. The fact that the Baltic states have long been playthings of bigger powers hardly validates the claims of any of those powers.

But the Soviet Union itself is an unpalatable bouillabaisse of disparate peoples with only one thing in common—sullen, smoldering resentment of detested intimacy with one another. No democratic ratifying process produced—could have produced—a free union of these peoples. Such a process did produce an organic union in America where, regardless of sectional differences, people shared a common cultural, religious and linguistic heritage and drew from a common fund of political philosophy and rhetoric.

To a Lithuanian's lament that half a century of socialism has produced only empty shelves, Gorbachev responded, "So shall we break up the union because of sausage?" Gorbachev doesn't get it. Sausages would not be nearly enough to buy off people incandescent with long-suppressed longings. If the Soviet Union's captive nations secede they may pass quickly from slavery into anarchy, then to their own despotism. Self-determination can (see postcolonial Africa) propel people into tribalism. Democracy not only presupposes a certain level of civility, it teaches it. But the seething peoples of the Soviet Union, their tempers frayed and their characters debased by decades of tyranny are, as democrats, preschoolers. Also, nations are not Tinkertoys to be pulled apart and reassembled casually. Woodrow Wilson, one of history's overreachers, preached "ethnic self-determination." (As a boy, in his father's parsonage in Augusta, Georgia, he heard his father's prayers for the secessionist armies.) But Hitler invoked "ethnic self-determination" on behalf of Sudeten Germans in the crisis that was then "settled" at Munich.

There must be some statute of limitations on historic grievances. There is an ominous potential for Eurasia to be ulcerated by many Ulsters, even Beiruts. However, time and delicacy can be great reconcilers. The turbulent Scots became Her Majesty's loyal subjects. In Spain, Catalan and Basque particularities have been respected with rights that defuse separatism. But *nothing*, nothing now or in prospect, commends to the captive nations continued association with the Soviet Union, that most comprehensive of failures, the most unnatural of nations.

Nations are made in two ways, by the slow working of history or the galvanic force of ideas. Most nations are made the former way, emerging slowly from the mist of the past, gradually coalescing within concentric circles of shared sympathies, with an accretion of consensual institutions. But a few nations are formed and defined by the citizens' assent to a shared philosophy. The United States is a nation of immigrants whose social diversities are subsumed beneath a shared dedication to a proposition. They consider that proposition "self-evident," that is, convincing to all minds unclouded by ignorance or superstition.

The Soviet regime has tried to produce an idea-based nation. Since the shell of the Russian state was seized in 1917 by a tiny thugocracy of ideologically intoxicated Bolsheviks, the Soviet Union has been held together first by force and random terror, lately by bureaucracy, inertia and despair. But the regime also has tried to weld together its wildly unlike and unsympathetic captive peoples, using a hot torch of ideology. But the ideology is arrogant, crude and false. So, to what proposition in Soviet public philosophy could the agglomeration of peoples spread across 11 time zones give nation-making assent? The analogue of the shop shelf barren of sausages is the Soviet library shelf barren of books containing a philosophy to which rational adherence is possible.

It can modernize only by scrubbing itself clean of communism. But it can remain intact only by suppressing the secession of cohesive peoples stirred by ancient creeds. It can do that only by hammering those peoples in the name of the New, asserting communism's claim to have deciphered the future. Gorbachev's dilemma is stark and insoluble. The best the Soviet Union can hope for is the choice between imploding and exploding but the economic sclerosis the political paralysis and the indecisiveness of Gorbachev, who is still committed to Communist forms, means that the Soviet regime might not choose. If so, it will face both fates—implosion and explosion—simultaneously.

January 29, 1990

Capitalism's Modern Times

The crises enveloping all societies professing "scientific socialism" have distracted attention from a small, germane event in this country. It is an application of the science of ergonomics to capitalism. The United Auto Workers has negotiated with Chrysler the use of ergonomics to reduce repeated trauma disorders. This is an event connected in a quiet way to the noisy clash of socialist and capitalist ideas.

Approximately one-third of all compensable industrial injuries result from physical stress. Such stress often comes cumulatively from repetitive motions. Ergonomics, the science of making machines and jobs fit people rather than the reverse, often is a matter of small marginal adjustments in the design of a tool or the angle at which a worker bends his or her back or wrist and shoulders.

The important variables in work are posture, pace, repetitiveness, movements, vibrations and energy expended. "White finger," for example, is loss of feeling and control in fingers and hands because of collapsed blood vessels. This can be caused by vibrations from power tools. Blackened fingertips result from tissues deprived of oxygen.

That and many other afflictions could be called Henry Ford's syndrome, or Charlie Chaplin's disorders. Ford pioneered flowing production and Chaplin, in *Modern Times*, depicted industrialism as a nightmare experience for workers caught as cogs in relentless machines. (According to historian William Manchester, audiences in industrial Pittsburgh did not find funny Chaplin's parody of a workman's five-minute break in which his hands continued to mime the machine's motion, slowing down just enough to enable him to lift a glass.)

Ailments arising from repetitive modern processes are not distinctively American but are especially American. Mass production, says historian Daniel Boorstin, altered the essential experience of life. Hitherto life had been composed of a series of unique moments. True, there had been a certain sameness to the days, seasons, years of a 14th-century peasant tilling a field behind oxen. But modern manufacturing brought an especially intense sameness.

Central heating, refrigeration and air conditioning radically reduced the significance of seasons. Electric lighting liberated mankind from the tyranny of two natural demarcations, sunlight and darkness, so factories could hum "around the clock." But before that could happen, clocks had to become so prevalent that people became accustomed to dicing their days—their lives—into minutes. (Wristwatches became common after 1900, partly because soldiers in the Boer War used watches to synchronize movements.)

With the coming of moving production lines, working time came to be thought of as a series of closely calculated units. The units were indistinguishable. So, too, were workers whose lives were tethered to the relentless line. Interchangeable parts of uniform dimensions moving past workers made economic efficiency primarily a matter of speed. That speed depended on the rate at which the slowest function along the line could be performed.

An undeniable good—the unleashing of productive energy—came from this economic organization. But one cost of this—repeated-trauma disorders—is only now, late in the age of mass manufacturing, becoming properly understood.

Until recently many repetition-related injuries were regarded as natural results of aging, unrelated to work. And only now are specialists seeing new potential for such injuries, as with computer keypunch operators who may make 23,000 finger strokes in a day.

Flowing production brings the job to workers, but often brings a badly designed job. Designing jobs is the business of ergonomics, a science for mitigating the costs of modernity.

Such costs were once related to the socialist impulse which often was a reaction against the conditions of modern labor. Socialists thought workers were debased—"alienated from their social product"—not merely by being denied just economic rewards, but also by the suffocation of craftsmanship. The satisfactions of craftsmanship were, they said, casualties of soul-destroying repetition in the severe division of labor made necessary by mass production.

Actually, the socialists' complaint was—is—with industrialism, not capitalism. But socialism promised special solicitousness for workers' interests. In fact, labor has been especially exploited in the "socialist bloc," where real labor unions have been suppressed. And one of the heroic stories of the capitalist "bourgeois" world is the role of free unions in making capitalism more attractive—more just—than mere market forces would have done.

The explosion that is blowing away "scientific socialism" in Eastern Europe began in Poland when Solidarity demonstrated a great proof: The right of labor to organize is as sharp a chisel as the right to emigrate is for cracking the concrete of tyranny. Lech Walesa is in America being toasted by, among others, conservatives who only value unions abroad. Conservatives should ask the bartender at the country club to uncork some champagne so they can offer a quiet toast to organized labor. It has made capitalism a more marketable idea by making it a less traumatic system.

November 16, 1989

Bonapartism in Poland

Shortly after the end of the Second World War, "Chips" Channon, a Conservative Member of Parliament, attended a society wedding in London with Lady Cunard. Gazing upon this gathering of the upper crust, and marveling at the speed with which life had returned to normal, Channon said contentedly, "After all, this is what we have been fighting for." Lady Cunard replied dryly, "What? Are they all Poles?"

Poland is back in the spotlight and is, for a change, a pleasing sight. This is Poland's third turn at center stage. The first two were problems for the democracies, which wished Poland would go away. It did, twice, in tragedy.

In 1939, Britain, having refused to resist Hitler when resistance would have been effective concerning the Rhineland and Czechoslovakia, joined its fate to Poland's. The futility of that led, five years later, to a second futility. At Yalta, the democracies insisted on free elections in Poland, behind the lines of the Red Army. The devouring of Poland's democratic forces was Stalin's declaration of Cold War.

Now, however, Poland is back in the headlines, in triumph, with elections in which communists running unopposed managed to lose. These elections cause one to wonder merrily whether Poland has sped from a one-party (Communist Party) state to another one-party state (Solidarity by a landslide) without pausing for the novelty of democratic factionalism.

Solidarity is trying not to run up the score against the candidates of the pathetic regime, which has humbly petitioned for electoral mercy in the form of a fix—some parliamentary seats handed to it on a platter. Poland's indigenous democratic culture is required to show extraordinary subtlety. Today in Poland there is an unprecedented coexistence of totalitarian and democratic forces. This poses for Solidarity a problem anomalous to the politics of parliamentary systems. How does Solidarity, enjoying the overwhelming support of the majority of the people, act like a subordinate force, a loyal opposition?

For now, however, Marxist theorists must execute yet another revisionist somersault. Socialism, according to Marxist orthodoxy, is the transitional stage between capitalism and communism. Now it seems that Bonapartism—the replacement of politics by military administration—is a transition stage back from socialism to capitalist pluralism. On December 13, 1981, Bonapartism came to Poland when martial law was imposed by General Jaruzelski.

Bonapartism, as practiced by the great scoundrel himself, at least had ambitious aspirations beyond domestic tranquility. It did concentrate power to discipline revolutionary ferment. But it also strove for a modern bureaucracy that would rationalize society and produce a meritocracy of "careers open to talents." And society was supposed to be energized for domestic grandeur and foreign influence by the majesty of a great military leader.

Jaruzelski, lacking greatness and unable to locate anyone willing to be led, has enjoyed only the prominence of a ship's figurehead carved from wood. However, history may accord him the grudging respect sometimes granted to one Napoleon—Louis Napoleon, who came in handy for France after the disturbances of 1848.

Marx was referring to Louis Napoleon when he said that historic personages occur in history twice—first as tragedy, then as farce. But it is foolish to call Louis Napoleon farcical merely because he was not like his namesake. He was a social conciliator whose regime was a stew of monarchial trappings, republican ethos and political absolutism leavened by economic liberalism.

Jaruzelski's authoritarianism also was an incoherent jumble. It was force ostensibly in the service of, but actually required by the evaporation of, communist ideology. It was authoritarianism devoid of authority, a regime rendered irrelevant by Polish society's astonishing ability to generate a political system apart from the state. If Jaruzelski's regime negotiates itself into an accommodation with Solidarity, and then dissolves into democracy, his bland Bonapartism will have been a small wave that carried Poland toward a better future. Europe has recently been rich with such surprises.

In the mid-1970s, with many capitalist economies mismanaged into stagflation, it seemed that "Eurocommunism" might be the wave of the future in, say, Italy. There, the 1948 elections had produced a crucial Cold War victory over communism. But the real drama was soon to be played out on another peninsula, the Iberian, where "Eurocommunism" proved to be less important than Neo-monarchism.

Spain, guided by King Juan Carlos (now more than ever he deserves the Nobel Peace Prize, for his example), and Portugal became the first European nations to pass from dictatorship to democracy without first suffering military conquest. Portugal's passage may offer a closer parallel to Poland's because Portugal's was not guided by a royal figure of national unity. A lovely thought: In Poland, the monarchic function was fulfilled by a trade unionist.

Old Europe, it seems, has surprising reservoirs of novelty, and a sufficiency of the ancient virtues of prudence, subtlety, patience and magnanimity.

June 11, 1989

The Man Who Is Not Paganini

WARSAW—Poland's president, General Wojciech Jaruzelski, is also Poland's sphinx. His eyes hidden behind tinted glasses, the usually stony set of his mouth betraying no emotion, he certainly does not smile promiscuously. But at a recent meeting with five Americans, the stone cracked and he smiled, even laughed.

A man, he said musingly, is on a tightrope stretched high above a street, with no net below. It is raining, the wind is gusting. And he is playing a violin. (Jaruzelski crooked his left arm and with his right he vigorously drew an imaginary bow across an imaginary violin.) "And people say, 'He's no Paganini!' " The General laughed at his jest.

The tightrope metaphor is a tantalizing exercise in reticence, a quality essential to survival in the Soviet orbit. Toward what is the tightrope walker edging? Democracy? The General, dressed like a banker, does not say that. But he sounds like a Polish patriot as he favors his American guests with a litany of the difficulties—civil war, racial strife, depression—American democracy has experienced in 200 years. Again, his message is—at most—implicit. It seems to be: We are doing, quickly and stealthily, what you have done with much turmoil when you were less constrained by time and circumstances.

Jaruzelski sounds like a conservative Republican when giving examples of excessive entitlements—long, paid pregnancy leaves, for example—that must be pruned if Poland is to become productive. The rococo system of controls must be dismantled and the thick fabric of subsidies must be unraveled. But this means a blast of inflation. Because things must get worse before they can get worse before they can get better, Jaruzelski, speaks like a Chicago alderman bent on assembling a broad social base for the government.

Poland is suffering shortages of almost everything—meat, machinery, poetry—but perhaps its most pressing need is a new, more inspiriting metaphor to replace the medicinal metaphors. Everyone here talks about the coming doses of "bitter medicine."

When necessities such as milk and meat are, in a blink, four to ten times more expensive, it may seem unfeeling, even fatuous, to call for a more cheerful vocabulary. However, another name for the bitter medicine Poland has just begun to taste is: freedom. And over the long haul, freedom is fun. It works.

A foreign-ministry official, pausing with a forkful of Baltic herring, reminds a visitor, "We are not alone in the world." Reticence about the Russian bear to the east comes naturally in a nation that has had the misfortune to exist (when it has existed: It disappeared from the European map from 1795 to 1918) near large, voracious neighbors.

Someone once said, rather hardheartedly, of Poland's history: If you pitch your tent in the middle of Fifth Avenue, you should expect to be hit by buses. Tanks, in Poland's case. Europe's northern plain is perfect for blitzkriegs.

But today East Germany's population is leaking westward through the porous papier-mâché curtain between Hungary and Austria. And between Poland and Russia, the Baltic states are in a roiling boil. They are reminding the world, at exactly the right moment, of this exquisitely embarrassing—to the Kremlin—fact: The Soviet Union is the only nation that was allied with Hitler when the war began but did not as a result suffer a rupture of its regime.

The Soviet regime, with all the troubles piled on its plate, probably cannot afford to think much about, let alone intervene in, Poland. But Soviet pressure need not come noisily, with clanking tanks. It could come silently, in reduced flows of iron, oil and cotton.

The Solidarity now faces an identity crisis. It cannot be both what it has been and what it now is: both a trade union and a government, a militant arm of a faction and a conciliating institution.

Poland's Communist Party has acquiesced, so far, in Solidarity exercising power. Is Poland still a communist country? If by that phrase one means a country with a majority of convinced communists, there never has been a communist country, anywhere. However, today the aims and values of Poland's government resemble more closely those of all the NATO governments than those of any Warsaw Pact government, with the possible exception of Hungary's.

However, Poland's communist apparatchiks still control enough institutions to cause the new government to fail. Do the communists want it to? We come back to the sphinx, The Man Who Is Not Paganini.

One longs to insinuate this thought in among Jaruzelski's information about the United States: The eyes of visitors to Washington are drawn irresistibly to a towering monument to a general. His greatest act was one of renunciation, a refusal to keep or receive powers that would have had a stunting effect on his nation's nascent democracy.

August 31, 1989

"Communism"? Never Heard of It

Hungary's new ambassador has not been here long enough to have gotten the hang of the Washington art of using words to conceal thoughts. When, in a Sunday morning television interview, he was accused of giving an evasive answer to a question, Ambassador Peter Varkonyi said with unfeigned cheerfulness, "It is, it is. I should be evasive on that."

Having been blindsided by the Ambassador's treacherous resort to candor, the interviewers fell to badgering him about philosophy: Is Hungary moving away from communism? The Ambassador allowed a look of puzzlement, mingled with injured pride and sorrow about the confusions besetting mankind, to steal over his suddenly woeful countenance. Then he said, in effect:

What's that you are suggesting? That Hungary has ever been—what was that peculiar word you used?—"Communist"? How do such odd rumors get started? Who is saying these hurtful things?

The ambassador's actual words were: "As a matter of fact, we are not —we never called ourselves a Communist country. We called ourselves a Socialist country . . . the Communist Party was called the Hungarian Socialist Workers Party, and it was not called the Communist Party."

The new party line in parts of Eastern Europe is that there has been an amusing mix-up—a silly misunderstanding, really: There never has been a Communist Party. In the current issue of *National Review*, Radek Sikorski, a Polish emigré, recounts his return to Warsaw where, in the inner recesses of the Communist Party's headquarters (where the night porter was watching *Miami Vice* dubbed in Polish), he asks a party official to pose for a photograph in front of the portrait on the wall:

"No, not under Lenin!"
  "But aren't you a Communist?"
  "No, I'm not a Communist."
  "But you are one of the top leaders of the Communist Party."
  "It's not a Communist Party. It's called the United Workers Party, and comprises two traditions, Communist and Socialist. I regard myself as a Social Democrat."

What is—was?—a Communist (person, nation)? It is, truth be told, hard to say because the Master was himself tantalizingly vague about that (you would have thought) crucial matter.

Marx was so busy predicting capitalism's collapse, he forgot to describe what would come next. Aside from the withering away of the state (it, being by definition an instrument of class oppression, would disappear when classes did), all he said was: Under capitalism man is a hunter or a fisherman or a shepherd or a critic, whereas in a Communist society he can be a hunter in the morning, a fisherman in the afternoon, raise cattle in the evening and be a critic after dinner.

Marx certainly did not burden his disciples with a too-detailed blueprint. But now we know that in a Communist society everyone does the same thing most of the time: They stand in queues. Or they go to Hungary and head west.

To the list of 19th-century theories slain by 20th-century facts, add one 20th-century theory now deceased: Twenty-five years ago there was a cottage industry among academics manufacturing variants of the theory that the Soviet and American systems were "converging." The former was supposed to "mellow" and the latter "progress" toward some mild social democracy, two bland leviathans living happily ever after.

Today, the Soviet Union is desperately in need of the book no one thought to write. As a Russian recently said, "There have been many books written on the transition from capitalism to socialism, but not one on the transition from socialism to capitalism."

Consider two stunning facts: East Germany, from which the highly skilled and educated young—tomorrow's elites—are fleeing, is the most productive and materially modern East European nation. And last week Boris Yeltsin (the "populist" described as the Soviet Union's Huey Long: actually he is their Imelda Marcos, a shop-till-you-drop communist) came to America: "All my impressions of capitalism, of the United States, of Americans that have been pounded into me over the years . . . all of them have been changed 180 degrees in the day and a half I have been here."

And where was the "here" where he had this epiphany about the commodious life and the sweetness of our people? New York City, believe it or not.

Today, East Germans, residents of what supposedly was communism's closest approximation to a success story, are "voting with their feet." The phrase was used in early 1917 to describe the behavior of the soldiers in the Tsar's disintegrating army. The phrasemaker was Lenin. What goes around, comes around.

September 21, 1989

What "Community" of Nations?

President Bush is more emphatic than specific in his reiterated prayers for the "success" of Gorbachev's *perestroika*. Specificity may not be necessary if one assumes that anything would be better than what the Soviet Union was in its first seven decades. But that assumption may be mistaken. If the Soviet Union is going to be more improved in its efficiency than in its intentions, putting enhanced productivity in the service of old expansionist ends, the assumption is dangerous.

The President's thinking was deployed in his Texas A&M speech declaring "containment" a mission accomplished. Now, he intimated, the task is to tidy up the loose ends left by the unraveling of totalitarianism. The aim is "the integration of the Soviet Union into the community of nations."

The phrase "community of nations" may seem harmless, if hackneyed. One risks seeming churlish pointing out that it is a sentimentalism, and almost an oxymoron. Different nations involve different notions of justice. A "community" consists of people held together by a broad, deep consensus about justice under a common sovereignty.

Bush's hope soars beyond community: "Perhaps the world order of the future will truly be a family of nations." But the idea of nations comprising a "family" compounds confusion; it is political sentimentality cubed. Families and political institutions are polar opposites. Families are associations of intimacy and affection. Relations between nations can never be like that.

Radically better relations with the Soviet Union should be a snap if the President is correct that *perestroika* is moving the Soviet Union toward "democratization." However, *perestroika* is not *glasnost,* and *glasnost* is not democracy until it is carried far beyond its current episodes, and then institutionalized. Democracy is not a yearning or mood, it is a complex, durable system of institutions—political (beginning with competing parties), judicial and journalistic.

Now, it would be misleading to weigh Bush's words more carefully than they were used. But words are all we have to think with; they do reveal habits of mind and they can bewitch our intelligence.

In Texas, Bush marveled, "Who would have imagined a Soviet leader who canvasses the sidewalks of Moscow and also Washington, D.C." The relevant *Oxford Dictionary* definition of "canvass" is "the action of personally soliciting votes before an election."

Bush's licentious use of the language of democracy is tame compared with that of the Columbia University professor who said the following about why Reagan and Gorbachev got on so swimmingly:

"Gorbachev and Reagan were both country boys from their Midwest regions, both governors of sorts and both anti-establishment populists determined to restore a mythic golden age. Both stirred up the bureaucracy against them and elicited fervent support and fervent opposition."

Rather a lot of wool is packed into the words "of sorts." Being the elected servant of California's electorate and being the appointed instrument of the Politburo are dissimilar apprenticeships. Strange that the Soviet establishment let loose that "populist." And what was the Soviet "golden age"?

Another former governor, Jimmy Carter, who was recently revived by Bush as a counselor, has declared that Gorbachev is "the most humanitarian of the world's leaders." That is about as batty as the Columbia professor's opinion. But the professor at least does point, in his peculiar way, to the supreme question of contemporary politics: "Who is Gorbachev?"

More precisely, the question is: Given what we know about the socialization—education and political—of the Soviet ruling elite, what is it prudent to suspect about the settled aims of the man who has emerged as supreme over that elite?

It used to be said that the four stages of socialism are utopian, scientific, real and curfew. Now, we are told, there is a fifth stage: "Hey, about the last 70 years? We just changed our minds."

It was natural for Reagan, the sentimentalist and romantic, to think that relations between nations could be reduced to sentiments shared by leaders, and to assume, with the parochial cosmopolitanism of a good American, that anyone not actually pointing a cocked pistol to your head probably has sentiments pretty much like yours. The pace and tonality of Bush's response to Gorbachev suggests greater sobriety, a quality not communicated by his language.

However, as the social ground heaves beneath the governments in the capitals of two burnt-out communist revolutions, the language that matters most is body language. It is the stirring of—virtually the creation of—the body politic in the Soviet Union and China. The result may be that fifth stage of socialism. Or the result may be a curfew.

May 21, 1989

New School Ties

During the 1980s, Washington got used to male attire that made a political statement. Earnest conservatives wore neckties emblazoned with likenesses of Adam Smith, a pioneer of free-market economic theory and a moral philosopher. Ideological neckwear is now another American idea that has gone east.

At a meeting in Davos, Switzerland, of European leaders from east and west, Vaclav Klaus, Czechoslovakia's new finance minister, was wearing a University of Chicago necktie. He never went to that noble institution, but it, in a sense, came to him.

The name "Chicago school" has recently referred to the free-market teachings of that university's economists, such as Milton Friedman and George Stigler, both winners of Nobel Prizes.

Richard Perle, who was a bête noire to the "socialist bloc" when he was an assistant secretary of defense, and who now is invited to contribute articles to publications that until recently excoriated him, congratulated Klaus on his necktie. Klaus responded: "The Vienna School may be dead in Vienna, but it is alive in Prague." And so the circulation of ideas comes full circle.

The "Vienna school" of economics, exemplified by Friedrich von Hayek and Ludwig von Mises, taught not only the efficacy of free markets as rational allocators of resources, but also the morality of capitalism by virtue of its connection with free political arrangements. These teachings took a detour through the Hyde Park section of Chicago on the way to Prague, where the intellectual flame was kept by a small group—let's call it a cell—of free-market students within the communist youth organization.

Communism is like bagpipes, only even worse. A mother once asked Sir Thomas Beecham, the British conductor, what instrument—violin? trombone?—her son should take up. She said she was worried about the possible wear and tear on family nerves from her son's first efforts. Sir Thomas recommended bagpipes: "They sound exactly the same when you have mastered them as when you first begin learning them."

Communism came to power in the Soviet Union as an irrational approach to modernization and has become more irrational as the 20th century has become more modern. It was dreadfully inefficient, even as an approach to forced-draft development of heavy industry in a backward country. It has become steadily less suited to society as the quantity and velocity of information has mattered more and more to economic life.

Communism was a moral imperative to some of its adherents, but to the Soviet regime it has always been primarily a doctrine of modernization. This explains Gorbachev, his motives, his strengths—and his by now glaring limitations as a leader.

He is a modernizer who knows that the essence of the Soviet system, "democratic centralism" (control of a command society by a party claiming a monopoly of the interpretation of history), is incompatible with modernity. Modernity requires broad dispersal for decision-making. Gorbachev seems reconciled—one cannot, on the evidence, put it any stronger—to such dispersal.

Speaking with asperity, Gorbachev recently said to the Communist Party Central Committee that "Pluralism of opinion is not dissent but democratic centralism understood in a new way." Note well: He defends "pluralism of opinion" only by distinguishing it—by undisclosed criteria—from dissent, which is, by implication, deplorable.

For all his narrow-gauge radicalism, Gorbachev is a recognizable Russian phenomenon. He is a modernizer looking west, as Peter the Great did. However, he is not also a moralist. He has received much, in fact quite enough, praise for saying what every store shelf in the Soviet Union says: Communism does not work. But he has never said communism is wrong.

By indicting existing arrangements solely in terms of materialist criteria—yes, we have no bananas—Gorbachev convicts himself, in advance but not far in advance, of failure as defined by those criteria. In Davos, Nikolai Shmelve, a member of the Soviet Parliament, predicted that the Soviet Union might soon require "100 percent rationing of everything—a labor camp economy." So the distinction between the camps in Soviet society may disappear before the camps do.

To reconcile his restive citizens to what is certain—grinding scarcity for the foreseeable future—someone needs to make the moral side of the argument: Freedom is a natural right, right for our nature and an end in itself.

Gorbachevism is dangerously thin gruel because it lacks what Vaclav Klaus and kindred spirits find so satisfying about the Vienna and Chicago "schools": a fusion of economic analysis and moral philosophy.

February 15, 1990

New Truths About the Wired World

As Congress convenes and the pulse of government quickens, consider the growing sovereignty of social forces over sovereign governments. Technology-driven change is changing the weight—physical and political—of goods, institutions, countries and regions.

Norman Macrae of the *Economist* reports that in 1903 the Mercedes Corporation concluded that there never would be a world market for more than 1 million automobiles. The limiting factor? There would never be more than 1 million people trainable as chauffeurs.

Manual labor was the norm until remarkably recently. In the 1960s in Western Europe and America, 70 percent of all employed people were use-of-hands workers, 30 percent use-of-brain workers. That ratio is being reversed.

Walter Wriston, writing in *Foreign Affairs*, notes that 85 percent of all the scientists who have ever lived are alive today, that scientific knowledge is doubling every 13 to 15 years and that the resulting social change is diluting the sovereignty of nations. In one important instance, *glasnost* was forced on the Soviet regime by photos taken from a privately owned satellite, the French SPOT, launched in 1986. Pictures of the Chernobyl nuclear plant forced the Kremlin to stop lying about the extent of the catastrophe.

The ability to mandate the value of currency was a traditional aspect of national sovereignty. Today communications technologies have produced an instantaneous international market rendering constant judgment about the values of currencies. In this wired world, Wriston writes, there is no place to hide as currency values are controlled by the "information standard."

Wars have traditionally begun when borders were violated. But today borders are porous because money and ideas—as powerful as armies—cross them electronically. Markets are no longer geographic locations. Rather, markets are data on millions of computer screens, worldwide. The markets render pitiless judgments on political actions by altering monetary values. Such global markets are, as Wriston says, a form of free speech telling the unregulatable truth about nations' politics.

Workplaces, like marketplaces, can become geographically indeterminant. Workers can be connected by computers to jobs far from their residences, and these are economic incentives for allowing people to "commute electronically." Macrae notes that the rental cost of the square foot of office space occupied by a wastepaper basket in the City of London or downtown Tokyo can rent an entire apartment a few blocks away.

Technology even alters the strategic importance of regions. As Wriston says, not long ago the conventional wisdom was that lights would go out all over the world if the Suez Canal were closed. That wisdom did not anticipate supertankers capable of carrying oil economically around the Cape of Good Hope.

Alan Greenspan argues that the rapid expansion of international trade is produced, in part, by technology, particularly the shrinkage of the size of products. In 1950, radios were made with vacuum tubes. Today, radios fit in shirt pockets, calculators fit in wallets. A fiber-optic cable as thin as a hair replaces a thick bundle of copper cables. Copper-producing nations lose their weight. (Wriston notes that the material for computer chips is the world's most common substance: sand.)

New architectural designs, engineering techniques and building materials mean more usable space with less concrete and steel. Space heating improves, so winter clothing becomes lighter, with the help of new chemical technologies.

Greenspan says the recent improvement in the economic well-being of most nations occurred without significant change in the physical bulk or weight of gross national product. "If all the tons of grain, cotton, ore, coal, steel, cement and the like that Americans produce were combined, their aggregate volume probably would not be much greater on a per-capita basis today than it was, say, 50 or 75 years ago."

High-value and easily transportable goods lend themselves to cross-border commerce more readily than do bulky products. "The cost of moving gravel across continents makes it hard to see foreign quarries as much of a backup for excess domestic demand. But the ease with which small electronic components can be moved by air integrates a significant part of the world's capacity."

The decline in the bulk and weight of goods is a result of what Greenspan calls "the conceptual contribution to economic activity." It has the political consequence of complicating one familiar assertion of national sovereignty: protectionism. In 1900, Greenspan writes, economic value was created, archetypally, by moving iron ore by rail from the Mesabi Range to Pittsburgh, where it was joined with coal to make steel.

Today, economic value is increasingly created by moving data, analyses and insights hither and yon, electronically. The products of economic production, says Greenspan, "are becoming progressively impalpable." So are elements of national sovereignty.

January 5, 1989

Totalitarianism Falls to the Suction Effect

Having been for decades indifferent to the masses, and having more recently been incompetent at addressing those aspirations, Communist nations have at least been free from the afflictions of consumer societies, such as traffic jams.

The first traffic jam in Soviet history occurred on October 15, 1941, on roads leading east out of Moscow. Hitler, who 150 days earlier had been an ally, was approaching from the west and the Soviet elite was fleeing to Kuybyshev, 600 miles east.

Today, East Germany's Communist regime has managed to generate traffic jams at the border between Czechoslovakia and West Germany. East German citizens are fleeing with the entreaties of the political elite ringing in their ears.

We are witnessing perhaps the last distinctive feature of totalitarianism, the "suction effect." The nephew leaves, so the aunt does too. Three members of the amateur soccer club leave, so four more, sensing that even that fun is gone, leave too. Four members of a factory work crew head west, so other members of the crew, facing longer hours and worse conditions, follow them.

Last August, the border between Austria and Hungary suddenly became the most important place on the planet. There, where the Iron Curtain became porous, the resulting suction began pulling down the Berlin Wall. A wall that you can, in effect, walk around is only an eyesore.

The Germans, said a wit who did not much care for them, are vigorously obedient. No more. The more the East German regime tries, in its sinister and transparently insincere way, to be mollifying, the more urgently more Germans feel the itch to flee.

The regime probably is incapable of understanding how it sounds when it offers to measure out more freedom with coffee spoons. The intended beneficiaries of this rationing are not reassured. All they hear is a thugocracy, one that has lied for 40 years and maintained the Wall for 28 years, asserting the right to ration freedom.

The regime says it will no longer be a crime for East Germans to flee the country (with about enough money to buy breakfast), but it will still be a crime to "directly violate the border." That murky distinction means:

The Wall stays. And the barbed wire and attack dogs and machine-gun towers.

The regime might as well announce the obvious: Liberalization is a ploy, a tactic designed to slow the flow of emigrants by lulling them into the sense that things will be radically different. But the Wall will remain as the regime's insurance that liberty is revocable.

Last week, on the 472th anniversary of Martin Luther's defiant act of nailing 95 theses to the door of the Wittenberg church in which he is buried, East German protesters nailed just seven demands. In 1517, the issues were many, theological and abstruse—transubstantiation versus consubstantiation, and all that. Today the issues are secular, simple and few.

The Communist ruling class, imbued with the categories of authoritarianism, if no longer the convictions of Marxism, is tone-deaf to the Jeffersonian assumption of the masses who believe in natural and inalienable rights that exist independently of the will of the state.

Today there may be more Marxists on the Harvard faculty than in Eastern Europe. In one month, Hungary's Communist Party has lost more than 95 percent of its members. When it changed its name from Communist to Socialist, it asked its members to reregister. Big mistake. One party official, who understandably desires anonymity, says the problem is the policy of requiring members to take the affirmative step of exchanging membership cards: "We were overgenerous by making it possible for them to leave decently and with a clear conscience." Think about that.

Egon Krenz, he of the shark's smile, was until recently the enforcer, the keeper of the East German regime's truncheons. Today he is a born-again reformer, serving up such hash as: The regime will offer radical reforms but will "preserve socialism" and its "achievements." The Wall is the defining achievement of socialism.

Last year, while making a triumphant passage through chanting, swooning West Germans, Mikhail Gorbachev was asked when the Wall would come down. He said: When the conditions that made it "necessary" are gone. That repulsive thought did nothing to dampen enthusiasm for Gorbachev.

What made the Wall "necessary" was—is—the existence of an alternative—any alternative—to communism. That is why today there is under way the greatest movement of European people since the surge of refugees who headed west as the Red Army arrived 44 years ago.

November 9, 1989

Germany: From Spiked Helmets to Soft Caps

Was there method to the manner of former West German Chancellor Helmut Schmidt, who was fond of sporting a soft fisherman's cap from his native Hamburg? It was perhaps a way of saying, "See how far we Germans have come from spiked helmets!" For four decades, Germany's most important export has been reassurances.

When, this week, Chancellor Helmut Kohl endorsed reunification for "the continuation of German history," anxious Europeans wondered, "Which history?" That of cultural achievement or political destruction?

But current events should be reassuring enough. We—including the two bystanders standing on the decks of their ships at the Malta Summit—are witnessing the triumph of a 40-year tradition of West German freedom over a political catastrophe imposed on East Germany.

On August 13, 1986, East Germany's regime celebrated—yes, celebrated—the 25th anniversary of the Berlin Wall with such incongruities as parades and a commemorative postage stamp depicting a winsome moppet handing flowers to border guards. There will not be 30th anniversary festivities, and some Western worriers seem sorry about that.

Germans are making nuisances of themselves by moving swiftly and peacefully toward unification, thereby upsetting diplomats who prefer the familiarity of the status quo. The Germans have been called a perpetually dissatisfied people who have a yesterday and a tomorrow but no today. The impermanence, even unreality, of the postwar present has been apparent in the defensive, reassuring slogan, "Bonn is not Weimar." Bonn is even Bonn—not really the capital of Germany. By being so provincial, it is ostentatiously provisional: It is the capital until Berlin can be.

It will be before long. Kohl has a reputation as a plodder, but he has seized this moment to move toward the end of the postwar era. And many people see in this movement the reappearance of dangerous German volatility and vitality.

Volatility? Germans are only seeking rights, including self-determination, that the West's civic religion teaches are inalienable. Political light-years ago (last May), a NATO summit communiqué reaffirmed the hope that "the German people" would regain "unity through self-determination." In the distant future (say, 1992) that may happen. That will knock into a cocked hat (where it belongs) the banality of "Europe '92"—

Brussels as the center of the Universe, national sovereignties surrendered to Eurocrats.

European freedom is being enlarged because history is running against Brussels. (And is running for Margaret Thatcher, and also for a statesman whose vision of Europe may be vindicated in the 1990s, Charles de Gaulle.) Quickened nationalisms may be compatible with a "broader" Europe of economic unity but not a "deeper" unity of political integration.

In a dialectical process that should be satisfying to students of German philosophy, the Berlin Wall (itself a delayed response to the uprisings of 1953, which the Communist regime blamed on contaminating contacts with the West) gave rise to forces that have toppled the Wall and the regime that built it.

The Wall led to West Germany's Ostpolitic that fueled, through human contacts, explosive pressures behind the Wall. That is why for years German foreign policy was *"détente über alles."*

The East German regime contributed to its own downfall by acknowledging a rising sense of Germanness. It restored the statue of Frederick the Great to Unter den Linden: It celebrated Luther Year in 1983, the 500th anniversary of his birth. It muted the ideological teaching that all reactionary forces in German history passed through Hitler into the Federal Republic and all "progressive" forces culminate in the Democratic Republic; it commemorated the July 20, 1944, assassination attempt on Hitler as a great event for all Germans.

If Europe's future belongs to producers, not warriors, that future may be made for—and by—Germany. The *Economist* says, "Germany is set to win in peace the European supremacy that has twice eluded it in war." Of course Germany will be the head of the European house. What else can it be? A big Switzerland? That is an oxymoron. But a big Germany need not be ominous. Norman Stone, professor of modern history at Oxford, says of Germany:

"She is, easily, the outstanding European country. She fulfills the role that we [Britain] used to fulfill of combining economic efficiency, educational excellence and all-around seriousness with political liberalism and respect for people's rights; she is now, in my opinion, the modern European country."

Stone's analysis may be too sanguine, but it is not silly and it is a timely antidote to reflexive, facile angst at Germany's expense. If Helmut Schmidt's hat was not sufficiently reassuring, 40 years of freedom should be.

December 3, 1989

Germany: Seeing the Solution As a Problem

Regarding Germany, Western leaders, who seem to believe that history can be tamed by communiqués, are dotting i's and crossing t's and missing the point.

The European Community recently revised its formulation to say that the German people should recover unity through "free expression of the popular will" rather than through "free self-determination." The difference, whatever it means, may be related to Secretary of State Baker's belief that German reunification is not just for Germans to decide.

That departure from the principle of self-determination was stated as the four conquering powers—the United States, Britain, France and Hitler's ally at the start of the war, the Soviet Union—announced their "common understanding of the importance of stability." At a moment when Western values are at last causing creative instability, only the Soviet Union has a stake in "stability."

President Bush, who is a Pekingese curled around the ankles of China's tyrants, is a German shepherd barking impertinently at the German people, a majority of whom have compiled a 40-year record of democracy and the rest of whom would like to participate, right now. Unification, says Bush, must be gradual. Oh? Soviet-imposed tyranny has stolen 40 years from the lives of East Germans. That is enough.

Giulio Andreotti of Italy says, "It would be a mistake to settle the German problem too quickly, if it meant turning Europe upside down." But Europe has been turned upside down by progress toward Western goals. Myopic, plodding politicians persist in talking about the German "problem" when what is at hand is a solution to the problem of the unnatural, indefensible division of an organic entity, Germany. The Basic Law of the Federal Republic declares that state is provisional, pending—if the EC politicians will pardon the expression—"self-determination" of all Germans.

Beneath all the measured diplomatic boilerplate about the inconvenience of a united Germany's economic power, and what reunification might do to the "stability"—that golden calf, again—of the Tinkertoy project of European federalism, there is a plain prejudice, against Germans. In the kangaroo court of some world opinion, Germany can only be guilty, at any time, because when it is peaceful and democratic, the calm is considered an ominous prelude to a storm.

Germany is considered dangerously volatile. "Protean Germany, as mutable as the sea," wrote Luigi Barzini as recently as 1983. But what Germany's critics are really saying is the reverse, that German history has an implacable continuity. That is no longer true, if it ever was.

For 40 years Germany has submerged patriotism in heroic materialism, reducing national purpose to an ever-rising standard of living. This low but steady absorption was applauded by many non-Germans who wish for Germany what they deprecate in their own societies. They wish Germans to be so distracted and enervated by consumption that they shall have no other energies or longings.

West Germany's postwar history has indeed been a transforming discontinuity. Geoffrey Wheatcroft of the London *Daily Telegraph* argues, rightly, that few young Germans—"democratic, pacific, sybaritic"— would lift a finger, let alone a weapon, to recover the territories lost in the East when, at the end of the war, Poland, in Churchill's phrase, took a step sideways. "Bismarck," writes Wheatcroft, "said that the Balkans were not worth the healthy bones of a Pomeranian grenadier. Today, Pomerania does not look worth the healthy weekend of a prosperous Düsseldorf car worker."

Fifty years ago, "Why die for Danzig?" was the last gasp of appeasers of Germany. Today, most Germans do not care a particle for Gdansk (as Danzig now is), home of Lech Walesa.

If the point of the game is a Germany wedded to the West, the West should show a less crabbed spirit regarding reunification which is, in any case, inevitable. Enough of the worship of stability and of "gradual" progress toward justice long denied.

We now see why Bush's laughable problem with "the vision thing" is not funny. Communism is buckling beneath the weight of aspirations that America, by its mere existence, arouses. And America's President? Remember when presidents were supposed to lead the West in championing change? Today's President is courting the tyrants in Peking (because of them, most of the people who were suffering under communism at the beginning of 1989 are suffering even more at the end of 1989) and nervously longing for "stability" in central Europe.

Remember the argument about where Bush is from—Maine, Connecticut, Texas? He is from Washington. He is a career government man, and it is with government, not ideals or the people they stir, that he identifies.

December 14, 1989

The Quadrille of Nations

Marx is confirmed, kind of, by the collapse of Marxist regimes: states are indeed withering away. East Germany, the fourth country to secede from communism in as many months, is becoming a bourgeois democracy (that is now an aspiration; until recently it was an epithet) and collapsing toward reunification with another, the Federal Republic. For 40 years East Germany has been a Potemkin state, a façade of legality. In the 1970s, recognizing the lethal threat of German national sentiment, the regime changed its description of itself from "a Socialist state of the German nation" to "a Socialist state of workers and farmers." It has had only one raison d'être, to be a Soviet salient in the Cold War. It is Socialist or it is nothing. It is now nearly nothing because East Germans have been over into the present—Berlin's Kurfürstendamm—and it works.

East Germany's befuddled, apolitical intelligentsia, its thinking stunted by decades spent frozen like a fly in amber, talks vaporously about some "third way," some "humane socialism." But the masses want none of it. At a Leipzig rally a man identifying himself as a "plain craftsman" wins loud applause when he says socialism has failed and any "new socialism" will, too. "We are not," he says, "laboratory rabbits." Neither are they *East* German.

Diplomats, blinkered by their prejudice in favor of existing arrangements, whatever they are, are often the last to see what is happening. Today they are earnestly asking a question that history has already answered: Will Germany be reunified? It already is. Institutional details remain to be resolved but in what matters most, consciousness, Germans suddenly are one people again. The crucial steps in the making of the United States (1776, 1789) were made possible by the fact that people were thinking like Americans. States of mind precede states.

Gorbachev says reunification is for "history to decide." It did, long ago. The boldness of this generation of Germans is ratification of 20 generations of evolving nationhood. Politicians who think history can be tamed by legalisms are trying to lasso a locomotive with a cobweb lariat.

In Brussels—that preposterous pretender to the role of Rome in a new empire of homogenized Europe—President Bush said Germany's movement toward reunification "must" be gradual and "should occur in the context of Germany's continued commitment to NATO, an increasingly integrated European Community, and with due regard to the legal role and responsibilities of the Allied powers." That is the muffled voice of the State Department, speaking with its head in the ground. Today it is gradualism that is imprudent, given the collapse of the East German government. ("Who was Egon Krenz?" asked a sardonic banner at a protest rally while Krenz was the head of state.) What now is this NATO to which leaders say they are committed, world without end, amen? The world that made NATO necessary may have ended. Does "due regard" for Allied rights refer to the vestigial occupation rights? If so, the less said the better. As for "European integration," George Walden, a British MP writes: "One of the major incentives to postwar European integration was the threat from the East: It is not easy to see how its sudden diminution can be used to justify a stampede towards federalism."

President Mitterrand, meeting last week with Gorbachev, said his position had not changed, which of course meant that it had. Previously he had said, "I have no fear of German reunification." Now he says: but only if Germans accommodate "the interests of others." France is not famous for sacrificing its sovereignty on the altar of other people's interests, but its anxiety is understandable. It is axiomatic that France wants a Germany strong enough to keep the Soviet Union at bay but weak enough to be held in check by Luxembourg. De Gaulle hoped that a special Franco-Soviet relationship would preserve Europe's balance of power. But what if the special relationship is between a reunified Germany and the Soviet Union? There are precedents—Rapallo in 1922, the Hitler-Stalin pact of 1939—for sudden reversals of German-Soviet relations. After the war a French officer in occupied Germany worried about the day when Germans might do that again: "We all know that every time they come to an agreement with the Russians they arrive in Paris."

Germany invaded France three times in 70 years (1870, 1914, 1940) but it is farfetched to worry about a fourth invasion. Still, it is natural that the French and others worry about the Fourth Reich bestriding Europe, with Berlin shoving aside Brussels as the center of gravity. Events are rekindling Bismarck's aspiration for Germany to be Europe's "honest broker," this time as a bridge between East and West. There is a history of German economic and cultural penetration in the East. As a Bundestag member says, "German history and culture are more tightly linked with our neighbors in Central Europe than with EC nations such as Portugal and Spain."

It is not yet 1990 and already "Europe 1992," the statists' gray dream of a "deepened" European integration inflicted by Eurocrats in Brussels, looks like an anachronism. Should Germany, with its quickened sense of self and of its capacity for collective action, now aspire to the role of Gulliver, bound down by a thousand threads of red tape spewed forth from Brussels?

Timothy Garton Ash says the puncturing of the Berlin Wall did for Germany what the Pope's 1979 visit did for Poland: It caused an epiphany (Ash writes of the "pentecostal quality" of the Berlin experience), a sudden comprehension by the people that they all felt and thought the same way. They quickly understood that they could be, collectively, a body politic, strong with acting in concert. The result in both cases was solidarity. In Poland a trade union midwifed the rebirth of a nation. In Germany the result soon will be reunification. So as we turn the corner on the last decade of the century we are heading back to the future, to the 19th-century quadrille of nations. Despite the castles being built in the air by the bland utopians of Brussels, those dreamers of European unification, the newly assertive nations are not about to wither away.

December 18, 1989

"Wir Sind Wieder Da"

On the first day of the Warsaw Pact invasion of Czechoslovakia in August 1968, a Czech enjoying coffee and a croissant at a border-town café was startled when a tank rolled by and a German-speaking head popped from a turret to say, *"Wir sind wieder da."* Here we are again. As the Soviet Union tries to orchestrate worries about German reunification, it is well to remember that the only time since 1945 that German forces violated a border, they did so under Soviet orders.

Debates now raging about reunification are surreal for several reasons, beginning with the fact that reunification is not in doubt. Another reason is that so much rubbish is being written about Germans.

The January 22 issue of *Time* magazine contains a bizarre two-page report on "Voices of East Berlin" under this headline: "Talking to young and old alike, an American visitor discovers an abiding love of East Germany—and little desire to reunify." Oh? The Wall was a dike holding in "abiding love"? "Abiding love" is driving East Germans west at a current rate of 400,000 a year?

Time's reporter "discovers" what a shabby remnant of the Western intelligentsia wants to cling to: faith in "real" socialism as a "middle way" between capitalism and communism. *Time*'s report is the (dare we hope?) last in a long shabby line of stupid travelogues written, from the 1920s on, by people who prove their radicalism by writing nicely about places they would not live in for a month.

A second surreal aspect of all this is the role of the Soviet Union. Citing "the revival of sinister shadows of the past," the Kremlin has had the impertinence to suggest an international referendum on German reunification.

The Soviet Union is the only nation that began the Second World War as Hitler's ally but did not suffer a rupture of its regime. Its alliance ended at Hitler's initiative and to the surprise of the Soviet Union. The Soviet Union spent four postwar decades sowing tyranny and violence around the world. And now it presumes to say that before Germany, now in its fifth decade as a good world citizen, can enjoy full sovereignty, the Soviet Union must have a say?

At the moment, the Soviet Union is suffering acute indigestion, 50 years on, because of the Baltic states it swallowed with Hitler's connivance. This is not a propitious moment for the Soviet government to speak of any other nation's "sinister shadows of the past."

At a moment when the Red Army is being used against some of the centrifugal forces ripping the seams of that unnatural entity, the Soviet Union, Moscow has no standing to speak against the coming together of the German people—a real nation kept sundered by Soviet power. A regime that cannot provide soap or sustenance to its captive people, a regime facing the prospect of urban riots of desperation, has nothing to contribute to the discussion of Germany, save a timetable for removing its occupation army.

Outside the Soviet Union, there is much economic envy and fear of economic competition masquerading as anxiety about Germany's national character. And in East Germany, political desperation is part of the masquerade.

Gregor Gysi is leader of East Germany's shriveled Communist Party, which will be humiliated in the March 18 elections. Gysi accuses West German political parties of interfering in East Germany's internal affairs. West Germany parties are, he says, "looking for partner parties" when they should be negotiating with the East German regime.

Whom does he think he is speaking for—or to? Gysi is at the ragged end of a long line of East German quislings and he is serving the occupying power to the end, citing "the danger of rightist radicalism" as justification for the old Soviet agenda of Germany neutral and completely disarmed.

This is more surrealism, this pronouncement from Gysi, a ghost of a state that has withered away. States of mind come before, and matter more than, states, so Germany already is reunified. It is unseemly for Chancellor Kohl to continue meeting with Communist representatives of a regime that was content to run the state as a prison until Hungary, with an assist from Czechoslovakia, opened a door last summer.

The reunification of Germany has been greeted in the West by a crabbed spirit of suspicion and lawyerlike talk about vestigial occupation rights. The Soviet Union, the most comprehensive failure in the history of human organization, is accorded respectful hearings when it asserts a right to audit Germany's evolution. The smudged pages of modern history are replete with reasons for alertness about German isolation, resentment, chauvinism, injured pride and consequent aggressiveness.

But if one were perversely trying to provoke those failings, what better way to do so than by questioning Germany's sovereignty and by giving only grudging, wary welcome to the emergence of a democratic, pacific, unified Germany?

February 8, 1990

Are Germans Always Dangerous?

Germany has always been a puzzling concept and a problematic fact, not least to Germans. Konrad Adenauer was a Rhinelander with ambivalent feelings about eastern Germans. When in the interwar years he traveled to Berlin, as the train crossed the Elbe he would mutter, "Now we enter Asia."

Now an ancient people enters a new age. East Germany, "an ideology in search of a nation," has expired. Germany, which sent Lenin and hence communism into Russia during one war and sucked Soviet power into Europe's center in another war, finds its current fate both like and unlike that of the Soviet Union. In Soviet disintegration and German unification, the same wholesome fact is manifest: civil society, the enduring customs and associations of peoples, can survive independently of, and against, states. The durability of the German sense of *volk*, of being a people, is particularly remarkable because it has only sporadically found expression through nationhood under a single state. There was no such a state for 45 years, since 1945. Before that, one existed for just 74 years, from 1871 to 1945.

The supposed "question" of German reunification has been earnestly debated for several months by the professionally earnest. They are the diplomats, politicians and international clerisy of conference-goers, seminar-attenders and think-tank administrators. They find existing arrangements (NATO, the Warsaw Pact) comfortingly familiar. They think it is impolite, even lèse-majesté, for history to settle some things before they have had time to schedule seminars and make up their minds. However, German unity became a closed question at dusk, November 9, when the Berlin Wall began to be transformed from a brute fact into a million souvenirs.

For three months polite people have been discussing peripheral questions: Whither NATO? Wither NATO? Ditto the Warsaw Pact? However, the central question is: Are Germans inherently, incorrigibly menacing? Is there some character trait transmitted down the generations, some national chromosome, as it were, that makes Germans not only different but dangerous? It is a question as serious as the damage Germany has done in modern times.

Certainly the German people are "different"; otherwise they (like Italians, Spaniards, Americans) would not be "a people." Considered collectively, Germans have propensities and predispositions. Four decades of democracy is one. Granted, democracy is no guarantee of civility or domesticity within the European house. Nazism grew from a small faction into a mass movement then into a government under the Weimer Republic. But nothing in the civic life of postwar Germany justifies the prejudice that discerns a terrible continuity in German life.

Much of the purported anxiety about unified Germany is expressed with reference to Germany's savage past. But some of the anxiety seems disingenuously phrased. Many people now theatrically worrying about whether Germany will play by the rules of pacific, bourgeois, commercial Europe are actually worried that Germany will play too well. Hence the desire to sink Germany knee-deep in that fudge of federal bureaucracy now being cooked up by the gnomes of Brussels in the name of "Europe '92."

One conservative was clearsighted about the course of change. Germany's recovery of a robust but civilized sense of nationhood accords with de Gaulle's vision, not of a Europe of shriveled sovereignties but rather of L'Europe des Patries. That vision, once dismissed as anachronistic but now looking prophetic, should be championed today by Margaret Thatcher. But she, so right so early about so many things, has been tardy in recognizing the inevitability of German unification and has been grudging about accepting it. This is doubly strange because she is a splendidly unapologetic nationalist and an implacable opponent of the statism that has suffocated so much of Europe's energy. She understands that statism, now in retreat in the political arenas of Europe's nations, can be insinuated into Europe's future by the supranational apparatus being erected in the name of "Europe '92." She should seize the day and rejoice in a revitalized German nationalism as a counter to the statists attempting to subvert the sovereignty of nations.

Much of today's resurgent Germanophobia is a cynical ploy for political and commercial advantage. But there may also be in it a dash of perverse nostalgia for Europe's lurid past, when horribly high stakes gave politics higher purpose, or at least higher entertainment value.

Sebastian Haffner, a German writer, notes that Europe before World

War I was much more political than today. It was an exciting, at times intoxicating panorama of imperial powers in permanent rivalry, perpetually jockeying for position and constantly ready for war. The domestic life of each nation was dominated by sharp class divisions. "In one way or another," writes Haffner, "politics was the subject at any table of regulars at a middle-class café and in any proletarian tavern. The private lives, not only of the workers but also of the middle classes, were much narrower and poorer than they are today. But in the evening, as a compensation, everyone was, with his country, a Lion or an Eagle, or, with his class, a banner-bearer of a great future. Hitler who had nothing else to do, was that all day long. Politics was then a substitute of living . . ."

The point is not that Hitlerism "could have happened anywhere." It could not. And it did happen *there*, in a particular place, because of particular social pathologies. Germany's sickness was unique and much the worst in Europe. But it sprang, in part, from a European malady, one from which Europe has recovered. The malady was spiritual, or at least emotional, malnutrition. It gave rise to the use of vicarious politics to compensate for impoverished private lives. Today Europe, not least Germany, has the blessedly bland politics of bourgeois peoples whose everyday lives are sufficiently exciting, or at least satisfying—some would say enervating.

However explained or depicted, European politics is much blander and better than it was, because the public mind is more mature. The lions have gone, the eagles have flown away, the banners have been furled.

February 26, 1990

Realism in Machiavelli Country

ROME—Italy, until recently the sick man of Western Europe, is so robust that social scientists should be dizzy. A mere decade after last rites were being pronounced, it is flourishing in a manner that may make it a model for Europe's fast-unfolding future. It may be especially suited to absorb the political and cultural shocks of 1992, the unified market of the 12 nations of the European Community.

Italy had Europe's first formidable Fascist Party. As recently as a dozen years ago, when "Eurocommunism" was a cresting wave (Italian communists got 34.5 percent of the votes in 1976), Italy had the last formidable Communist Party.

Ten years ago Italy was the only European state under serious siege by terrorists. There were 2,500 terrorist incidents in 1978, including the kidnapping and murder of Italy's leading politician, Aldo Moro. The fever did not break until the rescue of the kidnapped American general, James Dozier.

Until the 1950s, Italy had a preindustrial economy. A decade ago, a serious commentator, Luigi Barzini, concluded that Italy was "going down the drain like Bangladesh" and should be the first developed nation to "turn itself back into an underdeveloped nation." Barzini compared Italian workers to savages who do not connect sexual intercourse with the brain of a child nine months later: They "do not connect the dull discipline of factory work with their cars, their holidays and their homes."

But Machiavelli's country is receptive to realism, including the distinctive realism of the 1980s, the rediscovery of the virtues and rigors of markets. In 1980, there was the "March of the 40,000," when Fiat workers went into the streets of Turin demanding, against their union leaders, the right to end a strike on terms favorable to Fiat's drive to modernize at the cost of jobs.

Today, Italy is the world's fifth-largest industrial market economy (behind the United States, Japan, Germany and France) and it is a conundrum for social science. Catholic Italy has a higher standard of living than Protestant Britain. What, now, of the connection between the Protestant ethic and the spirit of capitalism? What of the adage that Catholics sleep well but Protestants eat well?

Actually, Italy may be the fourth-largest market economy, ahead of France. It is hard to measure and easy to underestimate Italy's GNP because of the size of the unmeasurable "black economy." It hums along largely in the interstices of state supervision, and may account for at least 20 percent of GNP. One study showed that 54 percent of civil servants had second jobs, 33 percent sold goods within their ministries, 27 percent ran other businesses during office hours. By tax-avoidance and regulation-evasion, the "black economy" amounts to an unofficial but effective supply-side program.

Italians show less interest in and more cynicsm about politics than other European peoples. Italians as a people are ancient; the Italian state is young. Having been governed over the centuries by Spaniards, French and Austrians, and having been unified only since the 1860s, they tend to regard the state as a semiforeign presence. But the Italian attitude toward the state expresses an entire stance toward life, and may be something Europe will soon need more of.

In his new collection of essays, *Europe, Europe: Forays into a Continent*, Hans Magnus Enzensberger notes that for 200 years Northern Europeans (he is a German) have fallen under Italy's spell. Disregarding public inefficiencies and corruptions they would not tolerate at home, they have condescended to Italians as charming, creative, stylish but, at bottom, unserious.

However, Enzensberger writes, Italy is not the West's drive-in theater, a place for brief entertainment. Rather, it may have the mildly anarchic brio required for life in Europe's emerging megastate.

A specter is, or should be, haunting Europe: the specter of . . . Brussels. Not the cute bourgeois Brussels of fine chocolate and linen, but the gray Brussels of bureaucracy, the home of the administrative machinery of the "new Europe." In 1992, the 12 nations are supposed to begin playing by the same rules. The rules will proliferate exponentially.

Social scientists, writes Enzensberger, have assured us that the price of progress is life within "the armor of institutions." We must reconcile ourselves to life inside a labyrinth of walls, visible and invisible, as bureaucracy grows along with social complexity. The bureaucracy is the good shepherd and "the good shepherd's benevolence stops where his own corporate existence is called into question."

Italians are Europe's least state-broken people, a fact directly related to the fact they are perhaps Europe's most entrepreneurial people. They are the least likely to be inert clay in the hands of Euro-planners and other dreamers of statist dreams from which Europe in the 1980s has been tardily awakening.

September 14, 1989

Inventing Europe

As late as 1911, Belgium was the only country on the continent operating on Greenwich time. Belgium was nine minutes behind Paris which, by the way, was five minutes ahead of French railway time, which was 16 minutes behind Dutch time. In 1912, in a step toward a more "European" sensibility, the continent rationalized itself: All European clocks were synchronized in appropriate time zones, with Greenwich. In 1914, however, the inexorable march toward European "unity" suffered something of a setback.

If at first you don't succeed . . .

Today European nations are back at the business of inventing "Europe." In this heady atmosphere of hands-across-the-wall it seems querulous to question the giddy assumption that political and cultural blessings automatically accrue from any coming together of European states. But in all the cheerful, facile talk about a "common European house," scant attention is being given to how little historical ground there is on which to build this house.

The rush of events is thrilling (a droll U.S. diplomat says he is nostalgic for last week), but by focusing on the things that politicians and bureaucrats are comfortable dealing with—arms control, currency arrangements, "Europe '92" and all that—we miss what is most thrilling about Europe's emerging new sense of itself. It is the resilience of national particularities—the rooted institutions of civil society—that have uprooted tyrannical regimes.

Europe has never been "Europe" in the sense of an entity united politically or even culturally. Perhaps the continent was closest to some sort of commonality, at least in fundamental outlook, when it was called not Europe but Christendom. However, what did such "unity" mean in centuries when the average European did not travel, or receive communication from, more than few miles from his village? When Christendom was shattered, Luther was the hammer and theology was the chisel, but nascent nationalisms made the shattering swift and lasting.

Luigi Barzini (now, there was a European) argued that the narrow postwar goal of European unity had been achieved. Its primary aim was sufficient political and economic integration to prevent a fourth (after 1870, 1914 and 1939) war between France and Germany. The "European idea" was clankingly expressed after World War II in prosaic institutions: Before the "Common Market" came the "Coal and Steel Community," as though a "community" could be organized around industrial commodities.

Forty years later, that name has an anachronistic ring, evoking a vanished world when steel was king and the power of silicon was unknown. But the idea of the European "community" and "market" suitably expressed an idea—liberal materialism. That was and still is the belief that economic forces fuel history and that the secret of the good society is the submersion of all mankind's turbulent energies into the enjoyment of private consumption and welfare-state services.

It was a plan for peace through enervation. It was not a noble vision but after two world wars, nobility seemed less urgent than tranquility.

War has been the homogenizer of Europe. As John Lukacs says, in 1939 there were more European nations than there were letters in the alphabet, and there were few Europeans. National differences were profound. (They still are. Might Europe be happier today if there were more rather than fewer nations—if, say Yugoslavia were disassembled?) Certainly the greatest happiness for the greatest number would be served if a score or so sovereign republics were spun off the Union of Soviet Socialist Republics.

Because of genocide, and the mass movements of peoples during and immediately after the last war, and the alteration of borders because of the war, most European nations are more homogenous than they were 50 years ago, when the war that had erupted from European animosities had King George VI practicing pistol shooting in the garden at Buckingham Palace.

There are still quite enough animosities to keep the European "house" raucous. Fareed Zakaria of Harvard's Center for Science and International Affairs notes that on the streets of Budapest vendors sell maps of "Greater Hungary," which includes a large slice of what Romania is today pleased to call Romania. A Hungarian diplomat, asked why his nation might want to remain in the Warsaw Pact, instantly answered: For protection from Romania.

The Warsaw Pact is an interesting alliance that exists partly to protect members from one another. But then, NATO does too, or originally did. (See: France and Germany 1870, 1914, 1939.)

Perhaps peace-through-enervation, the peace of the satiated consumer, will prevail. If not, Europe's future conflicts will start with all watches synchronized. Call it progress.

November 19, 1989

Margaret Thatcher: A Nation's Nanny

LONDON—Norman Tebbit, chairman of the Conservative Party, is the serrated edge of Margaret Thatcher's conservatism. He has paid a terrible price in politics. In 1984, he was severely injured and his wife permanently paralyzed by an IRA bomb. However, as Thatcher prepares to try to become the first person to lead a British party to victory in three consecutive elections, Tebbit has the satisfaction of her accomplishments.

She has, he says, refuted "the theory of the inevitability of the drift to the left, the theory that conservative governments only slow or ameliorate socialism." The ratchet effect now works the other way, he says, because many of Thatcher's psychological and institutional effects are as "irreversible"—an important word to Thatcherites—as anything can be in democracies that rest on the sand of opinion.

For example, to promote a "property-owning democracy," 2 million houses previously owned by public authorities have been sold to residents. An observer says, "The results can be seen in fresh paint, new front doors and neatly kept gardens." Labor opposition to the sales has ended.

Because Thatcher came to office shortly before Ronald Reagan became President, and because she will seek a third term before the Republican Party does (probably this May or October; necessarily by June 1988), the similarities between her and Reagan's experiences are intriguing.

She and he were produced, to significant extents, by their predecessors' failures. Nineteen seventy-nine, the year of Carter's "malaise" speech, began in Britain with the "winter of discontent," when even gravediggers went on strike. Both Thatcher and Reagan benefited from the disenchantment of many intellectuals with the state, which had come to be regarded as a captive of client groups it had nurtured.

Bearing in mind that "lucky" is what we often call people who are bold enough to seize opportunities, Thatcher and Reagan have been lucky regarding oil, little islands and arrogant unions. The decline of OPEC facilitated Reagan's fight against inflation; anarchy on Grenada provided an occasion for U.S. assertiveness; the suicidal obtuseness of the air-traffic-controllers union allowed Reagan to establish his forcefulness. Thatcher's coming to power coincided with the peak output of North Sea oil; Argentine generals handed her the "Falklands factor" prior to her reelection campaign; her defeat of the miners' strike reestablished the sovereignty of government over a union that had destroyed a Conservative government in 1974.

Thatcher, like Reagan, has aimed to disabuse the public of the postwar belief (more prevalent here than in America) that ever-higher public-sector spending could guarantee economic growth. Her moral point—she is a "conviction politician," meaning a moralist—is that individual productivity is the source of collective prosperity.

However, her expenditure-cutting bark has been worse than her bite. Under Reagan the rhetoric of parsimony has prevailed but federal spending as a percentage of GNP has hit an all-time peacetime high, and the percentage of GNP taken by taxes today is equal to what it was under Carter. Similarly, Thatcher has paid a price in popularity because of her reputation for severe frugality, although government revenues have risen at a faster rate under her than under the preceding Labor government.

But Tebbit and others stress attitudinal as much as institutional changes, moral changes not easily expressed numerically. Reagan, by riding out the 1982 recession with a slogan ("Stay the course") rather than a relief program, refuted the notion that inflation is a disease democracies cannot combat. By proving that it is possible to be reelected while 3 million (13 percent) are unemployed, Thatcher has shattered the stultifying consensus of postwar British politics, the commitment to use government to produce full employment. This has been part of her program to alter British attitudes toward work.

She has shaped Britain's public conversation as decisively as de Gaulle shaped France's precisely because consensus is not her aim. She asks, "Do you think you would ever have heard of Christianity if the Apostles had gone out and said, 'I believe in consensus'?" Tebbit says that Thatcher's goal of "killing socialism" is achievable, but that so far socialists have changed only their language, not their aims.

Labor talks less about nationalizing economic assets and more about "social ownership." That refers to backdoor ways of giving government and other groups (unions, consumer organizations, environmentalists) rights to involvement in business decisions, thereby vitiating the rights of the real owners. With a wintery smile, Tebbit says, remember the Conservative wit who warned that the adjective "social" negates the meaning of the noun it modifies, as in "social worker" or "social science."

Tebbit's jest is the sound of the serrated edge slicing through baloney.

March 12, 1987

Prime Minister of the Wrong Country

LONDON—When Nature was serving up charm and intellect Neil Kinnock, the Labor Party's leader, took a double serving of the former, leaving little room on his plate for the latter. Margaret Thatcher did the opposite. She is no intellectual, but her considerable importance in the history of democracy derives from the degree to which she has sought and wielded power in the name of ideas.

Kinnock, 45, exemplifies the '60s sensibility, the cloying right-mindedness that reduces politics to a report on the politician's emotional life. It considers "caring" to be a sufficient qualification for governing and disdains as callous the computation of costs. Thatcher is arguably Britain's greatest peacetime prime minister. She is certainly the most consequential democratic leader of any nation in this decade and the most important woman in politics in this century. She has shown that a soothing personality is dispensable in democracy. Reagan's charm has made his electoral successes susceptible to disparagement by factions eager to drain his successes of seriousness. Thatcher's porcelain personality—hard and a little bit brittle—has immunized her against such dismissive analysis.

Aside from the inadvertent delivery of democracy to Argentina (a fallout from the Falklands War), her four principal achievements have been the conquest of inflation, the taming of the unions, enlargement of the public's interest in economic growth rather than redistribution (a result of the spread of ownership) and attitudinal changes regarding individualism and nationalism.

Inflation is the systemic disease of democracy: Demands for government outlays always exceed demands for commensurate taxation. She tamed the unions by defeating the most militant (the miners), by democratizing them and by allowing a reserve army of the unemployed, 3 million strong. However, gratitude is not an attribute of electorates. This was the first election since 1966 that did not involve the great constitutional question of whether the government was sovereign or existed on sufferance of the unions. But governments suffer an attrition of success. So thoroughly has Thatcher prevailed over inflation and the unions that these threats seem minor, and so do her achievements.

Regarding the project of reforming the welfare state, Thatcher, like Reagan, is mostly bark. And even without much bite she has (says Vernon Bogdanor, Oxford politics don) "created a consensus, but against her." Thatcher has not seriously attacked either the theory or the practice of the welfare state, perhaps because her most important goal—the restructuring of the economy—causes dislocations that make a "safety net" especially necessary.

Thatcher is the first prime minister whose name denotes a doctrine. ("Churchillian" denotes a leadership style.) The essence of Thatcherism is creation of an entrepreneurial, property-owning democracy. This can make the decline of socialism irreversible. Since 1979 the home-owning portion of the population has risen from half to two-thirds, thanks in large part to the sale of public housing. In 1979 only 7 percent of the electorate owned shares in businesses. Today 20 percent do, partly because of the privatization of many nationalized companies. The economy she has made has done much to unmake the Labor Party. In the wringing-out recession of the early 1980s, Britain lost 25 percent of its manufacturing jobs. However, since 1979 there has been a more than 25 percent increase in the number of people whose employment and life-style qualify as middle class.

After all the standard economic indices have been calculated, there remains in politics a matter that is hard to measure and therefore easy to underestimate. It is the psychic income from citizenship. Reagan and Thatcher set out to practice the politics of psychotherapy, to give their countries pride transplants. In 1980 Reagan was responding to 17 lacerating years—Dallas, Watergate, Vietnam, stagflation, Iran, "malaise." Thatcher has been responding to three decades of Britain as the "sick man of Europe," and especially to the convulsive strikes of the 1979 "winter of discontent." In 1980 Reagan told Americans that it is neither intellectually mistaken nor morally disreputable to feel good about their national identity. Britain's long decline made Thatcher's task more herculean than Reagan's.

When Thatcher's hero Churchill left office in 1955, Everest had been conquered by a British expedition, a young queen was on the throne and many believed that a "new Elizabethan era" had dawned. But with the trauma of 1956—Suez—suddenly it was dusk and Britain sought attachments with things larger than itself—Europe or the "special relationship" with the United States. Harold Macmillan came to power because of Suez and his anti-ideological muddling along a "middle way" accelerated Britain's decline. There is symbolism in the fact that six months after he died someone utterly unlike him, a "conviction politician" and nationalist, has won a third consecutive term, an achievement without precedent since Britain became a mass democracy.

A problem inherent in democracy is discontinuity: The rhythms of problems do not fit electoral cycles. However, Thatcher has an unusually long crack at the problem of reforming British character to make it entrepreneurial. The problem is unusually intractable. In 1879 a post-office official told the House of Commons that the nation did not need telephones: "Here, we have a superabundance of messengers. The absence of servants has compelled Americans to adopt communications systems." There is much inertia in a nation's nature, and Thatcher may be, as Bogdanor says, "prime minister of the wrong country." Her anti-institutional cast of mind—she has been impatient with the civil service, the established church, the BBC, the unions, the industrial elite with their leisurely lunches—is un-Tory. Her emphasis on society's small units makes her Britain's first Jeffersonian prime minister. Her zest for up-and-at-'em enterprise makes her suited to lead the United States, or Singapore, but many of her people want a quieter, less strenuous life than she has in mind for them. Still, her mind is made up and before she steps down she will have been prime minister from the end of one decade through the entirety of a second and into a third, neither taking nor allowing rest.

June 22, 1987

British Socialism Comes Down in the World

LONDON—The morning after Margaret Thatcher won another lease of up to five years on the Downing Street house she has inhabited for eight years, a wit wondered, "After 13 years in No. 10, does she get the right to buy?" That is a resonant question about the lady who, as the scourge of socialism, has required local authorities to sell municipal housing to occupants.

As the dust settles from her most recent dustup with the Labor Party, the electoral result stands revealed as a large event in the history of a large development in the late 29th century: the death of socialism.

In 1983, Labor failed to unseat a Conservative government that had presided over an economic contraction sharper than that of 1929. In 1983, and now again, Labor has failed to translate 3 million unemployed into a winning issue. Thatcher does well with skilled workers; the Alliance (Liberals and Social Democrats) does well with the intelligentsia (known in Britain, delightfully, as the chattering classes).

In London this year, Labor did even worse than in 1983 when Thatcher had the Falklands factor and Labor was saddled with the inexpressibly unconvincing leadership of Michael Foot. This month Labor lost three working-class seats in London, including the seat held years ago by Clement Atlee, leader of the postwar Labor government. That is what happens when you raise property taxes 62 percent to hire an army of homosexual-rights and race-relations bureaucrats.

When a party plunges into steep decline, even its victories injure it. About one-quarter of the seats Labor won June 11 are now held by freshman MPs, many of them from the hard left. Already their voices are raised to blame the party's trouncing on insufficient commitment to "real" socialism. The Tories must be tempted to permit the televising of Parliament, the better to give the hard left ample exposure.

Some British socialists say socialism should not be judged by its works but by the purity of its ideals. But the central idea is as implausible as the works have been disappointing.

Socialism is, as the saying goes, "about equality." It carries the heavy baggage of having to believe that wealth and opportunity should be allocated somewhat coercively, to minimize the influence of talent. Socialism's implausible theory is matched by failures of practice. The collective purchase of "key goods," such as housing, and public ownership of the "command heights" of the economy have lost whatever allure they once had.

In the 1950s and 1960s, British socialism tried to turn itself inside out by becoming more meritocratic than capitalism. It stressed "planning," which meant: Economic decision-making should be concentrated in a government composed of the best and brightest, so that reason could replace inefficient motives ("great") in animating the economy. But the lesson of planning is that the risk-averse bureaucracies are unsatisfactory sources of economic dynamism.

Elsewhere in Europe, there has been an "Americanization of the left," the identification of the left with the middle-class, often noneconomic, issues such as environmentalism, racial and sexual discrimination and opposition to nuclear weapons and power. But in Britain, the left, once an example of merely arrested development, has been regressing.

George Watson of St. John's College, Cambridge, notes that for the first time in this century it is trendy to be Tory. As for socialism, "It has come down in the world, and top people have deserted it. It now belongs, if anywhere, to a world of the semi-literate and the semi-educated: to South American priests dedicated to new-fangled liberation theology, to tribal oligarchies in black Africa, and in Europe to the dropouts of higher education—a sort of Lumpenpolytechnik of bedsitter Trotskyites to whom mid-Victorian concepts of class and consciousness still look like the latest thing."

For the first time since Disraeli, Watson says, British conservatism is ideologically fervid, confident not just that conservatism is good for the stock market but that it is true. The embodiment of this confidence is the woman who, if her current government runs a full five years, at the next election would be younger than Churchill was when he first became prime minister.

The day after her third victory, she was asked if she would be prime minister in the year 2000, when she will be 75. "You never know," she said. "I might be here; I might be twanging a harp." As long as there are socialists to defeat, heaven can wait.

June 18, 1987

Romanticizing the Missile Crisis

Clio, the muse of history, is in bed with a splitting headache, prostrated by the task of trying to correct the still multiplying misunderstandings of the Cuban missile crisis. Most Americans believe 'twas a famous victory won by a resolute President prepared to take the world to the brink of nuclear war. Actually, there was not much of a brink, and no triumph worth celebrating.

In last Sunday's *New York Times Magazine*, J. Anthony Lukas reported on a reunion of former Kennedy administration participants in the crisis. The meeting was last April at a Florida resort with the wonderfully inapt name of Hawk's Cay.

Because the crisis began when the Soviet Union began putting missiles in Cuba and ended when the missiles were removed, it was considered an unambiguous triumph achieved by a President more hawkish than some dovish advisers. (The terms "hawks" and "doves" were popularized by this crisis.)

Now much is being made of a letter from former Secretary of State Dean Rusk, a letter read at the April reunion. The letter is said to show that Kennedy was a dove.

In the crisis, Robert Kennedy notified Soviet Ambassador Dobrynin that U.S. missiles in Turkey would be withdrawn within months of withdrawal of Soviet missiles from Cuba, but it was imperative (obviously for domestic American political reasons) that the linkage of the withdrawals not be announced. Rusk's letter reveals that if the Soviet Union had insisted on public linkage, Kennedy would have complied.

That historical morsel is only redundant evidence of what should by now be patent: Kennedy succeeded because his military advantage was huge and his goal was tiny.

The Soviet Union was not going to war at a time when U.S. advantages were 3 to 1 in long-range bombers, 6 to 1 in long-range missiles and 16 to 1 in warheads. The Kremlin must have been astonished—and elated—when Kennedy, in spite of advantages that would have enabled him to insist on severance of Soviet military connections with Cuba, sought only removal of the missiles. He thereby licensed all other Soviet uses of Cuba.

The stunning revelation in Lukas's report is not Rusk's letter; it is something said at the reunion by Ted Sorensen, the aide closest to Kennedy.

On Aug. 31, 1962, five weeks before the administration discovered the missiles, New York's Republican Senator Kenneth Keating, trusting information received from intelligence and refugee sources, said offensive missiles were going into Cuba. Republicans were making an election issue out of Soviet shipments to Cuba. In September, Kennedy warned the Soviets, with interesting preciseness, not to put in Cuba "offensive ground-to-ground missiles." Now, Sorensen says that the President drew a line where he soon—in October—wished he had not drawn it:

"I believe the President drew the line precisely where he thought the Soviets were not and would not be. That is to say, if we had known the Soviets were putting 40 missiles in Cuba, we might under this hypothesis have drawn the line at 100, and said with great fanfare that we would absolutely not tolerate the presence of more than 100 missiles. . . ."

Sorensen is a member of the McGovernite wing of the virtually one-wing Democratic Party. But he also is an assiduous keeper of the Camelot flame. Thus it is fascinating that he says, in praise of Kennedy, that Kennedy wanted to practice appeasement but calculated incorrectly.

This is amusing in light of Arthur Schlesinger Jr.'s rhapsodizing about Kennedy's handling of the crisis that Kennedy, according to Sorensen, wanted to define away: "He coolly and exactly measured. . . . He moved with mathematical precision. . . . This combination of toughness and restraint, of will, nerve and wisdom, so brilliantly controlled, so matchlessly calibrated. . . ."

Even assuming Sorensen is wrong, Schlesinger's romanticizing is not right. In 1978, MIG-23s (nuclear-delivery vehicles far more menacing than the 1962 missiles) were introduced into Cuba. Kennedy's noninvasion pledge, given as part of the crisis-ending deal, guaranteed the survival of this hemisphere's first communist regime and makes attempts to remove or reform the second seem disproportionate.

The Reagan administration, which began by talking about dealing with Nicaragua by "going to the source"—Cuba—is reduced to clawing for piddling sums for the contras, a recipe for another protracted failure. Today, most "peace plans" for Central America postulate the moral equivalence of U.S. and Soviet involvements in the region, another legacy of the missile-crisis "triumph" that killed the Monroe Doctrine.

A few more such triumphs and we shall be undone. The romanticizing of the missile crisis makes such triumphs more likely.

September 3, 1987

Good News Makes Some Liberals Morose

For us reactionaries, warmongers, merchants of death and feudal land-lords these are, as Peter Simple (who is one of us) says in the London *Daily Telegraph*, hard times because, try as we might, we can hardly keep from being happy. Man does not live by bread alone, but also by the nourishment of animosities, and the objects of our animosities are crumbling across the Communist world.

Some liberals, too, seem disoriented. They are even made morose by recent events.

The New York Times offers a column by Lucinda Rector, who is in her twenties, has a graduate degree and works for a New York law firm. She says she envies East German youth because they only had a concrete wall to conquer, whereas her life is blighted by America's "far more subtle, elusive walls keeping me from independence." The Berlin Wall certainly was not "elusive."

She says jobs that are "female-based" and do not pay enough are walls. And "as for a job in the arts, where my true interests lie," she is advised (by people who have seen her art?) "to marry rich." Such walls "build another wall: the wall of doubt."

Her aging parents mean that "familial responsibility—another wall—exacts a high price on my personal freedom." Her depression deepens "when I think about raising children" in America. There is "the economic wall": Children cost money, so "what corporation must I join in order to receive child care? Were I to get divorced, how close might my kids and I come to the poverty line?"

And college costs—oh, my. No wonder she says, "Then, of course, there is the question of abortion." Of course. She worries that "a wall of politicians"—slay that metaphor!—may interfere with her abortions, so "Is it any surprise that a wall of anger builds within me?"

Within Michael Gartner, president of NBC News, dismay builds. Young people protesting in Eastern Europe cause him to think dark thoughts about nonprotesting American youth—and cause him to work up the mandatory guilt feelings about his own shortcomings: Could it be that today's young generation is just as "apathetic" as his generation was in the "placid" 1950s?

Writing in the *Wall Street Journal*, he asks, "Why are they not saying,

'We, too must march'?" Well, it could have something to do with the fact that American youth do not suffer under a Communist government, and are even kind of happy, perhaps because they do not understand, as Ms. Rector does, those "subtle, elusive" American walls.

Gartner subscribes to the whole sentimental myth of the Sixties. He really believes that then "the young people of America" changed the world. They did so by "postponing their careers" to join the Peace Corps (well, a fraction of 1 percent did) and "risking their freedoms" (oh?) protesting the Vietnam War. The premise seems to be: People protesting in Eastern Europe are a reproach to America's nonprotesters because America is healthy only when "the young people" think it is sick.

The closest some liberals can come to cheerfulness is apparent in the "Notes and Comment" section of *The New Yorker*'s "Talk of the Town." This is how that magazine tries to feel good about the collapse of communism:

"That the Cold War may be ending, and that 40 years of nuclear dread might diminish, and that anticommunism, an engine that has propelled so many American political careers, could fall into disuse—a newspaper reader hardly dares to be so hopeful."

The New Yorker has long since (since it decided *The Greening of America* was a masterpiece; and since it tried to inflame antinuclear hysteria with Jonathan Schell's hyperventilating prose) become a laughingstock for its politics. But this is especially absurd.

The New Yorker's tone of voice, at once laconic and grating, is just right for expressing a sordid tenacity. Nothing will move it to modify its strongest passion, which is anti-anticommunism. It drips with disdain for American public life.

The New Yorker must be very sad to see Eastern Europe infected so thoroughly by the virus that *The New Yorker* thinks has made American public life so disagreeable. Never in history have so many people been expressing such furious anticommunism. *The New Yorker* must be thinking: All those Eastern Europeans now coming up for air and saying how very "evil" was the "empire"—don't they know that by such "Cold War rhetoric" Ronald Reagan brought about . . . never mind. *The New Yorker*, seeing that for the foreseeable future anticommunism will be a sine qua non of every political career in Eastern Europe, may not really want to say that liberation is such a good thing.

The changes now thrilling the world were made possible in part by U.S. foreign policies that *The New Yorker* disdains. They were the anticommunist foreign policies of (let us have at least a partial honor role) Truman, Acheson, Eisenhower, Dulles, Kennedy, Rusk, Johnson.

December 7, 1989

John Foster Dulles: Re-moralizer

An equestrian statue stands high on Washington's Connecticut Avenue, facing south toward the White House which the man on horseback coveted, and beyond toward the Potomac which, had he not been unhorsed by the President he despised, might today be an international boundary. With Eastern Europeans putting away stupid statues of disagreeable people, let us celebrate Lincoln's birthday by banishing this statue of his tormentor: General George B. McClellan.

It celebrates someone whose vainglory, political ambition and military incompetence put the Republic at risk. His contempt for Lincoln ("baboon," "gorilla") manifested itself repeatedly in insufferable rudeness, such as refusing to receive Lincoln's visits to his home. To which rudeness Lincoln responded by saying he would hold McClellan's horse if he would just fight and win.

His one great victory, Antietam, was characteristically incomplete and partly the result of a fluke (copies of Lee's orders were found in a Maryland field, wrapped around three cigars). It precipitated something McClellan opposed, the Emancipation Proclamation. He was a great organizer, but was forever organizing, citing exaggerated estimates of Confederate strength to justify delays. "All quiet along the Potomac" was a great song but lousy strategy. It sowed a sense of inferiority in Union forces.

He was a paranoiac with real enemies whom he called "traitors."

Lincoln sacked him, then he lost to Lincoln in the 1864 election. Forty-three years later, for no conceivable good reason, a statue was erected that has cluttered the city long enough.

Just kidding. Constantly rearranging the public furniture, shuffling public symbols in and out of favor, is a disagreeable European habit, a reflection of ideological fads and political immaturity. In America, surely, we know better than to be so foolish. We should not, for example, send to society's attic the bust of John Foster Dulles that today adorns the airport that—for now—bears his name.

Talk about an untimely idea: Victory in the Cold War is coinciding with a proposal to repeal an honor accorded to a man who insisted there was no substitute for victory. Senate Minority Leader Bob Dole of Kansas is among those urging that Washington's Dulles Airport be renamed for Dwight D. Eisenhower, who was born in Texas 100 years ago this year but who spent his formative years in Kansas.

John Foster Dulles's grandfather was President Benjamin Harrison's secretary of state. His uncle was Robert Lansing, Woodrow Wilson's secretary of state. If Taft rather than Eisenhower had won the presidency in 1952, Dulles still would have become secretary of state.

He had prepared all his life for that office. He had served Roosevelt and Truman, had helped lift a reluctant Republican Party up from isolationism by supporting the Marshall Plan and NATO, had insisted that the word "justice" be as prominent as "peace" in the U.N. Charter.

His preeminence was particularly impressive because it owed nothing to his personality. Stephen Ambrose, Eisenhower's biographer, says that aside from Eisenhower almost everyone found Dulles unbearably pompous and dull—"dull, duller, Dulles" was the jape. Churchill deliberately lisped Dulles's name and when told that Allen Dulles was to head the CIA he said, "They tell me that there is another Dullith. Is that possible?"

But Dulles's starchy personality was suited to implementation of the policies that came from the carefully amiable, always guileful man for whom he worked. "The truth," wrote Ambrose, "was that Eisenhower, not Dulles, made the policy, as anyone who knew anything about the inner workings of the Eisenhower administration realized." Eisenhower shrewdly used Dulles as a lightning rod to draw away the hostility that vigorous prosecution of the Cold War generated among much of the intelligentsia.

Dulles, like Eisenhower, only more so, was despised by much of the chattering class. Dulles's sin was his "moralistic" vision of the Cold War, and of the evil empire responsible for it. But Eisenhower fully shared Dulles's belief that no real peace would be possible until the Soviet system changed internally.

One reason the 1980s ended so well for the West is that they began with the election of a President who joined the Republican Party when Dulles was helping set the tone of it. Ronald Reagan re-moralized the Cold War after the demoralization called détente—which coincided in the 1970s with unprecedented Soviet aggressiveness. Re-moralizing the Cold War was necessary for re-summoning the stamina for winning it.

America was never more American than in the 1950s when America was at the wheel of the world and was sure it was right, and was. By all means rename something for Eisenhower, the man who embodied the Fifties. Rename something as big as he was, something as broad as his inspiriting grin that contrasted so with Dulles's grimness. Rename Kansas. Call it with Midwestern informality: Ike.

But leave Dulles in peace and in his place of honor.

February 11, 1990

Maxwell Taylor: From Hot War to Cold

Abilene, Kansas, and Clark and Keytesville, Missouri, are within a circle just 220 miles in diameter. They are the boyhood home of Dwight Eisenhower and the birthplaces of Omar Bradley and Maxwell Taylor, respectively. When Hitler was weighing the risks of war, he did not give due weight to that fertile circle.

Taylor, grandson of a Confederate soldier, was a soldier-statesman worthy of comparison with George Marshall. His death at age 85 has come at a moment when the news of the day—the latest venture in arms control—touches some of the issues about which Taylor was, years ago, a prescient thinker and lucid writer.

Taylor, a man of thought and action who jumped out of airplanes and quoted Polybius to Congress, moved quickly up life's ladder. He was just 44 when, in September 1945, he became West Point's second-youngest superintendent. (The youngest, in 1919, was the 39-year-old Douglas MacArthur.) And Taylor was a young general when a new form of fighting—airborne—made him the first American general to fight in France.

In the book *Six Armies in Normandy*, John Keegan argues that each of the armies operating there in the summer of 1944—American, Canadian, British, French, Polish, German—was "a mirror of its own society and its values." Certainly American paratroopers were.

Confusion is normal in combat and was extraordinary among the parachute forces dropped past the beaches on D-Day. But the fluidity of the confusion suited a strength of the American character. As was the case five months later during the crisis of the Battle of the Bulge (where Taylor again played a large part), American forces excelled when required to organize themselves into small groups and then improvise their tactics. Keegan says that what Taylor's paratroopers did was appropriate for Americans:

"Like pioneers in an unknown land, ignorant of its language and landmarks, uncertain of what the next thicket or stream-bottom might hold, confident only in themselves and their mastery of the weapons in their hands, the best and bravest among them had stifled their fears, marched forth and planted the roots of settlement in the soil that was there for the taking."

Many of today's weapons are as unlike those of 1944 as today's transportation is unlike the mule-drawn trolley in the Keytesville of Taylor's youth. However, Taylor insisted on the importance of the elemental—the infantry—even, indeed especially, in the nuclear age.

In *Swords and Plowshares,* his 1972 memoir, he said: "My conclusions as to our future prospects as a world power are not encouraging. . . . We are running the grave risk of permitting our democracy to destroy itself though its own excesses." He was particularly concerned about preserving "the ability of a democracy to resort to arms for reasons other than survival."

The flawed execution of a flawed strategy in Vietnam did not, he said, repeal the fact that noncoercive means are insufficient to cope with the ideological and other motivations of international violence. And "without the limited war option and the forces that go with it, we have little substance with which to defend our interest."

Taylor, a unifier of theory and practice, was author of the doctrine of "flexible response." It was primarily an attempt to cope with "wars of national liberation," such as North Vietnam's war of conquest against South Vietnam. However, his point is germane to the current rush to remove intermediate-range missiles from Europe. They are one component of the spectrum of U.S. options in containing the Soviet threat. The spectrum extends from reliance on conventional forces, in which the Soviet Union has an overwhelming advantage, to the threat to use strategic nuclear forces, a threat decreasingly credible in the face of growing Soviet strategic superiority.

Taylor, who faced his share of danger, understood that the world is not necessarily made safer by reducing the range of choices that leaders of free nations have when responding to the use or threatened use of force by aggressive totalitarians. "To a Communist enemy," he said, "the Cold War is a total, unending conflict with the United States and its allies—without formal military hostilities, to be sure, but conducted with the same discipline and determination as formal war."

If those words, and hence the man, seem out of tune with the times, so much the worse for these times.

April 26, 1987

American Power: Machiavellian and Moral

SUITLAND, MD.—This nation needs a spacious attic, and one corner of it is here. Some corner: 25 buildings house the Smithsonian's reserve collection of aircraft. A Soviet antiaircraft missile sits next to John Kennedy's campaign plane, *Caroline*. There is a Grumman Avenger of the sort the young George Bush was shot down in. But the sight that causes a visitor to catch his breath is the dull silver fuselage of a B-29 bearing the stenciled name *Enola Gay*.

The atomic age, which began in secret in a New Mexico desert at dawn 40 years ago July 16, announced itself 21 days later when the *Enola Gay*'s bomb bay opened. The fuse—the lens David Greenglass had sketched for the Rosenbergs' spy ring—unleashed neutrons that created in 22 pounds of uranium an explosion that occurred in one-tenth of a millionth of a second.

The flight of the *Enola Gay* began, in a sense, in 1932 in Cambridge, England, in Cavendish Laboratory, when James Chadwick discovered the neutron, the key to penetrating the atom's nucleus and unlocking energy for matter. Thirteen years later, when the B-29 fliers asked what they had volunteered for, they were told their 509th Composite Group was "going to do something different."

When they reached Tinian, in range of Japan, Tokyo Rose was on the radio reading the doggerel that Americans on Tinian had written to ridicule the 509th's strange training mission:

But take it from one who knows the score,
the 509th is winning the war.

Well, yes. At the stunning moment in New Mexico, when Robert Oppenheimer had thought of "the shatterer of worlds," a general simply said: "The war's over."

As the *Enola Gay* approached Japan the copilot was writing a letter to his parents. He wrote this sentence: "There will be a short intermission while we bomb our target." Next, he wrote this in a wild hand: "My God."

The government committee that had kept the secret of the bomb project (neither Admiral Nimitz nor General MacArthur knew about the bomb until July) said it should be considered not just as a weapon but "in terms of a new relationship to the universe." Forty years on, it would be extravagant to say the new technology of mass destruction has had such a transforming effect, spiritually or practically. Why should it have? Conventional munitions on the ground at Verdun killed many more people than nuclear weapons have. The same was true at the Somme, 17 years before the neutron was discovered.

Pug Henry, protagonist in Herman Wouk's *War and Remembrance,* says: "Either war is finished, or we are." It is too soon to say whether we are, but war certainly is not. It flourishes beneath the nuclear umbrella. However, the first two bombs were war-enders and life-savers. They prevented perhaps a million American casualties and probably spared Japan at least 10 times the 210,000 deaths they caused.

Each bomb killed fewer people than were devoured in each of two B-29 raids on Tokyo.

Those raids were previews of what the autumn would have brought, but for the bomb. Japan had 2.3 million regular army soldiers, 250,000 garrison troops, 5,000 kamikaze aircraft. Children were being trained to strap themselves with explosives and roll under tanks. There were potentially 30 million partisans with the will to die shown by Japanese soldiers on Okinawa and Iwo Jima.

U.S. officials were too uncertain of the new technology to risk a nonlethal demonstration for Japan that might have been a dud, producing hardened Japanese resolve. There were just two bombs. Until after the second bomb fell, Japan's regime remained resolved to have a face-saving (and perhaps compromise-achieving) bloodbath.

The use of the bombs was seized upon by persons eager to portray America as a crude giant whose technological power is disproportionate to its moral maturity, a nation with a cold, Machiavellian heart beating slowly beneath a thin lacquer of idealism. But Machiavelli's bad reputation is the unjust price he paid for being an unsentimental moralist in the world addicted to moral evasions.

He said that a material and mental capacity for violence underlies a great nation's power. The moral imperative is to economize violence by distinguishing between legitimate and illegitimate uses. Legitimate uses are to reduce violence and preserve or promote good objectives.

In a few years, the *Enola Gay* is to be displayed with other aircraft at a new museum at Dulles Airport in Virginia. It will be visited by hundreds of thousands of fathers and their children and grandchildren who would not be alive had the two bombs not made unnecessary an invasion of Japan. The museum will be a school teaching sobriety, where Americans can ponder the *Enola Gay's* role in a deed profoundly Machiavellian and moral.

July 14, 1985

Remembrance of Another War Worth Winning

LONDON—In Whitehall, a steady trickle of tourists shuffles through the subterranean rooms where Winston Churchill and his war cabinet conducted business while the bombs fell. Taped voices of Neville Chamberlain and Churchill and Hitler echo through the concrete corridors.

Across the river in the Imperial War Museum, visitors must make reservations for "The Blitz Experience," a simulation complete with smoke, sounds of air-raid sirens and make-believe bomb concussions. It is very popular. It lasts eight minutes.

A recurring theme in modern thought, in writings as diverse as those of Freud and Proust, is the insistent, disturbing prompting of uncontrolled memory. And a recurring political task is the recapture of the past through cultivated memories, those mystic chords that bind people into communities. However, commemorations, such as those of the events of 50 years ago, can give false clarity to the past.

What really began in September 1939? The late A.J.P. Taylor was a contrarian, but he had a point when he said the Second World War began in April 1932, when Mao Tse-tung and Chou Teh declared war on the Japanese in the name of the Kaingsi Soviet. Taylor said the war in the European theater began in March 1938 when the army of a great power, Germany, crossed a frontier—Austria's—to force political change. John Lukacs says that what began 50 years ago was "the last European war." As a European war it lasted until December 1941, at which point it became a world conflagration and the fate of Europe fell into the hands of the United States and the Soviet Union.

What certainly began on September 1, 1939, was the quick conquest of Poland. By December 1939 only two European states were really involved in combat—the Soviet Union and Finland. British and German troops did not meet until April 20, 1940, in Norway. And as Taylor wrote, until 1942 a wife in London was more apt to be a war casualty than was her husband in the army.

The outcome of the war was settled in the first week of December 1941, on December 5, when the Red Army launched a general offensive on the Moscow front, and on December 7, when America was dragged into the war.

No one knew what the world was slipping into 50 years ago. A *Wash-*

ington Post headline of September 3, 1939, said: BOTH SIDES AGREE NOT TO BOMB CIVILIANS. The war that in its first month featured charges by Polish horse cavalry ended with two atomic blasts. In 1941, the U.S. Army had 20,000 horses, the most since the Civil War.

Paul Fussell, in his quirky, dyspeptic, fascinating new book, *Wartime*, is an archeologist of the American and British psyches, unearthing evidence of their conditions during the war. He confirms the judgment that it was a war in which disillusionment set in before the first shot was fired.

In 1914, Rupert Brooke spoke for many when he thanked God for the outbreak of war, rejoicing in it as an awakening from "a world grown old and cold and weary," relishing war as a cleansing, invigorating experience, "as swimmers into cleanness leaping." However, the nations that turned wearily to the Second World War had read *All Quiet on the Western Front* and seen the movie of it, as well as *Grand Illusion*. They had read Dos Passos's *Three Soldiers*, Hemingway's *A Farewell to Arms*, Robert Graves's *Good-bye to All That* and other literature conveying the taste of ashes from the last war.

The Second World War was, Fussell says, a war of impersonal forces, shaped by developments in mass production and propaganda. It was Krupp against General Motors, a war in which anonymity, the annihilation of individuality, was underscored by the name given to the men who conquered the ground: G.I. (government issue) Joes.

Eugene Sledge, a Marine whose memoirs Fussell has rescued from obscurity, recalls Okinawa, where replacements were killed before their units learned their names. "They were forlorn figures coming up to the meat grinder and going right back out of it like homeless waifs, unknown and faceless to us, like unread books upon a shelf."

Yes, of course the war was a ghastly experience, a maelstrom of modern forces that a poet has called "the conspiracy of the plural against the singular." But it was waged on behalf of singularity. Suppose our side had not won.

As Lukacs writes, it is inconceivable that in the First World War, a nationalist war, a bar of German music (the first bar of Beethoven's Fifth Symphony—three short notes and one long note: Morse code V for victory), could have been adopted as a call of defiance by the nations fighting Germany. But the Second World War was waged in defense of a civilization of which Beethoven is an exemplar. It was a war worth winning.

September 3, 1989

Treblinka's Unquiet Earth

TREBLINKA, POLAND—The earth here is unquiet. Wind and rain, and insects and small burrowing animals stir the sandy soil, bringing to the surface small white and gray substances. They are flecks of compressed ashes, and bits of bones. In a circle 15 feet in diameter, a visitor to this site of a Nazi death camp sees on the ground parts of an adult's finger and a child's rib.

Recently an American delegation was here and at other Holocaust sites to receive artifacts from the Polish government. They will be permanent exhibits at the Holocaust Memorial Museum that will open adjacent to the Mall in Washington in 1992.

One such artifact is freight car 11688. Thanks to meticulous German record-keeping, meticulousness necessary for an administrative task as complex as genocide, we know that this 27-foot cattle car was used on the 60-mile shuttle—trains of 60 such cars, each car carrying 100 Jews—between the Warsaw ghetto and Treblinka.

Some said that literature itself would be the final victim of the "final solution," that imagination must flag and words must fail in attempts to encompass it, that silence is the only possible response. Not true. There can be sermons in stones, as in the shattered bricks and masonry that are the shards of the Warsaw ghetto, taken for the Museum from just a few inches below the surface of rebuilt Warsaw.

From Majdanek are coming canisters that contained Zyklon-B gas pellets, blue stains from which are still on the walls of the gas chambers. Also coming are 2,000 of the 820,000 pairs of shoes piled to the rafters of Majdanek barracks. More than 10,000 artifacts have been received from survivors in America and elsewhere in response to an appeal. They will be sifted for suitable displays in a building designed by the firm of I. M. Pei, a design of solemn commemoration but also evoking the industrial nature of the crime.

It has been said that we make our buildings, and then they make us. The Museum will make memories for rising generations, expanding their consciousness of the awful possibilities of human action. Thus it will be, fundamentally, a museum serving philosophy. It will start from extreme particularity—shoes, bricks, canisters, an event: Hitler's war against the Jews. However, it will stir visitors to the most general reflections on the nature of man and (hence the Museum's proper place on the Mall) the great questions of governance.

The cooperation of Polish authorities with the U.S. Holocaust Memorial Council has been overshadowed by the controversy concerning the establishment of a Catholic convent at Auschwitz, in a building originally used to store Zyklon-B. Cardinal Glemp, who wants to abrogate the agreement by which the convent was to have been removed by now, is a useful anachronism. He is a living museum exhibit of lumpen anti-Semitism (Jews are cosmopolitan outsiders, they control the mass media, they are responsible for anti-Semitism). Lumpen anti-Semitism made possible the seizure of power by virulent anti-Semites.

Without questioning the good motives of the nuns, who wish to pray for all victims, Jewish leaders rightly see the convent as yet another act having the effect of diminishing the Holocaust, sinking it back into the stream of history by blurring its monstrous clarity. That clarity is a function of the Holocaust's particularity: All the resources of a modern state were turned toward the destruction of one people, the Jews.

Yes, others were killed. But if there had been no Jews in Europe, there would have been no Holocaust. There would have been no Hitler. No Treblinka.

At the peak of its frenzy, Treblinka was the worst of the Nazi works. In an area you can walk across in 10 minutes, they probably killed more people than live today in Cincinnati. Here, there was not, as there was at Auschwitz, an atom of demonic utilitarianism in the form of slave labor for industry. Here, the slaughter was single-minded.

At Treblinka one sees . . . nothing. And everything. Nothing, in that the Germans tried to erase every trace of the camp. All that are here are memorials—rough-hewn stones for each Jewish community annihilated—and ashes and bones. And a silence. A curator says birds do not sing here. I believe him.

But here you also see everything. Treblinka is the starkest testimony to the radical evil that gives the Holocaust its stunning uniqueness, its apartness from all other human experiences. The radicalism was in its furious focus on Jews.

There would have been no Holocaust if there had been an Israel—a haven. Standing in the doorway of a prisoner's barrack at Auschwitz-Birkenau, it is stirring to see far across the camp, through the stubble of brick chimneys that are all that remain from any wooden barracks, the blue-and-white flag of Israel borne by young Israeli visitors.

Architecture, it is said, is frozen music. The Museum will not be a dirge. It will be an anthem to the resilience of a people, and of people.

September 10, 1989

Sowing Seeds of Democracy

The National Endowment for Democracy, one of this decade's good deeds, last week celebrated its fifth birthday as quietly as it does its work and with the scant public acclaim that usually comes to institutions that are unobtrusively useful.

This private and bipartisan grant-making body, which is funded by Congress, was originally viewed with suspicion by people too fastidious to countenance any U.S. "interference," however delicate, in the "internal affairs," however promising, of any nation, however situated. Today, NED's spending is the biggest bargain in government. It is one reason why the percentage of the world's population classified by Freedom House as living in "free" countries is 38.3 percent, an all-time high.

The people at NED know too much about the complexities of popular government to claim inordinate credit for the undeniable progress of democracy in this decade. But they are teachers of the learned art of democracy. They know how to prepare the stony ground of authoritarian societies for the seeds of democratic skills—organization, mass persuasion.

NED's mission is to direct open support, financial and technical, to groups working to enrich the institutions of civil society beneath the brittle crust of oppressive regimes. NED contributed to the crumbling of that crust in Chile in October.

In the referendum against the Pinochet dictatorship, democracy won a narrow (54 percent) victory because of a huge turnout (92 percent of the electorate). The margin of victory can reasonably be credited to polling and other assistance from American political consultants organized by NED. Funds from NED helped 200,000 poor voters acquire the small photographs required of voters. This cost just $25,000.

NED is one reason why Poland today has a thousand independent cultural institutions—publishers of books and periodicals, film-makers, schools. Such small efforts can, cumulatively, crack political concrete.

Carl Gershman, NED's president, believes that for many centuries many factors—"the Crusades, which decimated the nobles; the printing press, which spread knowledge to all classes; the discovery of America, which gave opportunity to millions"—have had a tendency to help democracy. But he also knows that a tendency is not an inevitability. And he knows that this century, with its most important political innovation, totalitarianism, has posed the danger that new tendencies (bureaucratization, refinements of terror, propaganda and other means of social control) might mean that democracy is an arrangement accessible only to a minority of privileged nations.

The year 1975 was pivotal. Indochina fell to communism and Indira Gandhi's state of emergency turned the world's largest democracy into the world's second-largest dictatorship. But regimes in Portugal, Spain and Greece were democratized. For the first time in history, Western Europe was cleansed of dictatorship.

Larry Diamond of the Hoover Institution, writing in *The Washington Quarterly,* notes that since then there has emerged "a kind of global Zeitgeist for democracy." Starting from various points, there have been varieties of progress in the Philippines, South Korea, Taiwan, Thailand, The Dominican Republic, Grenada, Haiti, Argentina, Bolivia, Brazil, Ecuador, El Salvador, Guatemala, Honduras, Peru, Uruguay, Nigeria, among other nations.

In North Atlantic nations, democracy often came gradually and from above, with the slow widening of competition among elites. Today the task in the Third World is the transition from authoritarianism by means of gradualism from below. What Diamond calls the "efflorescence of associational life" requires "the reconstruction of a boundary between the state and civil society." Such reconstruction is NED's speciality.

Authoitarian regimes become porous as civil society becomes enriched with independent business, labor, religious, cultural and other mediating institutions serving as buffers between the individual and the state. As the autonomy of society grows, so do channels for articulating interests. Something else grows—the most potent solvent of hegemonic regimes, the broad and rapid diffusion of ideas, aspirations, information and awareness of possibilities.

Modernization destabilizes all but modern—pluralistic and democratic—societies and regimes. Modernization accelerates the circulation of people and information and the evolution of political consciousness. This confronts authoritarian regimes (South Korea has been a case study) with what Diamond calls "a legitimacy contradiction, a kind of Catch-22."

If such regimes do not produce socioeconomic dynamism, they lose legitimacy because such progress is their justification for monopolizing power. If they do produce dynamism, it has political repercussions in intensified demands for participation which the regimes cannot satisfy without liquidating themselves.

NED is a forthright but deft instrument for helping others bring about peaceful liquidations. Yet its tiny budget ($15.8 million), the source of so much leverage, has been repeatedly cut. Surely the government can find a more eligible target for frugality.

December 18, 1988

Woodrow Wilson's Hour Comes 'Round

Ronald Reagan says the Soviet Union has, as people used to say, mellowed out, becoming a sort of overarmed Canada, a puzzlement but not much of a menace. That, you might have thought, would easily be this year's most notable political pronouncement. But speaking at the State Department the other day, Michael Dukakis said something almost as attention-grabbing:

"Somebody called me 'Wilsonian' the other day. Well, [Woodrow Wilson was] another governor who didn't do badly in foreign policy—at least at the beginning."

Oh? Wilson began by picking a moralizing amateur, William Jennings Bryan, as secretary of state. Then Wilson himself got busy, turning his improving impulse toward Mexico where a general, Huerta, who was in the pay of British oil interests, had set himself up as dictator.

Wilson announced, grandly, that he would "require Huerta's retirement" by "such means as may be necessary." Referring to Mexico as a "distracted republic," Wilson, the professor from Princeton, vowed to "teach the South American Republics to elect good men!" If an American President talked that way today, Dukakis would lead the Democratic Party in suffering the vapors.

To prevent a German merchant ship from landing supplies for Huerta at Veracruz, Wilson ordered the U.S. Navy to seize that city, and Wilson—are you sitting down, Michael Dukakis?—did not ask Congress's permission. If Wilson "at the beginning" is Dukakis's model, a Dukakis foreign policy would be stimulating.

Wilson then offered to intervene on behalf of a revolutionary named Carranza against Huerta, if Carranza would promise to be a gentlemanly—perhaps almost a Princetonian—revolutionary. Carranza disdained Wilson's offer and overthrew Huerta on his own. Then a Carranza subordinate persuaded Wilson's agents that he, the subordinate, was a tamed and decorous revolutionary who deserved Wilson's support against Carranza. The subordinate was Pancho Villa. The honeymoon was brief.

Carranza drove Villa into his native northern Mexico where, in January 1916, Villa, in an attempt to provoke Wilson, rode over into New

Mexico and killed 19 Americans. So Wilson sent an expedition into Mexico. Before his presidency ended, he had also intervened with troops in Haiti, the Dominican Republic, Cuba and the Soviet Union.

What was it about Wilson "at the beginning" that Dukakis admires? And at what point in Wilson's career does Dukakis's approval lapse?

Dukakis may have a Wilsonian attribute that Wilson would have been better off without. Dukakis sometimes seems like someone who does not frequently entertain doubts about his correctness, and does not suffer disagreement gracefully. Wilson lost what was supposed to be the crowning glory of his career, the League of Nations treaty, because he was so insufferably sure he was entirely right, and was too stiff-necked to compromise with U.S. senators as he had with European leaders.

It is easy, too easy, to ridicule Wilson, a moralist who toiled to bring democracy to the wide world while personally insisting on the intensification of racial segregation in Washington. And Wilsonian principles quickly decayed—under Republicans, mind you—into such 1920 vapidities as the Kellogg-Briand Pact condemning "recourse to war for the solution of international controversies."

But as Pat Moynihan has written, Wilson's singular contribution to our national experience was a definition of patriotism suited to America's 20th-century destiny: patriotism as "the duty to defend and, where feasible, to advance democratic principles in the world at large." Regarding a willingness to undertake frequent and often unilateral American action, Dukakis, like today's Democratic Party generally, is utterly un-Wilsonian.

Wilson's politics of morality did lead him into overreaching. But however poignant, there is nothing contemptible about the image of him on his hands and knees in the middle of the night in his suite in Paris, poring over maps as the Versailles Conference tried to make a new world and instead made the conditions for a new war. In his complacent policy of favoring only "multilateral" actions with "the allies," Dukakis ignores one of the lessons that the Versailles Conference illustrated: The chance of success in an enterprise often is inversely related to the number of parties participating.

Wilson's moral imperative was of a scope and intensity worthy of this nation, which is more than can be said for the Democratic Party's current morality of underreaching. As regards the use of American power to advance American values abroad—as in aid for the contras or the rescue of Grenada from totalitarianism or the punitive raid against Libya's terrorist regime, all of which Dukakis opposed—the real Wilsonian is the man whose middle name is Wilson: Ronald Reagan.

June 19, 1988

The Good Neighbor Policy in Panama

This intervention is a good-neighbor policy. America's role in Panama—in effect, administering a recount on last May's elections—is an act of hemispheric hygiene and it comes at a propitious moment. It punctuates a decade of recovery of national purposefulness and a year of militant democracy.

Coinciding with what can be considered the climax of the Cold War, the intervention turns a page in the book of American history and begins, on a fresh sheet of paper, writing another chapter in America's oldest story. It is the story of American attempts to comprehend the rights and responsibilities that come with the possession of great power and the enjoyment of democracy.

The decade was not three months old when the debacle of Desert One—an eight helicopter invasion of a vast nation—seemed, like the hostages the helicopter were sent for, to symbolize national decline into futility. The first year of the decade was dominated by a presidential election that was in part a referendum on how the nation should think about its goodness and usefulness in its third century.

This is the third use of force by a NATO nation in this hemisphere in this decade: Before Grenada and Panama, there was the Falklands war. Because of American interventions in this decade, this hemisphere has two more democracies—Grenada and Panama—than it would have if America husbanded its power differently, two more than would exist if recent presidential elections had produced different results.

The President gave a dry, nicely understated summation of his catalog of Noriega's offenses: "That was enough." However, what the President said, although sufficient for the moment when he said it, is not, in the context of American history, quite enough. There is a richer, an unapologetically nationalistic, case to be made.

Outrages against Americans, caused by Noriega's stirring of the situation to the point of declaring a state of war, were intolerable because, among other reasons, the clock continues to run on the schedule for transferring control of the Canal. Another stage is reached January 1. The President faced a domestic storm and a diplomatic conundrum in trying to comply with treaty obligations without ratifying the legitimacy of an outlaw regime.

The graphic record of 1989, so replete with pictures of freedom ascendant, includes pictures of Noriega's savagery in the streets against the men who beat him in an election. Those pictures were worth six words: Panama's regime is devoid of legitimacy.

America's national interests, narrowly construed, may not conclusively justify this intervention. That is an argument not against the intervention but against the narrow construing of national interests.

As was the case regarding Grenada, the need to protect American lives has been given as a sufficient reason for intervention. The presence in Panama of many Americans in connection with important national assets (the military's Southern Command, the Canal) was perhaps a politically necessary justification for intervention. But American lives and assets might have been protectable by measures short of intervention. And it is certain that bringing Noriega to American justice on drug charges is no serious reason for mounting a major military operation.

However, a constant of America's national character, and a component of American patriotism, has been a messianic impulse, sometimes mild, sometimes not. It rises from the belief that national identity is bound up with acceptance of a responsibility to further democracy.

There always have been many Americans who reject that premise, who say America has no responsibility toward democracy abroad beyond (in John Adams's words) wishing it well. But an American majority has always thought otherwise, and America's oldest argument is about the circumstances in which American power should be employed on behalf of American values.

By stressing, among the reasons for intervention, the restoration of democracy, the President put himself squarely in a tradition with a distinguished pedigree. It holds that America's fundamental national interest is to be America, and the nation's identity (its sense of its self, its peculiar purposefulness) is inseparable from a commitment to the spread—not the aggressive universalization, but the civilized advance-ment—of the proposition to which we, unique among nations, are, as the greatest American said, dedicated.

That is why, although the President's reasons for the invasion are sufficient to justify it, the first reason he gave is the one that explains it: It was an act of neighborliness.

December 24, 1989

The Revision of Reputations

The pilgrimage is over. The long march of the West's "progressive" intellectuals has come to a bedraggled end in Nicaragua, a peasant nation about as far, socially, as a nation can be from the conditions where the revolt against modernity was supposed to take root.

Marxism has been just that revolt for those who look upon it sympathetically (usually from a safe distance, in modern "bourgeois societies"). The revolt—romanticism in drag, dressed up as science—was against the supposed cold rationality and soulless banality of a capitalist, industrial, commercial world.

The revolt was supposed to succeed first where the industrial revolution came first, in Europe, probably in Germany, with its large proletariat. But the supposed engine of history, the industrial workers of the world, would have none of it, preferring material progress and freedom, and understanding the connection of the two.

So intellectuals in fatigues (Castro, Ortega) foisted Marxism on peasants who were perceived (from the safe distance of faculty clubs) as "unspoiled" by the "false consciousness" of capitalism. But given a chance, the peasants say, "Please, spoil us, as quickly as possible."

To the non-Marxist left, including many church groups, the charm of the Sandinista regime was its anti-Americanism. How galling for those people that the regime has been toppled by a candidate known in Nicaragua to be backed by the United States. Where now can the glazed gaze of the last political pilgrims turn? To North Korea? Meanwhile, so high have been the stakes of American politics, and so mistaken have been the stances of one faction, that in victory we have a surfeit of what normally accompanies defeat—recriminations.

The collapse of the Soviet system under the pressure of Western military preparedness has elicited, from those who fought that preparedness, the preposterous thought that the collapse proves that the preparedness was disproportionate to the task. Now the alibi industry on the left, which did not quite kill aid to the contras soon enough to save the Sandinistas, must deal with this truth: Without Reagan, there would have been no contras to put pressure on the regime, pressure that eventually led to elections. The contras were not sufficient to cause that outcome, but they were necessary.

The ongoing attempt to make Reagan a figure of fun, an attempt now entering its second quarter-century, founders on a huge fact: The world is going his way, in no small measure because it was his way. From Eastern Europe to Central America, "the evil empire" has collapsed because Moscow lost its nerve and capacities. The collapse of other communist regimes then resulted because the Soviet Union was "the focus of evil in the modern world." The next result of this unraveling may be among Soviet clients in the Middle East.

The reputations of many people and the interpretations of many events are undergoing revision. The U.S. effort in Vietnam looks more worthwhile in light of the subsequent bloodbaths and waves of boat people. They discredit those who, in their zeal to see America defeated, professed to see humanitarianism on the other side.

One can now see why the overthrow of Allende's incipient Leninism in Chile, coming just as Vietnam was being conquered, was such an unnerving event in Moscow and throughout the international left. It shattered the myth of inevitability. The leftward ratchet of history was broken: All movement in that direction was not irreversible.

Another crack in the left's confidence (confidence was everything, material accomplishments being paltry) came when communism crested short of power in post-Salazar Portugal. Can it be just 15 years since "Eurocommunism" was "the wave of the future"?

If the last three U.S. presidential elections had turned out differently, today there would be a thugocracy in Grenada, Panama would be Noriega's plaything and Sandinistas would be screwing down the lid of Stalinism on Nicaragua. That said, this too must be: The contribution of the winner of the 1988 election could be, to say no more, better.

The vast majority of people who a year ago were suffering under communism's cruel stupidities are today suffering even more. They are Chinese—and, lest we forget, Tibetans, who are under China's grinding heel. We know that all the nations of the world are now porous to news. (Turn up those American transmitters!) Our friends—if such they still are—in China, the democratic forces knew what happened in Nicaragua as soon as it happened. Now is the time for the Bush administration to acknowledge the futility of its gentle policy toward China and turn up the pressure, including those transmitters.

The change of regimes is cause for joy in two communities in Miami. Many Nicaraguans can now go home. And the Cuban-Americans, for whom America is home and Cuba is an imprisoned family member, know that Castro is next. Moscow should be told that all cooperation with the United States is now contingent on the ending of all aid to Cuba.

One of the creations of "progressive" political pilgrims was the pro-Castro "Fair Play for Cuba Committee" (which attracted Lee Harvey Oswald). Now, this instant, we need a fair-play-for-Cubans policy.

March 1, 1990

A Tale of Two Julys

On June 22, 1812, at the beginning of his invasion of Russia, Napoleon was on a reconnoitering ride when a hare darted between his horse's hoofs. Startled, the horse threw Napoleon to the ground. To some it seemed an ominous omen. "A Roman," wrote one of Napoleon's aides, "would have abandoned the expedition." But Napoleon was a modern man.

The invasion of Russia, one of history's huge acts of overreaching, was the quintessential Napoleonic act—folly on a grand scale. And Napoleon was the vessel of the French Revolution, the concentrated essence of its spirit.

The Revolution spread an exhilarating, energy-releasing sense of emancipation from superstition and old, retarding structures. It proclaimed an enlarged scope for shaping events by the human will, the will enlightened by reason. No omens would be seen in hares.

The evil of the Revolution was in its disproportion: hubris, overreaching. It had an irrational confidence in reason shorn of the legacy of tradition that should inform reason. The Revolution quickly became a rage of wipe clean the social slate so the state could write whatever it willed. The citizenry would be so much clay in the hands of the strong-willed.

But crumble the cake of custom, smash the crust of restraining tradition, and what bursts forth is molten willfulness. Julien Sorel, protagonist of Stendhal's *The Red and the Black* (1831), is one of the first modern men in fiction, upwardly mobile with a vengeance—like the Corsican who became the emperor Sorel so much admired. "Man's will is powerful, I see it written everywhere," Sorel exclaims.

Written in blood. By the time Napoleon was a spent force, millions of French citizens and Europeans had died. Was what began at the Bastille "necessary"? No.

The best aspect of this bicentennial is a book, *Citizens*, by Simon Schama. This history of the Revolution restores to the story the central history-making role of the speech and conduct of a self-conscious political elite. Schama argues that the Revolution was not predestined, not determined by economic forces. Rather, it was made by the political choices of strong-willed men moved by ideas.

History told from "the top down" is truthful but offends leftist historians. Their agenda requires "history with the politics left out," the disparagement of greatness, choices, ideas as mere "epiphenomena." Such disparagement elevates the importance of the masses. And, even more, it inflates the self-importance of the priesthood of academics who decipher ("deconstruct") the hidden and impersonal forces of history.

The great lesson to be underscored by bicentennial meditations is that individual men and women, and the ideas they choose, matter. The ideas and example of the Revolution have mattered, terribly.

There have been many subsequent terrorists for virtue, using practical evil to pursue a speculative good, beggaring the present generation for the sake of the future (Burke's words), attacking despotism and all institutions that might prevent despotism from recurring (de Tocqueville). Such modern menaces trace their pedigrees to July 14, 1789.

Two 18th-century Julys gave the world two models of revolution. The first was the success.

The American Revolution was a conservative act, arising organically from a tradition it aimed to recapture. It began as a demand for the ancient rights of Englishmen. It became a real revolution when it ruptured institutions and loosed ideas that would shake other regimes. But it was a moderate revolution, conducted in the name of the morality of a process of government—popular sovereignty.

The French Revolution was hardly fastidious about the means to its extravagant and ultimately preposterous ends. When Napoleon emerged to "pick a crown from the gutter," he embodied the Revolution's ideal of an enlightened despot. As Felix Markham, a biographer of Napoleon, notes, Voltaire deplored the restoration of the Parlements, Rousseau said a great legislator must educate the public's general will (that was Robespierre's rationale for the Committee of Public Safety), and in 1790 Mirabeau urged Louis XVI to lead the Revolution.

An emphasis on results over process elevates willfulness over persuasion and produces the reign of force, then chaos. The greatness of the soldier who waged the American Revolution was that he would not accept all the power he could have had. HMS *Bellerophon* carried Napoleon into exile. Washington rode to retirement at Mt. Vernon.

Visitors to Napoleon's tomb see words carved in marble. They are the names of battles. Visitors to the Jefferson Memorial—Jefferson, whose pen put the American Revolution in motion—see words carved in marble. They are passages from Jefferson's acts of persuasion, his philosophy of freedom. The difference speaks volumes about why it is wise to celebrate July 4 and deplore July 14.

July 13, 1989

PART 3

American Governance: Going Through the Motions

Ronald Reagan: The Captain Who Calmed the Sea

There is a special openness to the horizon in the Middle West, an openness that reveals no obstacle to travel in any direction. The remarkable flatness of the prairie suggests that God had good times in mind—smooth infields for countless baseball diamonds—when he designed Illinois, where Ronald Reagan spent his formative years. There Reagan acquired a talent for happiness. Since then he has traveled far and had a good time all the way.

The nation is, by and large, better off because he did. Most Americans feel that way, which is why today, for the first time in 60 years, a president is preparing to turn over his office to a successor from his party. The cheerfulness that has defined Reagan's era of good feelings has been, on balance, salutary. But it also has been a narcotic, numbing the nation's senses about hazards just over the horizon.

Most presidents come to Washington bright as freshly minted dimes and leave much diminished. To govern is to choose and choosing produces disagreements, disappointments, even enemies. Furthermore, the modern president is omnipresent in the public's consciousness and the public confuses prominence with power. Therefore too much is expected of presidents. They are blamed when it becomes clear, as it always does, that events are in the saddle, riding mankind. However, Reagan is leaving Washington more popular than he was when he arrived (having won just 50.7 percent of the 1980 vote). Like Eisenhower, he is leaving on a crest of affection.

It has not all been smooth sledding. The silly phrase "Teflon president" was coined by a Democrat and was a way of saying that the people are fools, bewitched by Reagan's magic. They are not fools and they do not cotton to a party that says they are. During the 1982 recession, Reagan was not protected by any political Teflon. His popularity plummeted, as it did four years later during the Iran-contra revelations.

One reason Reagan today is standing tall in public approval is that he is standing. He has gone the distance. The last time Americans were watching the completion of a president's second term they were reading *To Kill a Mockingbird*, listening to "Itsy Bitsy Teenie Weenie Yellow Polkadot Bikini" and watching the movie *Psycho*. It has been a long time. Too long. Reagan is not only upright at the final bell, he is bouncing on the balls of his feet. He has proven that the presidency is not such a destroyer after all.

The most common, indeed jejune criticism of Reagan is that he did not properly allow the presidency to fill his days, let alone his nights. His immediate predecessor, Jimmy Carter, proudly, even ostentatiously made the presidency seem crushing. It was Jefferson's "splendid misery" without the splendor. Reagan made being president look a little too easy for some tastes. He drained it of the aura of melodrama that journalists relish. (Melodrama enlarges them by making them participants in stirring events.)

Reagan has been president for 4 percent of the republic's constitutional history. He did not shinny to the top of the greasy pole of American politics by accident or lassitude. He first sought the presidency in 1968. He fought fiercely for the Republican nomination in 1976, losing one of life's close calls. (If 794 votes had switched in the New Hampshire primary Reagan might have been president when oil prices doubled and hostages were taken in Tehran.) In 1980 the man and the moment met for two reasons—foreign policy humiliation and domestic inflation. Both created a demoralizing sense that the nation had lost control over its destiny.

Inflation generated the fuel of political change in America, middle-class anxiety and anger. Inflation was blamed on Washington and reinforced the core conservative message of hostility toward government. Today, however, the dialectic of democracy is working. The Democratic Party has benefited from Reagan in two ways. The dampening of inflation, and the general geniality of the most visible symbol of government, has caused confidence in government to increase. That makes the future a little less forbidding to the Democratic Party. Second, the Democratic Party has moved like a tide pulled by the rise of the Reagan moon. In a democracy a leader's success can often be gauged, in part, by his effect on the opposition party. Reagan has rendered the Democratic Party more ready to govern in the 1990s than it was in the 1970s and 1980s. He has done this by drawing it back toward 1960.

John Kennedy was a "growth Democrat." All Democrats were then. His Treasury Secretary was a Republican, Douglas Dillon. The last large tax cut for individuals before Reagan's occurred in 1964 and was Kennedy's proposal. It has been downhill for Democrats since 1964. The party was captured by people who repudiated its postwar foreign policy of anticommunist containment and in domestic policy, were "fairness Democrats." They elbowed aside growth Democrats and advocated programs of distributive justice. After two drubbings by Reagan and one by his vice president, Democrats again emphasized growth.

American politics often follows a serpentine path into the future. The

Founding Fathers fought a profoundly conservative revolution, founding a new regime to protect ancient rights. Civil war produced the ideological, social and economic bonds of national unity. The Depression produced a president who was—still is—emblematic of liberalism. He saved capitalism by beginning to build a conservative "social insurance state" that has reconciled people to the vicissitudes of economic dynamism. And in the 1980s the man emblematic of conservatism has caused conservatives to come to terms with the post–New Deal role of the central government—the welfare state. He also liquidated the Cold War.

And there are other aspects of Reagan's career. This most cheerful of presidents is the product of the first and most consequential protest movement of the decade of protests. Before the campus and urban unrest of the mid and late 1960s (both kinds of protests helped bring Reagan to California's governorship), there was the conservative insurgency in the Republican Party. Another oddity: The oldest president ever elected—a president who not only remembers but reveres one of the last premodern presidents, Coolidge—has had a sure sense of modernity, in the presidency and elsewhere.

If a 19th-century congressman were returned to Capitol Hill today, he would be stunned (and appalled) by many changes—the swarm of staff, the glut of legislation, the general pell-mell pace of life. However, he would say, "Congress does essentially what we did—just more of it." But were Coolidge returned to the White House he would not comprehend what a modern president does. The office has been utterly transformed by the growth of governmental responsibilities, at home and abroad, and by the power to communicate to a wired nation.

Reagan recently said that he sometimes wonders how presidents who have *not* been actors have been able to function. I do not know precisely what he meant, and he probably doesn't either, but he was on to something.

Two of this century's greatest leaders of democracies, Churchill and de Gaulle, had highly developed senses of the theatrical element in politics. FDR did, too. So have evil leaders in the age of mass effects, Hitler, Mussolini and Castro all mastered ceremonies of mass intoxication.

A political actor, be he good or evil, does not deal in unreality. Rather, he creates realities that matter—perceptions, emotions, affiliations. An actor not only projects, he causes his audience to project certain qualities—admiration, fear, hatred, love, patriotism, empathy. In some nations the actor's role has been assigned to a constitutional monarch. But the role is not incompatible with republican values. Reagan has been diligent about the task of making vivid the values that produce cohesion and dynamism in a continental nation. That task is central, not peripheral, to the problem of governance.

Reagan may seem like the least complicated of men, an open book that by now has been completely read to the country. But there remains one particularly puzzling aspect of his personality. It may have something to do with his having been—with his being—an actor. In any case, it is this: He is genuinely amiable but also remote. He is a friendly man with few close friends. Perhaps only one. He married her.

Reagan's White House years have been the Reagans' years. Their lives are thoroughly woven together. And Nancy Reagan, in her chosen public role, has acted on an understanding she shares with him. It can be called the sophistication of simplicity.

The media often are the last to learn things. They certainly took their time even getting a partial understanding of this good and remarkable woman. When she first came to Washington she was the victim of an extremely dumb and lazy caricature by the media. She supposedly was just another Beverly Hills lady who lunched a lot, someone with a Black Belt in shopping earned on Rodeo Drive. Then the media, in one of those pendular swings that takes them from one misjudgment to another, portrayed her as a policymaker and palace intriguer—a woman who should go shopping and leave men's work alone.

The full truth about her role is known only to her and him. It is for her to tell if she chooses. She probably will tell only a carefully calibrated portion of it. A quarter of a century at the center of serious politics has schooled her in discretion and reticence. However, this much can be said for sure. She has been *with* him, physically there and mentally engaged, every step of the way. She has been in motel corridors in the middle of the night in the middle of campaign crises. She has been upstairs in the White House, where the hum of governance is heard day and night from downstairs. Her astuteness, her quick and penetrating political intuitions, have been focused on her husband's personal fortunes.

She has made one public issue her own. Before the professional political class awakened to what the public had already discovered, she recognized that drug abuse would be the most alarming phenomenon of the 1980s. Before the bankruptcy of "supply side" drug policies—interdiction and all that—became apparent, she went to work on the demand side. She knew that the solution must come from altering the behavior of young people by changing their attitudes: "Just say no."

"Say *what?*" asked the sophisticates, much amused by yet another example of Reaganite simplicity. They were right about one thing. Nancy Reagan is Reaganite. That is, she shares her husband's understanding of the arduous patience required for democratic social change. "Even now," writes James Q. Wilson, "when the dangers of drug abuse are well understood, many educated people still discuss the drug problem in almost every way except the right way. They talk about the "cost" of drug use and the "socioeconomic factors" that shape that use. They rarely speak plainly—drug use is wrong because it is immoral, and it is immoral because it enslaves the mind and destroys the soul. It is as if it were a mark of sophistication for us to shun the language of morality in discussing the problems of mankind."

Sophisticates have been late learners about the wisdom of plain speaking about drugs—"Just say no." When—how—did Ronald Reagan learn what he knows about simplicity and leadership? Perhaps it is not learned; perhaps it is largely a matter of temperament.

An ancient Greek poet said, "The fox knows many things, but the hedgehog knows one big thing." Reagan is more foxy than he has contrived to seem. Like Eisenhower, he understands the advantages of being underestimated by the chattering classes. But Reagan is much more of hedgehog than a fox. He knows a few simple, powerful things. He understands the economy of leadership—the husbanding of the perishable hold any president has on the attention of this complacent, inattentive nation. He knows it is necessary to have a few priorities, a few themes. He knows how often—again, the peculiar patience of politics—you must repeat them when building a following. He knows what Dr. Johnson knew—that people more often need to be reminded than informed. He knows the importance of happiness in a nation where the pursuit of it was affirmed at the instant independence was asserted.

Reagan has been derided as a Dr. Feelgood. The description is more warranted than the derision. Reagan believes the American people are "lumpy with unrealized potentialities." (The phrase comes from another Californian of simple but powerful understandings, the late Eric Hoffer.) The fruits of American talents will be bountiful when Americans are optimistic. When they are optimistic they make the most of freedom. They stay in school longer, have more babies, start more businesses— varrrooooom!

It is no accident that Reagan rose to the pinnacle of power at a moment when there was a rising wave of intellectual pessimism. Numerous theories were being offered as to why the trajectory of the American experiment has passed its apogee. Reagan's greatest gift to his country has been his soaring sense of possibilities. To see where he got it, look at what he has seen in a long life.

In the six decades since he left home for college, America's real GNP has increased sixfold, three times the rate of population growth. Since the Second World War the world (the calculation is by Norman Macrae of the *Economist*) has added seven times as much producing power as was added in all the previous millennia of *Homo sapiens*. More acceleration is certain as more societies enter the information age, an age in which (Macrae again) a moderately competent researcher using an ordinary computer can check more correlations in an afternoon than Einstein could check in his lifetime.

Reagan's sunniness about future possibilities is not silly. But possibilities are not certainties, or even probabilities, unless political leaders see the world steadily and see it whole, and tell the truth about the dangers the future holds. In domestic affairs, meaning primarily economic management, Reagan is not recognizably conservative. He is not even a Keynesian. He is a Panglossian. And he has presided over a debilitating feast as the nation has eaten much of its seed corn.

Congress has passed every balanced budget he has submitted. Congress has quarreled with him a bit about the composition of spending, but not much about the amount. The first Reagan budget was essentially Carter's. The eighth was a product of the Reagan-Congress "summit" following the October 1987 stock market convulsion. The middle six budgets tell Reagan's story. Those budgets produced deficits totaling $1.1 trillion. The budgets Reagan sent to Congress *proposed* 13/14ths of that total. Congress added a piddling $90 billion, just $15 billion a year.

As Pat Moynihan has said, something fundamental happened in American governance when a conservative Republican administration produced deficits of $200 billion—and nothing happened. Nothing, that is, dramatic and immediately visible. Much happened in the way of silent rot as we mortgaged much of our future vitality. But for the political class, the event was a splendid liberation: All the rules were repealed. It was a particularly perverse event coming from conservatives: There were no longer restraints, practical or moral, on government spending. Under Reagan the interest component of the budget has more than doubled to 14 percent. The fiscal 1989 interest cost—a regressive transfer of wealth to buyers of government bonds—exceeds $150 billion. That is more than the combined budgets of nine departments—Agriculture, Commerce, Education, Energy, Interior, Justice, Labor, State, Transportation.

By knocking the budget into radical imbalance, Reagan has placed a restraining hand on the 1990s. But it will not restrain the growth of the welfare state. The population is aging and the elderly are the principal beneficiaries of welfare state payments, particularly pensions and medical care. Instead, the restraining hand will strangle defense spending, beginning with Reagan's most cherished project, the Strategic Defense Initiative.

The last large creative act of domestic policy in the Reagan years occurred in 1986. With tax simplification government took a big step back from supervision of economic choices. Rather than use the Tax Code to fine-tune the fairness of life, the policy would be: Use the Code to raise revenue and stimulate growth. Growth will deliver rough justice and the welfare state will rub much of the roughness off that justice.

Conservatives argue, plausibly, that people at the bottom of the social pyramid benefit from policies that energize those at the top—the investing, entrepreneurial class that makes a market economy hum. Since the end of the 1982 recession the economy has hummed. The number of workers earning just the minimum wage has fallen 22 percent. But by now, after 73 consecutive months of growth, we know that growth is not enough.

John Kennedy, in the full flush of postwar confidence, said, "A rising tide lifts all boats." Now we know better. We do not know how to raise those who are stuck in the mud. Conservatives have refuted the redistributionist simplicities of those who thought they knew how to help the underclass. But it would be nice if conservatives did not think that refutation exhausts their responsibilities.

Regarding the perennial American problem—race—limited progress has been made, and it may seem paradoxical to call it progress: The civil-rights era ended in the Reagan years. That is, the problems afflicting poor blacks are no longer regarded as primarily matters of race. It is broadly understood that if all the members of the urban underclass were magically given white skins, their life prospects would not appreciably improve. For decades conservatives contented themselves with saying: Liberals emphasize equality of condition, we emphasize equality of opportunity. In the Reagan years conservatives have come face to face with the fact that equality of opportunity is much more complicated than they thought. It must be, in part, a government artifact.

The Reagan years have involved a rolling referendum on government. The results are clear and they are not what conservatives wanted. Americans want low taxes and a high level of services. Big surprise. Big deficit. The deficit is the numerical expression of a cultural phenomenon—the American determination to live beyond our means, to consume more than we produce. Once upon a time conservatives prided themselves on a flinty realism about the costs of life. No more. Costs are not a cheerful subject. Costs imply limits and obstacles not suggested by that openness of the prairie horizon.

Liberals have practiced "tax and tax, spend and spend, elect and elect" but conservatives have perfected "borrow and borrow, spend and spend, elect and elect." Conservatives are supposed to have clear heads to compensate for not having warm hearts. However, in the Reagan years there has been what Moynihan calls a hemorrhaging of reality regarding the fiscal requirements for strength and prosperity. This is a consequence of the narcotic of cheerfulness.

In foreign policy, too, there has been a tendency to allow wishes to be the father of thoughts. Granted, the world seems less dangerous than it did in 1980, and Reagan is partly responsible for the improvement.

The allocation of political praise or blame often is done on the basis of the *post hoc, ergo propter hoc* fallacy: The rooster crows and then the sun rises, so the crowing causes the sunrise. Reagan did not singlehandedly cause the rise in the fortunes of freedom in this decade. Many forces have been gathering strength for many decades. Still, Reagan has been a leading participant—Margaret Thatcher has been another—on the winning side of an ideological argument. Distilled to its essence, the intellectual sea change in this decade has been recognition of this: Pluralism means progress. Modernization requires markets. Free markets require some political liberty—and they generate demands for more of it.

In May, at Moscow State University, Reagan said that mankind is emerging "like a chrysalis" from the economy of the Industrial Revolution and is entering the information age, the economy of the mind. "The key is freedom—freedom of thought, freedom of information, freedom of communication." Such freedoms cannot be tentative and tactical concessions by an uncontrolled government, they must be institutionalized. Otherwise "freedom will always be looking over its shoulder. A bird on a tether, no matter how long the rope, can always be pulled back."

How true. But how wildly wrong he is about what is happening in Moscow. Reagan has accelerated the moral disarmament of the West— actual disarmament will follow—by elevating wishful thinking to the status of political philosophy. Here he is assessing Gorbachev: "He is the first leader that has come along who has gone back before Stalin and . . . he is trying to do what Lenin was teaching . . . Stalin actually reversed many of the things. . . . I've known a little bit about Lenin and what he was advocating, and I think that this, in *glasnost* and *perestroika* and all that, this is much more smacking of Lenin than of Stalin." Lenin the liberal "advocate" and teacher, Stalin the aberration? The mind boggles and the spirit sags at the misunderstandings—of Soviet history, of the 20th century. Reagan blandly says that Gorbachev has just "come along." How is it that the Soviet Union suddenly fell into the hands of such a pleasant fellow? That does not puzzle our cheerful president. Hey, good things happen to nice people.

At the United Nations in September, Reagan spoke of the "synergy of peace and freedom." He said that "history teaches" that where individual rights are respected, "war is a distant prospect." History—1914 for example—really teaches a less clear lesson. It teaches that freedom is a fragile flower. We shall see if a nation hooked on the narcotic of cheerfulness can face unpleasant facts that the future is certain to put in front of it.

The future has been called the mirror with no glass in it. The future is especially unknowable in an open society. Democratic government runs on opinion, so all its achievements rest on shifting sand. Conservatives, especially, should have a keen sense of impermanence. Even success is problematic. When, in the mid-1960s, Reagan became Mr. Conservative, it was clear what conservatism was. In foreign policy it was anticommunist and particularly anti-Soviet. There was to be no nonsense about détente. In domestic policy conservatism advocated balanced budgets, radical pruning of the welfare state and redress of Supreme Court excesses regarding the "social issues," particularly school prayer and abortion. The fate of those last two issues tells much about Reagan and his years.

At the peak of his powers he did not get the Senate, controlled by his party for six years, to pass even the mildest constitutional amendments pertaining to school prayer and abortion. Truth be told, he did not try hard. They are hot, divisive issues. They are useful to a conservative candidate who wants to energize particular constituencies. But as president, Reagan, the cheerful consensus conservative, tried to avoid heat and division. That was understandable after the nastiness of the preceding two decades.

In his second term, speaking to an audience of intense conservatives, Reagan said that "returning civility to public life and the political discourse is a high and worthy goal." Using Jefferson's phrase, he said Americans are all "brethren of the same principle." And he said each of us should be true to Teddy Roosevelt's injunction to play fair and "be a good man to camp out with." He has been that, a happy camper.

However, a great communicator will communicate complicated ideas, hard choices and bad news. Reagan has had little aptitude and less appetite for those tasks. But, then, communication is not really Reagan's forte. Rhetoric is.

Rhetoric has a tainted reputation in our time, for several reasons. One is the carnage produced by murderous demagogues. Another is the public's uneasiness about modern means of mass manipulation, including propaganda and advertising. But rhetoric is indispensable to good politics and can be ennobling. Ancient political philosophers, such as Aristotle and Cicero, and the best modern politicians, such as Lincoln and Churchill, understood that rhetoric can direct the free will of the community to the good. Rhetoric is systematic eloquence. At its best it does not induce irrationality. Rather, it leavens reason, fusing passion to persuasion.

Rhetoric has been central to Reagan's presidency because Reagan has intended his statecraft to be soulcraft. His aim has been to restore the plain language of right and wrong, good and evil, for the purpose of enabling people to make the most of freedom. In his long career of crisscrossing the country, practicing the exacting ethic of democratic persuasion, he has resembled a political John Wesley. For all his deplorable inattentiveness regarding many aspects of his office, he has been assiduous about nurturing a finer civic culture, as he understands it. Here, then, is the crowning paradox of Reagan's career. For all his disparagement of government, he has given it the highest possible purpose, the improvement of the soul of the nation.

When passions cool and the dust raised by current contentions settles, judicious historians are apt to place Reagan in the front rank of the second rank of American presidents. The first rank includes those who were pulled to greatness by the gravity of great crises. Washington and Jefferson were pulled by the hazardous flux of the founding era. Lincoln was pulled by disunion and the need to define the nation's meaning. Theodore Roosevelt was pulled by the need to tame the energies of industrialism, Woodrow Wilson by America's entry into the vortex of world affairs, Franklin Roosevelt by the Depression and the dictators.

Reagan is the last president for whom the Depression will have been a formative experience, the last president whose foremost model was the first modern president, Franklin Roosevelt. Roosevelt's first words as president ("the only thing we have to fear is fear itself") emphasized the tone-setting role of the office, and the need for high public morale. America was far less troubled in 1981 than in 1933, but it needed reassurance. It needed to recover confidence in its health and goodness. It needed to recover what was lost in the 1960s and 1970s, the sense that it has a competence commensurate with its nobility and responsibilities. Reagan, like Roosevelt, has been a great reassurer, a steadying captain who calmed the passengers and, to some extent, the sea.

January 9, 1989

George Bush's Rightmindedness

New presidents serve up rich sauces of symbolism, high in political cholesterol. George Bush has begun with a blizzard of words and gestures communicating high-mindedness.

We are at the English-muffin phase (folks swooned when Jerry Ford popped his own muffin into the presidential toaster), which also has been a cardigan sweater and jelly-bean phase of young presidencies. This humanizing—perhaps miniaturizing—of presidents is a recurring skit for a public that periodically pretends it wants ordinariness in that extraordinary office.

The Bushes—up with horseshoes, down with designer clothes—are quite traditional in their ostentatious unostentatiousness. Their carefully choreographed "simplicity" projects the image of indifference to image. This is Carter Redux, as in the religiosity (Bush's first presidential act was to lead the nation in prayer), the walking on Pennsylvania Avenue, the country music, the open house, the stern talk about ethics. Carter's presidency confirmed this law: Frenetic reliance on symbolism indicates uncertainty about what you want to do.

Amidst the familiar metaphors (breezes blowing, pages turning, doors opening) of Bush's inaugural address there ran a vein of familiar moralism. It equates rectitude with right, and assumes that having the right attitude is tantamount to doing the right thing. Bush's feet may be in cowboy boots, but his head is in New England, home of right-mindedness and (not coincidentally) Abolitionism.

The Abolitionists were not much help in ending slavery while preserving the union, but they were pure in thought. The Abolitionist mentality was visible in the one specific vow in Bush's inaugural, concerning cocaine: "This scourge will stop."

It won't, but Bush has struck a pleasing pose, as he did in the campaign when he said, "If I'm elected President, if I'm remembered for anything, it would be this: a complete and total ban on chemical weapons." Bush's national security adviser, Brent Scowcroft, speaking last Sunday, said he supposed a verifiable ban to be "impossible." That is the unvarnished truth. But Bush has an arresting attitude, if not a practical position.

Bush also stood foursquare for rectitude when he came out against "bickering" and for bipartisanship in foreign policy. Bush, like many who came of age politically during the Second World War, assumes that bipartisanship is the American norm. That is a misreading—perhaps a nonreading—of American history.

The fiercest dispute of the 1790s—some historians say it raised the specter of civil war—swirled around the Jay Treaty with Britain. The War of 1812 stirred semisecessionist sentiment in New England, which became almost a neutral zone. The Mexican War (1846–48) was denounced by Whig critics (including Congressman Lincoln) as, among other things, unconstitutional. The war with Spain (1898) and the acquisition of territories brought bitter debate about the very nature of the nation. Between 1914 and 1917, modern isolationism found its voice, heard again in the late 1930s. Advocates of a "Pacific first" strategy troubled FDR's conduct of the war. They had an ally in General Douglas MacArthur, who was heard from again during the angry debates about Korea.

Much has been made of the fact that Bush's inaugural address contained the word "sacrifice": "Are we enthralled with material things, less appreciative of the nobility of work and sacrifice?" But one reason he was inaugurated was his pledge not to ask a central sacrifice of citizenship—taxes. "No new taxes" was a pledge not to let public needs impinge upon private materialism. Bush's pledge does mean a sacrifice—of national security. Scowcroft, when asked if Bush's tax pledge and his promise of a strong national defense are conflicting goals, said: "Of course. Of course they conflict." But, as attitudes, each is popular.

After praising sacrifice, Bush said, serenely: "We have more will than wallet; but will is what we need." However, in government will without wallet is usually ineffectual. And willing an end without willing the means to that end is mere attitudinizing. Bush was praised for saying at the Republican National Convention, "I don't hate government." That is an admirable attitude, but actions count. Governments run on money and Bush's solo significant campaign promise was to keep the government's wallet thin.

That is why when he promised "a new activism," he spoke of the need for voluntarism and generally displaying "better hearts and finer souls." The new activism will not be by the government that he does not hate but will not fund.

Bush has hit the ground running in place, promising rectitude—handsome attitudes—and raising anew this question: Beyond "serving," is there something he wants to do?

January 26, 1989

George the Good, If He Does Say So Himself

The first month of the reign of George the Good has featured frequent testimonials from the new president to himself regarding his ethical sensibilities. His homilies imply that America will soon be better than it recently was because he is more morally exemplary than the last fellow. Washington is an echo chamber when the media and others succumb to the power of suggestion, so we are now told by many sources that the tone of the town is amazingly more noble than it was just a few months ago. This month of moral exhibitionism has been partly a cause and partly an effect of Washington's obsession with ethics, as Washington understands that subject.

Once upon a time what were called important questions of ethics in government concerned the important things government does. The subjects of ethical arguments were war and peace, treatment of the poor or even such specific questions as whether to ban semiautomatic assault rifles of the sort used in the Stockton, California schoolyard massacre. Last week Washington, showing today's sense of ethics, wallowed in retrospective angst: James Baker, while Treasury secretary, owned stock in a big bank. No one thinks he acted dishonorably. The fretting is about appearances. There might have been an appearance of a conflict of interest if anyone had thought to be troubled by it. Last week's retroactive scrupulosity occurred when it was "revealed" (yawn: it was in Baker's disclosure form) that he owns stock in the bank and the bank has lots of loans to Third World countries. As secretary of state he will be involved in formulating policies regarding such a debt.

Because of Bush's punctiliousness about avoiding any appearance of any unseemly appearances, Baker is selling the stock. But the only serious question in such a case is: Is Baker the sort of scoundrel who would prefer his investment portfolio over the national interest if they conflicted? If he is, selling his stock hardly suffices. He should be put in stocks in Lafayette Square across from the White House and pelted with dead cats. If he is a scoundrel. But he is not. So why waste mental energy worrying about his stocks?

Last week Baker's deputy, Lawrence Eagleburger, had Beltway ethicists in a tizzy because (are you sitting down?) while in the private sector he was a consultant to multinational companies. Some of them (follow the bouncing ball) do business in countries (bounce) where the United States has policies (bounce, bounce) that Eagleburger (bounce, bounce, bounce) might help shape. Eagleburger's response has been to say, "Well, rescue me." He promises that at State he will not have any dealings with certain companies operating in more than a dozen countries. Presumably he will be poised to bolt from the room if any sensitive subject arises. It is a matter of appearances.

Speaking of which, does Washington mind appearing out of its mind? Nowadays ethics, the incredibly shrinking subject, involves questions such as: When John Doe left government service, did he have oral or written communications with an agency with which he had been "directly" involved while in government? Did he lobby about an issue with which he had been "substantially" involved? Did he do it on the 366th rather than the 365th day after he left government? In Washington the ethical quality of an action can change dramatically, like Cinderella's carriage, when a clock strikes midnight.

Immanuel Kant, call your office. Washington cannot keep track of all its categorical imperatives. Actually, Washington has platoons of Kants. They are ethics officers. My college in England had someone called a "moral tutor" whose tutelage consisted of common sense, such as: Be careful climbing the college wall after curfew. Washington's moral tutors are crucial. Given the Talmudic density of the ethical fine print, a government rookie who wants to remain law-abiding needs a government rabbi. An ethics officer will guide him through the thicket of laws, lest he have an ethically dubious cup of coffee with a proscribed kind of person or with an acceptable kind of person who in the course of the conversation touches upon a proscribed subject.

Such rules actually are wonderfully liberating for politicians. Politicians can do as they please, which means as is politically convenient, regarding budgets and assault rifles and other things, without brushing up against what today counts as a question of ethics. Politicians can then be certified as ethical by compliance with nit-picking rules written to prevent bad appearances. Such rules are the result of moral grandstanding by Congress, which does not live under them. They are written, by and large, by young staffers fresh from law school who know little about life and less about government. They think an awful lot about money. They do not have much of it and are fearfully worried lest anyone else be corrupted by it. This impulse dovetails with today's strong streak of journalistic voyeurism (dressed up in the fancy frock of "the public's right to know") about everyone's bank account.

Once upon a time Washington's charm was that people here thought mostly about power, its sources and uses, rather than money. It wasn't pretty, but at least it wasn't New York, where money is on most minds. One reason Bush has begun by talking so much about ethics, microscopically observed, is that it beats talking about budgets and other aspects of governance. Bush has been stressing how different (and better) his sensibilities are than those of the last lot in town, how much kinder, gentler, more compassionate and ethically sparkling. But he has embraced his predecessor's loopy budget assumptions, which will drive policy. That, however, is only substance.

The style is the thing, as Bush has shown in puncturing the myth that the media are carnivorous. For a month now Washington has been waist-deep in a syrupy goo of junk journalism about the new decency, sensitivity, compassion, morality, etc. But as Month One ended, Bush was opposing a ban on those assault rifles and was proposing in his budget to follow pretty much the path marked by his predecessor. You remember him: He was less kind, gentle, etc.

Once upon a time it was thought that budgets did more than ethics officers to define the ethics of a government. Not today, as we watch the trivialization of government by the miniaturization of ethics.

February 27, 1989

Government As an Ethics-Free Zone

Speaker Wright's "personal ethics" are now the focus of attention in this continental superpower. Many people, including Wright, say that whatever is to be done, 'twere well it were done quickly. Nonsense. Let's all wallow in it, for weeks, months if possible.

'Tis said there should be no element of Republican revenge in this. Why ever not? It is said we must avoid an orgy of recrimination and a ruinous escalation of nastiness on the ethics front. I say let the ruination begin. Let there be scorched earth, salt sown in the soil, not a stone left standing on another stone on Capitol Hill.

I do not know if Wright is guilty of anything, but I hope that if he is innocent he is ruined and if he is guilty he goes unpunished. Let there be no nonsense about justice at this late date from the fine folks who brought us the Bork lynching, the Tower inquisition, the Meese tormentings, and much else in the name of highmindedness.

What part of the destruction of the Bork nomination did you find most admirable, if only for its imaginativeness? Was it anti-Bork advertising campaigns that the sponsors admitted were lies? Was it anti-Bork groups snooping around to learn what movies Bork had rented, hoping to find something naughty? (They found Fred Astaire.) Then there were all those fraudulent reports by free-lance ethicists who said they saw John Tower misbehave on occasions when they could not have seen Tower. Ah, but that was then, this is now. And two wrongs do not make a right, right?

Right. But a 14th or 18th or 23rd wrong, if the 14th or 18th or 23rd victim is a prominent Democrat, may make a cease-fire on the "personal ethics" front. And perhaps we might even get a redefinition of ethics to include behavior with an important effect on the public weal.

Suddenly a lot of Democrats are not having any fun anymore. Won't some referees blow the whistle, call time out, reset the clock, do something? The best thing about Wright's travail is that it may cause a few hundred Democrats to decide that ethics is not such a good dodge after all.

It is lovely that Wright's case is coming to a boil as the latest bipartisan budget fraud is being perfected at both ends of Pennsylvania Avenue. And as, in a courthouse at the foot of Capitol Hill, the trial of Oliver North is coming to a close. Did North lie to Congress? Yes, he says so. But the lying was extraordinary and the quantity was small beer compared to the mountain of mendacity routinely shoveled out to the American people by the Bush administration and both parties in Congress concerning the annual evasions of the Gramm-Rudman deficit-reduction "law."

In the last two years under that law, the deficit has actually increased. Congress and the executive branch have conspired for their mutual convenience (that is what bipartnership, so much celebrated just now, really means) to fudge the assumptions and cook the books in ways which, if practiced in the private sector, might get the practitioner sent to prison.

This is the time of year for senior-class trips to Washington by high-school students. They come in brightly colored buses that sometimes park bumper-to-bumper, like benign, pretty snakes stretching down Capitol Hill. If there were criminal sanctions attached to Gramm-Rudman, there would be a snake of bumper-to-bumper paddy wagons lined up to cart Congress and some of the executive branch to jail.

Wright and North may have misbehaved with sums involving single commas. But ethics—pardon me, I mean "personal ethics"—stop with the second comma. Budgetary shell games involving three commas—billions—do not count when the subject in Washington is "ethics."

The adjective "personal" gives the game away. The subject of "personal ethics" is a device for changing the subject from the ethics-free zone of matters central to the nation's welfare. In that zone, the stakes are high and the choices are hard so there is tacit bipartisan agreement that ethics have nothing to do with it.

Actually, "personal ethics," is understood in terms of financial fastidiousness, are probably better than ever in American politics. However, today's relatively pristine ruling class will not write an honest, let alone a responsible, budget.

Better "personal" ethics and worse government—that is the result of deciding that ethical rules are about relatively little things.

April 20, 1989

The Bush Presidency's Hollow Center

President Bush, who needs handlers as much as he disdains them, deepened suspicions he sought to allay when he bounded, yet again, into the press room and quickly found himself denying that his administration is in disarray. It does him no good to give the country more exposure to himself than he can fill with interesting or merely plausible things to say, so he should go to earth for awhile.

The substantive thinness of his presidency was guaranteed by his way of winning it—"no new taxes"—and the thinness was proclaimed as policy in his inaugural address: "We have more will than wallet." Today's $5 trillion economy is 75 percent larger (40 percent bigger per capita) in real terms than in 1967 when Bush became a congressman. The nation's wallet is remarkably thick. The government's wallet is thin by political choice and will be kept so by Bush's policy.

Hence the imaginative energies of the political class here are increasingly squandered on intellectual dishonesties to justify evasions of the deficit problem. And the centrality of that problem guarantees a Bush presidency hollow at its moral center.

In *The Public Interest*, Joseph Wright and Aaron Wildavsky denounce, with passionate disgust, the stultification of political debate by the deficit, which, like anticommunism in the 1950s and civil rights in the 1960s, has been the issue shaping debate on all other issues, from aid to friendly governments to help for the homeless. The Bush administration looks bewildered because its goals number 2, 3, 4, 5 through the full list all are nullified by goal No. 1: keeping the government's wallet thin—"no new taxes."

This guarantees more governmental monomania. Washington usually has at most a one-track mind and Bush's taxophobia guarantees that the deficit will stifle rational debate about choices for the public household. And such debate as there is, about meeting Gramm-Rudman deficit-reduction requirements, is surreal. Bush's economic forecasts incorporate GNP growth assumptions wildly incompatible with Federal Reserve policies that are necessary to achieve Bush's projected inflation rate (1.7 percent by 1994).

Interest rates are ever-larger levers on events in a nation addicted to debt. Total debt—government, business, household—has risen 200 percent in a decade, and much of the debt is pegged to the prime rate. In this decade interest, not defense, has been the fastest-growing portion of the federal budget. Rising rates make that portion grow faster while the consequence of rising rates—slower GNP growth—causes revenues to grow slower than Bush's budget presupposes.

Compounded intellectual incompatibilities—administration assumptions incompatible with one another, and with predictable Federal Reserve policy—are by now a Republican ritual. This is an odd ritual for a party that advertises its realism as an alternative to Democratic wishful thinking.

The Reagan administration's first forecasts, made in March 1981, assumed that between 1980 and 1986 there would be a rate of GNP growth (25 percent) and a decline in unemployment (from 7.2 to 5.6 percent) and a balanced budget (by 1984, no less). These forecasts were utterly incompatible with the monetary policies that would be necessary to achieve serious progress toward the Reagan administration's most serious goal, reduction of inflation from 13.5 to 1.9 percent.

As things turned out, by 1986 real GNP growth had been just 16.5 percent, unemployment was not much below the 1980 level (6.9 percent) and the 1984 budget had been $185 billion dollars out of balance. The problem was that the Fed had practiced what Reagan preached, emphasizing the primary goal of suppressing inflation.

And today? There they go again, those Republicans.

The administration projects declining interest rates. They are rising. Even if they remain where they were when the administration made its projections, the deficit-reduction projection would be $9 billion off because rates did not decline. The administration projects 3.5 percent real growth in GNP for five years. Fed chairman Alan Greenspan says such growth "presupposes an increase in productivity which could conceivably happen but is quite unlikely."

Bush wants America to think beyond quarterly reports and annual budgets, to the long term. Good idea. Let's start.

The deficit, which today is larger as a percentage of GNP than ever before in peacetime when unemployment was this low, is sopping up in government borrowing a debilitating share of domestic savings. America's savings rate has fallen substantially, from an already alarmingly low base, in the 1980s. Hence investment has been inadequate. Hence productivity growth has been too slow: The growth of output per hour has been at half the 1960s rate.

Because of investment neglected and growth forgone, Herbert Stein says: "For every $100 billion of deficit we run, we reduce national income by $15 billion a year forever." Forever. That is the long term.

March 12, 1989

Conservatives Making Big Government Cheap

The political rhetoric praising small government is "a kind of civic religion, avowed but not constraining." Senator Daniel P. (Pat) Moynihan uses those words to describe FDR's 1932 pledge to balance the budget. However, the description also fits conservatism as it confronts America's fundamental choice: How much economic growth do we want, and how much government?

Since the New Deal, conservatives have argued that national policy has unduly sacrificed economic growth to the growth of government. Moynihan (D-N.Y.) argues in a recent lecture that since 1981 conservatism has "acted in a manner that intensified the trends it most deplored." Pledged to reduce government and increase the rate of economic growth, conservatism has been "bringing about just the opposite." Moynihan says that the paradox of conservatism in power is this: "In effect, big government was made cheap."

The growth of America's GNP was 4 percent in the 1950s and 1960s. It dropped below 3 percent in the 1970s and has been barely above 2 percent in the 1980s. Since 1960, the overall increase in U.S. manufacturing productivity of 2.7 percent a year has been less than that of nine European countries (for example, France 5.5; Britain, 3.6) and about one-third that of Japan (8.0).

Now, what has happened to government recently? Between fiscal 1980 and fiscal 1986, federal outlays rose from $590.9 billion to $979.9 billion. The federal debt has soared from $914.3 billion to more than $2 trillion. In Moynihan's words, we borrowed $1 trillion from the Japanese and had a party—a party of consumption, including a flood of foreign goods.

Ronald Reagan's first presidential act, executed on Inauguration Day, was a federal-employee firing freeze. He said it "will eventually lead to a significant reduction in the size of the federal work force." Well. At the beginning of fiscal 1981, federal employment, civilian and military, was 4,966,000. At the beginning of fiscal 1986, it was 5,210,000, with most of the increase civilian.

Why does government grow? In August 1986, Reagan at the Illinois State Fair boasted—yes, boasted: "No area of the budget, including defense, has grown as fast as our support of agriculture." He added that "this year alone we'll spend more on farm support programs . . . than the total amount the last administration provided in all its four years." The farmers interrupted his 11-minute speech with applause 15 times.

As Moynihan says, growth of government is a natural, inevitable product of the political bargaining process among interest groups that favor government outlays that benefit them. This process occurs under all administrations. What is different today—so different in degree that it is different in kind—is the radical discontinuity between conservative rhetoric and results.

"Once through the $100-billion deficit barrier," Moynihan says, "then the $200-billion barrier; once through the $1 trillion debt barrier, then the $2 trillion barrier—the politicians were free to soar. After all, no serious harm had come of it." This is what Moynihan means when he says "big government was made cheap." Because of the numbing deficits, the money did not seem to matter much.

There are many facets of the modern world that explain why the civic religion of small government is unconstraining. Knowledge, says Moynihan, is a form of capital, and much of it is formed because of government investment in public education. Our knowledge-based society is based on a big-government provision.

Also, knowledge begets government. An "information-rich" society by its own dynamic learns about matters that make government goods and services either economically rational, as in government support for scientific agriculture, or morally mandatory, as in medicine.

Not long ago, most American workers were farmers. Today about 3 percent are, and they feed all of us and many more around the world. The most important cause of this revolution was knowledge generated and disseminated by government.

The social sciences and medical science have produced knowledge that has, in turn, driven government in the direction of activism. Antipoverty programs became a moral choice only after we learned how to measure poverty. Time was, Moynihan notes, when the biggest hospital expense was clean linen. Now we have knowledge of kidney dialysis, and numerous other technologies. We can choose to keep people alive, and so we do, and it costs money.

As society's wealth has increased, so have demands on government. There are limited amounts of clean air and water. But a "people of plenty" accept fewer limits than a society of scarcity. They make the collective purchase of environmental improvements.

These are tendencies of societies such as ours. Tendencies are not inevitabilities. But, Moynihan warns, a society that refuses to recognize its tendencies intensifies them.

November 20, 1986

The Pastel President

"Clang" go the horseshoes. "Yip" go the puppies. "Ahhhhhhh," go the students of style. The only consistent theme of the Bush presidency is its moral and intellectual superiority to the "imagery" of Ronald Reagan. So it is odd that there is such fascination—encouraged by Bush—with Bush's "style." Bush makes much (and his image-tuners help him) of his disdain for "handlers" and his preference for what is called a "spontaneous" and "unscripted" presidency. (Churchill on an adversary: "He spoke without a note and almost without a point.") Of course no politician was ever more passive clay in the hands of handlers than Bush was in 1988.

However, today John Sununu, Bush's chief of staff, says, with a straight face, that Bush is being criticized "for not aggressively manipulating the media." Gosh, yes, that criticism has been harsh. Bush's style is loudly proclaimed understatedness. "Look! Look here! See how I shun the spotlight!" Bush says "more is going on than meets the eye," as we will see "when we look back from the year 2000." That is, judge me when I am long gone.

Last fall Bush said he was running "because I believe in the honor of it all." That is the reason students run for class president. Student elections are usually popularity contests. The Bush presidency rests on 60,000 thank-you notes, aptly called "stroke notes." It is politeness in lieu of political purpose. The politeness does have limits. Before and after the China trip Bush called Jimmy Carter, not Reagan, a discourtesy noted in California. For months Bush's administration has oozed disdain for the man who made the Bush presidency possible. Bush and his aides have stressed how much kinder, gentler, smarter, compassionate, energetic, etc., etc., etc., Bush is. Richard Nixon, an unlikely auditor, has written to Bush telling him to mind his, and his aides', manners. Such a tone of pettiness is set at the top, partly by being tolerated there. Pettiness is the tendency of people without large purposes. And Bush is a notorious nurser of grudges. In a New Orleans hotel suite he personally struck from his convention speech a gracious sentence praising Bob Dole.

Bush, like the rest of Washington, has been preoccupied with "ethics," or more precisely with microethics, petty financial matters, not great questions of governance. Bush's determination to continue running huge deficits which rob the voiceless, voteless rising generations? That is not what Bush considers an ethics problem. Another bipartisan budget fraud, evading requirements of the deficit reduction law? That is not what Congress considers an ethics violation. Jim Wright's nickel-and-dime scams, those are what arouse Washington ethicists.

Political nature abhors a vacuum. An obsession with miniaturized ethics floods in to fill a void of public purpose. What also flourishes in such a voice is morality understood as right-mindedness: having the right attitude amounts to doing the right thing. Thus Bush on the oil spill: "So what you do is the best you can, express the genuine concern that you feel on the environment—and I do feel concern. . . ."

At the age of 64 Bush is 10 years older than the average for 20th-century presidents in their first year. But Bush seems to be a bystander watching to see who Bush turns out to be. Recently he made this self-refuting assessment: "Maybe I'll turn out to be a Teddy Roosevelt." Try to imagine TR saying something like that. TR's overflowing joy was in being an original. Explaining the TR reference, Bush said: "I'm an Oyster Bay kind of guy." Bush understands TR not in terms of TR's political passions but rather his country estate. TR's political portrait was painted in primary colors. Bush, the pastel president, thinks of TR in terms of "life-style."

Last December Alessandra Stanley, writing in *The New Republic*, anticipated what has come to pass, a "Presidency by Ralph Lauren." The "Laurenification of America" responds to a craving for "Wasp aesthetics and pseudo-English gentility." There is "an insatiable mass-market hunger for upper-class totems," such as hunting prints and crested T-shirts from The Gap. Stanley rightly blames Reagan's Norman Rockwellesque 1984 campaign for helping to blur the line "between commercial advertising and political philosophy." Reagan's "Morning Again in America" commercials were indistinguishable from the many ads associating products with gooey nostalgia for white picket fences and paperboys on bikes. But Reagan could do that in 1984 because for 20 years he had been politically specific. In 1980, to the despair of his more "creative" advisers, he emphasized simple ads with him talking to a camera, telling what he wanted to do.

When Bush intones that "it's time to govern," he is implying: "unlike the previous president." But Bush is exactly like the previous president in being content to have the government gridlocked by the deficit. A recent *New York Times* news story began: "The Bush administration, citing budget constraints, does not plan to . . ." It could be a generic lead sentence. In this case, it pertained to Bush's intention to violate the commitment to modernize surveillance satellites, a commitment made in conjunction with ratification of the INF treaty. Is Bush prepared to sacrifice national security to his taxaphobia? Probably. All causes— education, drug treatment, environment—seem subordinate to the cause he cares most about, keeping budget constraints severe.

Bush is said to incarnate noblesse oblige. But where is the nobility in refusing to insist on the civic obligation to pay taxes sufficient for the government's great purposes of security and justice?

In 1894, when Congress was considering a tax of 2 percent on incomes of more than $4,000 (1 percent of the population), a wealthy New Yorker threatened to leave the country. A Nebraska congressman, William Jennings Bryan, said: "Of all the mean men I have ever known, I have never known one so mean that I would be willing to say of him that his patriotism was less than two percent deep. . . . If 'some of our best people' prefer to leave the country rather than pay . . . we can better afford to lose them and their fortunes than risk the contaminating influence of their presence." Today's supposed patrician has something to learn from The Great Commoner.

April 24, 1989

America's Weak Commitment to Progressive Taxation

What a difference a word can make. The middle of April—tax time— might be less lacerating if we used a delightful anachronism and spoke of having our "faculties" assessed rather than our incomes taxed.

Taxing incomes was originally spoken of in America as taxing individuals' earnings "faculties," as in the new Plymouth colonies' taxation on persons "according to their estates or faculties." It would flatter Americans to be told they are paying because, and to the extent that, their faculties are substantial. And saying so would teach a moral truth: Generally people prosper, and pay more taxes, because of reasons for which they cannot claim responsibility.

Our faculties are bestowed by our parents, through DNA and nurturing, and by society, through schooling and the culture. Sorry, you who are particularly vain about your rugged individualism. Life would really be rugged if social reality reflected your self-congratulatory ideology of lonely, unassisted accomplishment. But it does not.

The principle on which progressive taxation rests is that those who make the most money get the most from society not merely in terms of money but also in "faculties," and thus owe a proportionately larger debt. As Turgot, finance minister of the much maligned Louis XVI, told him: "The expenses of government, having for their object the interest of all, should be borne by everyone, and the more a man enjoys the advantages of society, the more he ought to hold himself honored in contributing to those expenses."

In the United States, the income tax was not, needless to say, enacted out of a sense of honor. It was passed by a political movement confident that its members would not pay it. In fact, it was a tax to cut taxes (counting tariffs as taxes).

After the Civil War, regional and class interests (the manufacturing North and the affluent commercial class) converged to produce reliance on tariffs for the lion's share of federal revenues. The income tax was advocated as a painless (for 99 percent of the population) way of paying for lower tariffs that also would reduce the cost of the common man's consumption. And so it was, briefly.

The income tax enacted in 1913 taxed personal income at 1 percent and exempted married couples earning less than $4,001. A graduated surtax, beginning on incomes of $20,000, rose to 6 percent on incomes of more than $500,000. The $4,000 exemption expressed Congress's conclusion that such a sum was necessary to "maintain an American family according to the American standard and send the children through college." It was about six times the average male's income.

But as quickly as Americans could say "Sarajevo," war caused government expenditures to soar and international trade (and tariff revenues) to shrink. By 1919, the minimum taxable income had been reduced to $1,000 and the top rate was 77 percent.

Nevertheless, at tax time in 1939, only 3.9 million Americans had to file. Six years later, 42.6 million did. War turned the class tax into a mass tax. The Cold War and, even more important, the welfare state would keep it that way.

Shortly after the income tax was enacted, Senator Elihu Root told a friend that they both might go to jail for failing to master the tax form, but jail would "be an intellectual center, for no one understands the Income Tax law except persons who have not sufficient intelligence to understand the questions that arise under it."

Complexity increased and the principle of progressivity was largely vitiated by the practice of writing arcane loopholes into the law. By the mid-1960s a senator complained: "The first nine pages of the Internal Revenue Code define income; the remaining 1,100 pages spin the web of exemptions and preferences."

The web was spun primarily for two reasons. Wrinkles in the code were Congress's way of legislating social policy without appropriating public funds. And the ideology of individualism—the myth that incomes reflect rugged individual attainment, not socially conferred and shaped "faculties"—made Americans weakly committed to the principle of progressivity. So weakly that it was virtually abandoned in 1986 in the name of reform.

The strong—wealthy, high-achieving, socially competent individuals—contribute much to society because they have benefited much from society. So they should pay a lot of the upkeep of the civilization that confers as well as rewards their faculties. But that notion may itself be an anachronism in a nation that seems to believe that taxation, with or without representation, is tyranny.

April 13, 1989

Abandoning the Income Tax, Absentmindedly

If the Democratic Party disappeared, would that make a difference? What is the party for? These dyspeptic questions are occasioned by the party's participation in the bipartisan abuse of its emblematic achievement, Social Security.

Begin, as everything does these days, with the bipartisan business of breaking the law. The Gramm-Rudman deficit-reduction law was enacted in 1985. Not one of its targets has ever been hit in spite of "creative accounting"—budgetary frauds—of a sort that might get someone in the private sector sent to prison.

Gramm-Rudman, which originally permitted a deficit of only $36 billion by fiscal 1990 (now one week old), was revised, in the name of realism, to permit a $100 billion deficit (plus a $10 billion fudge factor). The administration claims the deficit will be $99.7 billion, the Congressional Budget Office claims $117.8 billion, so we have a $18.1 billion disagreement, right?

Wrong. We have a mock argument between people who know that the important number is around $300 billion. With a few honorable exceptions, the political class is united in ignoring, as Gramm-Rudman permits them to do, the part played by all the trust-fund surpluses, the largest of which is the Social Security surplus, generated by a regressive payroll tax.

This nation had a mighty argument concerning enactment of the 16th Amendment—the income tax—which implemented an ethical judgment. Now the nation is almost absentmindedly reducing the importance of the income tax relative to the payroll tax.

A Democratic-controlled Congress is untroubled by the flood of revenues from that tax, revenues surging through the federal budget and out into operating expenses for the government. These expenses include debt service of about $180 billion in interest payments, largely to wealthy individuals and institutions.

Republicans have seized the low ground, aggressively embracing the beggar-the-next-generation policy of borrow, borrow, spend, spend, elect, elect. But give Republicans their due. They campaigned on a promise to do precisely that. But you would think Democrats would be bothered about using Social Security for this regressive transfer of wealth.

The deficit (as misleadingly calculated) for fiscal 1989 was about $160 billion. It was $160 billion even though the Social Security surplus ($50-some billion and rising about $10 billion a year, $115,000 an hour) was counted in with the rest of the government's revenue. If the Social Security surplus (and unspent tax revenues in Medicare, civil service and military retirement, highway and airport trust funds) were taken out of the equation, the government's unmasked operating deficit would be approaching $300 billion.

But watch your—our—language. The real name for the Social Security "surplus" is "reserves." Unfortunately for taxpayers and retirees beginning around the year 2030, the reserves are not being reserved. They are supposed to be there when the current ratio of workers to retirees shifts toward fewer workers and more retirees. Then the reserves are to be drawn down, to zero around 2050.

But because the reserves are being treated like a surplus—like a windfall—the nation is sleepwalking toward one of three, or a combination of three, nasty choices. The three are: huge tax increases to fund Social Security's promises from general revenues; or staggering amounts of borrowing to fund the system; or repudiation of the great compact with the people and contraction of Social Security into a means-tested welfare program.

By then, today's political class will be long gone. That is why the country proceeds with a misuse of resources on a scale guaranteed to damage its standard of living. This misuse will mean worse industry, science, medicine—everything—for our children's children than they would have had if we were not foisting upon them, through improvident borrowing, a large portion of the costs of our standard of living.

Senator Rudman (R–N.H.) has always called Gramm-Rudman "a bad idea whose time has come," because it exerts some pressure for deficit reduction: without it the deficit would have risen faster than it has these last two years. But how do you count the cost of the increase in Washington's CQ—cynicism quotient?

It is probably a felony—a crime against consumerism—to print a misleading health claim on a box of cornflakes. But bipartisan deception of the nation about the real size, regressive financing and ruinous consequences of the deficit? That is routine. The President says to his fellow politicians (who nod contentedly): Hey, we weren't sent here to bicker.

October 8, 1989

Dr. Moynihan Suggests Surgery

The first tick of the clock on New Year's Day triggered another phase of one of the nine tax increases of the nine Reagan-Bush years. And this year will be just 23 days old when Senator Pat Moynihan proposes a bill to repeal this most recent tax increase, and thereby begin to stop "the leakage of reality from American life."

He would repeal the Social Security tax hike. That increase was proposed by the 1983 Greenspan Commission, of which Moynihan (D-N.Y.) was a member. He also would further cut the Social Security tax rate on January 1, 1991. This would sharply increase the reported budget deficit (by $62 billion through 1991 alone), but only by revealing what the government's real operating deficit is.

Moynihan's measure would stop the swelling of a huge Social Security surplus. By including that surplus (and those of other trust funds) in the unified budget, the real deficit—approaching $300 billion—is cut in half, cosmetically.

The Greenspan Commission proposed the Social Security tax increases to build reserves for the population "bubble" of baby-boom retirees next century. But the reserves are not being reserved. They are being spent, masking the real deficit. So either way, large tax increases will be needed in the future. By making it official that Social Security is an intergenerational transfer-payment program, on a pay-as-you-go basis, Moynihan would make the real deficit—the gap between government outlays and non–Social Security revenues—visible.

Moynihan is practicing sauce-for-the-gander politics, doing for Democrats what Reagan and Stockman did to Democrats. In 1981, Reagan and Stockman said, to themselves, in effect: Maybe our tax cuts will be self-financing—so stimulative to the economy that no deficit will occur. But if not, the deficits will serve a political good by applying pressure for restraint on the growth of government.

Moynihan denounced this reckless abuse of fiscal policy for political purposes. But now he, too, is willing, and rightly so, to reduce the revenue base of the government for therapeutic purposes. In 1983, he supported the schedule of Social Security tax increases on the assumption that the surpluses would be put to some use other than the perpetuation of fraud, the disguising of the government's operating deficit.

Ideally, Moynihan's proposal would confront the government with the need either to make politically difficult spending cuts or adopt more candid, rational and equitable revenue sources to shrink the real huge deficit, suddenly made visible. Alas, as the 1980s showed, there is a third course—a borrowing binge to finance the deficits. However, a necessary precondition for sound policy is a willingness to face facts, such as this: After five years under Gramm-Rudman, the government's operating deficit is growing.

Some liberals may flinch from Moynihan's radical budget surgery. Because taxophobia is the strongest political passion today, some liberals believe the flow of Social Security tax dollars is necessary for domestic spending programs. But liberals cannot remain liberals and remain collaborators in the current process whereby Social Security revenues are used for the slow, surreptitious semirepeal of a great liberal achievement: the 16th Amendment, and heavy reliance on the income tax.

That has been happening, with the connivance of a Democratic-controlled Congress. Federal taxes in the first year of the Bush administration are about what they were in the last year of the Carter administration, around 19 percent of GNP. What the "Reagan revolution" changed radically is the incidence of taxation. Income taxes were cut and made less progressive. The regressive Social Security tax rate (the same rate for all payers; and income above $51,300 is exempt) increased 25 percent in the 1980s. Now the burden of the Social Security tax (including the employer's share) is larger than the income-tax burden for 74 percent of all taxpayers.

Conservatives, too, should rally 'round Moynihan, and not just because some of them have never met a tax cut they didn't like. Thoughtful conservatives fear that the Social Security surplus, perhaps supplemented by a "peace dividend" carved from the defense budget, may be used by liberals to fund new government programs, perhaps addressing the most pervasive anxiety of the 1990s—health care for an aging population, parents who caused the baby boom.

Spending, say, $50 billion on a continuing basis for a politically well-crafted program could, says Texas's Republican Senator Phil Gramm, "move millions of votes." Gramm fears a paradox: The anticommunist rebellion against statism in the Soviet bloc could give rise to a defense-cutting euphoria that, combined with Social Security surpluses, results in too much government here.

That is one possible choice. But before the choosing begins, Moynihan's bill, a blow for candor and equity, should be passed. It would deprive Democrats and Republicans of the choice of continuing the pretense that the deficit is disappearing.

January 11, 1990

To the Boca Raton Station

The five-paragraph dispatch was buried deep in the *Wall Street Journal*, as befits news of class struggle in this moment of capitalist triumphalism. The small, laconic headline was: MOYNIHAN PLAN OPPOSED BY MANUFACTURING GROUP.

The board of the National Association of Manufacturers had met and frowned mightily against Senator Moynihan's proposal to cut Social Security payroll taxes. Such a cut would partially unmask the real deficit, would cost the government $62 billion over the next two years, for starters, and would (one can hear the NAM say) cause grass to grow in the streets of America's cities.

The NAM statement says, with more fervor than rigor, this: Changing the schedule of Social Security tax increases adopted in 1983 would "erode whatever confidence remains that any tax structure adopted by the Congress will actually remain in place for more than a few short years."

Actually, the NAM is broad-minded about tax changes. It favors cutting the capital-gains rate which was set in 1986. But speaking about the Moynihan proposal, the NAM says: It is bad because it would lead to changes in the venerable income-tax structure adopted in 1986. (That was, evidently, before the birth of the principle that all tax changes, other than in the capital-gains rate, are reprehensible.)

The NAM's statement is admirably forthright: "The sharp increase in the deficit would generate intense pressure for offsetting spending cuts and/or tax increases, with the likeliest result politically being income-tax increases, especially on corporations."

Precisely.

The NAM story was datelined Boca Raton, Florida.

A famous book on Europe's revolutionary tradition is titled *To the Finland Station*, a reference to the Petrograd (as it then was and may again be) railroad station where Lenin arrived in 1917, bearing the revolutionary impulse. When the history of America's nonrevolutionary tradition is written, it should be titled *To the Boca Raton Resort and Club*. That is where the ruling class goes to recuperate from the rigors of capitalism and to plan the defense of trickle-down economics against the ingratitude of those who are trickled upon.

The NAM's position is understandable and defensible—indeed, it could have been stronger. It could have truly said: Corporations do not pay taxes, they collect them, so increased corporate taxes may be in many ways regressive, depending on how they are passed.

But the NAM is understandably reluctant to raise the subject of regressivity while defending current Social Security taxes.

The NAM is putting up a proper defense of its constituency's interest. What is indefensible is the Democrats' invertebrate response to Moynihan's idea. Does the Democratic Party differ in any interesting way from the NAM? Are the constituencies the same?

Felix Rohatyn, the financier and Democrat who helped New York City through its fiscal crisis in the 1970s, says any analysis of the increasing regressivity of social policy should examine state and local taxes, too. He says the effect of Reagan-Bush policies has been to enlarge the mandates of state and local governments, while shrinking the federal resources for them. Thus local governments have been driven into deeper reliance on regressive sales and property taxes.

Many Democrats (there they go again, off on another retreat to think; here they come, behaving in a way that indicates they played volleyball instead) say Moynihan's proposal would provoke a "crisis." In Washington, "crisis" is a noun denoting any situation in which politicians must make choices that are preceded by a modicum of thought about large questions and followed by the need to say something intelligible about the principles that dictated the choices.

Yes, cutting Social Security taxes without knowing what compensatory action would be taken would be risky. Or, as Democrats like to say soberly, it would be "irresponsible." They should remember the wisdom of Trollope's Duke of Omnium: "There is such a thing as a conscience with such a fine edge that it will allow a man to do nothing."

Moynihan's Democratic traducers say: Gee, if we open large questions of taxation and distributive justice, who knows what the majority might do to us? The rumor persists that Democrats are the majority. But rumors often are wrong, such as the rumor that Democrats comprise the "opposition." That canard is refuted by this fact: Oppositions oppose.

Democrats lack confidence in themselves, and who shall say they are wrong? They do, after all, know one thing best: themselves. But politics would be more satisfying if they had the brio of the Catholic priest who, when asked how one could come to know the Church's view of heaven and hell, said: "Die."

February 18, 1990

Listen to the Bridges

New York, New York, it's a wonderful town [songwriters are not under oath], the Bronx is up and the Battery's down. And so, almost, is the Williamsburg Bridge. That 85-year-old suspension span across the East River connects Manhattan with America, which may not be in the national interest, but nearly a quarter of a million people use it daily. Used it. Since last Tuesday only pedestrians and bicyclists do. It is not quite collapsing—yet—but it is unsafe for vehicular traffic, and that is a considerable defect in a bridge.

The discovery last week of its corroded condition was serendipitous. The discovery occurred while the three surviving Democratic presidential candidates were clashing around the Empire State promising to make America into a paradise and, in their spare time, pacify the Middle East. The mere crumbling of a bridge is too mundane a matter to arrest the attention of candidates who are bent on the betterment of all mankind. However, the sounds made by that tired old bridge (it was screeching and squealing ominously) should be listened to. It tells us more about our future than the candidates do. The nation has a huge bill coming due for the neglect of its infrastructure, meaning bridges, roads, airports, waterways, water and sewer systems—all the things that make everything else possible.

This neglect, which reflects a weak ethic of common provision, may be a consequence of our individualism. Individually, Americans are exercising more and eating more sensibly to maintain their personal infrastructures while the nation's physical plant deteriorates. In the years dead ahead that physical plant is going to force itself upon our attention. It will be something to think about while we creep along in increasingly congested traffic, or wait for our delayed flights to take off at overburdened airports.

The *National Journal* reports that one out of four bridges is considered dangerous. More than 4,100 are closed. Every two days a bridge collapses. Sixty-five percent of the Interstate Highway System is in need of rehabilitation. The average age of the 184 principal locks on the inland waterway system is 40 years. The Army Corps of Engineers says 3,000 dams in populated areas are hazardous. Air traffic has doubled in the 14 years since the last new commercial airport (Dallas–Ft. Worth) opened. Los Angeles needs to spend $111 million more every year just repairing streets or 60 percent of them will be unusable by the end of the century.

The Environmental Protection Agency says $108 billion will be needed between now and then just for construction of new sewage treatment plants.

OK, some of these numbers may involve overreaching and attention seizing and an appetite for pork. Still, there are many needs and not enough money. The cost of public-works investment is substantial, but so is the cost of underinvestment. Millions of worker-years are lost as congestion and detours sap economic efficiency. The cost of Los Angeles County congestion is estimated to be nearly half a million hours a day and half a billion dollars' worth of working time (and 72 million gallons of gas) a year. Unfortunately, blocking the road to a solution is a mountain— Mount Deficit.

The deficit is the numerical expression of a cultural tendency, the national tendency to live for the moment and beyond our means, consuming more than we produce and investing too little, heedless about the future. A government devoting 14 percent of its budget to pay interest on its debt—to rent money—has not enough money for the physical prerequisites of efficient and commodious living. Four federal trust funds—highway, transit, aviation and waterways—had a combined cash balance of about $24 billion at the end of 1987, all of it from user fees that can be spent only on infrastructure. But our leaders, ever imaginative at cooking the books to make the deficit seem smaller than it is, are hoarding the money. This is done so that deficit estimates will be smaller and the Gramm-Rudman knife will be easier to avoid.

An earlier, more robust America had more energetic leaders regarding "internal improvements." In 1808 Jefferson's Treasury Secretary, Albert Gallatin, issued his *Report on Roads and Canals*, a proposed network of projects, most of which were built over 60 years. It is unfortunate they were not built sooner. In 1816 John C. Calhoun, who eventually would sow seeds of secession, introduced a bill for internal improvements at federal expense. He warned that New York and other Northern states had public and private financial resources sufficient for such improvements, but that the South did not. Without federal help, the South would be consigned to inferiority, and "disunion" might result. President Madison, taking a crabbed view of federal power, vetoed the bill as unconstitutional. Denied federal help, the South's dependence on slavery grew, as did its sense of separateness.

Disunion is not a danger today. Decay is. That is a pity because public works are the sort of things government is good at. The Tennessee Valley Authority and the Interstate Highway System were not just good in themselves, they were good for the morale of government, which periodically needs some inspiriting successes. Alas, in election years we have this sort of dispiriting experience:

You are driving warily down a street cratered with potholes deep enough to serve as silos for the MX missile. Your car radio is emitting the sounds of candidates promising to provide "meaningful jobs" and "a sense of community" in "model cities" in a disarmed world. And you are thinking (if thinking is possible as you jolt along, your radio chattering and radial tires disintegrating): Thanks a lot, but could we please start our trip to utopia on a well-paved street leading to a structurally sound bridge?

April 25, 1988

Hamiltonian Conservatism and "Internal Improvements"

On March 9, 1832, a 23-year-old candidate for the Illinois General Assembly told Sangamon County voters "my sentiments with regard to local affairs." His first sentiment was "the public utility of internal improvements," particularly "the opening of good roads [and] the clearing of navigable streams." Thus did Abraham Lincoln's public life commence with concern about what is now called "infrastructure."

Today Transportation Secretary Samuel Skinner, from Illinois, has the challenging task of selling a taxaphobic nation on the rationality of spending much more on infrastructure. Americans already spend $800 billion for transportation products and services each year. Eighteen percent of GNP is spent on transportation, which employs one-tenth of the work force. It is perhaps natural that the public considers infrastructure a banal subject. Natural, but unhistorical.

In 1816, John Calhoun introduced legislation for a federal program of internal improvements as a means of avoiding disunion. President Madison, believing Congress not constitutionally empowered to do such things, vetoed it. So prosperous Northern states built their own improvements and the South sank into inferiority and increasing dependence on slavery.

Historian James McPherson writes that prior to 1815 most roads were rutted paths impassable in wet weather. Commerce depended on sailing ships and riverboats. The cost of moving goods 30 miles inland equaled the cost of moving them across the Atlantic. Transatlantic trade exceeded inland commerce and economic growth barely exceeded population growth.

But then came all-weather macadamized roads. The Erie Canal ignited construction: 3,700 miles of canal by 1850. Next, railroads freed commerce from frozen canals in winter, cut travel time from New York to Chicago from three weeks to two days, and cut the price of shipping a ton of wheat from Buffalo to New York from $100 to $10. The difference between the wholesale price of pork in Cincinnati and New York plummeted from $9.53 to $1.18. Suddenly urban workers had more money to spend on manufactured goods.

Today the condition of the infrastructure is just as dramatically connected with economic vitality. Unfortunately, the wearing out of America, which is one aspect of today's incontinent pursuit of current consumption, is accelerating. Since 1960, investment in infrastructure has fallen more than 50 percent as a percentage of GNP, which explains much of America's drop in productivity. Illustrations abound.

Of America's 575,000 highway bridges, 42 percent are structurally deficient (closed or restricted to light traffic) or functionally obsolete. A bridge fails every two days. Consider one bridge with a light load of 2,000 cars and 200 trucks a day: If trucks must detour, adding five miles to their routes at 50 cents a mile, costs increase $182,500 per year. If cars must detour (figuring 20 cents a mile), the annual cost is $730,000.

Over the last two decades, traffic has grown five times faster than highway capacity. In the next two decades, congestion is projected to become five times worse. Airports anticipate a 72 percent increase in passenger volume in this decade; by 1997, 33 major airports are expected to experience, cumulatively, 20,000 hours of delays annually. More billions of gallons of gasoline and billions of dollars' worth of aircraft fuel and flight-crew time will be wasted yearly.

Time is indeed money and already billions of dollars are being lost because people and freight are congealed in traffic. There are 3 million truck, bus, taxi and delivery-vehicle drivers stuck there, being paid by the hour. Transportation is 15 to 30 percent of the price of agriculture products. A worker delayed by even 10 minutes each way during 45 years of commuting wastes the equivalent of two working years. Slow, unpredictable traffic prevents businesses from relying on "just in time" delivery of raw materials and parts, a technique for reducing inventory costs.

You get the picture. The first Republican President certainly did. A crimson thread of consistency connects Lincoln's passion for internal improvements with his later mission of binding the nation together as a land of opportunity. The 9th Republican President, in his exuberance, understood the value of infrastructure abroad: Teddy Roosevelt built the Panama Canal.

Transportation and other infrastructure issues should bring out a strong Hamiltonian streak in American conservatives who too often talk

the anachronistic language of Jeffersonian small-government sentimentality, of nostalgia for another America. In the debate now beginning
about transportation policy, we shall see if the 18th Republican President
is the kind of conservative who understands the need to spend in order
to conserve and enlarge the nation's sinews.

March 11, 1990

The Basin Runneth Over

LOS ANGELES—Fascinating problems of the fast-unfolding future can
be seen in the Los Angeles Basin and in the working of the law of
cumulation: When many millions of people in a metropolitan area do
anything—start their cars, mow their lawns, spray their hair, paint their
houses—there are big consequences.

Speaking of paint, it is time to acquaint you, gentle reader, with yet
another cause for anxiety, something else to make the world around you
seem menacing. Paint pollution—stuff released into the air by drying
paint and solvents on houses, cars, aircraft and other products—is a
major source of hydrocarbon pollution in the Basin, 14 times larger than
the oil refineries. It could be worse: it once was. Thirty years ago a can
of paint contained one-third solids and two-thirds "carrier" which, when
evaporating, dirtied the air. Now the ratio of the benign to the polluting
ingredients is better. But it is not good enough. The Basin is second only
to North Carolina–Virginia in the manufacture of furniture. Improved
coatings would mean—will mean, when government promotes
research—less gunk in Los Angeles lungs.

The Los Angeles Basin is far from Washington, D.C., and the presidential pinnacle of government that is so much on American minds just
now. But out there one of America's most interesting governmental
agencies is wrestling with problems of the modern megalopolis. It is the
South Coast Air Quality Management District. Its jurisdiction is the
Basin. Standing alone the Basin would be the world's 11th-largest economy. It is the nation's biggest manufacturing center. In the 1970s, when
manufacturing employment declined nationwide, it grew by 20 percent
in the Basin. The SCAQMD is responsible for a region of 13,000 square
miles, larger than nine states. Its population of 12 million—5 percent of
the nation—is larger than that of 47 states. Just 20 years ago there were
fewer than 4 million people there. Eighteen million are expected by
2010. In this teeming polyglot sprawl of population, government is testing its ability to manage growth.

We are still learning about pollutants that are formed in the air from other pollutants emitted from vehicles and stationary sources. For example, the sunshine that attracts people to southern California produces ozone by photochemical reaction from 2,286 tons of hydrocarbons and nitrogen oxides pumped into the air every day. The Basin's biggest problem is vehicular congestion. It degrades the environment, involves economic waste and takes a huge human toll in stress and frustration.

Every day millions of people move many millions of miles through this Basin in vehicles propelled by exploding fuel. The explosions are less polluting than they used to be but there are limits to how clean they can be. Today's cars emit only 20 percent of the pollutants of 1960s cars but there are so many more cars (and trucks and motorcycles and planes and boats) and the pollutants cumulate. In the last 10 years the population of the Basin has increased 13 percent but vehicle-miles have increased 39 percent. This is primarily because of the entry of women into the work force and because housing costs cause many people to live far—often a two-hour commute—from their workplace.

Congestion has spurred the growth of several industries, such as car telephones (and car fax machines—really) and books on tape, as commuters try to make use of time spent trapped in traffic. Billions of dollars' worth of productivity are lost in the hours wasted inching along coagulated freeways. Too many people are commuting alone: today 10 vehicles are delivering an average of 11 people to work. However, one employer, Arco, uses financial incentives and disincentives (subsidized car pooling, charges for parking) to get 20 workers arriving in every 10 vehicles. Four-day workweeks of 10-hour days would reduce vehicle-miles. Studies are being made of the productivity of people who work at home because computers could make many people into "electronic commuters." Again, remember the law of cumulation: When millions of people change their behavior a bit, it makes a big difference.

The need for big differences is changing political choices. Conservatives tend to be libertarians who think that government should go stand in a corner and let private desires and market forces rip. Thus it was an eyebrow-raising event when conservative Governor George Deukmejian said it is time to get trucks off the freeways at peak hours.

The conservative dilemma is that trying to solve congestion with more concrete—more freeways—would mean higher taxes. It would cost $100 billion just to hold the line at today's level of congestion 10 years from now. And there would be hell to pay if anyone tried to run new freeways through this now densely populated Basin. Most Americans are fierce libertarians where their cars are concerned. They believe what the current Mr. Goodwrench commercial proclaims: "It's not just your car, it's your freedom." They believe that freeway lanes reserved for car-poolers are the signature of Big Brother. Next thing you know we will have to ask bureaucrats for permission to have babies.

No we won't, but, speaking of babies, 660 percent of the population growth in the Basin is not from people moving in, it is from people already here having babies. The archetypal California house has a lawn littered with bicycles. But when the bike riders turn 16 they want cars. And a few years later they want jobs and houses. U.S. birthrates are lower than those in many less-developed nations, but an American baby is more of a challenge to the environment than is a Third World baby. Economic development always means putting stress on the planet.

In the last decade of the century, development will put new kinds of stresses on American politics. Los Angeles is the laboratory for coping collectively with the large cumulative consequences of individuals' behaviors. F. Scott Fitzgerald called Los Angeles—then a mere toddler of a town—"the Great Gatsby of American cities." The description was not an encomium. It connoted vulgarity and an overflowing adrenaline that could be menacing. But Los Angeles's vitality, born of diversity (in one high school's student body 85 languages are spoken), makes it the laboratory where we test formulas for taming the future.

January 30, 1989

Dayton's Mundane Machines and Your Taxes

DAYTON, OHIO—History is spread across this country as evenly as honey on toast. You can not drive for long down any highway without coming upon some site of the distinctive American genius for democratizing history-making. Dayton, for example, is the site of one of those commonplace developments that altered habits of thought as well as action.

Something that happened in this middling-sized city in the middle of the state that begins the Middle West shows how middle-class concerns shape the history of our commercial society. Dayton may be most famous for the bicycle shop in which the Wright brothers tinkered with the technology that would, in time, democratize the experience of long-distance travel. But Dayton also deserves fame for a more mundane machine.

A list of cities that have shaped our world would include London and New York (finance), Washington (freedom), Moscow (revolution), Paris (art), Vienna (philosophy and psychology). And add Dayton, birthplace of the cash register.

In the 1870s, James Ritty was running a saloon here and wondering why business was brisk but profits were slim. He suspected that his bartenders were dipping their fingers in the till. Driven by distress to a breakdown, he embarked on a vacation voyage to Europe. While on board, he became fascinated by a machine in the ship's engine room that recorded each rotation of the propeller shaft. It was an epiphany. Perhaps a machine could be built that would record each sale in a saloon.

Cutting short his vacation, he dashed back to Dayton and invented the cash register. "Ritty's Incorruptible Cashier" was soon refined to record all transactions on a paper roll. Retailing—among other things—was on the way to being transformed.

Ritty soon sold his struggling business for $1,000 to a clever fellow who added a bell that rang when the cash drawer was opened. The official history of Dayton's National Cash Register Company (now NCR) said that the bell "like the historic Revolutionary shot fired at Lexington . . . would be heard around the world."

What was heard around America was the new phrase "ringing up a sale." Historian Daniel Boorstin writes: "Americans had thus found a way to give a new publicity to the shopkeeper's smallest transaction. Shopping now was a semipublic, communal activity, announced by the ringing of bells."

The company soon was owned by John Henry Patterson, a coal dealer who found that his business became profitable only after he replaced his cashbox with a cash register. A company report from 1888 contains this gem: "A hotel keeper when asked why he did not discharge his bartender who had purchased a $1,000 diamond pin, out of a salary of $10 per week before he had been at work six months, said that if he did so, he would only have to lose another $1,000 on the next man because the new man would do the same thing."

Patterson encountered resistance to cash registers in businesses whose employees considered the machines a slur on their characters. However, he was not one to be defeated. When his doctors ordered him to do daily calisthenics, he ordered his executives to join him at five A.M. One executive whose performance displeased Patterson arrived at work one morning to find the charred remains of his desk and other office effects in a smoldering pile in front of the factory. Nowadays that is called negative feedback.

Patterson added to his machines devices for printing customers' receipts and classifying sales by sales persons and departments. All this, according to Boorstin, "reinforced the nation's number consciousness." As a result, people "began to think quantitatively about their activities, their products and their income. They were putting themselves in count-less new statistical communities." The most important came to be called brackets.

Next came calculating machines. As more and more precise informa-tion became available about the quantity of things, Americans acquired the habit of thinking quantitatively, especially about incomes. In a nation of mobile immigrants, where people moved around geographically and up and down the social scale, income (rather than Old World categories of "property" and "wealth") was the most useful way of quantifying stan-dards of living.

By the end of the 19th century, a powerful political movement for a new kind of taxation was forming around this way of thinking. And in the 20th century, as Boorstin says, "income consciousness, no longer merely a byproduct of technology or of government statistics, became a civic obligation, under penalty of fine and imprisonment"—and under an an-nual mid-April deadline.

Do not blame Dayton's ringing machines for your income taxes that are due soon. But there is a connection.

April 6, 1989

Playing With Guns

President Bush, balancing when he should be choosing, says he is seeking "an accommodation between the police and the sporting inter-est" regarding assault rifles. So much for the interest of ghettos, where such guns are frequently fired.

The urban poor are, as usual, invisible while their betters plan their betterment. But the poor have a special interest in firearms policy. They would gain from a prompt ban on assault rifles and would suffer from gun control focused, as it usually is, on handguns.

The reasons for acting forcefully against the former are reasons for leaving the latter alone. Assault weapons are not yet prevalent and never will be needed for legitimate civilian activities. Handguns are widely dispersed and poignantly necessary for some people.

Don Kates, Jr., notes that New York's pioneering Sullivan Law (1911) was an example of gun control advocated by conservatives who associated handguns with foreign-born anarchists, labor agitators and criminals. Newspapers of the day denounced "low-browed foreigners" with guns, guns in the pockets of "ignorant and quarrelsome immigrants of law-breaking propensities."

Today, too, there is a class bias in the gun-control argument. Literature from the National Coalition to Ban Handguns includes this gem:

Q. Does the banning of handguns discriminate against minority members of society?

A. No. Handguns would be illegal in the hands of the total populace, including all racial and religious groups, the rich and poor alike.

Wonderful. It would impartially disarm white, safe Park Avenue and the South Bronx, a war zone.

Kates makes a disturbing but not unsupported argument as follows: Many urban Americans live where government cannot, or will not, enforce its proper monopoly on the use of force. Given this failure, or abdication, by government it is unseemly for the safe majority to deny the endangered minority the handguns needed for self-help.

A Chicago judge writing in a legal publication stresses that his readers "would not go into ghetto areas except in broad daylight under the most optimum conditions—surely not at night, alone or on foot. But some people have no choice. To live or work or have some need to be on this 'frontier' imposes a fear which is tempered by possession of a gun."

Kates cites data that indicate that "handgun-armed citizens actually thwart almost as many crimes annually as handgun-armed criminals succeed in committing. Citizens acting in legitimate self-defense kill about three times more assailants and robbers than do police." He says prison surveys show that criminals fear armed victims more than police and that fear of armed civilians deters criminals into nonconfrontational crime. Burglars rarely encounter armed victims because burglars target unoccupied premises. Even so, more burglars meet armed resistance than are arrested and sent to prison.

About half of America's households possess at least one gun. Among those owning at least one gun, the average is three. About 50 million households have handguns. Prohibition of handguns would be a bigger failure than prohibition of gin. "Handguns, unlike liquor," notes Kates, "are reusable, and their continued use does not involve the visibility of perpetual illegal purchase."

Assault rifles are different. Daryl Gates, Los Angeles police chief, says: "A reasonable right to bear arms does not mandate that weapons designed and built for the express purpose of killing human beings on battlefields be made available to the general public. In fact, the general public is already prohibited by the National Firearms Act from owning most weapons made for that purpose."

But assault rifles have enthusiasts (the Bush administration even worries about the interests of "gun collectors"), so a President whose primary objective is popularity is resorting to a tested technique: When the subject is politically problematic, swallow it up in a larger subject.

Hence the administration's position is: Assault weapons are misused by drug dealers, so let's not ban the guns; let's win "the war" on drugs which must be won (in the words of Attorney General Dick Thornburgh last Sunday) "on the battlefield of values."

Meanwhile, back on the nonmetaphysical battlefield where many poor people live, the poor must be bemused by Bush's idea that his temporary ban on the importation of some rifles is a "cooling-off" period. It is not cooling their streets, but it is not supposed to.

No wonder the National Rifle Association is so pleased by Bush's policy. The policy is to cool off public opinion until some fresh menace— say, a tainted banana from some banana republic—appears, a menace that threatens substantial interests, like the serenity of the comfortable.

March 23, 1989

The Weathervane of the Western World

Our leaders are talking a lot about hunters. They have to talk loudly to be heard over the Washington gunfire that this year, through last Friday, had killed 113. People, not deer. Three questions come to mind: Would it give deer too big a break if hunters were restricted to rifles that cannot fire quite as fast as those semiautomatic assault rifles that can enfilade a forest? And: Why are they called assault rifles? And: Do hunters ever say to their buddies, "Hey, let's go assaulting"? The rifles are called that because they are made to hurl a hail of bullets in front of advancing troops. Hence they are useful for settling commercial disputes between drug dealers. But back to today's subject, hunting. Surely any hunter who needs 30 or even five shots to kill his quarry is an antisportsman deriving sick delight from slaughtering something immobile enough to be riddled that way.

Why are we talking about hunting when the issue is urban mayhem? Because solicitude for "sportsmen" is, it seems, uppermost in Washington minds, including the President's. Regarding assault rifles he has been at his inarticulate and muddled worst. Shortly after the California school-yard massacre, Bush gave the press some of that much praised "access" and gave the country a dismaying glimpse of his "mode." He said: "Whenever there is a crime involving a firearm, there are various groups, some of them quite persuasive in their logic, that think you can ban certain kinds of guns, and I am not in that mode. I am in the mode of being deeply concerned and would like to be part of finding a national

answer to this problem." Perhaps Bush is considered gentlemanly because he praises persuasive logic while disregarding it.

Public opinion, shaped by carnage in the nation's capital, is changing.
So, predictably, a presidential aide has dutifully announced that Bush is
"deeply torn" by this gun issue. But in what depths is the tearing taking
place? In the constitutional law of it? Let us not dignify his poll-reading
as a lonely meditation on individual liberty. Bush's views are undergoing
what he calls a "pulse change" (that is Bushspeak for trimming) because
his ancient fear of the gun lobby is balanced by a fresh fear of public
revulsion.

The New York Times reports, with depressing plausibility, that some
GOP congressional and White House leaders recently retreated to Virginia to think and came to a conclusion: "We're in trouble, we need an
issue, and we need one fast." In mid-March of Year 1, with the needle
of the administration's philosophic fuel gauge registering empty, they
thought: Bush's theme-a-week presidency can milk some mileage from
semiautomatic rifles. So Bush, the weathervane of the Western world,
acquiesced in an aide's (William Bennett's) tentative, almost timid idea:
Ban a few (imports) for a while (pending study). The policemen Bush
used as props last fall in his campaign against Willie Horton favor bolder
action. So do doctors. Because of these rifles' volume of fire and muzzle
velocity, emergency wards must use Vietnam War medical techniques
on wounds of a sort once associated only with battlefields.

Any controversy worth a whole week should involve the Constitution.
This does. The Second Amendment says: "A well-regulated militia, being necessary to the security of a free State, the right of the people to
keep and bear arms, shall not be infringed." The original intent of that is
unclear. Was it to guarantee to individuals the right to bear arms, or to
states the right to organize militias? The Constitution came from the
Philadelphia convention without the Bill of Rights, to which that amendment belongs. The enumeration of rights was a price of ratification,
allaying fears that the Constitution went too far toward centralization of
power. So the amendment seems more concerned with the rights of
militia-forming states than of gun-toting individuals. Perhaps we should
amend the amendment to say: "The right to bear arms shall be enjoyed
by all those, but only those, who are active members of a well-regulated
militia." If you want to play with guns, join a well-regulated militia, one
that drills on the village green, in December sleet and August heat.

Just kidding. Law must not diverge far from culture so, although the
culture is becoming more grown-up about guns, the law will for a long
time be too permissive. But must we talk about hunting when the issue
is the importation, domestic manufacture and sale of weapons no sensible
society should permit in circulation? The reason we do is political fear of

a lobby. It is an old story. So is this. In a bourgeois city, violence by the underclass against itself is a "concern" to correct thinkers. But when bullets come near the bourgeoisie, that's a *crisis*. However bullets rarely do.

Our leaders are talking about hunters' rights. Most hunters, like most lawmakers, are white and middle-class. While terrified poor black families live and die amid gunfire, white politicians who live and work in tranquil neighborhoods weigh, with Solomonic judiciousness, the right of sportsmen to have military arsenals against the right of poor people not to have neighborhoods sounding at night like the third afternoon at Gettysburg.

A Brooklyn man says, "The kids on the street are becoming connoisseurs of machine guns. They hear a sound and say, 'That's an Uzi'." Bush says, with that ineffable imprecision that sounds funny but isn't, that some people "think you can ban certain kinds of guns." *Think* so? Of course certain kinds of guns can be banned. Any congressman who believes a ban is beyond the wit of mankind should so signify by saying, "I resign." We'll find cleverer congressmen. A ban will not disarm criminal users, at least not soon. But neither is the ban on cocaine now effective. That is not a reason for surrendering. Law's expressive function matters. It is time to express disgust with levels and kinds of violence known in no other developed democracy. And a law banning assault rifles would at least say to the suffering minority that the safe majority cares.

But it doesn't care much or we would not be weighing sportsmen's pleasures against poor people's terrors. If 1 percent of the gunfire heard in Washington's black neighborhoods were heard in, say, white Chevy Chase, the Marines would be deployed there faster than you can say "Halls of Montezuma." Or faster than you can say, as Bush does, "It is time to govern."

March 27, 1989

Slow-Motion Death in Miami

MIAMI—Light from passing traffic shimmers off a yellow satin Los Angeles Lakers warm-up suit on yonder street corner. The wearer of that conspicuous garment is an undercover police officer and before the night ends he and more than 50 colleagues on the Miami Street Narcotics Detail will have sent 68 people to jail, thereby sending a message to the community: Buying drugs is risky business.

The officers congesting the sidewalk at an intersection in the rough

Liberty City neighborhood are dressed in denims, fatigues and other forms of street-corner casual. The only constant is running shoes, which is fine: There will be some "runners" tonight—drug buyers who bolt.

Tonight's walk on the wild side is an exercise in fighting drugs on the demand side. Attempts to destroy drugs in source countries or interdict them en route to this country are insufficient. When a rich country has a multibillion-dollar demand for a product produced by peasants in poor countries, the supply will pour forth. There are not enough U.S. soldiers to seal U.S. borders. Interdiction has been both a resounding success and a demonstrable failure: Quantities seized have increased dramatically, yet the price of cocaine has fallen. So Miami's police department has taken to the streets to target buyers.

At 5:30 P.M., officers establish a command post in a dusty school yard, with facilities for fingerprinting and buses (business will be brisk) to cart customers to jail. Other officers are away arresting the dealers at the intersection that the police will take over for tonight's sting.

A week ago, 250 arrests were made in a sting a few blocks away, but that was a Friday—payday—and tonight, a Thursday, will be relatively slow. Relatively. There will be 68 arrests. Tonight's is the 66th sting. The first 65 resulted in 4,388 arrests. The important number is the small one: 40. Only 40 customers have been caught twice. Stings are repeated until a neighborhood's drug traffic dries up and the traffic is not just displaced to other neighborhoods. Many customers are being "scared straight."

However, conversations with arrested customers compel a dispiriting conclusion about the limits of deterrence. Deterrence depends on a degree of rationality. But some customers have minds hopelessly clouded by addiction, and others are virtually immune to society's information systems, including the media that publicize these stings.

Watching the corner at dusk from a second-story window, an officer sees a man take just two steps from a car and concludes, "He's a buyer— you can tell from the way he walks that he has tunnel vision." Another customer walks right past a news photographer, a white man in a black neighborhood, to make a purchase.

Stings conducted in places like Coconut Grove target yuppie customers who wear khakis and Topsiders when they go in search of weekend party supplies. But places like Liberty City are where sales are most blatant.

As a tall, thin man with a scraggly beard wanders by, an officer murmurs "rock monster." The man's weight loss and glittering eyes ("like a cat's") are signs of "crack" addiction. Rock monsters steal all day and seek crack cocaine by night.

Real addicts are conspicuous by the absence of chains or other gold jewelry. It has all been sold. But many of the customers at this corner tonight are different. They are, so far, occasional users, but still danger-ous to the community as well as themselves. When a community comes to have a critical mass of even recreational users, the pool of dollars calls into existence a merchandizing operation for a mass market.

Only one person arrested this night seemed high at the time. He said he had used "powder" (regular cocaine) three hours earlier. He had the slurred speech and gauntness of a man frying his brain in increasingly frequent chemical bursts. Yet he said something also said by many oth-ers: "I won't use crack."

Anyone can afford crack. A dime-size rock costs $10. But information—probably word-of-mouth—is getting around about its deranging powers. Even this evidence that people are learning has a disheartening side. Repeatedly one heard arrested customers saying they used "only" reg-ular cocaine because "it don't kill as fast."

That is powerful testimony to crack's reputation, but also to the awful, fascinating fatalism of people who, caught in the culture of poverty, calibrate the pace at which they will ingest slow-motion death.

March 31, 1988

Desperate Euphoria in the Ghetto

MIAMI—Tears stream down both cheeks of the woman who stands with her hands bound behind her back by a plastic thong. Her jeans are neatly pressed. She is the mother of four children aged nine, six, one year and three weeks and she has been caught in a police sting, arrested for trying to buy cocaine from one of the undercover police officers swarming around a nearby street corner.

She says, as almost all those arrested do, that she does not do drugs, she only came here at the request of "a friend." Another arrested cus-tomer says, "It just don't pay to do a friend a favor," and the officers smile the thin, weary smiles of people who have heard it all before.

The purpose of such stings is to give drug buyers "a taste of the system." The buyers' hands are bound (how tightly depends on whether they have, in the laconic language of the police, "an attitude problem"). They are marched to a small, crowded, noisy, dirty room in an aban-doned building where arrest forms are filled out.

The trauma of arrest-fingerprinting, seizure of automobiles used to facilitate felonies, the wrath of a spouse, is condign punishment for peo-ple who may never get much other punishment, given the way the mills of justice grind, or fail to. And the trauma is the message of the sting: Buyers as well as suppliers should know that the heat is on.

To one side stands a man who looks like a black Wyatt Earp. Beneath an at-least-ten-gallon cowboy hat is Clarence Dickson, Miami's chief of police.

When in 1960 Dickson approached graduation from the city's police academy, he joined in the class photograph. But he was not in the class photo distributed on graduation day. Another photo had been taken later because his black face was not welcomed. It is a welcome sight today in neighborhoods, white and black, where his men and women are implementing his vow to "take back the streets" by ending blatant drug sales.

He leads a police force traumatized by scandals that followed the hasty hiring of 600 officers in response to the 1980 influx of Cubans from the Mariel boat lift. That frenzied expansion of the force, which swept in some bad apples, and the corruption that comes with huge surges of illegal cash, produced this appalling statistic: In the last two and one-half years, about 100 officers (10 percent of the force) have been arrested, indicted, suspended or have resigned under pressure.

However, no tonic improves police morale quite like aggressive law enforcement, and Dickson has at hand a merry—yes, they are, in their way—band of enforcers, the Street Narcotics Detail. These are men happy in their work because they are welcome in the communities where they do it.

The Detail is composed of black and white officers, but when the task is a sting, and the place is the ghetto, the black officers must do the dealing. A black officer watching his colleagues scoop up drug buyers says, matter-of-factly but also pointedly and unanswerably, that what we are watching is made possible only by affirmative action. If Miami's police force had remained what it, like so many other police forces, was until too recently—too white—this kind of law enforcement would be impossible.

Tonight most of the white officers are driving the unmarked cars that sprint, like quarter horses heading off a steer, when a customer makes a dash to escape in his car. Some of the black officers conducting tonight's sting grew up in this neighborhood. One of them says the plague of drugs is influencing society "as much as the Industrial Revolution did." His emphasis on the comprehensive nature of the drug influence—on the community's economy, manners and mores—is not wrong.

One danger is that many in the ghetto will develop ambivalent feelings about the drug business, just as many in the 19th century did about industrialism. A black officer recognizes a clean, well-dressed infant on the sidewalk and says he remembers seeing the child dirty and ill-clothed. Perhaps the boy has benefited from the trickle-down of drug money. Dealing is a career open to talents, and sometimes produces a sad, desperate euphoria in the ghetto.

But the officer believes that only "half a generation" has been lost, and the tide is turning, thanks in part to the full-court-press of entities like the Detail. A sign that he is right is a slender 12-year-old who, walking past a white man at the wheel of an unmarked car, sizes up the situation and says, "Get 'em, officer."

April 3, 1988

Mothers Who Don't Know How

The almost silent video is short and sweet. And searing. It gives a glimpse of one reason for America's urban regression, the family pathologies that drive the intergenerational transmission of poverty. At first glance the scene the video captures is sweet, a mother feeding her infant. Ten minutes later, at its end, you understand: the mother does not know how to mother.

Jim Egan, a clinical psychiatrist in Washington, says the video, from a steady camera focused on a 22-year-old woman and her six-month-old baby, was made as part of a study of "failure to thrive." The mother feeds the baby, which sits on her knee, with a spoon from a bowl. The spoon moves steadily, the baby makes no sound and neither does the mother. The only noise, every minute or so, is the soft sound of the baby vomiting. This occurs each time the baby turns with its hands extended, reaching for contact with the mother's warmth. The mother reflexively—not unkindly but stiffly—holds the baby away. Then the baby regurgitates the food swallowed since the last rebuff. Vomiting, says Egan, is the baby's tactic for maintaining at least the attention of feeding.

Egan sees many babies with bald spots on the back of their heads, evidence that the babies are left for long stretches on their backs. A child-care—actually, noncare—product popular in some ghettos is a pillow made to hold a bottle next to an infant so the infant can take nourishment without an adult in attendance. But the baby in the video is more fortunate.

The baby's mother, like most young mothers in Washington and many other inner cities, is unmarried. But she is not a moral failure, not what was once called a "fallen woman." One cannot fall from down where she started. She has an emotionally disturbed mother, under whose care the child suffered dreadful diaper rashes. The study of "failure to thrive" is, for her, a school of mothering.

It is perhaps natural to think that parenting is a natural talent, a spontaneously acquired, unlearned skill. It is not. It is learned, as language is, early, and largely by parental example. Parents generally parent as their parents did. As the woman feeds her baby she gives the sort of verbal stimulation she probably got from her mother: none.

Depressed, unstimulating or unavailable mothers produce in babies "maternal deprivation syndrome," which suppresses their infants' development. A mother reared in poverty is apt to have a barren "inner world" of imagination and emotional energy, a consequence of impoverished early experiences. And such a mother nowadays may be the only nurturing adult in an infant's life. A study of turn-of-the-century Massachusetts showed that 90 percent of households included three or more adults—two parents plus perhaps a grandmother, a bachelor uncle, a maiden aunt. Today many homes have but one adult, and infants are handed around to various caretakers. This can be disorienting and developmentally damaging early in life.

Until the 1940s it was widely believed that it did not matter who raised babies, if basic competence was assured. A good orphanage would do. However, subsequent studies documented the bewilderment, withdrawal and depression of infants who begin but do not adequately complete bonding with their mothers. In too many homes today, says Egan, "the lights are on but no one is home." People are there, but not there. Inattentive parents are producing children who are like that: They seem normal but they are not what they should be, what they could have been.

Verbal stimulation of middle-class infants produces in their babble the sounds of the phonetic alphabet much earlier than those sounds occur in the babble of lower-class children. Will children reared in poverty catch up in school? Probably not. They are not just behind; they are, in a sense, crippled. Animals reared in nonstimulative isolation have been shown to have less brain weight than those reared amid the stimulation of company. Those reared in the stimulative environment have a higher ratio of differentiated (specialized functioning) to undifferentiated brain cells. Egan's chilling inference is that an infant can fail to develop some early brain functions as a consequence of social deprivation.

Children, says Egan, are like computers in that what goes in comes out. And each child gets only one floppy disk. He says there is a critical period early in the developmental process of every infant: The merry-go-round goes around only once and the infant does or does not get the brass ring of the full enjoyment of the potential that was his or her birthright. This fact should shock American sensibilities because it refutes the assumption that equality of opportunity is a fact as long as there are no obvious formal, legal, institutional impediments to it. Hence the vast—and increasingly misplaced—faith in schools as the great equalizers of opportunity for upward mobility in a meritocratic society. But studies of early childhood development indicate that school comes too late for many children. Before they cross their first schoolyard, severe damage has been done to their life chances. Even superb schools could not correct the consequences of early deprivation, and superb schools are not frequently found in the neighborhoods where children damaged by their social environment sustain their damages.

Failing families concentrated in a particular class cause urban regression, but Americans recoil from the fact of class. We see our society through ideologically tinted spectacles that filter out unpleasant evidence, such as: 15 percent of IQ points are experientially rather than genetically based, and the preschool experiences of ghetto children can cost them a significant portion of those points.

Studies of "failure to thrive" babies and their mothers suggest a strategy for combating the syndrome, but the studies also indicate that the strategy cannot be a public health policy. Very early intervention, involving close and protracted supervision of young unmarried mothers, can "jump-start" their mothering skills. But there are too many single mothers who need this long, painstaking, labor-intensive and therefore expensive attention.

As regards incompetent parenting, there also are, Egan emphasizes, gilded ghettos. Their residents include "privileged" children of parents too affluent for their children's good, parents able and eager to give children anything but attention, measuring out what these parents are pleased to call "quality time" in dribs and drabs. There are more ghettos—and more damages to children—than meet the eye.

April 23, 1990

Where Bayonets Are Beside the Point

One March morning some distinguished Washingtonians convened a meeting with a senior adviser to the President in the boardroom of Riggs Bank a block from the White House. Alarmed by violence sparked by the drug epidemic, they asked the presidential adviser if he would advise the President to bring in military forces to patrol Washington. The adviser emphatically said he would not because to do so would be to forsake a precious democratic principle: that the military should not be involved in keeping domestic peace.

That meeting occurred March 17, 1970.

Today the truly terrible ideas do not even have the virtue of originality. Garrisoning the city is again being proposed. There is a way to make conditions here even more acutely embarrassing to the nation: Flood the world with pictures of armed soldiers in open jeeps patrolling the city.

What, exactly, would the soldiers do? "Supplement" the police? How would that work? Would they arrest people? Would they summon the police when they saw something "suspicious"? Such policing judgments are not for amateurs. By what criteria would the occupation of the capital be declared a success and terminated?

The presidential adviser at the March 1970 meeting is now a senator, Pat Moynihan. He says Washington's problems are worse today than they were then. But even earlier, by 1965, the trends were visible that have produced many of the afflictions of Washington and other inner cities.

Robberies in Washington rose from 1,072 in 1960 to 12,236 at the end of the decade, largely as a result of heroin, primarily a male addiction that caused an increase in one-parent families. Crack may be producing "no-parent children."

Drugs are both cause and effect of something unprecedented. For most of two centuries, Americans believed in what came to be called "American exceptionalism." It was the belief that this nation is exempt from the grinding, persisting problems that have troubled older, class-riven societies. Actually, America got most of those problems, but got them later.

"For most of the 20th century," Moynihan says, "the social problems of the United States—always excluding that of race—had first appeared in Europe, as had the first responses." America eventually adopted such responses as workmen's compensation, unemployment insurance, Social Security and heavy government involvement in provision of medical care.

Now, says Moynihan, "we have a new set of problems and there's no European 'solution' at hand." The problem is social regression of a sort without precedent in urban history.

Industrialism and urbanization created many social problems, but also created economic growth and a social surplus for government to divert for the elimination of problems of material deprivation. However, what makes today's form of poverty-amidst-plenty so frustrating is that it cannot be solved or even appreciably dented by normal welfare-state transfer payments.

The intergenerational transmission of poverty is produced by the disintegration of family structure. In Washington, 68.3 percent of minority births are illegitimate (in Baltimore, 80 percent). In what is called a "typical elementary school" in Washington's Anacostia section, 90 percent of all pupils are from single-parent homes.

Twenty-five years ago, the Economic Opportunity Act, the core of the War on Poverty, was enacted. It was, Moynihan says, the beginning of the third phase of the American attempt to eliminate particular kinds of poverty and distress associated with industrialism. The first phase was in the Progressive Era, from Theodore Roosevelt through Wilson. The second was from Franklin Roosevelt through Truman. The third was under Kennedy, Johnson and Nixon.

It was a remarkably continuous project. And remarkably successful, Moynihan says, "where we simply transferred income and services to the elderly—a stable, settled population group." But the project had little success where "poverty had its origin in social behavior," meaning, primarily, family structure.

Today family disintegration is one of the principal correlates of poverty. In 1988, 24 percent of America's 63 million children lived with only one parent, double the 1970 percentage. Most single-parent households are headed by women, and such households have a poverty rate of 55 percent. The Bureau of the Census estimates that only 39 percent of children born in 1988 will live with both parents until their 18th birthday.

Family structure almost certainly now is, as Moynihan and many others suspect, "the principal conduit of class structure." That poses the most immense challenge ever to confront American social policy, a problem of unprecedented complexity, for which there is no "European solution" to emulate.

One thing is certain: Bayonets are beside the point.

April 9, 1989

Fighting Drugs: Blame America First

The martial metaphors miss the point. For all the rhetoric about a "war" on drugs, the government's job is primarily one of pressure and persuasion, comparable to the job the government undertook 35 years ago when the civil-rights crisis could no longer be deferred.

In democracies, where public opinion must be palliated, there are necessary futilities. One such is the warlike aspect of drug policy: the use of AWACS and the Navy and perhaps even the infantry for interdiction of drug shipments.

Interdiction today may be stopping 1 percent of the drug flow. Assume something highly improbable—that extensive use of the military could boost that to 5 percent. Every gram interdicted would be as expensive as a gram of moon rocks.

If we committed large forces for a long time to the depths of Colombian jungles, we probably could succeed in driving the processing apparatus . . . into Peru or Bolivia or elsewhere. In 1984, U.S. and Colombian efforts smashed a "cocaine industrial park" in the jungle—14 laboratories, seven airplanes, barracks for hundreds of workers, 11,000 drums of chemicals, 14 tons of cocaine. The result? A small, brief (five-month) price rise.

In a decade, cocaine traffic has grown from handbag-sized parcels to shipments like the four tons found in a shipment of Brazilian lumber. In 1988, 55 percent of high-school seniors surveyed said cocaine was "fairly easy" or "very easy" to obtain, up from 45 percent in 1984.

Acreage allotted to production of coca leaves has increased enormously. Peru, which produces 60 percent of such leaves, has a per-capita income of $900 a year. America's drug dollars are about equal to the combined GNPs of Peru, Bolivia and Colombia. Those nations' police and judicial systems will not soon suppress an activity that is employing hundreds of thousands of people and is woven into the fabric of those nations' economies.

But, then, political-economic factors here—America's unwillingness to put its money where its mouth is—will keep the drug "war" quite limited. William Bennett, the epigrammatic drug "czar," says "crack is worse than taxes," but his commander-in-chief emphatically disagrees. So there will still be long waiting lists at drug-treatment facilities which, properly funded, could dampen demand.

This is not new. In 1980, Ronald Reagan denounced drugs mightily. But in 1981, the Drug Enforcement Administration was not exempted from budget cuts. Surveillance was cut; so were undercover buys. Republican taxophobia qualifies as a dangerous addiction.

Actually, we already are winning the "war." And as is generally the case in wars, the casualties are disproportionately—and increasingly—among the poor. The use of cocaine and other drugs by high-school seniors has fallen to the lowest level in more than a decade. The information-acquiring segments of the population have got the message: Drugs are dangerous and dumb. Their cachet is gone. Drugs, like cigarettes, are déclassé. A potent weapon in the "war" is adolescent status anxiety.

But people who make it to senior year in high school are not the most at-risk group. Drugs and attendant pathologies are increasingly confined to inner-city enclaves—Beiruts without heavy artillery. Let us assume (it cannot be assumed) that the nation will remain aroused when it realizes that the crisis is one of poor neighborhoods devouring themselves. Is there any model of government success in confronting a task of large-scale behavorial, and hence attitudinal, changes?

The conspicuous government successes of recent generations have included the Second World War and the reconstruction of Europe; TVA and rural electrification; the Manhattan and Apollo projects; the Interstate Highway System. All these were essentially material achievements. Even the radical reduction of poverty among the elderly was essentially a material act—mailing checks to a stable population group.

These achievements are not models for victory in the "war" against the myriad social pathologies of which drug use is part cause and part effect. But there is one heartening analogy. At bottom, the purpose of civil-rights legislation, usually enacted in advance of public attitudes, was attitudinal change. Such legislation was statecraft as soulcraft. It succeeded—not completely, but to a remarkable extent and remarkably quickly.

The drug crisis is not a crisis of Latin American production or of interdiction. It is a crisis of American behavior, of appetites produced by bad attitudes. But political action can change attitudes; it has done so regarding drugs, in segments of society, in this decade.

The crucial prerequisite is political leadership prepared to blame Americans first.

September 7, 1989

A Gang Banger Goes to Jail, Briefly

LOS ANGELES—Across his nearly expressionless face flicker mingled traces of boredom and lightly sleeping menace. Sam (not his real name), wearing blue prisoner's garb at the Los Angeles County Jail, is sitting out his latest sentence, for a drug offense, in one of the two wings reserved for the 700 or so strictly segregated members of two warring gangs, the Bloods and the Crips. Only because I have prompted him, Sam is thinking, as much as he ever does, about tomorrow. He has been a mugger, armed robber, car thief, drug dealer—is he, I ask, running out of career moves? "Naw, the world is too big to run out."

Sam's sabbatical ends soon and he will be out and about, being what he has been since he was expelled from the 10th grade for constant fighting. He is what is known here as a "gang banger."

He cannot count the number of times he has been shot, but he still has in him two of the nine slugs from the first time, which he survived because "the Lord was with me." The Lord would have saved the LAPD a lot of trouble by being elsewhere. Sam is 35, weighs 250 pounds and is the ugly new face on an old phenomenon, urban gangs. Time was when they were part of a rite of passage, a subculture that inner-city adolescents outgrew. But in this drug-swamped decade, gang banging is a career.

Call this the gentrification of juvenile delinquency. The juveniles are staying on, juvenile no more, and acquiring Uzis, Soviet AK-47s and other automatic weapons. "Delinquency," which suggests sporadic naughtiness, does not describe the new epidemic of viciousness, both random and purposive. The violence expresses both the tribalism of small primitive groups and the big business of cocaine and other drugs. What the life often lacks in longevity it makes up for in intensity. Overhearing a detective talking on a telephone, Sam recognizes the name of a murder victim and says, with only slight interest and no surprise, that it is the second of his cousins killed in 10 days. Fifteen-year-olds drive BMWs and make bail from pocket cash. Young teenagers have been arrested with $10,000 in their jeans. No wonder young dealers wear phone beepers in school.

Every ethnic group in this seething city of unmelted blocs contributes to the many hundreds of gangs that have perhaps 70,000 members. But the black community is bleeding most, because of the Bloods and the Crips. The jail world of steel and concrete echoes to the clinking shuffle of lines of men manacled at the ankles, protected from other lines of manacled and color-coded criminals. In this jail, as in the neighborhoods, Crips, who wear blue accessories, would slaughter on sight Bloods wearing any of their trademark red. Why? No reason is required. Atavism often is a sufficient explanation for the random "drive by" shootings that are a favorite mode of self-expression. There is, of course, the traditional territorial imperative, the gangs' struggle for "turf." What is new is the killing for commerce, for market shares in the cocaine and crack business. Also new is an unsentimental view of gangs.

Thirty years ago on Broadway a musical was in its first year of a long run. It was *Romeo and Juliet* set among Manhattan's fighting gangs. *West Side Story* was a facet of the romantic interpretation of gangs. Intellectuals who found the '50s—peace, prosperity, Eisenhower: yuck— boringly bourgeois found "alienation" fascinating. They were reading too much Camus and were too much taken with the idea of "existential assertion" through spontaneous violence, such as the murder by Meursault, Camus's "Stranger" (or the murder by Belmondo in the movie *Breathless*). If academic interpreters, pursuing alienation and tenure simultaneously, could not sit in Paris cafés wearing black turtlenecks and sipping black coffee and thinking black thoughts, they could at least sympathize with juvenile delinquents as rebels against the anonymity, anomie or whatever of modern life. Those "kids" did after all (sorry, James Dean) have a "cause." They were avoiding the suffocation of life as "the organization man" (remember that book?). A boy in a "black leather jacket and motorcycle boots" (remember that song? remember Brando as *The Wild One*?) was preferable to *The Man in the Gray Flannel Suit* (remember that novel?).

Viewed through the lenses of the social sciences, juvenile gangs were seen as rebukes to society by society's young victims who were condemned to *Growing Up Absurd* (remember Paul Goodman's polemic?) in industrial societies composed of a "dust of individuals" (Durkheim's phrase). Gangs also were considered "protest masculinity" on the part of young men lacking role models. Or, in a less exotic theory, gangs were regarded as a rational response to society's inadequate "opportunity structure."

Three decades and intellectual light-years separate *West Side Story* from *The Bonfire of the Vanities*, Tom Wolfe's mesmerizing novel about the urban sense of pervasive menace: "It was that deep worry that lives in the base of the skull of every resident of Park Avenue south of 96th Street—a black youth, tall, rangy, wearing white sneakers." No one will make a musical from *Bonfire*.

The cost to the black community, and America, is incalculable. It is caused by people like Sam. And of course virtually all victims of black violence are blacks struggling to rise past the savagery of large, lazy, brutal men-children like Sam. His speech is barely semiliterate but, such is the downward seepage of the social sciences, it includes a smattering of jargon for allocating blame to "peer pressure" and "the media" (they give gangs a bad "image") and "society." But whatever made him what he is, he, like thousands like him, now is an "institutional man." He is an unreformable recidivist, unfit for society. He is an example of a rapidly expanding class of semisociopaths, utterly indifferent to social norms or any notion of right and wrong, and with the time horizon of a child. He sheds his lethargy and becomes slightly indignant when it is suggested that his future is not in doubt and that he will be back in jail soon and often. He protests, "I am patient. I might get a job." (Pause.) "For six or seven months." But, he adds, "If I can't get what I want, I'll quit." What does he want? "A thousand dollars a day." Really? Really. "It's out there." Indeed it is. And the huge demand for drugs produces a terrifying supply of Sams.

March 28, 1988

Hooked on Legalization

The dynamics of public opinion lag behind events, so the drug crisis probably peaked before anxiety did. And now, when drug use is decreasing, calls for surrender—legalization—are increasing.

Alcohol does much more damage—illness, accidents, violence, lost productivity, premature death—than cocaine and heroin combined. Yet many advocates of drug legalization favor (this is economist Milton Friedman's formulation) treating drugs "exactly the same way you treat alcohol."

Alcohol is much less addictive than heroin or cocaine and, besides, has long been a pervasive, rooted social phenomenon in a way that cocaine need not become. Surely it is perverse to argue for decriminalizing one drug on the ground that it currently does less damage than a drug that is legal.

Friedman argues that criminalization is "not working," that it costs society more than legalization would and that government has no right to interfere with free choices that do not interfere with the free choices of others. Thus Friedman is logically committed to unleashing existing drugs—and as many "designer drugs" as perverse chemists concoct in the future.

What of Friedman's bald assertion that the fight against drugs is "not working"? Drug use is declining from peaks reached in this decade. The number of heroin addicts is approximately the same as it was in 1972 when defeatists warned of exponential growth—and "epidemic"—and when Friedman urged legalization.

Containment of drugs is indeed costly. So has been containment of communism—costly, but a bargain. If drugs are legalized, asks James Q. Wilson, "in what proportion of auto fatalities would the state police report that the driver was nodding off on heroin or recklessly driving on a coke high? In what proportion of spouse-assault and child-abuse cases would the local police report that crack was involved? In what proportion of industrial accidents would safety investigators report that the forklift or drill-press operator was in a drug-induced stupor or frenzy?"

Legalizers urge: Tax drug sales and use the billions to provide "treatment on demand." But Wilson argues that "demand" for treatment often is a result of judicial coercion, and society could not compel treatment for consumption of a legal commodity. Wilson makes these and other decisive points in a dazzling essay in the February 1990 issue of *Commentary*.

Wilson proves that Friedman, the high priest of market capitalism, is talking rot about markets and price mechanisms. If Friedman had been heeded in 1972 the price of heroin would have fallen 95 percent. Friedman concedes only that lower drug prices "might" increase demand. But then again, he thinks demand for cheap legal drugs might not increase because drugs would lose the appeal of being "forbidden fruit."

Friedman really thinks that appeal, and pushers, create demand. But as Wilson says, friends, not pushers, recruit addicts. Pushers dislike dealing with nonaddicts because they might be undercover policemen.

Wilson says that most veterans who acquired a habit in the drug bazaar of Saigon kicked it when they came home. At home, the criminal law made continuing the habit involve risking one's personal and professional lives and one's bodily safety by "making an illegal contact with a disreputable dealer in a threatening neighborhood" to buy a possibly contaminated drug. Does Friedman think demand would not rise if the people making and selling aspirins were making and selling heroin and cocaine?

Legalization would cause drug prices to crash; then taxation would raise them. How far? Government, calculating rates of consumption at various tax levels, would decide the "right amount" of addiction. If government priced drugs above what criminals could profitably sell them for, there would be two markets, and there would be no laws suppressing demand by stigmatizing use.

Legalizers say young people would be excluded from the free market for drugs. Oh? And today no young people obtain cigarettes or alcohol?

When asked about advertising legal drugs, Friedman flinches. He favors prohibiting advertising of drugs in newspapers or on television because people must see such advertising "whether they chose to see it or not." What rubbish. Friedman is caught. Advertising exists to inform and influence choices. If drug use is a private choice concerning which society should be permissive, drug sellers should be free to compete for market shares.

Friedman's monomaniacal worship of "free choice"—even regarding addictive substances—is less a philosophy than a fetish. It demonstrates the intellectual poverty of libertarianism, the antipolitical and antisocial doctrine of severe individualism.

As Wilson says in the core of his essay, no society is a mere aggregation of independently formed individuals. Society, without which human character is inconceivable and by which character is formed, depends on a certain level of dignity, responsibility and empathy. Determining that level is difficult, "but if crack and heroin use do not fall below it, what does?"

This also does: Today, interest in legalization is increasing as drug abuse becomes increasingly concentrated among poor minorities. That is proof that many privileged people are failing to measure up to minimal standards of responsibility and empathy.

December 21, 1989

Life Becomes More Regressive: The Case of Drugs

Jay McInerney, the novelist, knows about fashions, being a chronicler, product and shaper of them. He says drug use is going out of fashion. But the bad news (it is hardly news, it was so predictable) is that unfashionable people are inheriting the whirlwind.

This is especially so regarding crack. "That's strictly a class thing," says McInerney, 33. "I don't see it among anybody I know."

McInerney is quoted in a *Washington Post* report on the emergence of a "two-tier" drug culture. That is part of a broader phenomenon, the emergence on many fronts of a two-tier society as modern life becomes increasingly regressive, and not merely in monetary terms.

McInerney's *Bright Lights, Big City* is a picaresque tale of a Holden Caulfield of the '80s, a young man with a habit of "hoovering" cocaine. But McInerney reports that the Holdens have cleaned up their acts: "People my age, we've been through the cocaine wars and we've seen it can hurt you and even kill you. It's become unfashionable among the people who made it fashionable. It's really not around much any more."

It's around, not far from the Manhattan haunts of people like McInerney. "People my age, we've . . ." He means only people of his small social experience. But he is right about "the people who made it fashionable," people like him.

James Q. Wilson writes that most of the most dangerous drugs— heroin, cocaine, LSD, for example—have first been used by affluent, educated people. Drug use was promoted by people who considered themselves liberated from deadening restraints (including the law). Such people were intellectual at least in the limited sense that they possessed—or were possessed by—theories, about drugs as keys to peace, self-discovery, self-expression, fulfillment.

When self-discovery turned into self-destruction, these experimenters, "being affluent and educated, had access to treatment programs and support systems that gave them a good chance of finding their way back to normality." But, says Wilson, to people less advantaged, the pursuit of bliss was a one-way path to an abyss.

"What began as a clever experiment for affluent Americans quickly became a living nightmare for disadvantaged Americans. Drug use has not spread because drug pushers have forced it on us, but because the apostles of unconstrained self-expression . . . celebrated the value of self-indulgence."

There is a pattern here. It is axiomatic that the rich get richer. They have money to put to work making more money. However, there is a more encompassing axiom: In this information age, the advantaged become more so, and the disadvantaged fall from the inability to use the information.

Life is increasingly regressive because the benefits of information are distributed disproportionately to those already favored by many advantages. The more certain kinds of information matter, the more unequal society—life—becomes.

In the last quarter-century, since the 1964 Surgeon General's report condemning smoking, it has become clear that the most cost-effective thing government does is disseminate health information. Smoking has become déclassé. Alcohol, high blood pressure, red meat, fiber, oat bran, seat belts, safe sex—the list is long. In a broadly educated middle-class country, information about such matters produces behavioral changes on a dramatic scale.

More and more is being learned about the relationship of particular problems, and of "wellness," to particular patterns of behavior. The more such information is available, the more life-chances are improved—but only for people equipped by upbringing and training to act on information.

Consider AIDS. It is not a democratic disease, threatening us all equally. It is behaviorally based. It is hard to get and easy to prevent. Easy, that is, if information is heeded, which it is by advantaged people.

That is why apocalyptic talk about a "breakout" of AIDS into the general heterosexual population is waning. It is being replaced by anxiety that society will lose interest in AIDS as it becomes increasingly a disease of marginal, inner-city populations such as intravenous drug users and their sex partners. Such people are caught in the culture of urban poverty precisely because they are inadequately educated and lack the ability to regulate their behavior on the basis of important information.

The meals of the poor are unhealthy not merely because they often are meager, but because they are not prepared by people influenced by information about healthy eating. And so it goes. What has always been true is becoming more broadly important: The more information matters, the more advantages flow to the advantaged. As ever, but increasingly, modern life is regressive.

January 8, 1989

The Pleasures of a Killjoy

Letting the chips (of other people) fall where they may is an imperative of contemporary journalism. In that scorched-earth, take-no-prisoners spirit, I must report having seen Dr. C. Everett Koop eat a Saturday lunch consisting of a martini, a hamburger and french fries. His departure from killjoyism was wonderful to watch.

For eight years it has been fascinating to watch Koop, who has just resigned as Surgeon General. He looks like an Old Testament prophet and sometimes seems to be—as some of those scolds were—comprehensively miffed about the way humanity is behaving.

Man is the only animal that needs a Surgeon General because man is the only animal that does not instinctively eat, drink, smoke (ever see an elk light up?) or behave sexually the way he should. As Surgeon General, Koop left office doing what he had done so well so often, calling a lot of bluffs. He did so by clarifying public choices and individual responsibilities about health.

Recently, 99 senators and a unanimous House of Representatives urged him to do something about drunk driving. He did. Now they probably regret having urged him.

He has recommended, among many other things, new taxes, restrictions on advertising of beverages, and reduction of the permissible blood-alcohol content (BAC) of drivers from 0.10 to 0.04 percent. His severity gets general support from a RAND Corporation study that argues this premise: Taxes on a particular activity (such as smoking or drinking) should cover the costs of that activity to others.

The RAND study argues that the social costs of smoking (principally health care, lost productivity and fire damage) are almost balanced by cigarette taxes and the savings (Social Security, pension benefits, nursing-home care) that accrue to society because smokers die prematurely. (After age 20, a smoker loses 137 minutes of life per pack.)

However, drinking costs society about twice as much as drinkers pay in alcohol taxes. These costs include a huge burden on the criminal-justice system. Many heavy drinkers die very young, before they contribute much to pension funds, and others retire early and become drains on pension and disability funds.

About 24,000 annual traffic deaths (one every 22 minutes) are alcohol-related. These are about half the traffic deaths each year and include approximately 7,400 victims who were not drinking. (Only—only!—about 2,400 people die annually because of other people's smoking.) And 534,000 people (one per minute) are involved in alcohol-related crashes.

Koop's strongest case is for increased taxes on beer, the preferred drink of young people. Drunk driving is the leading killer of adolescents. More than 40 percent of all deaths of people aged 15 to 20 are in crashes and at least half involve alcohol. Federal taxes on beer and wine have been unchanged since 1951, so in many supermarkets a six-pack of beer costs less than a similar quantity of soda.

New taxes and restrictions on advertising are debatable. What is indisputable is that public education—the Surgeon General's principal task—works. In this broadly educated, information-acquiring middle-class country, dissemination of public-health information is the most cost-effective thing government does.

It is one reason drug use seems to have peaked. (Another reason is demographic: The percentage of the population in the prime drug-using years, 14 to 20, has declined.) Much drug-related violence is by dealers fighting over shares of a stagnant or declining market.

Medicine is reducing the amount of illness that is not behaviorally based. And the dissemination of information is reducing behavior that causes illness. But that reduction is primarily among classes that are skilled at acquiring information and modifying their behavior on the basis of it. As a result, the least educated (and poorest) Americans have an increased proportion of the nation's health problems. AIDS, for example, is increasingly a disease of inner-city intravenous drug abusers and their sexual partners.

There is, then, this paradox. Behaviorly based illness is not the result of bad luck, but of bad choices. As education reduces the role of randomness in public-health problems, society becomes more regressive. The disadvantaged are least able to take advantage of one key to health: information.

Still, information, wrapped in exhortations, is the Surgeon General's business. Koop's campaign—crusade, really—for a smokeless society by the year 2000 has done much to stigmatize smoking to the point that some employers will not hire people who smoke either on or off the job. This practice has provoked tobacco-growing Virginia to ban discrimination against smokers. There is a blizzard of lawsuits accusing employers of violating employee privacy rights, and some smokers are claiming they are handicapped and entitled to special treatment.

All this constructive irritability is part of Koop's splendid legacy. He has quickened the nation's understanding of the connection between individuals' choices and public health.

July 16, 1989

The Trauma in Trauma Care

HOUSTON, TEXAS—From the crumpled cowboy hat, drooping mustache, big belt buckle and faded jeans, down to his scuffed boots, Dr. James H. (Red) Duke, Jr. looks like one of those mournful cowpokes sung about by Willie Nelson, who is, in fact, Duke's buddy. Duke does his damnedest to seem like a bumpkin but he is a professor of surgery and a leading advocate for better trauma care. And he has been made melancholy by something alarming, the unraveling of the nation's trauma-care system.

Duke was present at a particularly notable attempt at trauma care. He was at Parkland Memorial Hospital in Dallas, on November 22, 1963. There was nothing that could be done to save that patient. Today at Houston's Hermann Hospital there is too little for Duke and other trauma specialists to do. Hermann has had radically to reduce the number of trauma cases it will receive. This is because the cost of caring for uninsured patients has become crushing.

If misery loves company, Houston has that consolation, lots of it. Los Angeles's collapsing trauma network recently received another blow when a Pasadena hospital announced its withdrawal from the emergency-care system. Its trauma unit lost $3.7 million last year. The inadequate number of remaining trauma facilities will buckle beneath the burden of an intensified flood of cases. More than 25 percent of Angelinos do not have health insurance, and the uninsured often lead traumatic lives.

Trauma care is costly. The machines and multitalented personnel are expensive and have to *be there*, always. Hermann, a private not-for-profit hospital, lost $7 million on its trauma unit in a year. It exhausted the option of charging other patients more to make up for the losses. Hermann's woes are paradigmatic. They would not be nearly so acute if Houston did not have its share of the nation's 37 million people without medical insurance and of the millions more who are underinsured. Or if Medicaid covered more than 38 cents on the dollar. Or if there were not a drug epidemic. Or if Houstonians had fewer guns. (According to one estimate, one in three Houston cars has a gun in it. Says a doctor, "I don't use my horn since I moved to Houston.")

Trauma—serious injury—is America's costliest public health problem.

It is the leading cause of death of people aged 1 to 44; it is the fourth most common cause of death generally. Trauma takes more than 4 million potential years of life annually, more than heart disease, cancer and stroke combined. Half the deaths of children up to the age of 15 are from accidents. Approximately 150,000 Americans die from trauma each year (about a third in motor vehicles).

Doctors speak of the "golden hour" when the seriously injured can be saved. Trauma treatment has been refined in war. In World War I the lag between injury and surgery was 12 to 18 hours; in World War II, 6 to 12 hours; in Korea, where trauma medicine took a quantum leap forward with MASH (mobile army surgical hospital) units, 2 to 4 hours; in Vietnam, 65 minutes. Mortality rates declined sharply as those delays did. But today two-thirds of the country, geographically, is at least 50 miles from a trauma center or even an adequate emergency room. Because of inadequate technology and personnel, upward of 25,000 injured Americans per year die *after they reach hospitals.*

As trauma units are downgraded to emergency rooms—many of which need not have a surgeon present—trauma victims are deposited at congested facilities that many poor people now use for all their health care. Today many emergency rooms are themselves emergencies—disasters to which disaster victims are taken. With patients on pallets in hallways, patients waiting 18 hours for treatment, some people are going to die in ambulances that are seeking hospitals that will receive them. It all makes Duke mad.

His voice creaks like a rusty cattle gate and what he says is often pungent, as in: Everyone who buys a motorcycle should have to sign an organ donation pledge. The most common American injuries, he explains, come from "blunt trauma"—the body hitting something hard. ("It ain't the falls that's so bad, it's the sudden stop that hurts.") But in the inner city ("the knife and gun club" in the parlance of emergency rooms) 75 percent of all traumas are "penetrating"—blades and bullets. Sensible living is causing heart disease and cancer to decrease but trauma is increasing more among people who, Duke says dryly, "can't settle their differences in a Christian way."

Health planners did not plan emergency facilities sufficient for two epidemics that were not visible just 10 years ago, crack cocaine and AIDS. As recently as 1985 AIDS patients accounted for only 2 percent of the time spent in emergency rooms of New York City's public hospitals. Just two years later they accounted for 44 percent. These two epidemics, crack and AIDS, coincided with another epidemic that burst upon the nation and has deepened the crisis of health care—the epidemic of taxophobia among taxpayers.

Life involves a lot of hard trade-offs, as doctors know who work on the fine line between life and death. But Duke, who understands the necessity for Hermann's restrictive new policy, nevertheless says that when it went into effect, "part of me died." Trauma medicine might seem to be a depressing specialty because so much trauma is the result of reckless, brutal, often intentional disregard for human life. But Duke thrives on it. Cowboys, according to his buddy, Willie, like smoky old pool rooms and clear country mornings. Duke likes the slam-bang medicine of trauma care because, he says laconically, "You can make a difference and you can make it in a hurry."

Today he and others at Hermann, in Houston's dazzling medical center, are not hurrying as often as they want to, through no fault of their own. America's hospitals are suffering institutional traumas. This is yet another of the multiplying examples of what happens when society flinches from facts, such as the cost of things, and refuses to pay its bills. What then happens is that life becomes more regressive: The debris from falling standards hits those at the bottom. An official of the Pasadena hospital says of its withdrawal from trauma care, "this means that there will be some [patients] who die. The question that the public has to answer is, are [those patients'] deaths worse than raising taxes?" The President says "we have more will than wallet." He has it backward.

March 12, 1990

"Life Is Priceless" Is Useful Nonsense

"Who," asked Senate Majority Leader George Mitchell (D–Maine) when questioned about the cost of clean-air legislation, "can calculate the dollar value of a child's health and life?" Well now. Whose child, mine or yours?

We calculate the value of loved ones and strangers differently. Parents will pay more to educate their children than they would be willing to have government pay, in taxes, for all children. Government does not legislate for "a" child.

Mitchell's question was rhetorical and his point is not just that such a calculation is complex. Rather, his implication is that attaching monetary values to such moral values is morally dubious, even repellent. However, policymakers do that constantly. They do not advertise that fact; they often do not admit it even to themselves. But it is sometimes—not always—well to dwell upon it.

Let us stipulate that the clean-air compromise to which the Bush administration has subscribed is sensible. Its cost to industry (to be passed along in various ways) would be about $21 billion. That may be, as some say, a bargain, purchasing health-care savings and preventing much lost productivity as a result of pollution-related illness and premature death. That may be so, but two things must be said.

First, we have seen this movie before. Washington is always awash with programs "certain" to pay for themselves, programs that will not really cost what they seem to cost. A jobs program will "pay for itself" in increased tax revenues and decreased welfare payments; a tax cut will be self-financing because wondrously stimulative; health savings will exceed the costs of this or that environmental program.

Second, one thing is certain: The $21 billion spent for cleaner air cannot be spent on other things. Many environmentalists argue that health and longevity are values so valuable that no alternative augmentations of social welfare can be weighed against them. Like all extremisms, this could produce perverse outcomes.

It is obviously preposterous to say that any incremental improvement in health, however marginal, is worth any cost to, say, economic vitality, however severe. Economic vitality produces jobs, wealth and other satisfactions; economic vitality underwrites government, the arts and sciences, including sciences pertaining to health. It is crude biological materialism to assert that health and longevity are values superior to all others.

But even if one grants that premise, policymakers face morally difficult trade-offs. Comparative returns on health must be considered. The $21 billion spent on cleaner air is $21 billion that cannot be spent on immunization, infant mortality, care for poor pregnant women. If we really believe that health and longevity are values immune from cost-benefit scrutiny we should, for starters (on an endless list), limit automobile speeds to 35 mph and ban left turns.

Last week, a bipartisan commission voted 8–7 to recommend providing health insurance and long-term care to all in need. It would cost business $20 billion and government $66 billion. Because the government has inadequate resources (of revenues, and of the will to increase them), the commission's proposal is being dismissed as a mere audit of needs it would be nice to fill. An additional 70¢ tax on a gallon of gasoline (raising the price, in real terms, to what it was in 1980) would pay for it. But no elected official is going to say that such a gasoline tax, or some other equivalent revenue-raiser, is morally obligatory lest we be guilty of putting a dollar value on health and life.

Policies concerning health take odd caroms. The use of automobile safety belts is good, but because of it there are fewer dead drivers and passengers, so there are fewer organs available for transplants. Smoking is a health catastrophe, but an end of smoking would be a blow to Social

Security and private pensions: Their actuarial assumptions count on millions of smokers dying before they collect much, or any, of their entitlements. Antipollution technologies required on cars since 1980 have raised car prices, thereby encouraging many people to continue driving older cars. Pre-1980 cars are one-third of those now operating and they produce 86 percent of automotive pollution.

Environmentalism is a worthy concern. But it is one among many, and attaching the adjective "environmental" to legislation and demonstrating a health benefit from the legislation does not give it irresistible momentum for enactment.

The idea that "life is priceless" comes under the category of useful nonsense. It is useful to talk that way, thereby inclining our minds to place high value on life, precisely because we constantly must act in ways that cause that value to be jostled and compromised by competing values.

March 8, 1990

The Flag, the First Amendment and the President's Viscera

President Bush says he feels "viscerally" about flag-burning. That bulletin about his inner life is not helpful because the viscera are not arguments. There is a serious (although unconvincing) argument for Bush's idea, but Bush shows no sign of knowing it. Its crux is that we must draw some lines asserting the general claims of the community against the doctrine of extreme individualism.

It is serendipitous that the flag controversy has coincided with yet another Supreme Court wrangle about abortion. Both issues involve a particularly American tension between the values of individualism and community. Actually, the rights of communities are by now so attenuated that there is not nearly enough tension.

Speaking about the leftist whose arrest for flag-burning started this, Representative Don Edwards (D–Calif.), a liberal, is distressed that "a nincompoop in Dallas, Texas, could do something that could trigger this reaction." Edwards does not understand. Five confused men in robes triggered this.

Their constitutional doctrine (by now it really is this, whether the justices know it or not) is that any behavior expressing an attitude that can be given a political coloration is protected "expression." A congressman wonders if fornication at high noon in Times Square is protected. The answer is that fornication would blend into the background there, but would be protected if the participants said they were trying to shock the bourgeoisie into a higher consciousness.

After half a century of misconstruction, the First Amendment cannot be helped by a piddling-fiddling amendment about the flag. It needs serious thought about why the Amendment's framers, who used words more carefully than the Court does, used the word "speech" rather than "expression." The answer is that speech, meaning the use of words, is the sine qua non of reasoning and persuasion, and hence of democratic government. Democracy is, after all, the point of the Constitution, to which the Amendment is appended.

The fundamental problem is a social atmosphere saturated with a philosophy of extreme individualism. In many manifestations this philosophy is antidemocratic because it overrides the right of the community to speak and act. This philosophy has been absorbed by many judges, including some called conservatives, who have supported the assault on the rights of the community.

The Court's decision that 48 communities—states—and the national community cannot codify their reverence for the flag came 16 years after the Court ruled that 50 communities—the states—could not codify their values regarding abortion. So, is it surprising that a low-level judge overthrows the governance of the community of major-league baseball because he has a hunch that an individual's right to "fairness" might not be sufficiently respected in a process that has not yet taken place?

Where does a judge get such presumption? From the Supreme Court that sorts through Christmas displays to make sure crèches are surrounded by sufficient secular symbols. Thus does the community's symbolic life in its public space become incoherent or barren.

Individualism understood as absence of restraint has spawned innumerable new "rights." They are rights against, and preferred over, the community's right to nurture and act on the collective values that give it meaning and vitality.

Bush so loves the flag he wraps himself in it, like Linus, and so loves the Constitution he overflows with ideas for improving it. He favors three amendments (preventing flag desecration, protecting the right to life, requiring a balanced budget), and a fourth if he is serious about a line-item veto.

There is no flag-burning problem sufficient to justify the radical step of amending the Constitution. And conservatives should be especially wary of using amendments as gestures, even to assert that communities, too, have rights. A flag-protection amendment is a gesture on behalf of communities' rights generally. When liberals join in loading the document with gesture-amendments (ERA was one), it will become as long as *Moby Dick*.

No words on parchment will stymie litigious individualism. A change of constitutional words without a change of judicial and other minds will be unavailing. Go ahead, enact this amendment: "Nothing in this Constitution shall be construed to prevent states from protecting the flag from desecration." Then stand back. There will be an avalanche of litigation to determine if the use of the flag in advertisements, on clothing, with political slogans spray-painted on it, dragged in the dirt, or whatever, constitutes "desecration."

Conservatives should content themselves with saying that liberals want to read pornography by the light of burning flags. Say anything; just keep your hands off Mr. Madison's document.

July 2, 1989

Crime Wave in the Locker Room

Crisp autumn Saturday morning, second cup of coffee, sports pages full of football news.

Crime wave update from the University of Oklahoma: no more shootings or cocaine busts, but the criminal-justice system is booming some more Sooners, this time two convicted of rape. At Notre Dame, coach Lou Holtz is not having fun. His number-one ranked Irish are brawling with opponents (before kickoffs, on the field). University officials are delivering a forearm across the windpipe to the idea that Holtz was in any way connected with illegal payments to players at Minnesota, his last coaching stop.

Colorado is challenging Notre Dame for dominance. More than two dozen Colorado players were arrested in a recent three-year period, charges ranging from trespassing, assault and burglary through rape. Hmmm. No news this day from Florida. But in a 22-day period the University of Florida fired its football coach (the one hired five years ago to replace a cheater) for cheating, and its basketball coach and three of his assistants, and lost two quarterbacks this autumn for gambling. It is hard to keep up that pace of scandal.

But the big story this morning is the NFL's permanent suspension of Washington Redskins' defensive end Dexter Manley, for a third drug offense. He is the second Redskin lost to drugs this month. Team officials suspected trouble when Dexter missed an appointment with his reading tutor.

Where did Manley learn that there really are no rules, that drug laws are not serious, that football players can do an end-run around reality? In school.

Before becoming a Redskin, Manley spent four years making a lot of tackles and money for Oklahoma State University. Restaurateurs and motel operators in Stillwater thank him. He left school without a degree (like most NFL players) and still unable to read.

Now Manley has fumbled away millions of dollars. No more of the custom-tailored suits he has been sporting for years. "I'm not gonna say how I got them. It was my senior year in high school, so you put it together. I had 37 scholarship offers. So, that's how it works."

Does college football form character? Sure does, by teaching cynicism. Nearly one-third of NFL players responding to a survey say they received illegal payments in college—slipped under dormitory doors, passed in congratulatory handshakes, left in helmets.

Come for a stroll along the banks of the open sewer that runs through many campuses. Read *The Hundred Yard Lie* by Rick Telander, formerly lead college football writer for *Sports Illustrated*. Formerly. His book is his declaration of incurable disgust.

I know, robust reader—yes, you there, looking at your watch, counting the hours until kickoff—you are thinking: Lighten up. At least the players are being prepared for a profession—football—and meanwhile are generating pots of money for the math department.

False, twice. About one in 50 players makes it to the NFL, where the average career lasts about three years. And virtually all the money from college football bypasses the school's general funds and flows into the athletic department.

Telander propounds a paradox: Absence of money—amateurism; the pretense thereof—is the root of the evil of hypocrisy enveloping college football. But his solution—pay the players at least a pittance from the $500 million generated by Division I teams—would, like most reforms, make matters worse.

He is, of course, correct in saying that the players are exploited labor. (Disproportionately black labor. About 40 percent of Division I players are black. About 4 percent of students at those schools are black.) But while his proposal would help players, it would not bring hygiene to higher education.

The only solution is to sever universities from this mega-entertainment industry. If the NFL wants farm teams, let it do what baseball does: Pay for them, far from campuses.

Four reforms would help: coaches paid comparably with other faculty and given tenure; no freshman playing or practicing; no spring practice, and no fall practice before classes start; no special admissions or curricula

for athletes. Some players currently take such courses as Billiards, Jogging, Advanced Slow-Pitch Softball (imagine the reading list for Elementary Slow-Pitch Softball), Trees and Shrubs and—my favorite—
Recreational Leisure.

These reforms are utopian. "Student athletes" who attend real classes?
Coaches as faculty members rather than entrepreneurs? Teams as ap-
pendages of universities rather than the other way around? Preposterous. There is too much money and passion on the other side.

Passion? A juror in a criminal trial swore in an affidavit that he had
been pressured by fellow jurors to change his vote from innocent to
guilty so that they could watch the Ohio State–Michigan game.

College football, like most other smarmy features of American life,
prospers by popular demand.

November 23, 1989

Too Bad Rousseau Was Not an Eskimo

Descending on Stanford to smite it hip and thigh, Secretary of Education William Bennett may have felt as the 19th-century wit did when
surrounded by curates: like a lion in a den of Daniels. He came to charge
that the Daniels had been intimidated into dropping a Western civilization course required of all freshmen that emphasized the reading of 15
classics by Homer, Dante and other (the reformers noted, austerely)
white males.

The new course will be CIV (Culture, Ideas and Values), which its
most ardent advocates say will be innocent of the previous course's sin,
Eurocentrism, which is a close cousin of racism and sexism. Professors
will be directed to include works by "women, minorities and persons of
color." Were not the Navy an instrument of imperialism, Stanford might
adapt its slogan: "Join Stanford and see the world."

But will you see it through ideological filters? There is nothing inherently alarming about curriculum revision, and any selection of canonical
texts invites intellectual argument. The worrisome aspect of Stanford's
debate is its political undertone.

Some CIV advocates understand that the idea of a canon is incompatible with the central tenet of modernity, and for that reason they rejoice
in anything that dilutes or disputes any canon. That tenet is this: The
world is a bazaar of cultures, a cafeteria of "values," and no hierarchy of
choices can be established by reason.

A backlash against this notion is apparent in the astonishingly large readership for Allan Bloom's book *The Closing of the American Mind.* Bloom's thesis is that modern nations, and none more than ours, have founded themselves on reason, so a crisis in the university, supposedly the seat of reason, is a profound political crisis. If any "commitment" to "values" is a nonrational act arising from factors other than reason—acculturation, race, sex, class bias, whatever—then all choices are political and all politics is essentially nonrational.

Disparagement of the power of reason to reach authoritative conclusions about the best way to live leads to disparagement of the idea of classic texts being valuable for comprehending the good life. Such disparagement may seem an expression of intellectual humility. Often, however, it is an act of aggression by people who are sure they are right about one thing: The West represents an overestimated, overbearing and perhaps inferior tradition.

Stanford would have been spared much trouble if Rousseau had been an Eskimo, if Lear had raged upon a blasted heath in Peru and if an Indian had written *Middlemarch.* The trouble is, in part, that they have become pawns in an academic power struggle.

In the mixture of motives behind Stanford's curriculum revision there is a new wrinkle on special-interest scholarship. Such scholarship began with "black studies" and "women's studies." Not content with ginning up ersatz disciplines, the political academics would now dismantle courses which, being organized around canonical texts, affirm this fact: America is predominantly a product of the Western tradition and is predominantly good because that tradition is good.

Isaac Barchas, a Stanford undergraduate studying classics, sees exactly what is wrong with looking for texts to allocate in an academic spoils system to satisfy racial, sexual and ethnic groups. It is disrespectful of the idea of a text independent of its context. It also is an affront to the unifying theme of the West's rich tradition. The theme is that reason matters supremely, whereas individuals' accidental attributes, such as race, are irrelevant to the great enterprise of thoughtfulness.

The "great books" approach to undergraduate education has, says Barchas, this great advantage. Students are taught by great authors with the assistance of professors, rather than vice versa. When texts are chosen from a long and constantly changing list assembled to satisfy shifting standards of "relevance," the academic experience becomes rootless. Indeed it teaches rootlessness.

Furthermore, pedagogy that focuses on the social context that supposedly produced and explains the text's significance, rather than on the text itself, elevates the professor unduly. It places him in the grand—too grand—role of the supplier of social theories which are supposedly indispensable for interpretation of the texts. Thus today's teachers with their agendas, not the texts, become the sources of illumination. Then there is the intellectuals' self-dramatizing notion that they should comprise an "adversary culture."

All this is a recipe for politicizing universities. Stanford has not altogether jettisoned the anchor of canonical texts. However, it has taken a step on the downward path toward defining a university not as a transmitter of culture but as a "demystifier" of culture and an advocate of the politically ascendant agendas of the moment.

May 1, 1988

Allan Bloom in the Bazaar of Culture

Recently American readers have been partial to "how to" books such as those explaining how to achieve thin thighs quickly or sexual ecstasy slowly. But suddenly this summer—summer: the season for spilling Coppertone on Danielle Steel novels—there is an astonishingly different best seller. It is Allan Bloom's *The Closing of the American Mind.* Readers taking this book to the beach are going swimming with Nietzsche, Heidegger and others.

Bloom's subtitle is *How Higher Education Has Failed Democracy and Impoverished the Souls of Today's Students.* Revenge is, indeed, a dish best eaten cold and this book is, in part, Bloom's delayed revenge against academics who found no moral resources for resisting the 1960s' mobs that broke universities to the saddle of "relevance," meaning the political passion of the hour. But Bloom, a political philosopher at the University of Chicago, is really refuting the entire intellectual tradition that brought on the 1960s. This tradition is, he says, responsible for mankind's "300-year-old identity crisis."

Bloom and a few kindred spirits are resisting the triumph of relativism and intellectual egalitarianism. To the modern mind, those are related moral imperatives. Relativism is considered a requirement for a free society because the only modern sin is intolerance, and intolerance results from denying that all "values" are of equal dignity.

Relativism, says Bloom, extinguishes the purpose of education, which is the search for the good life. Democracy needs education that produces people with the knowledge, habits and character necessary for democracy. But when tolerance replaces natural rights as the basis of democracy, then "going with the flow" replaces rules developed by reason. These are rules for living in accordance with natural rights—that is, in ways that are right for creatures of our nature.

"Commitment," says Bloom, is a word invented to serve modernity, which asserts the absence of any natural motives in the soul for moral dedication. What modernity values is "authenticity," meaning intensity of commitment to whatever "values" one has picked from the unlimited cafeteria of choices.

Today, students are taught that there is no hierarchy of choices establishable by reason. The social sciences teach this leveling lesson: The world is a bazaar of cultures, no one of which can be demonstrated to be superior to another. True, some cultures place high value on tolerance, but relativism teaches that a preference for tolerance is as arbitrary as any other preference.

Openness—to experience, to arguments—used to be an instrumental virtue valued because it made possible the quest, through reason, for knowledge of the objectively good. Now openness is not an instrument, it is an end. Indeed, it is the only universal value, reason having been declared powerless to discern the good. But there is vanity beneath the intellectual humility: Openness makes the absence of principle look principled.

The American mind is being closed in the name of openness—closed to the idea of reasoned discrimination between ways of living. Bloom says students are taught that all beliefs issue from an abstraction called the "self," a monochrome kaleidoscope, and these beliefs have no validation other than being, by definition, "self-expression."

Students are taught that the production of values is an act of will, not of understanding. This is, says Bloom, "nihilism with a happy ending." Understanding is not distributed democratically, but everyone can be willful, just as everyone has a "self" to "express." Such teaching induces self-satisfaction that stunts learning: It instills the sense of having nothing to learn from the past or from philosophy.

Bloom writes about music, sex, scholarship, politics. He is passionate and witty. (Bloom, a smoker, says the campaign against cigarettes advances because our relativism does not extend to matters of bodily health, only to matters of the mind.) He has written a "how to" book for the few—not so very few, according to the best-seller list—who want to know how to be independent.

It is about the arduous task of achieving autonomy, understood not as capricious "commitments" but as governance of oneself in accordance with prescriptive nature. It is living in accordance with philosophy (truth) rather than in subservience to convention, myth, opinion.

Bloom's book, the publishing surprise of the year, is a paradoxical phenomenon, and may be politically portentous. The book's success is evidence against Bloom's severe judgment about the decay of the capacity for reflection about life's large questions. Furthermore, since the

1980s there has been a quickening anxiety about the trajectory of our evolving national character.

Candidates looking ahead to 1988 should look into a bookstore. Bloom's best seller is a timely sign of the high level at which many Americans can be addressed.

July 30, 1987

Professors Playing Politics

When professors play politics, the bitterness is often inversely proportional to the stakes. That was the case when some scientists recently denied Professor Samuel Huntington of Harvard membership in the National Academy of Sciences.

Actually, Huntington's vocation, properly pursued, makes him unsuited to the Academy as it evidently wants to be understood. And his civic virtue would make him uncomfortable in the Academy as it is currently composed.

Huntington is a distinguished political scientist who has served several presidents in national-security capacities, and his critics say he has committed other sins, too. He and a colleague recently published a scholarly article, "Dead Dictators and Rioting Mobs: Does the Demise of Authoritarian Rulers Lead to Political Instability," and did not note that the CIA helped fund the research. A scandal, no?

No. The CIA had a rule (now modified) against acknowledgment of support. The CIA has good reasons for not advertising its interests, and there are people eager to infer that if the CIA is interested in the consequences of dictators' deaths, it is interested in causing such deaths.

This article, as well as his support for the Vietnam War and his "conservatism" (he is a Hubert Humphrey Democrat) were important catalysts of opposition within the Academy. However, there also was the argument that "soft" scientists (social scientists such as political scientists) do not belong in the Academy with "hard" scientists such as physicists and mathematicians.

It is reasonable to suspect this argument was in part a cloak for political opposition, given that there are 177 social scientists among the Academy's 1,462 members. Opposition to Huntington was led by a passionate left-wing mathematician whose criticisms of Huntington's mathematical methodology were refuted by Herbert Simon, a Nobel laureate in economics.

Were Huntington's "hard" science opponents really interested in distinguishing themselves from social scientists, their position might be supported by some political scientists (including one lapsed professor of political science: me). Many political scientists do frame their research so the results can be reduced to arithmetic expressions that suggest explanatory or predictive powers comparable to the laws of physics or other generalizations of the natural sciences.

Professor Allan Bloom of the University of Chicago rightly says the issue is whether this leads to distortions of social phenomena, or the neglect of phenomena that cannot be mathematized, or the construction of mathematical models unrelated to the real world. Political science is divided between those who are enthusiasts of science and those who are interested in politics.

Many "behavioral" approaches are political science with a political agenda, albeit one understood dimly, if at all, by most practitioners. Behaviorism aims to explain the political order in terms of nonpolitical causes (economic, psychological or others), rather than the core concerns of political philosophy—convictions about and desires for freedom, equality, honor, distinction, justice.

Contemporary political science is a tossed salad of psychology, sociology, economics, decision theory. And over in a quiet corner is political philosophy—the contemplative life that is political science as Aristotle understood it.

Political philosophy, properly undertaken, is political because its subject is law-giving to achieve justice. It is science in that it involves the incorporation of empirical findings to facilitate the achievement of proper goals.

However, much modern political science is different and its aim and the aim of modern politics coincide.

The aim of modern politics, from Machiavelli on, has been to simplify politics by orienting it, away from ideals of excellence and nobility, to low but solid passions and goals. Modern politics conceives of man not as a political creature fulfilled by life in a well-ordered polity, but as a solitary "self," and it aims only to regulate selfishness. If selfishness always is—or can be encouraged to be—a constant powerful force, like planetary gravity, then a science of politics, comparable to Newtonian physics, is achievable.

Huntington, a political scientist who understands the irreducibly philosophical nature of his vocation, should be content to leave the Academy to the "hard" scientists whose vocations, although dignified, are different. However the Academy, by the undignified political bigotry that was a component of its action against Huntington, calls into question its fitness, and that of its subordinate organization, the National Research

Council, to receive public funds for research projects that result in advice on public policies.

The Academy was founded during the Civil War to advise the government in military-engineering problems. Since then, there seems to have developed an inverse relationship between the technical virtuosity and civic virtue of the scientists controlling the Academy.

May 7, 1987

Don't Worry: Half of All College Seniors Have Heard of Moby Dick

Hey (as The Education President, TEP, might say), what do you want, anyway: boring unanimity? Look on the sunny side: Most (58 percent) of seniors—college seniors—know that the Civil War occurred in the second half of the 19th century.

Don't worry, be happy (as TEP did say en route to becoming TEP): An 87-question examination given to an (alas) representative sample of 696 seniors at 67 colleges and universities reveals that slightly more than half have heard of *Moby Dick* and *David Copperfield*, and half could identify the Magna Carta and the Emancipation Proclamation.

After 16 years of American education, 60 percent of these seniors thought the Korean War began during the Roosevelt, Eisenhower or Kennedy administrations, or shrugged in bafflement. One-third confused Reconstruction with the Marshall Plan and one in four college seniors thinks that "from each according to his abilities, to each according to his needs"—Marx's daydream—is from the U.S. Constitution.

No extraordinary sunburst of inspiration is required to explain such numbers. Chester Finn, Jr., one of America's wisest voices concerning education, puts the crucial point plainly enough that even the education profession can understand: "Kids tend to learn that which they study, and they tend to learn it in rough proportion to the amount of time they spend studying it."

Only 2 percent of the 3,000 institutions of higher education have core curricula. Students can graduate from 38 percent of America's colleges and universities without having taken a single history course, as at the university where the "humanities" requirement (so to speak) can be satisfied with a course on interior decorating. So perhaps it is gratifying that only slightly more than half (55 percent) of the 696 seniors failed the 87-question examination (assuming 60 percent correct answers for a passing grade).

There are 27 million Americans with bachelor's degrees that certify
. . . not much. Colleges and universities are failing to do what high
schools fail to do in the first place. There, years ago, a survey of 11th
graders (80 percent of whom were studying American history that year)
found that 67 percent could not place the Civil War in the correct half-
century.

A large part of the problem, says Finn, is that the education profession
is pursuing the wrong goals. It is "obsessed"—Finn's word—with
whether the student's mind is functioning, and is not sufficiently em-
phasizing the business of actually learning things. Finn distinguishes
between skills and knowledge:

"Our educators in general are so transfixed by cognitive skill that they
have concluded that as long as you are thinking, it does not really matter
whether you know anything; as long as you are reading, it does not
matter what you are reading; as long as you are able to analyze, it does
not matter whether you possess knowledge worth analyzing."

It matters, especially concerning American history and the history of
Western civilization of which the American experience is a product.
Without an understanding of that civilization, the passions of the Puri-
tans, for example, are unintelligible.

That example is given by Prof. Paul Gagnon of the University of
Massachusetts, Boston. He has written with proper urgency about the
civic importance of awakening young people to history's fascinations.
Young people are susceptible to the enchantments of the muse Clio
because they are developing their identities and want to locate themselves in the stream of time.

The reason for studying history is not to extract from it tidy, potted
little "lessons" about this or that particular problem. On the contrary, the
basic lesson to be learned concerns the particularity of events. That
particularity prevents the compilation of pat answers to "recurring" situations.

The study of history is the best way and, other than by bitter experience, perhaps the only way to be inoculated against the terrible simpli-
fiers, those people who lead nations into trouble. It is better to learn
from history than from, say, the semisponsorship of failed coups the role
of accident and irrationality in history. A polity that is well-schooled
concerning the core of history—contingency—will be a prudent and
patient polity.

The study of history should, says Gagnon, encourage citizens to ap-
preciate "the necessary combination—sometimes accidental—of circumstances, ideas and leadership" that exists when democracy flourishes.
Such a combination does not occur automatically or last indefinitely, so
"the truly tough part of civic education is to prepare people for bad

times." Students should learn what has been required, and will be required again, to preserve democracy: "Hard work, high costs and genuine sacrifice—toil, tears and taxes."

To the indelicate use of that last word, The Education President says: "Er . . . it's time for recess."

October 15, 1989

The Politics of Cheating the Children

Walt Whitman High School in a Washington suburb is a sea of faded denim and raging hormones. Which is to say, it is a perfectly normal school—large, teeming, cheerful, middle class. At an evening activities night, students could sign up for the clubs that proliferate at Whitman like leaves of grass. Clubs cater to every conceivable interest. Young Republicans were bustling about. Young Democrats were nowhere to be seen. "There aren't any," explained a student. If so, one understands why. The wonder is that there are any students interested in politics in late 1989.

Has there ever been a political year so steeped in, so basted by, so saturated with dumbness? It began with a bang, or perhaps a splat, as a pay-raise proposal was buried beneath an avalanche of tea bags mailed to Congress by apoplectic constituents. Then the Senate, a.k.a. World's Greatest Deliberative Body, fell to counting John Tower's swizzle sticks. The House joined the ethics sweepstakes by meditating about Jim Wright's literary life: Is it naughty to sell books by the pound? The HUD scandal involves petty cash compared with the savings and loan scandal (already costing $1,000 per taxpayer and rising). Both these scandals stir less heavy philosophizing than Barney Frank's fixing of parking tickets for a male prostitute—What is privacy? What is the matter with Massachusetts?

Given all this, the Bush administration's adventure with the Panamanian coup actually raised the tone of Washington. (Talk about pots calling kettles black: Bush aides said the Panamanian plotters were disorganized.) And last week Congress threw caution to the wind and took a stand foursquare against the scourge of flag burning. But now things are getting ugly.

The unspeakable and of course unspoken truth is that if Congress had its druthers it would grab some grandmothers and grandfathers and roast them on a spit over a crackling fire kindled from smashed rocking chairs. Congress is shocked and saddened by sin whenever it sees it and it sees it now in geriatric "greed." The elderly have been caught in the act of acting like the people who are under 65. The nerve.

In the waning days of the Reagan Terror (the all-out, no-holds-barred, take-no-prisoners machete attack on the social "safety net") Ronald Reagan endorsed the biggest expansion of Medicare in a quarter century. He endorsed catastrophic care for his peers, the elderly. Congress piled in and piled on the benefits. Then they handed the elderly this gift—and the bill for it. That sort of thing dampens the gratitude of the recipient. For the affluent elderly the bill is steep and the benefits often redundant to services they have paid for privately. They are livid. The ingrates.

Disraeli thought it wise in a crisis to let people "see conviction slowly stealing over me." For months Congress has been changing its conviction. The House, which two years ago voted 328 to 72 to enact catastrophic care, has now voted 360 to 66 to repeal it. It was said that Gladstone's idea of impartiality was to be furiously in earnest on both sides of a question. Gladstone took both sides simultaneously. Congress takes them seriatim. What has disillusioned Congress about the elderly is this: When Americans turn 65 they do not, it seems, turn over a new leaf and quit behaving as badly as everyone else. It is one thing for the rest of us to perch like starving starlings on the legislative branch of government, our beaks open wide. But don't the elderly know that it is undignified when they do likewise?

Let there not be too much moralizing against codger power. The elderly are not more rapacious than the rest of us, they are just better at being so. A typical 1986 retiree, who in his working life paid the maximum social-security tax, had by October 1988 already received benefits equal in value to all his contributions. The age of eligibility for full benefits is rising, and social-security taxes have recently been raised a lot (by one of the biggest tax increases in the history of this solar system, signed in 1982 by the taxophobic Reagan). So a young worker today will be lucky to live long enough to get back as much as he pays in. The 12 percent of the population over 65 gets about 27 percent of the federal budget—45 percent of what is left when defense and interest payments are subtracted. This is a huge regressive redistribution of wealth: the elderly are better off than the rest of the population. This intergenerational transfer is perverse in a nation in which the poorest portion of the population is children. More than 20 percent of Americans under 18 live below the poverty line. There are more poor children than there are people over 65.

We are cheating children by running a whopping deficit to finance our consumption. This guarantees inadequate investment in the future. But any serious deficit reduction would involve cuts in programs for the elderly. Don't hold your breath. After the firestorm over catastrophic care, Congress is not going to mess with Granny. The elderly vote more than others; they give more money to candidates (the average age of Republican contributors is 55); they have more time and social skills to use badgering legislators. As usual, but now more than ever, government is the servant of the strong. Incumbents get the lion's share of dollars from political-action committees. Most incumbents are Democrats, who are supposed to look after *les misérables*. So? So today Republicans are hot to cut the capital-gains tax and Democrats say the key to a better America is bigger Individual Retirement Accounts. Imagine how entranced Harlem and Chicago's South Side and East Los Angeles are by this bidding war between the two parties (there are two, aren't there?) seeking the affection of the comfortable. This is "class war"? It is the upper middle class against the upper class. To the barricades!

Congress's last large act before it slinks out of town will be passage of the "reconciliation" bill, the blob that will eat the beltway. This pile of pork (at one point it had swollen to 1,975 pages) is a monument to how well reconciled Bush's Washington is to business as usual. The bill rights many historic wrongs. For example, it reduces from five years to three the full depreciation of rental tuxedos of the sort Walt Whitman students wear to the prom. Yet, inexplicably, the students do not see the romance of politics.

October 23, 1989

A School for Families

CHICAGO—Derek, a young black male, has fallen into the clutches of the law, which takes a dim view of the way he operates his vehicle. Derek, six, is a menace to other tricyclists on the well-waxed linoleum in the basement of the Corporate Community School in Chicago's North Lawndale district. The law is Elaine Mosley, the school's principal, who is bending Derek's ear concerning "appropriate" behavior, a word heard often here. Mosley is a huggable (children cling to her like vines) sergeant major (as Derek can attest). Last week the president and governors were at an education "summit"—an inflated title for a molehill event. Back in the real world Derek and about 200 other little citizens were getting an education of a sort too rare in ghettos. It stresses self-management and the schooling of parents, too.

The CCS is about four miles geographically and light-years socially from Chicago's chic lake front where Joe Kellman, now 69, lives. When he was growing up in Lawndale it was a tangy goulash of Jews, Poles,

Italians. He had to leave school at 14, but now heads a $100 million glass business. Today the district is black and teeming with children whose hopes hinge on early intervention in their lives. The school is Kellman's dream. It is low-tech, labor-intensive education funded by hardheaded corporations and run by clearsighted blacks who know how hard it is to teach children who come to school down mean streets.

Primus Mootry, project director, says, austerely, that the neighborhood is not an undifferentiated mass of "writhing poor." However, all its children experience "the traumas of just growing up black and poor." Just. In a neighborhood where 80 percent of the children are born to single women, the school struggles to help family environments approximate the clean, orderly environment of the school. That is quite a chore. One child has a 15-year-old sister who has two children. Another child saw her uncle kill: "My uncle stomped his face and blood was everywhere." A teacher with a nice sense of understatement says simply, "These are things that interfere with learning."

The school elicits parental involvement by providing services such as adult education that leads to high-school diplomas or at least helps parents keep pace with their children's reading skills. One child's mother— one of those strong women who will save our cities yet—was struggling to make a home in an abandoned house without heat or other amenities. The school arranged help for this urban homesteader. The school teaches "wellness." The children, most of whom have dental problems, recently visited a dental college. Proper brushing and flossing begin *now*.

In this the school's second year 50 new students were chosen by lottery from 1,400 applicants. Social agencies are enlisted to get the least motivated parents to apply. Soon the school will be giving free education to 300. By then the cost per pupil will be approximately what it is in Chicago's public schools. The CCS's teachers are paid about 10 percent above the public-school level. However for CCS teachers the psychic income is incalculably higher. In overcrowded, bureaucratically suffocating inner-city schools, burnout is the occupational hazard of the best teachers. The worst linger, going through the motions, and much time is wasted on nonproductive activity such as discipline. In public schools, says a dispirited teacher, they must spend more time worrying about what goes on in the washrooms than in the classrooms.

The CCS is funded by about 60 corporations, including some of Chicago's heaviest hitters—Baxter International, Sears, United Airlines, Quaker Oats, McDonald's, Whitman Corp. They know their choice is: pay now or pay later—support competent schools or run remedial education programs for employees. The *Chicago Tribune* says Chicago's public high school system amounts to "educational triage." Promising children from motivated families attend well-maintained and well-staffed magnet schools. But a large majority of Chicago's students are ware-housed in disgraceful conditions. A majority of that majority drop out. In 1986 half of Chicago's high schools were in the bottom 1 percent of U.S. schools in terms of students' scores on a standardized test. One Chicago business (its experience is not unusual) found only two of 70 high-school graduates competent to be secretary-receptionists.

Chicago may be making matters worse by electing "local school councils" for each of its 542 schools. This empowerment of parents sounds good in principle but in practice, says Kellman, the schools that most need help are in neighborhoods where many people "are having trouble managing their own lives." Kellman is a straight-ahead, rough-as-a-rasp, blunt businessman who believes, as businessmen often do, that business can teach the world a thing or two. In Kellman's case this is not Babbit-try, it is the truth. Corporate-management practices can help bring schools up to snuff. Failing schools, like ailing corporations, need "turn-around specialists." Success begins with a board of directors with the power to hire and fire staff until the right combination starts getting results objectively measured by standardized academic indexes.

About 70 percent of Chicago's public school students live in poverty. The city government's resources are inadequate. The state will not foot the bill: 80 percent of Illinois state legislators represent rural, suburban or middle- and upper-class urban constituencies. So corporate America had better levy a school tax on itself before America's competitiveness buckles beneath the strain of spending billions of dollars annually to do what schools are failing to do to equip young people for entry-level jobs. Also, Kellman believes we are in a race against time. Some demagogue may rise to protest "double taxation," saying, "We pay to educate *them* and to incarcerate *them.*"

But even if neither political prudence nor economic necessity dictated a sense of emergency, there still would be a single simple and sufficient reason for doing better by our schools: Derek deserves it. A high-spirited tricyclist is a terrible thing to waste.

October 9, 1989

Mayor Daley, Act II

CHICAGO—The chip off the old block is compactly built but does not look, as dad did, like something that walked—no, stalked—away from Stonehenge. And Mayor Richard J. Daley was never called, as the son is, Richie.

Things are (these things are relative) almost mellow as Chicago prepares for its mayoralty primary next Tuesday. The political machine, and much else, isn't what it once was.

In Ward Just's new political novel, *Jack Gance,* a character recalls the description of Prussia as less a state with an army than an army with a state. Not long ago, Chicago was a machine with a city. But in this year 13 A.D.—Mayor Daley died in December 1976—the machine, or as much as remains of it, is in the hands of the incumbent mayor, Eugene Sawyer, 53. That makes Richie Daley, 46, the reform candidate. If Daley wins the primary, Chicago will become the first large city to elect a white mayor after having elected a black mayor.

In 1983, Richie Daley helped make Harold Washington Chicago's first black mayor. Daley entered the Democratic primary against Mayor Jane Byrne, splitting the white vote. When Washington died after reelection in 1987, Timothy Evans, a black alderman who had been Washington's captain in the City Council, was backed by Jesse Jackson in his bid to be elected mayor by the Council. But Sawyer, backed by a few black aldermen and most of the white ones, won in a near riot, during which he fainted.

Today Jackson is supporting Sawyer in the primary. But if Daley wins, Jackson may support Evans, the candidate of the Harold Washington Party, in the April 4 general election. Jackson and some other black politicians are encouraging black voters to regard the mayor's office as a racial entitlement.

Meanwhile, although the Republicans have designated a candidate, another guy wants in. Edward "Fast Eddie" Vrdolyak, former Cook County Democratic chairman who recently turned Republican, is mounting a write-in campaign for the Republican nomination. That could drain enough white ethnic voters from the Democratic primary to cost Daley a close election. (The Daley-Sawyer race is close. The city is approximately 40 percent white and 40 percent black.) Conceivably, Vrdolyak could win the Republican nomination, setting up a Dodge City general election between him, the symbol of white hostility to Harold Washington, and two black candidates (Sawyer and Evans).

A Republican mayor? Not likely. The games being played by politicians are stirring fewer passions than in recent elections because citizens are increasingly serious. Chicago is somewhat healthier politically because it is becoming sicker socially.

The city government's budget has grown as city population has declined. The city's solvency depends on retaining and attracting job-creating and tax-paying businesses. That is becoming desperately difficult because of what most people recognize as the most important issue, the disastrous condition of Chicago's public-school system.

The system is 60 percent black, 24 percent Hispanic. Forty percent of the students flunk at least two major courses a year. Almost half do not graduate. Half the 65 high schools are in the bottom 1—yes, 1—percent of U.S. schools in student performance on the American College Test (ACT). The average high-school graduate seeking a job reads at the level of an average American eighth-grader. One-fourth of these graduates read at the sixth-grade average.

This city of broad shoulders is not stacking wheat anymore. It is increasingly a city of nimble fingers on computer terminals. Many new jobs are in financial services. Chicago businesses are at the breaking point in their ability to compete while building in the cost of doing what the schools do not do—teaching skills suited to today's workplace.

When William Bennett was U.S. Secretary of Education, he called Chicago's schools the worst in the nation. Are they? "Everyone knows that," says Daley.

He still lives two blocks from his father's house in the near Southside neighborhood where his mother, sister, brother and many friends from grammar school and high school still live. His politics, like his slightly doughy shape, lack edge, as do the politics of Sawyer. These are not divisive men.

That is good, because behind the gleaming lake front, Chicago is caught in a dynamic of decline. The next mayor—Chicago has had five in 13 years—is going to bump against the sharp shards of a fractured city.

February 23, 1989

New York, New York, It's a Declining Town

NEW YORK—It is cold, it is dark, it is drizzling, it is late October, he is late for his next appearance, he is low on money and at the moment he is losing the race for mayor. And what Rudolph Giuliani must do right now is convince a roomful of Jewish voters to think of him as Fiorello LaGuardia. Good luck.

LaGuardia—"The Little Flower"—was, like Giuliani, a Republican. There the resemblance ends. LaGuardia was a protean force, a politician in every chromosome. A reporter recalls that he "sat in a condition of more or less constant gesticulation." Here is a sample of LaGuardia's Sunday morning radio broadcasts:

"Ladies, I want to ask you a little favor. I want you please to wear your rubbers when you go out in this weather. If you don't wear your rubbers you may slip and hurt yourself. . . . Now another word about fish. . . ."

Giuliani's body language, and his language on the stump—earnest, dry, not a lot of laughs—says: Politics is not my profession. A former prosecutor, Giuliani is not as chilly as "The Little Man on the Wedding Cake" (Thomas Dewey, another crime-busting New York Republican), but it is laughable when he says that he, like LaGuardia, is a "fusion" candidate.

Who is fusing with whom? Republicans are outnumbered five-to-one here. Anyway, cold fusion does not work.

Six months ago, polls showed Giuliani shellacking Ed Koch, the three-term incumbent mayor. Then Koch got unhorsed in the Democratic primary by David Dinkins, Manhattan borough president. Koch's act was stale and Giuliani could have run on the theme, "Buttoned-down (or buttoned up, for that matter) is beautiful."

Dinkins, who would be New York's first black mayor, is commonly characterized as "cautious," although it is not usually considered cautious to forget to file tax forms—federal, state or city—for four straight years. That and other misadventures with legal niceties include an aromatic stock transaction (in 1983, he valued a stock holding at $1 million; in 1985, he sold it to his son for $58,000), and living in subsidized housing for which he is spectacularly ineligible. He has ties to some colorful political zanies on the lunatic left, including a convicted kidnapper who reacted indignantly when accused of anti-Semitism: "Anti-Semitism? I'm anti-white."

Were it not for the $12 million negative campaign run against Giuliani by the rich, feckless Ronald Lauder in the Republican primary, Giuliani might be winning. He still might win, poor fellow.

The city needs more of everything, from drug-treatment facilities to hospital beds for AIDS patients to jail cells to infrastructure investment. But most of all, it needs a vibrant middle class and that class already is in flight from taxes. Dinkins understandably does not like to talk about taxes or (he is ahead) much else. Giuliani plans to pay for the future by eliminating "corruption" and seizing the assets of drug dealers. Really.

The city's spiraling decline is stunning. In 1945, a Gallup poll found that 90 percent of New Yorkers called themselves happy. Would 10 percent today? Here is a genuine sample of graffiti back then: "Nuts to all the boys on Second Avenue—except between 68th and 69th Streets." According to a *Look* magazine survey in 1945, 92 percent of New Yorkers were in bed by 10:30 P.M. Today, muggers seem to make up more than 8 percent of the population.

I exaggerate. Slightly. New York is called the city where everyone mutinies but no one deserts. Wrong. Juan Samuel of the New York Mets wants to be traded. A team official explains: "He and his wife had a difficult time with the city. They were robbed a couple of times. He just didn't have a good experience in New York." Samuel has played second base, a position not for the fainthearted.

Who is having a good experience? There are 28,000 children in foster care. Infant mortality is 20 percent above the scandalous national average. In Manhattan and the Bronx, one in every 60 newborns tests positive for the AIDS virus. Last year, 5,000 babies were born with narcotics in their blood. Many were born to some of the 140,000 children under 17 who are cocaine, crack or heroin addicts. Forty percent of teenage girls will be pregnant at least once before they turn 20.

Forty percent of all the city's children live in poverty. Fewer than half the ninth-graders graduate four years later, although 85 percent of new jobs require at least a high-school diploma. Murders are up 20 percent in two years. Crime costs small business $1 billion a year. Wonder why? The chance of actually going to jail for a felony is 2 percent.

Mayor Jimmy "Gentleman Jim" Walker, who married a chorus girl and drove a Duesenberg and governed, sort of, from 1925 until he hotfooted it out of the country to escape fraud charges in 1932, said he would rather be a lamppost in New York than mayor of Chicago. Nowadays it's better to be a lamppost in New York than mayor of it.

October 26, 1989

Houston Hits the Comeback Trail

HOUSTON—What a difference just half a decade can make in the life of a city.

With the sort of bad timing that is the result of bad luck, the bad timing that any journalist can understand, Jan Morris, the travel writer, picked 1982 to celebrate Houston as "the best hope the time can offer."

She compared it to Queen Victoria's London, or New York or Chicago in their salad days. Houston was, she marveled, a city of centripetal forces, a city metastasizing, where the vocabulary "is habitually in the future tense" and the Sunday papers carried 40 pages of help-wanted ads. Few boomtowns ever boomed as Houston did between 1973 and 1982.

With the sort of bad timing that any politician can sympathize with, Kathryn Whitmire picked 1982 to become Houston's mayor. She came to power thinking that her task was to deal with the problems of pell-mell growth. She must be a glutton for punishment: She is starting her fourth two-year term. But she has the serenity of someone who can reasonably suppose that she has seen the worst.

Visitors to her office walk past a wall adorned with an admonition spelled out in large art deco lettering: "Cities and Thrones Stand in Time's Eye." Houston does not need to be reminded of the impermanence of prosperity.

Houston became a focus of the national epidemic of *schadenfreude* (the emotion of the '80s: taking pleasure from the misfortunes of others) because of the fall of oil and natural-gas prices, first in 1982 and again in 1986. Houston had typified the Texas "too much ain't enough" spirit, but suddenly see-through skyscrapers—new and empty—became symbols of the city in which John Connally, Bunker Hunt and other high rollers were brought low.

In the 1970s, the state government ran surpluses of up to $3 billion a year. But every $1 drop in the price of a barrel of oil cost the state $100 million in revenues and cost the state economy $3 billion.

Texas had considered itself recession-proof, or at least the place where the recession came last and left first. Actually, the economy of the "oil patch" (Texas, Oklahoma, Louisiana) was in an inverse relation to the nation's economy. In the 1970s, when rocketing energy prices drove the nation into stagflation, Texas produced less and prospered. Oil production fell from 1.3 billion barrels in 1972 to 945.1 million barrels in 1981, but revenues rose from $4.5 billion to $31.7 billion. Natural-gas production fell from 8.7 trillion cubic feet to 7 trillion while revenues soared from $1.4 billion to $12.6 billion.

However, in 1982 Jan Morris had detected something evanescent about Houston. She recalled that the glory days of cities come and go. When Charles Dickens arrived by train in Chicago, the conductor boasted to him: "You are entering the Boss City of the Universe." Morris said the future never lasts, that Houston's ascendancy would be as ephemeral as any other. She imagined Houston emptying itself "in an exodus as terrific as its influx," Mexicans streaming back south toward the border, oilmen fleeing in their Gulfstream jets.

But great cities do not disperse, they diversify. Today Houston's largest employer is the Texas Medical Center. In this respect, Houston, the South's largest city, resembles some Rust Belt cities. The largest employer in Cleveland is a medical center. The largest in Pittsburgh is the University of Pittsburgh.

The oil patch did not use its wealth to prepare for a future insulated from the vicissitudes of oil prices. "Oil," wrote the *Economist* of London, "made the oil patch rich; it also made it feckless, lazy and conceited." The oil patch entered the 1970s relatively poor and far behind the rest of the nation in education and other indices of development.

Much of the money and many of the mores of the West come from extraction industries—oil, gas, mining. Such industries involve hard physical work and good luck, booms and busts. They are not industries that encourage attitudes conducive to husbanding resources and investing in the social and physical infrastructure needed for steady prosperity over the long haul. Extraction industries are bastions of rugged individualism. They do not encourage in the community a propensity for collective provision.

But now Houston is developing a saving diversity. One moral of its recent roller-coaster history is an old moral. It is that in the lives of cities, or nations, things rarely are as good or as bad as they seem. Another moral the nation should draw from this metropolis-as-microcosm is that the future has a way of arriving unannounced. Its arrival is jolting when people have not prepared for it. One way to prepare is by governing with a two-word truism in mind: Nothing lasts.

January 17, 1988

Lyndon and the Liberal

The best biographers, it is sometimes said, are conscientious enemies of their subjects: scrupulous when sifting evidence, but unenthralled and disposed to suspicion. Robert A. Caro, the indefatigable and unforgiving biographer of Lyndon Johnson, has now published the second of his projected four volumes.

It is, as Caro intended, fascinating and dismaying. It also is some things Caro did not intend, a case study of flight from the inescapable ambiguities of political judgment.

Caro, 53, is a liberal devoting the prime of his professional life—14 years so far—to pulverizing the reputation of the most consequential liberal politician of the postwar era. Caro probably voted for Johnson rather than Goldwater in 1964. It is probably good that Johnson was president when the racial crisis reached a roily boil because, as Caro writes:

"Abraham Lincoln struck off the chains of black Americans, but it was Lyndon Johnson who led them into voting booths, closed democracy's sacred curtain behind them, placed their hands on the lever that gave them a hold on their own destiny, made them, at last and forever, a true part of American political life."

That true tribute appears in the introduction to *Means of Ascent*, this volume dealing only with Johnson's life from 1941 through 1948. Nothing in the more than 400 pages that follow gives the reader an inkling of how Johnson was capable of any goodness.

This volume tells three dismal stories: how Johnson lied about his brief military service, how he used political power to begin making a fortune in the federally regulated broadcasting industry, and (this consumes half the book) how he acquired a Senate seat by winning the 1948 Democratic primary. Caro demonstrates, with sledgehammer force, how Johnson stole the election, defeating Coke Stevenson, whom Caro reveres and romanticizes.

But had Caro been a Texas voter in 1948, he probably would have done what most Texas liberals did: voted for Johnson.

Coke Stevenson was a rancher and lawyer whose character may have been, as Caro insists, a splendid distillation of frontier individualism and rectitude. But in his political life, he was a familiar Southwestern type of his day, well to the right of the ground Barry Goldwater was later to occupy, and racist in a way common then but that Johnson never was.

Caro makes a plausible case that Johnson saved his career by stealing 35,000 votes. But the verb "steal" must be used gingerly in this context.

These were not 35,000 votes that otherwise would have been cast after the free deliberation of informed and uncoerced individuals behind democracy's sacred curtain. Many—almost certainly most—of those votes were going to be delivered as a block, at some boss's discretion, to someone. (In other elections they had been delivered to the sainted Stevenson.) The precincts that had better than 90 percent turnouts and larger than 90 percent landslides for Johnson had been "voting" that way for a long time, for other candidates.

Johnson got 494,191 votes, Stevenson 494,104. Subtract 35,000 votes from Johnson's total (never mind that Caro acknowledges that votes were stolen from Stevenson) and it would still have been a close race, largely because of Johnson's support among poor, labor and liberal voters. It is not extenuating but it is interesting that, as president, Johnson did as much as anyone to make impossible the kind of electoral corruption that flourished in Texas, and not only there (see Chicago, 1960). He did it by fostering a dramatic expansion of federal power over the electoral process.

Caro believes that many more than 35,000 Johnson votes were tainted by his "modern" campaign techniques (campaigning by helicopter, and with a broadcasting blitz). Caro's rhapsodical account of Stevenson meandering from one small town, and tiny audience, to another has a misty romanticism to it, until you ask: Why, precisely is it good to campaign in a way that communicates to such a tiny sliver of the electorate?

It is fun to execrate the frequent superficiality—and worse—of media politics. But broadcasting helped put bosses out of business by enabling candidates to talk directly to voters. Caro may pine for the days when a candidate had "no electronic devices to mediate between himself and them" (the voters). But then, the mediating was apt to be done by the bosses so repellent to Caro.

Caro's narrative prompts this thought: Perhaps something in liberalism, or the liberal temperament, disposes liberals to make aesthetic judgments about politics, subordinating substantive judgments to the romance of style.

Johnson was a bullying vulgarian, often crudely unethical, sometimes corrupt. He also was the most potent promoter of the liberal agenda since Franklin Roosevelt. Reality is often messy that way, and perhaps something in the liberal mentality has trouble coming to terms with such untidiness.

March 22, 1990

Mario Cuomo's Sparring Spirit

NEW YORK—It is rush hour, it is raining, traffic has congealed and Mario Cuomo, running late and looking uneasy, warily asks his driver if it is "French Connection" time. The driver, a willowy but steely lady state trooper, recognizes the reference to the hair-curling automobile-chase scene in the movie of that name, a chase along Manhattan's West Side, which is where she is now threading the governor through traffic en route to a statewide radio call-in show.

That show will be a suitable setting for considering the possibility that Cuomo has, as has been charged, a dreaded skin problem. Summon the specialists in political dermatology: Has Cuomo got thin skin?

Since becoming a national figure—since winning the governorship in 1982—he has had a reputation for sensitivity concerning his treatment by the media. His comportment during his runaway reelection this autumn convinced many people that his personality is too brittle for the bruising business of running for president.

The truth is that he is indeed somewhat thin-skinned—and that this is not altogether bad. He also is intellectually quick and combative, qualities that can cause slower and thinner-skinned journalists to call him thin-skinned.

Cuomo's bullying behavior against a hapless opponent this year was especially unpleasant coming from someone who has worked so hard the "love" and "compassion" pedals on the political organ. (We must be "strong enough to use the words 'love' and 'compassion.' ") He set absurd conditions for debates, held only one at the last minute and was insufferably rude when his opponent phoned him on a radio show.

Criticized for these and other matters, he has made angry calls to reporters and has called journalists "spoiled," "ingrates" and "incompetents" who "made me look bad." Such petulant behavior is especially peculiar from a man possessing the confidence and spirit he displayed during the call-in show on a rainy night.

Annabelle from Ithaca phoned to say she and others deserve a cost-of-living adjustment to their state pensions. Cuomo responded: Why? That was not part of the agreement when you took your job.

A retailer from near the Pennsylvania line called to complain that New York's sales tax causes shoppers to shop in Pennsylvania, so it should be reduced. Cuomo: Oh? Then Annabelle really will get nothing. And don't you want better schools, more jails?

A caller who accused President Reagan of heartlessness regarding the homeless got from Cuomo a guided tour through "the Judeo-Christian tradition" and the theory of federalism, including a devil's advocate defense of the Reaganite belief that compassion should be personal rather than governmental, and if governmental then locally administered. A caller demanding a pardon for Jean Harris elicited another dose of the didactic Cuomo, who explained the difference between a pardon and clemency, but not before boxing the caller's ears for implying that the Harris trial jurors were incompetent.

Cuomo rattled off facts supplied by a human library named Elaine Ryan, seated next to him. He handled the calls with no announcer or other intermediary. It was a graceful performance—assertive without being abrasive, teaching without condescension. It was the behavior of a man who should not brawl with journalists, or should do so not from pique but only for sport.

Recently he tried to change the subject regarding the press by delivering a speech. In it he restated some of his valid criticisms of the media (a herd mentality, irresponsible use of unnamed sources, the reflexive dismissal of most criticism as 'Nixonian') but did so more in sorrow than in anger, warning that if journalists do not shape up, courts may slap them down.

He had in mind increased judicial interest in less-exacting standards for finding the press guilty of libel. But his and others' reasonable criticisms of the press pertain to its distortion of their public performances, not personal defamation. Still, the speech, although oddly focused, was an attempt to be less prickly.

That quality is hardly the principal impediment to any desire he may have to be president. He is more liberal than the electorate. Regarding foreign policy, he is a blank slate and it is unclear who will write on that slate.

However, his sparring spirit can be overstimulating, even when he is being playful. Shortly after he became governor, a woman approached to introduce her small son, who by now probably has recovered from the experience which, as recalled by a fellow who was with Cuomo, went like this:

Cuomo: "How old are you?"
Boy: "Six."
Cuomo: "Six? How do you know you are six? Just because she (indicating mom) says so? Or do you feel six? And what is 'six'?"

At which point the boy, and who can blame him, burst into tears. He was suffering metaphysical overload, an affliction the national electorate may one day experience, and perhaps even enjoy.

December 7, 1986

Democrats Learn a New Language

The New Republic's search for the world's most boring headline turned up some beauties: DRAMATIC CHANGES FAIL TO MATERIALIZE ON HILL, GLOBAL GROWTH: A TASK FOR ALL, CHILL FALLS ON WARMING RELATIONS BETWEEN AUSTRALIA AND INDONESIA.. The winner was: WORTHWHILE CANADIAN INITIATIVE. But if the contest were still on, the winner would be the headline on a *Harper's* magazine symposium: WHAT'S WRONG WITH THE DEMOCRATS? Here . . . we . . . go . . . again. Was that the 784,452nd such symposium of the '80s, or is it the first of one-shudders-to-think-how-many of the '90s? Good grief. One does not ask much of Democrats, but can't they at least be boring in new ways?

Surprise: The symposium is not just the usual silliness. Consider, first, the nonsense that is *not* said. There is little talk of salvation through higher turnouts, of blaming Democratic defeats on mythical legions of liberals, sulking at home waiting to be intoxicated by 90-proof political liquor. Democrats may be educable after all. They may have noted that if 100 percent of the electorate had voted in 1988, Dukakis would have absorbed a worse drubbing, according to polling data. Not even selective mobilization would have sufficed. If the voting rate of the poor had matched that of the nonpoor, Bush still would have won by 5 million votes. He would have won—pay attention, you Democratic class warriors—if every voter from families with incomes of more than $50,000 had been banned from voting. If blacks and Hispanics had voted at the rate whites did, Bush still would have won by 4 million. This is one reason why Jesse Jackson is Yesterday's Man. He always runs as Mobilization Man.

There is, two elections too late, a new, sharp edge to some Democrats' talk about Jackson. Congresswoman Barbara Boxer of California suggests telling Jackson, "You run the risk of becoming a Harold Stassen." Roland Burris, Illinois state comptroller, is black and does a familiar, boring number: Democrats lose because too many Americans are racists. His number is not well received. When he says Dukakis lost Illinois because "a lot of black voters sat on their hands because of the mistreatment of Jesse," Congressman Barney Frank of Massachusetts snaps, "Jesse was not mistreated. He didn't win."

Burris: "People made a lot out of Dukakis not calling Jackson about the vice presidency."

Frank: "Then I'd say to the black voters, 'If you are going to refuse to vote for someone for president who'll act demonstrably more in your interest because somebody didn't phone somebody, I wash my hands of the situation. I am serious. We have encouraged people to be self-indulgent in our groups."

The groups seem to some Democrats like house guests who are wearing out their welcome by leaving wet towels on the bathroom floor and complaining about the selection of breakfast cereals. Bruce Babbitt, former Arizona governor and presidential candidate, says the party is lousy at winning the White House because it is too good at winning everything else by "the politics of disaggregation." Because the party has only discrete issues for particular interests, its whole seems less than its component parts. Frank suggests a grand theme: Come home, America.

True, McGovern tried that and swept Massachusetts. But in 1992, the first post–Cold War election, something like that theme might work. Frank, who seems to have spent time at a Betty Ford Clinic for Chronic Liberals, says: "We can now say, 'Harry Truman, we succeeded. Containment has worked, the Marshall Plan has worked, and the occupation of Japan has worked.' " It's time to come back home. We can reorient these resources toward education, improve our international competitive strength and be nicer to ourselves. And we can make it clear that we are doing this out of a sense of American triumphalism, not beating up on American imperialism."

Now, Frank's pearl of wisdom is stuck in a dumpling of foolishness. Do not try to talk about Truman, Marshall, containment, to the 1992 electorate, the median age of which will be 41. About half the 1992 voters were not born when Truman left office. All they know of that ancient history is what they learned watching MTV: nothing. And what resources are to be "reoriented"? The "peace dividend"? Imagine a big one. Now double it. It will be swallowed by the savings and loan shambles. So if Frank's agenda requires much money, there must be a tax increase, and Frank, a recovering taxaholic from mendicant Massachusetts, says that idea is political poison.

Babbitt: "Didn't San Francisco impose a tax surcharge for earthquake relief? Does that suggest anything to you?"

Frank: "Yes. If we have a *national* earthquake, we can raise taxes."

Boxer says: "In telling our story of American winning, we could also point out that the Republican story had some very sad endings. One in five kids lives in poverty—"

Frank: "No, we can't. We are always preaching doom and gloom; we sound like we are wearing hair shirts. We are a bit like the guy with the sign that says, 'The world's going to end on Thursday.' Well, it's the following Tuesday afternoon."

Actually, both Boxer and Frank are bang on, she intellectually, he politically. She cites America's worst problem, broad-scale urban regression that wastes lives and blights America's success as an urban civilization. Democrats are supposed to talk about such things. It is what they do, and if they do not, well, as Truman said, give people a choice between a Republican and a Republican, they will pick the Republican every time. But Frank knows that Democrats have too often described America's problems as indictments of a "sick society" rather than as blemishes on a prosperous, admirable nation. Democrats are trying for a grown-up tone of voice: Look, we are a successful society with some problems. Eighteen years ago McGovernites said, in effect, "Come home, America, because you are a paranoid, racist, imperialist menace to the world." Today's version can be: Come home with the flag ("I pledge allegiance to the . . .") flying triumphantly and address the few big flaws in this, the best nation. Read their lips: Democrats may be learning the language that wins elections, the language of nationalism.

January 15, 1990

A Law to Send Lawmakers Home?

The best reason for enacting Representative Bill Frenzel's bill is that he, a sound fellow, wrote it. The decisive reason for rejecting it is that it would retire its author.

Not to worry. Frenzel, a Minnesota Republican now in his tenth term, has submitted to ten Congresses his bill to limit congressmen to nine terms and senators to three. Once—he cannot remember when or who—he got one cosponsor. Frenzel, who came to Congress when two crucial committee chairmen (Banking and Currency, and Judiciary) had cumulatively 90 years of seniority, has an old idea whose time will never come.

Mandatory rotation of congressmen was required in the Continental Congress (a limit of three years' service in any six years). The 1988 Republican Platform endorsed the idea of limits on terms, but flinched from specifying them. This year, a dozen bills propose limits, most specifying two Senate and six House terms or three House terms of four years each. (The Senate would never agree to four-year House terms: Congressmen could run against senators without risking their seats.)

In the first House election after President Washington was elected, 40 percent of incumbents were defeated, allaying anxieties about an entrenched "government of strangers." In the 19th century, 40 to 50 percent of House seats changed hands at each election, often through voluntary retirements: 19th-century travel and life in Washington boardinghouses were experiences easy to forsake. After the turmoil of the early 1860s, House seniority began to rise. Establishment of standing committees made seniority matter and the expanding role of Washington made Congress matter more. But not until the turn of the 20th century did the average House seniority reach even five years.

What has changed since 1945 is the number of incumbents seeking reelection, ranging from a low of 382 (1978) to 411 (1956, 1966). Still, during Reagan's presidency 55 percent of the House turned over; since 1974, 81 percent; since Speaker Tom Foley was elected in 1964, 93 percent. Average seniority in the House in 1971 was six terms; today it is 5.8.

In today's Senate, the mean years of service is 9.8. A two-term limit would eliminate 20 senators. In the first four postwar decades, the success rate for senators seeking reelection was only 74.9 percent. If that rate held for the House, 100 would lose every two years. Senators are less secure because their constituencies are larger and more diverse and Senate races often attract two strong candidates.

There simply are lots of one-party House districts. In 1988, 56 of the 435 seats were uncontested; 20 winners topped 90 percent of the vote; 70 percent (306) won 65 percent; if landslides begin at 55 percent, there were 401 landslides. In 1986, 98 percent of incumbents running won; in 1988, 99.2 percent. Even in modern America's most tumultuous year, 1968, 96.8 percent won.

In today's House, the mean years of service is 11.6, but 34 percent of members have served seven or more terms, and they are the most important—some would say most stagnant—third. Most turnover comes off the bottom third, often from younger members (often Republicans facing a bleak future in a permanent minority) leaving to run for Senate or state offices. Forty Democrats and 19 Republicans have been here at least as long as Frenzel has. (Mississippi's Jamie Whitten was elected 33 days before Pearl Harbor.)

Frenzel would relish the pleasure of "taking a few with me" if his bill took him out. Limits on terms would indeed prune much deadwood, but also would chop down all the tall cotton: all great careers are long. Frenzel believes the ratio of mediocrity (or worse) to excellence is too high to protect the former for the sake of the latter.

Could be, but so could this: Limits on terms might confirm the axiom that all improvements make matters worse.

Compulsory rotation of offices would bring in "fresh faces," but another name for them is "rookies," people with a lot to learn in a town where there is a lot to know. Forcing out veteran legislators would increase the power of the "permanent government"—congressional staff, executive bureaucracies. Forced circulation of congressional elites also would please another entrenched elite—the press (and that is another reason for not doing it).

The idea of limiting terms recurs because there is deep in America's soul a streak of Jeffersonian sentimentality unsuited to today's Hamiltonian realities. Ideologically, Americans favor citizen-legislators because Americans like to think they favor a small central government comprehensible by amateurs who could not do much damage anyway. Practically, however, Americans are remorseless Hamiltonians, demanding an immense government (the bureaucracy grew—by 214,000—even under Reagan) and career legislators looking after constituency interests.

Incumbents win because Americans despise Congress but love their particular congressman, who toils tirelessly to deliver services. Incumbents are entrenched by democratic choices, and Americans have a constitutional right to democracy, not good government.

January 7, 1990

In the Grip of Gambling

It has been 308 years since William Penn began what he considered a holy errand into the wilderness. He founded a community in which government would try to be a force for moral improvement. Imagine what he would think of Pennsylvania in the grip of gambling fever fomented by the state's government.

State lotteries rarely reach the giddy heights attained by Pennsylvania's last week when the prize rose to $115 million. However, the state-lottery industry (Nevada likes to speak of gambling as the "gaming industry") is big business. Twenty-eight states and the District of Columbia, with 68 percent of the population, have lotteries. Americans gamble $90 per capita annually with governments. Cotton Mather, call your office: Your New England is a hotbed of gambling. Per capita spending on lotteries in Connecticut ($158) and Massachusetts ($234) is well above New York ($91) and Pennsylvania ($121).

States spend $200 million advertising their lotteries, creating and inflaming gamblers. However, the most potent advertisements are the gargantuan jackpots. Pennsylvania sold 11 million tickets in one morning to mobs of buyers, some of whom flocked to the state by car, bus, train and plane. Last December, when New York's jackpot was a piddling $45 million, the state's 5,600 vendors were selling 28,000 tickets a minute. In three days 37.4 million were sold. Government is not ineffective when the task is to turn citizens into lemmings. Those who win $1 million are .000008 percent of the 97 million lottery gamblers.

James Cook, writing in *Forbes* magazine, reports that in the fiscal year ending June 1988, state lotteries had sales of $15.6 billion, about equal to the gross of the U.S. primary aluminum industry. After subtracting payouts and overhead the states received about $6 billion for their general funds or particular uses (education, the elderly, transportation). Lottery earnings have been growing an average of 17.5 percent annually, a rate comparable to that of the computer industry. For the year ending this June, earnings may be $7 billion, more than the budgets of 40 states. Cook says lotteries were used to finance the founding of Jamestown, the Continental Army, Dartmouth, Harvard, Princeton and public works such as roads and canals. In 1832 Philadelphia's 200 lottery shops dispensed prizes of $53 million, equal to $600 million today. Lotteries are getting a small share of the estimated $200 billion wagered in America each year ($2.5 billion on the Super Bowl alone). Cook asks, "Why not harness frivolous instincts to serve worthy causes?" A fair question. What *is* wrong with raising so much money from consenting adults who evidently derive pleasure from being fleeced? Plenty is wrong with it.

One state's welfare is uniquely woven into gambling, but Nevada has an excuse: The silver was gone, the soil was lousy and the would-be divorcées were bored. After the Comstock Lode petered out, Nevada eventually discovered divorce as a way of making money from federalism. Nevada crushed the competition of a few other states in setting the shortest residency requirement, then looked around for a new way to mine money from the law, and found gambling. Now, one Nevada is kind of nice. But there is something sinister about more and more governments becoming more and more addicted to money from what was until recently considered a vice.

Reporting on "America's gambling fever," *Business Week* notes that gambling is part of the weekly, even daily routine of tens of millions of Americans. And new technologies, such as television gambling for couch potatoes and video lottery terminals (street-corner casinos run by state lotteries), may soon make gambling more ubiquitous.

Aggressive government marketing of gambling gives a legitimizing imprimatur to the pursuit of wealth without work. By blurring the distinction between well-earned and "ill-gotten" gains—a distinction blurred enough by Michael Milken, LBO's and other phenomena—government-run gambling repudiates an idea once important to this republic's sense of virtue. The idea is that citizens are distinguished more by the moral worth of the way they make money than by how much money they make.

People who want to delegitimize capitalist societies encourage the belief that much wealth is allocated in "speculative," meaning capricious, ways. That is, too much goes to people who earn their bread neither by physical nor mental exertion—neither by the sweat of their brows nor by the wrinkling of their brows in socially useful thought. Gambling is debased speculation, a craving for sudden wealth unconnected with investment that might make society more productive. Government-fostered gambling for huge stakes institutionalizes windfalls, and thus does recurring injury to society's sense of elemental equities.

Gambling fever reflects and exacerbates what has been called the "fatalism of the multitude." The more people believe in the importance of luck, chance, randomness, fate, the less they believe in the importance of stern virtues such as industriousness, thrift, deferral of gratification, diligence, studiousness. It is drearily understandable why lotteries—skill-less gambling; gambling for the lazy—are booming at a time when the nation's productivity, competitiveness, savings rate and academic performance are poor.

Finally, and most important, there is the degradation of democratic politics. Once upon a time social health was thought to be connected with the political courage to ask, and the civic virtue to grant, taxes sufficient to pay the price of national security and necessary public services. Nowadays the voice from the nation's bully pulpit preaches that it is unthinkable that people should pay taxes commensurate with their demands for services. And state politicians are pleased to winkle money from people irrationally excited by improbable dreams.

"Governments, like clocks," wrote William Penn, "go from the motion that men give them." Today many state governments are driven by delusions they have instilled. States do not pass truth-in-gambling laws that would require full, forceful explanations of the odds against winning. Once upon a time, mass irrationality was considered a menace to democratic government. In this age of lotteries, manufacturing mobs is a government goal and mass hysteria is an important ingredient of public finance.

May 8, 1989

"Realism" by the Polls

Perhaps Representative Harold Rogers, the Kentucky Republican, was just joking in the robust, exaggerating tradition of America's middle border. Let us assume so, for his sake. Otherwise he becomes one more reason to doubt Republicans' seriousness. What he said was:

"Every statesman in the world over the last four decades, from Churchill to Reagan, has attempted—with millions of troops and trillions of dollars—to free up Eastern Europe . . . and to no avail, until the first year of the Baker administration at State."

That scrumptious specimen of the *post hoc ergo propter hoc* fallacy (the rooster crows and the sun rises, therefore the crowing caused the sunrise) was contained in a *Los Angeles Times* report on how bullish Washington is about Secretary of State James Baker. The report contained another illuminating passage.

The scene was a breakfast table around which sat Baker and some congressmen, two of whom, both Democrats, asked: If the Cold War is over, why does the budget not reflect that fact, particularly regarding increased aid for the new democracies in Eastern Europe, and poor Third World countries?

According to the *Times*, "Baker's hazel eyes narrowed. His honeyed voice went cold." And his dehoneyed voice said: "You want to go out and argue for higher taxes to pay for foreign aid? Try that argument out in your district, Congressman."

Such swaggering "realism" sends shivers of admiration through some Washingtonians. But the important issue is not whether the congressman can afford, politically, to take that position regarding foreign aid, or whether the country can afford, economically, the aid. Rather, the crucial question is whether the country can afford to have a government that thinks so much the way Baker does.

Baker reflects the President, and policy-by-polls reflects thinness of beliefs. So does the hitching of U.S. foreign policy to foreign personalities, as in U.S. dithering about Lithuania, an unseemly policy of solicitousness for Gorbachev, whose survival is the President's only clear foreign-policy aim. More "realism."

Recently Washington went into one of its periodic seizures of loopiness, and this time the great question of the hour concerned the presidential epidermis: who gets under George Bush's skin. No one does, said Himself, through clenched teeth, when asked specifically about Representative Richard Gephardt, the House majority leader. But Gephardt (D–Mo.) clearly did, by saying things like: "Harry Truman lived by Sam Houston's maxim: 'Do right, risk consequences.'

The maxim of the Bush administration seems to be, 'Do polls, risk nothing.' " Truman, Gephardt notes, launched Point Four and the Marshall Plan (the seed of containment, which preceded Baker's thrilling dissolution of communism) when a Gallup Poll showed only 14 percent support for foreign aid.

Americans had long deferred purchases of houses, cars, even clothes, and had shed blood on the soil of nations then seeking aid. And Truman was then more unpopular than Nixon was to be during Watergate. But he would not be a president who "thinks he is too big to do the necessary persuading," so he deserved to be reelected, and was.

Today's popularity-hoarding President may yet learn that such political parsimony is false economy. Speaking of which . . .

We are in the midst of (although perhaps not yet even halfway through) the costliest debacle in the history of American governance. The savings-and-loan scandal is another black hole swallowing a share of our children's standard of living. New losses are much larger than even recently predicted. The eventual cost is unknown (estimates range from $300 billion to $500 billion), but three things are known.

We know that in this decade alone the bailout will, as Senator Lloyd Bentsen says, cost more than will be spent on highways, or on the war on drugs, or on preschool education.

We know that this diversion of capital from more productive uses will, like the Reagan-Bush deliberate deficits, lower the standard of living, economic and cultural, of coming generations.

And we know that one reason so many billions are hemorrhaging away is that the Bush administration is saving a few millions by scrimping on FBI agents and Justice Department investigators and prosecutors.

The savings-and-loan crisis is complicated, silent and slow-motion. It is the sort of murky mess about which there is no focused public opinion. So no polls tell the Bush administration to behave properly. So it doesn't.

April 1, 1990

Bush's Year One: The Echoing Emptiness

An unenthralled assessment of George Bush's first year as president is this: his campaign showed little promise and he has kept his promise. In foreign policy, he is perhaps the perfect president for America the by-stander. Domestically, not since the 1920s have Americans looked less to the national government for leadership, or believed less that what it does matters to their lives. So in Bush, the man and the moment have met.

A less mild assessment of Bush's Year One is that his administration illustrates—in a sense is—the echoing emptiness at the core of contem-porary politics. Its intellectual and moral flaccidity reflect (we do indeed have representative government) the sagging of America deeper into a peripheral role abroad and self-indulgence at home.

The words of American liberty are on the lips of millions struggling to dismember the Soviet empire. The administration seems worried that they will succeed. East Germany's communists, clinging to levers of power, must have been buoyed by the secretary of state's December visit. Lithuanian aspirations for independence are considered, by some in the administration, a disagreeable inconvenience to Gorbachev, the falling star to which the administration has hitched its wagon, and the nation. Two-and-a-half million Panamanians are better off because of the Bush administration. A billion Chinese are not.

Bush's presidency began rolling downhill during his Inaugural Ad-dress when he said, "We have more will than wallet; but will is what we need." Actually, by "will" he meant something less sturdy. He meant rightmindedness—having nice aspirations unconnected with resources.

During the Inaugural Address, Bush got his presidency-by-gestures going by extending a hand to a Democrat and praising "bipartisanship."

In domestic affairs, bipartisanship usually is collaboration in something disreputable but mutually convenient. Today's bipartisanship is an amiable conspiracy to cook the books, and run up the debt, and give people a dollar of government while charging them 75 cents for it, and get reelected.

Small wonder Congress likes Bush, who does not rock the boat. But being liked is not a bankable asset. The Congress that thinks he's a swell guy administered to him the stunning rejection of his nominee (John Tower) to be secretary of defense and, even more remarkably, refused to pass his tax-cut proposal (capital gains). Congress does not fear a man who ran behind the congressional winners in 379 of 435 districts.

The ideal first term for a president gets the pain over early and saves the euphoria for election eve. Ronald Reagan wrung out inflation by quickly putting the economy through the worst contraction since the Depression. By 1984, with the Los Angeles Olympics turned into a flag-waving festival, life seemed like an endless summer. Bush is having his euphoria now—the end of the Cold War, and all that.

But a harbinger of harder-edged politics is Senator Daniel Patrick Moynihan's proposal to cut Social Security taxes. This would deprive the government of a flood of revenue, thereby soiling the bipartisan fun of borrow-borrow, spend-spend, reelect-reelect.

With a mixture of obtuseness and arrogance, the White House first said derisively that "Mr. Moynihan's got a lot of ideas," an accusation never directed at this White House. Then the administration tired of the fear factor, saying, "Democrats seem to want to fiddle with the Social Security system." That is an interesting charge from an administration content to spend the Social Security surplus as though there will be no tomorrow.

Moynihan's proposal echoes loudly, like a gunshot in a cavern, because it elicits evidence of the emptiness of an administration with only one grand passion: a yearning to make a remarkably regressive tax system even more so by cutting the capital-gains tax.

Girding his loins for another round in that fight, Bush denounces "demagogues" who say that tax would favor the rich, which of course it would. Charges of demagoguery come awkwardly from the man who wanted to fiddle with—to coin a phrase—the First Amendment to stop the epidemic of one flag-burning.

When no necessity—no economic or international crisis—requires great energy from government, government naturally slouches along the path of least resistance. That is why the administration's brightest spot, Jack Kemp's HUD, is so admirable: it is bringing energy to bear on a project—empowering the urban poor—that is optional in the sense that it is necessitated only by conscience.

As regards much of the rest of the administration's handiwork, from Beijing to the budget, it is odd to recall that candidate Bush told an audience he wanted to be president "because I believe in the honor of it all."

January 21, 1990

Less About the Man in the Kremlin, More About the Boy in the Bronx

What shall we talk about now? The Cold War's end should change the conversation of the country as conducted through journalism. We have a welcome quandary: standards of news judgment need revision. The revision should be governed by nationalism turned inward. We should be writing a bit less about Gorbachev and Lithuania and more about Darryll McPherson and the Bronx.

The triumphs in Eastern Europe and the crackup of the Soviet Union in Lithuania and elsewhere are momentous events meriting serious coverage. But journalism has finite resources and a limited claim on the public's attention. America, sighing after 60 years of Depression, war and Cold War, will budget only so much energy to thinking about public things. Journalism is not offering a balanced menu of the appropriate things.

There is much inertia in the public mind, a mind that journalism both reflects and shapes. Like a large ship that plows ahead even after the engines have been abruptly stopped, the conversation of intellectual and political elites, who are comfortable with the familiar, continues along old lines. It concerns East-West relations, the arms control agenda, the fate of NATO, etc. Journalism partakes of this decreasingly useful continuity. The result is the journalistic equivalent of elevator music—easy listening for an audience that is barely listening. The television networks, in their manic and comic narcissism, hurl their anchors hither and yon for no discernible journalistic reason, adding nothing to America's understanding of what is important. The networks' bizarre behavior is symptomatic of a general journalistic disorientation.

To the extent that Soviet adventurism is abating, many of America's international concerns are becoming as much moral as prudential. And the stakes of American politics—of elections—are lower than they were. Lower, but not negligible. If the policies produced by our politics do not so directly involve questions of national survival, they do directly engage the issue of national worthiness: Are we behaving, abroad and especially at home, in ways that nationalists—we who believe in the distinctive greatness of America's past and premises—can equably countenance?

The Soviet Union is being transformed back into Russia—a big nation rather than a fighting faith. Thus the 20th century is being transformed into the 19th, a minuet of nations and shifting balances of power. This minuet will always be consequential, even dangerous, but it is not deeply interesting. It is not because it does not often raise philosophical, as distinct from merely prudential, considerations. From Plato on, the great works of political philosophy have dealt primarily with the domestic arrangements of societies. Relations between nations, unlike relations between citizens seeking justice consensually, rarely raise genuinely philosophical—the most interesting—issues. So a reallocation of journalistic attention from foreign to domestic matters is hardly a flight from seriousness.

In advocating such a reallocation one runs the risk of seeming sympathetic to that American temptation, isolationism. It is a perennial temptation because we are a nation of immigrants who came here to get away from there; besides, the isolationist impulse is essentially just the natural human desire to be left alone to cultivate one's garden. However, "natural" is not a synonym for "right." America should remain a superpower, in material capabilities and moral intentions, and should have a journalism suited to a nation with global reach on behalf of high values.

But we need to strike a new balance when weighing what news matters most. By all means let us monitor great events abroad. But it is no disparagement of, say, the Lithuanian drama to ask: Is a proper portion of the American public's precious and scarce resource—its attention— being allocated to things like the following?

Nineteen nations have better infant mortality rates than the United States. The infant death rate in Japan is less than half the U.S. rate. (How will the alibi industry—America's high-growth sector—blame *that* on Japan's "unfair trade practices"?) The infant death rate in the nation's capital, and in Detroit and Baltimore, is humiliatingly close to a Third World rate. It is higher than in Jamaica and Costa Rica. The rate among black American babies is worse than among Hungarian or Polish babies. Nothing that happens in Bangladesh should be as interesting to Americans as the fact that a boy born in Harlem today has a lower life expectancy than a boy born in Bangladesh. Between 1978 and 1988 the number of babies born with syphilis increased sevenfold, the number born with AIDS is increasing, and 100,000 babies born each year may be chronically handicapped because of their mothers' use of crack cocaine.

Such statistics should stir nationalist feelings just as strong as, if the inverse of, those feelings of pride stirred by the ascendancy of the American idea abroad. Too many facts about America are appallingly unworthy of, and should infuriate, a nation that thinks of itself, with reason, as the finest example of popular government, blending individual freedom and community responsibility.

One evening recently Darryll McPherson, 13, looking ahead to breakfast, headed for the store in his Bronx neighborhood to buy cereal and milk. On the way Darryll, who plans to be a police officer, was severely wounded in the chest and abdomen by five of the bullets filling the evening air from a drug-related shoot-out. "I heard the shots," his mother says, "but I always hear shots." She adds, "Before I leave home every morning I say a prayer because you don't know if you're coming back."

No mother in London, Paris or Rome—or Berlin, Prague or Budapest—always hears shots and wonders each morning whether she will make it back home through the fields of fire. It is disgusting. And it is news. There is a gnawing, growing sense that savagery and second-rateness are increasing in America. However, this sense is not gnawing hard enough or growing fast enough. There is a need for a new nationalism, a fierce, proud intolerance of lawlessness and also of the slipshod, the incompetent, the uncivil. Hence there is a need for a journalism that stokes that fire.

April 9, 1990

PART 4

The Miniaturization of American Politics

Surely He Didn't Say That! (Yes, He Did)

"Pssst!" says the man lurking in a soiled raincoat in a dimly lit doorway. "Wanna buy an attack video—see politicians naked?" It is a tape, unedited, of Democratic candidates debating at the Kennedy Center.

Buy it, but be warned. You will wear out your VCR's pause and rewind buttons as you mutter to yourself, "Surely he didn't say that!" and, reviewing, you see that he did.

The front-runner, Jesse Jackson, says, "Since 1973 we've lost 38 million jobs." The rap musician of American politics is into rhyming, not reasoning, and may count as "lost" any jobs that disappear as a result of economic dynamism that is causing the total number of jobs to rise. (Think of the lost jobs in the buggy-whip industry between 1900 and 1920.)

In any case, in 1973, 85.4 million Americans were employed; today 112.7 million are. When Jackson says "58 cents of every federal dollar is spent on military buildup" (actually, defense is about 28 percent of the budget), his five frightened rivals sit like stumps, pretending not to notice the nonsense. Presumably they are saving their gumption for when they stand up to Gorbachev.

Some people say it is condescending not to take Jackson seriously as the front-runner. The real condescension is in not judging him by serious standards. Not since George Wallace has there been a candidate so uninhibited by facts. Like Wallace, Jackson has the freedom that comes from knowledge that he will not be on the ticket.

Jackson asked those in the Kennedy Center audience to raise their hands if they owned an imported VCR. Then he asked for the hands of those who owned an MX missile. You see, he said, "we're making what nobody's buying." The audience, overflowing with liberalism, applauded, unconscious of the racism that made them patronize Jackson rather than laugh him off stage.

The *New Republic* magazine, which knows that its journalistic DNA will drive it to endorse one of these men 12 months from now, notes gloomily: "Jackson's positions are only slightly more egregious versions of the party consensus anyway." By "party" read "party activists."

At the Kennedy Center, Albert Gore (D–Tenn.) noted that most Democratic voters, unlike most of the party's activists, leaders and presidential candidates, approved of the use of force in Grenada and against Libya.

Paul Simon (D–Ill.), who says foreign policy should be based on "caring for people," lifted his pinafore and cried "Eeek!" when Gore let loose this mouse of a thought: The United States has vital interests that must be defended. This coupled with Gore's accusation that some Democrats can "not get over the idea that America must always pull back" and preach "the politics of retreat, complacency and doubt," were denounced by Gore's rivals, and especially Simon, as divisive.

Richard Gephardt (D–Mo.) took a fling at fierceness toward the Soviet Union: "We have got to ask" (an exquisite choice of verb) "them to get out of Afghanistan and to stop some of the things they've done. But by the same token, we've got to be willing to stop some of the things that sometimes we have done."

Unable to leave tepid enough alone, Gephardt, who probably worries that some Iowa "peace" lobby will suspect him of cold-warriorism, could not resist adding a dash of moral symmetry. But perhaps there is progress, of sorts, here: The "blame America first" Democrats have moderated. Now they are merely "by the same token" Democrats.

There is something wrong when a presidential candidate (Gephardt) is reduced to saying things like "There is something wrong when the most important businessman in this country is Ivan Boesky." Part of what is wrong is the "sound bite" nature of these debates, in which a candidate (Gore) finds himself saying he wants to "take my full 30 seconds" to discuss the Middle East.

Alas, a few seconds are sufficient rope for some to hang themselves with. Mike Dukakis explained that he opposes the Midgetman missile because he wants to spend the money on conventional forces. But he went a tad too far.

He said: If force is "ever used," it is apt to be conventional force, not strategic nuclear force. Evidently the Dukakis doctrine is that Midgetman probably never would be launched, so it would be a waste. That is, deterrence is not a "use." *The New Republic* reserves special disgust for Dukakis who, it says, "parrots the left isolationist line—not an isolationism from strength, which is the style of the right, but an isolationism of weakness and abdication."

A London food critic recently described a restaurant as offering "nouvelle cuisine with the food added." Who will add food to the Democrats' lite politics? It certainly is less filling than it should be.

October 15, 1987

Two Cheers for Iowa

Iowa bashing and candidate disparagement are in, again. As in: Weird, narcissistic, self-aggrandizing Iowa is covered with an eczema of candidates, all discussing their views at length, although a simple apology would suffice. And 1988 is, in a sense, the centennial year of a familiar complaint. In 1888, James Bryce, an Oxford professor, wrote about "Why Great Men Are Not Chosen Presidents." Bryce lived until 1922, so, as Stephen Hess notes, he lived to see perhaps the finest array of candidates (Theodore Roosevelt, Woodrow Wilson, William Howard Taft, Charles Evans Hughes) since the founding era. Today it remains an article of faith that the people who ought to be president do not get elected, or even run, and the nominating process is to blame.

But to begin with basics, the presidency is a political job and should generally be reserved for those who have made politics their vocation. If you are reluctant to run, you probably should not; if you lack fierce desire, you probably will not have the political energy to govern effectively. So the presidency is reserved for a small subset of professional politicians—those with presidential ambition.

It is said to be irrational for Iowa to be so consequential. But what should be done? We could chop the country up into, say, six regional primaries. The first such primary, whatever states it included, would be prohibitively costly and unmanageable for any dark horse, so it would effectively shrink still more the real pool of presidential possibilities: Only the famous and well-financed need apply. In the absence of regional primaries, some state is going to go first, and it might as well be Iowa.

Iowa's population is 25th among the states. Iowa is not so small as to be utterly unrepresentative of the nation (would you rather start the political season in Nevada?) and not so large as to make impossible the "retail politics," one coffee klatch at a time, by which a dark horse can, by dint of effort, rise. Iowa has an unusually high earnestness quotient, in part because it is such a political cockpit. In Iowa's small towns, as in much of the Midwest, the center of cultural life is the high school, where there is a heavy emphasis on current affairs. Furthermore, the waves of immigration that lapped upon the broad beach of Iowa came predominantly from northern Europe and included many Lutherans, Amish, Mennonites and others fleeing wars and conscription. There is to this day a strong liberal cast to many of Iowa's religious groups.

Many congregations meet before services for discussions of political issues.

Iowa is fourth in the nation in the percentage of people over 65, in part because the elderly have stayed while many young people went seeking better job markets. Iowa is a right-to-work state but the most heavily unionized of such states. In 1984 Iowa gave Mondale his sixth-highest percentage. Because Iowa's Democratic electorate is so strongly seasoned with liberalism, Democratic candidates are pulled to the left, which does not help in the South and West in November. But any state is apt to have some similar distorting features for one party or the other.

Some say we would select better candidates if we could call back into existence some of the political machines (Daley's in Chicago, Tammany Hall's in New York, David Lawrence's in Pennsylvania) that produced deliverable blocs of votes and delegates that could be bartered by bosses in smoke-filled rooms. But the bosses and their machines were rooted in social soil that has long since disappeared, eroded by several forces. One is television, which enables candidates to address the public without the mediation of parties. And the welfare state has multiplied rights— entitlements—where hitherto people depended on the discretion of party people (to get a job, to get a street paved, to get "relief," as welfare was then called).

In the bad old days, before "democratization" of the process, John Kennedy faced only two key primaries, Wisconsin and West Virginia. The latter ended Hubert Humphrey's bid. Kennedy, who was at best an inattentive senator, then won the nomination by beating Lyndon Johnson, who did not understand the dawning age of which Kennedy was a herald. Johnson thought that being a major player in the game of government (he was the last really powerful Senate leader) was still a larger advantage in the nomination process than being an athlete of the campaign trail. The bosses behind Kennedy recognized that he understood the new politics of a wired nation.

Campaigning today is one of the purest forms of individual entrepreneurship available in an age of bureaucratized enterprises. A candidate enlists a small staff, raises capital, invests it in marketing his product (himself) and the market decides. But it is all-absorbing individualism, and therefore further limits the list of realistic presidential possibilities: It severely handicaps governors. Since 1900 the two parties have given presidential nominations to 29 men, 13 of whom were or had been governors. But Mario Cuomo has a crippling disadvantage: a job. Illinois's Jim Thompson, the nation's senior governor in terms of service (11 years) is, you might suppose, a natural presidential candidate. He is from a state that has voted with the winner in 16 of the last 17 elections. He considered plunging into the process that begins next door in Iowa. He decided against it because he could not manage events in Springfield by phone from a Holiday Inn in Cedar Rapids. Dukakis is the first serving governor in 20 years to mount a serious bid for a nomination. Nelson Rockefeller failed in 1964 and 1968.

The best reason for nostalgia about the bad old days is that Bryce was so wrong. Thirty-nine men have become president and eight of them can reasonably be called great presidents: Washington, Jefferson, Lincoln, Theodore Roosevelt, Wilson, Franklin Roosevelt, Truman, Eisenhower. One in five is a fine record. Two other great men—John Adams and William Howard Taft—were quite satisfactory, if not great, presidents. Two other great men, Madison and Grant, were made presidents and did not do well. The greatest president had one of the least impressive prepresidential records: one term in Congress, one failed senatorial campaign. Why are great men not chosen? They frequently have been. Will the future be like the past? We should be so lucky.

February 1, 1988

The Rhythm Method of Politics

This age, which is full of faith in psychology, thinks that anything a person does, from the way he dreams to the way he eats artichokes, reveals, to the tutored eye, his moods. So, given the science of polling, many people probably think it is a snap to decode the nation's mood and forecast its immediate political future.

But it is not. So we try to achieve predictive powers by discerning patterns in the past that may extend into the future. In his book *The Cycles of American History,* Arthur Schlesinger Jr., distinguished historian and unreconstructed Democrat, argues that America has alternating rhythms, periods of activist government followed by periods of preoccupation with private interests.

The minimalist government of the late-19th-century "Gilded Age" was followed by the activism of the turn-of-the-century "Progressive Era." That yielded to the conservatism of the 1920s, which was followed by Roosevelt-Truman activism. Then came the conservatism of Ike's 1950s, then Kennedy's call to get "moving again" and LBJ's "Great Society." In 1968 there began another 20-year cycle of conservatism, Nixon through Reagan. And now?

Schlesinger says Theodore Roosevelt and Woodrow Wilson infected a generation of young people like Franklin and Eleanor Roosevelt and Harry Truman who, in maturity, produced their own activism. FDR in turn had political offspring such as JFK and LBJ. Schlesinger says: "In the same way the age of Kennedy touched and inspired a new generation. That generation's time is yet to come." If Schlesinger is correct about such cycles, the time for the political children of Kennedy arrives in 1988.

Reviewing Schlesinger's book in *The New Republic*, professor Alan Brinkley of Harvard notes that even if political disjunctions can be discerned at, say, 20-year intervals, that fact does not necessarily yield a theory with predictive powers. Three large events that drove American politics in new directions—two world wars and the Depression— occurred when they did for reasons unrelated to the existence of any American cycle. Patterns detected in the past may be mere coincidences like, Brinkley notes, "the causally meaningless fact that Presidents elected at 20-year intervals since 1840 have all, until now, died in office."

Schlesinger's cycle theory has predictive value only if there is, in Brinkley's words, an internal dynamic that makes the cycle self-generating. Schlesinger says there is. It is the ability of activist leaders to seed the future with inspired young people. Schlesinger says: "It is the generational experience that serves as the mainspring of the political cycle."

Schlesinger's theory of approximately 20-year cycles points to a consummation he devoutly desires—a liberal restoration in 1988. But historical rhythms are in the eye of the beholder and John Sears, veteran of Nixon and Reagan campaigns, has a theory of national character from which he derives his own theory of the oscillations of America's politics.

Americans, he says, are naturally optimistic and assume that change means improvement. Such optimism translates into support for whichever party promises an era of change. But the nation has not always assumed that change results only from activist government.

In 1861, the infant GOP took charge of preserving the Union and, in the process, ended slavery. The nation then entered an era of hyperactivity—immigration, industrialization, closing the frontier, building railroads. The nation identified the GOP as the party with an ideology (minimal government, laissez-faire) conducive to rapid change. The GOP dominated politics for 72 years. Between 1860 and 1932 there were just two Democratic presidents, Grover Cleveland and Woodrow Wilson, and both were results of Republican schisms.

In 1932 the Democratic Party acquired, first by default and soon through action, the status of the party of change. This was the result of the second great crisis since the Civil War—the Depression. The 1980 election punctuated a crisis of confidence that began with Vietnam and Watergate and culminated in the sense of impotence produced by high inflation and the Iranian hostage crisis. The 1980 mandate was for less government energy domestically and more internationally.

Notice the difference between Sears's and Schlesinger's perceived rhythms. Sears stresses the nation's penchant for social change, which sometimes has been, but at other times has not been, identified with an activist federal government. The generally conservative policies of the last three decades of the 19th century coincided with the most transforming changes (industrialism, immigration) in American history.

If, as Sears says, the American constant is a craving for change, the question for Schlesinger is whether in 1988, unlike in 1980, government will be considered an initiator of change rather than an inhibitor of America's creative energies.

November 27, 1986

Lincoln-Douglas Without Either

Houston, capital of the oil patch, has suffered enough, yet recently was host to the Republican presidential candidates who, in the semiprivacy of public television (for which privacy several of them should be thankful) continued their tussle to see who will run against the fellow who will be the Democratic nominee, Paul Simon (D–Ill.), more about whom anon.

The debate resembled the Lincoln-Douglas debate, except there was no Lincoln, no Douglas and precious little debating. Lincoln and Douglas, having nothing better to do, argued, at length. They would rattle on for three hours, just the two of them. But what can six fellows do, now that the national attention span has shrunk? In Houston they were sometimes allowed to ramble on for 45 seconds. These bursts were interspersed with home movies and some towel-snapping male-bonding heartiness. They gave excruciatingly ponderous answers to a question about which presidential portraits they would cherish. A candidate could have clinched the nomination by saying he'd pack away all the old pictures of politicians and hang one of Glenn Close.

The evening was a rousing success in identifying a man qualified to be president. But Bob Strauss, cohost of the event, is a Democrat and is not running, presumably because the Democratic field is so satisfactory. The semidebate had two demiwinners, George Bush and Pat Robertson, Bush because he did well, Robertson because he was legitimized just by being there. Robertson's relentless smile seems eerily unrelated to any external referent, so his continuous chuckling is no laughing matter, but it is nice to see a man happy in his work. Bush was crisp, assured and utterly unlike himself—the self of verbal fender-benders. Perhaps his pratfalls have been a cunning tactic to lower expectations that he would then triumphantly exceed. His handlers should keep their hands off him and remember what a Kansas City Royals manager said when asked what advice he gave George Brett on hitting: "I tell him, 'Attaway to hit, George.' " Bush used bare-knuckled name-calling to respond to Pete du Pont's ham-handed attack, calling him "Pierre," which is brutal, although that is du Pont's name.

Al Haig was highly Haigian when telling Bush "I never heard a wimp out of you" about something or other. Please, not in front of the children. When Haig goes to the mat to wrestle with the English language, or-thodox syntax gets its ligaments strained. Haig accused the administra-tion of "pummeling toward an arms-control agreement," but he also said something sensible, chastising Bush for saying (as Reagan does) that strategic defense is necessary because nuclear deterrence is "immoral." Deterrence has kept the peace and, anyway, we are stuck with it for the foreseeable future, so conservatives should quit stigmatizing it.

Haig broke the Texas indoor record for statistics-as-static when he said that none of the 12 generals who have been president got us into any of the eight wars since 1812, all of which proves that Haig is living in the wrong century. Between 1824 (Jackson) and 1892 (Harrison) there were only three elections in which no general was nominated. In this century, only Ike has been. Ike's personality was as amiable as Winnie-the-Pooh's. No one has ever confused Haig with Pooh.

Jack Kemp was uncommonly concise and, defying the odds, made it through the evening without mentioning gold. In the past he has forgot-ten the axiom that the secret of being a bore is to tell everything. On occasion he has been, shall we say, comprehensive on the matter of monetary reform. A British member of Parliament, unwinding from a stem-winding speech about bimetalism, asked Prime Minister Balfour, "How did I do, Arthur?" "Splendidly, Henry, splendidly." "Did you understand me, Arthur?" "Not a word, Henry, not a word." Kemp has been that way, but was much better in Houston.

Bob Dole (R–Kans.) presented himself as a gifted legislator, which is fine, but he made the mistake of talking like one, which made him hard for normal folks to understand. Legislators talk in shorthand, the argot of minutiae, as Dole did when, discussing abortion, he referred to "the Hyde language" and "the Hatch amendment," a reference not helpful to six or even seven viewers in Duluth.

Dole is one of the few genuine wits in public life and he relaxed when the boys began to roughhouse. Wit is grounded in a sense of irony, which is necessary for mental equilibrium in the political cockpit. Dole should throw caution to the winds and smile more. No face in public life is as changed as Dole's when it goes from repose to a smile. It is the difference between January and June. He should pummel us with smiles because he comes about as close as a candidate dares come to being a Bad News Bear. He says deficits will not go away because wished away and he tells Republicans that their party and government have neglected duties toward Americans who are, for whatever reasons, not high achievers. Furthermore, in Houston Dole tiptoed to the edge of lèse majesté by promising to be a "hands-on president." Unlike?

All of these fellows may be embryonic Ciceros, but none of them is as yet fulfilling the 2 A.M. political fantasies of Republican activists, as Paul Simon does for Democratic activists. All of us have guilty secrets, weird things we like to do when no one is looking. Some people like to watch *Falcon Crest*. Others read Gothic novels. I like Nehi grape soda. Turn off the lights and let a room full of intense Democrats do what lust dictates, they will nominate Simon. They are the way inflamed Republicans were in 1964. Those Republicans were sick and tired of being sedate, so they nominated Goldwater, thereby pioneering a moral principle later associated with the left: If it feels good, do it.

Democrats have not really had fun since 1960, and 28 years is a long time between drinks. Mark Shields (the Dole of columnists; he can't long remain solemn, try as he might) notes that most of today's Democratic candidates are like the "modern" Republicans of the early 1950s. They were diluted Democrats who bored Republican true believers to tears, and to nominating Goldwater. Simon dispenses the 90-proof New Deal–Fair Deal whisky—Democratic fun. Watching the Houston event, many hard-shell Republicans, whose pulses raced when Reagan was running, must have thought, wistfully: These candidates are an awfully responsible lot but not, at least at the moment, much fun.

November 9, 1987

Oh, Go Bowling, Both of You

If Bob Dole says one more word—even one more—about his rise from the social depths, he should be sentenced to go bowling. That punishment would be deliciously condign because Dole might bump into George Bush, who recently has allowed as how he is a bowling-alley kind of guy.

So, all of you Stanley Kowalskis, put your elbows on the formica top of Stella's kitchen table and imagine how George Bush feels suffering through a rerun of this issue. In 1980 Ronald Reagan, that horny-handed son of toil, sashayed out of his tarpaper shack—or was it a log cabin?—in Pacific Palisades to challenge Bush for the nomination. Reaganites, hurling epithets the way boys in school dining rooms hurl hard rolls, charged Bush with being "a clean-fingernails Republican."

One day in 1980, several journalists badgered Bush about his ability to "understand" folks who are jus' folks, because he "hasn't suffered" or "been tempered by difficulties."

Bush: Financial difficulty, you mean?

Journalist: Well, whatever we mean by the dark night of the soul, of that sort of personal difficulty.

Bush: Have you ever sat and watched your child die?

Journalist: Thank God, no.

Bush: I did, for six months.

Journalist: What did that do to you? Is that the answer?

Enough, already. Today's Dole-Bush debate about who looks spiffier in bowling shoes is (as a reviewer said of a dreary novel) "like a long hike home in wet socks and gym shoes, uncomfortable and unnecessary." Let's agree that they have both suffered enough, and that their argument has enabled us all to make the same boast.

Such arguments recur because they are rooted in Republican history. Democrats can nominate the gently born (FDR, JFK), but Republicans recoil from the idea. Robert Taft and Nelson Rockefeller, from opposite wings of the party, failed. Nixon knew the rule: When the going gets tough, the tough wrap themselves in their wife's "Republican cloth coat."

As you might expect, Republicans can not get the hang of the class struggle, so things get confusing. Taft, a president's son and a Yalie, was beaten by Dewey and Eisenhower, two men from modest backgrounds backed by the wicked East. But at least Taft was from Ohio; conservatives called him a tribune of the plain people. Willkie and Hoover made sacks of money (as Landon later did) but, as Dole understands, Republicans are permitted to make it, just not inherit it.

Coolidge rose by the effervescence of his personality (that's a joke, son) and Harding rose because things lighter than air do that. Charles Evans Hughes was the humbly born son of an immigrant clergyman. Not for 76 years, not since William Howard Taft, have Republicans nominated someone born to wealth.

Dole's point is that his life has etched on his consciousness an awareness that many deserving people need help from government. But he can sing that refrain in a different, less grating key, the one he improvised recently in a New Hampshire debate.

The candidates were asked to square their ritual denunciations of drugs and government spending with the fact that drug rehabilitation facilities are underfunded. Dole, who falls somewhere short of hip, did not know that his five-word punchline was a refrain from George Harrison's top-of-the-charts rock record: "It's going to take money."

As Harrison says, money "to do it right." The country wants candidates, especially Republicans, with the independent judgment to say that some things have not been done right.

As vice president, Bush is cast in the unenviable role of the Republican Party's dripping faucet, saying and saying and saying something that most Americans doubt: that no significant course correction, no temperament rougher than Reagan's, is required. If Dole is chosen, it will not be for his charm which, although real, is rationed (and is, like rationed sugar, especially pleasing when experienced). If Dole goes to the top of the charts, it will be because of a point he has yet to make.

He has made his point about Bush—that Bush has lived a life of lateral movement—a point that may or may not justify negative inferences about Bush's inner resources. But Dole's positive point about himself can not be merely that the experience of social hardships is itself a virtue. Dole's task now is to show how his private biography foreshadows public benefits—how a quickened capacity for empathy and a steely will can translate into the sort of presidency that ought to come next.

January 24, 1988

Boomerology, With Fries

CHICAGO—Enter Ed Debevic's restaurant and slip through a crack in time, back to the 1950s, to meat loaf, macaroni and cheese, Ovaltine and "wets"—french fries with gravy. And be the first on your block to have a blazing insight about the 1988 presidential election.

Let's talk the language of politics: Doo-wop, sha-na-na. This flavorful dialect was favored by Clyde McPhatter and Dion and others and was used in ballads such as "Stagger Lee" and "Shimmy Shimmy Ko Ko Bop." In Ed's, a meticulously recreated 1950s short-order diner, the music interrupted only when the maitre d' (wearing shades and a DA haircut) commandeers the audio system to bark: "At table five—the lady missing the grilled cheese. We'll get there, just hang in." Meanwhile, have a black cow made with Dad's Old-Fashioned Root Beer.

On a good week, Ed's serves upwards of 18,000 customers—if "serve" is the verb for what is done by the gum-cracking waitresses who audition for brassiness. The fare includes peanut-butter pie and other delicacies not for the fainthearted. This restaurant, an exercise in nostalgia, is now being reproduced elsewhere, including Beverly Hills. Details include bowling trophies. How kitsch. But hark: *The New York Times* reports that folks wearing Merrill Lynch T-shirts are clustered around the formica tables at New York bowling alleys.

Ed's, like the movie *American Graffiti*, caters to the powerful sense of identity among the 76 million "baby-boom" Americans born between 1946 and 1964. In 1988, they could comprise 60 percent of the electorate. A candidate who wins, say, a 60–40 split of that group probably becomes president.

A pioneer of boomerology—the study of them—is Pat Caddell, Democratic consultant. He says this generation is uniquely "self-contained." Because of its "critical-mass" size, "it has experienced itself as the center of events." Because of its size—which means, in part, because of its purchasing power—the generation has always been a center of attention, an experience that has bred "a certain arrogance."

Davy Crockett hats and Hula Hoops were instant, continental fads because of this generation, the first wired, television generation. Caddell says the movie *The Big Chill*, in which boomers evidently see themselves clearly, depicts a generation in which "pictures, remembrances, ideas and experiences are shared universally, and music is the greatest conductor of these."

The pack at Ed's, listening to "Leader of the Pack" and thinking about cherry Jell-O with walnuts, is enjoying the music and wets. But most of all it is enjoying its self-contained self.

Peter Hart, another Democratic consultant, notes that because of the boomers, the nation may be ready to "skip a generation" in picking its president. Were John Kennedy alive, he would be 69. He and Reagan and Lyndon Johnson and Nixon and Ford and Carter came from essentially the same generation. However, in 1988 we may elect the first president born after FDR's first inauguration. If booming Joe Biden gets his way, the next president will have been born after FDR's third inauguration.

Hart says elections are about moods, and popular culture is a measure of moods. In 1978, five liberal senators lost and, in California, Proposition 13, limiting taxes, won. These were portents. But television, says Hart, also foreshadowed the conservative future. Two especially popular shows were *Happy Days* and *Laverne and Shirley*. Both were set in the glow of the remembered 1950s. Hart surmises that both indicated a need for reassurance. That was a Reagan specialty in the presidential election that followed.

Hart suggests listening to the jargon of the young. In the 1950s, the young spoke of being "hip" and "cool" and "with it"—"it" denoting the right or "in" group. The 1960s echoed with the rhetoric of "doing your own thing" and "getting your act together," a vocabulary of self-absorption for a decade of disintegration. Today, Hart says, the punctuating expressions of youthful discourse are "for sure" and "really"— again, a reaching for reassurance. Something to think about at Ed's (Ed, by the way, is a fiction) in the glow of the pink neon announcing NO PREMIUM BEER HERE.

In 1983, before enlisting with Gary Hart, Caddell tried to talk Delaware's Senator Biden into running. Biden is six years younger than Hart and so can adopt a boomier-than-thou attitude. However, from George Bush's elephantine—in size and grace—staff comes an entertaining thought. Bush, 62, is boomiest because he has five children aged 26 to 39.

Still there may be a risk in relying on the support of boomers raised on rock 'n' roll and television. In 1984, Gary Hart's hot streak, from New Hampshire to late spring, was about as long as the run of success enjoyed by a hit record. Perhaps that is the boomers' attention span.

August 14, 1986

Jesse Jackson's Verbal Meringue

In his crusade for national betterment, Jesse Jackson has many suggestions, including this: If you see George Will drowning, throw him an anvil. He does not say quite that, but that is his gist.

According to the *Los Angeles Times,* Jackson recently addressed in Sacramento a $500-a-plate luncheon which "was closed to the press, but some reporters listened to the remarks and tape-recorded them from an adjacent partitioned-off area." Jackson berated the media for portraying minorities in a way "designed to poison the minds of the common people." The *Times* reported that Jackson "singled out conservative columnist George Will for special criticism."

Jackson said, "He is more dangerous to us than Jimmy the Greek and Al Campanis." The *Times* reported that "Jackson did not elaborate."

I will elaborate. But first a point about the niceties of slander. Jackson has kissed Yasir Arafat and hailed Fidel Castro, so I am content to be excluded from the ambit of his affections. But if he wants to call me a racist, he should have the courage of his convictions and do it publicly. If he wants to smear people privately, he should rent rooms with thicker partitions.

Jackson spoke two days after appearing on ABC's *This Week,* during which I asked him these three questions:

"You said in a recent debate that since 1973 we have lost 38 million jobs. In fact, today 27 million more Americans are working than were working in 1973. In what sense have we lost the jobs?"

"As President, would you support measures such as the G-7 measures in the Louvre accords?"

"Last month in the Kennedy Center debate, Mr. Jackson, you said that 58 cents out of every federal dollar is being spent on military buildup. Since the defense budget is about 28 cents out of the federal dollar, in what sense is your statement true?"

His answer to the first question was that some people are "working at lower wages" and "we've lost workers who once were driving trucks who are now driving hamburgers." Then he whipped up a verbal meringue, mostly air and references to "Wall Street analyses and these humongous numbers," and airline deregulation and the minimum wage.

His answer to the second question was, "Explain that." His answer to the third was slightly to fudge his falsehood, saying 55 cents of every federal tax dollar is spent on "military-related matters."

In Sacramento, Jackson told his mostly black audience that the media spread negative images of blacks, and that I am especially "dangerous" to "us." Actually, he is contributing to negative stereotypes by his implicit demand for exemption from standards to which white candidates are held.

People who say the reason Jackson can not be elected is that he is black should ask themselves this: How many candidates spout Third World rhetoric and fraternize with anti-American dictators and terrorists and then do well in presidential politics? Being black is his advantage as a professional campaigner: Suppose he were a white minister from Chicago attempting to make the presidency his first elective office.

Because he is black, his white rivals sit silently beside him, leaving his foolishness unremarked. The real racism in this campaign is the unspoken assumption that it is unreasonable to expect a black candidate to get rudimentary things right.

Jackson is doing something for which there are ample precedents. He is doing what Strom Thurmond, George Wallace, Norman Thomas, Henry Wallace, Robert La Follette and others have done. He is using the process of presidential politics to alter the nation's conversation, agenda and patterns of participation.

But because he is not going to be on the Democratic ticket, there is a journalistic question of what coverage of him is appropriate. The answer is: Lots of it.

Coverage should be proportional to his support measured in polls, which is considerable. Coverage is merited by his potential to influence events, which is substantial. He is saying things that many people like to hear and the fact that some of the things are silly just gives journalism the additional task of tidying up after him.

Before Jackson does too much more complaining about the treatment of him in the media, he should consider this. Jimmy the Greek got obliterated because he said dumb and offensive things, although they were said in a crude attempt to praise blacks. Jackson said dumb and malicious things about Jews and then collected matching funds for his nonstop campaigning. He should be thankful for double standards.

January 28, 1988

What Democrats Won't Say

Most Democratic presidential candidates speak the way most people do physical exercise, with plodding, joyless earnestness. But Jesse Jackson uses words the way a playground hot dog uses a basketball, with Michael Jordan's exuberance, as when Jackson says that when he is president he will end "economic brutality."

His noun is hyperbolic because its purpose is to breathe life into the adjective. Democrats are having trouble figuring out how to deplore economic conditions in this record-setting 65th month of expansion. The Democrats' language reflects not only uneasiness about some of Ronald Reagan's successes, but also a failure of nerve about addressing his failures.

When politicians employ verbal concoctions like "economic brutality," they do so because it is awkward to use more mundane words like "inflation" and "unemployment" (now at an eight-year low) to denote what they are complaining about. Both inflation and unemployment have, in the 1980s, confounded conventional wisdom by declining substantially simultaneously.

So the emerging Democratic theme is that the economy's surface gloss conceals the, well, brutalizing fact that the jobs being created (14 million of them since 1980) are somehow degrading and the wealth being created is being allocated inequitably. Thus, Michael Dukakis says we are sinking toward "an America where all we do is flip each other's hamburgers and take in each other's dry cleaning for $3.35 an hour."

However, the Council of Economic Advisers (CEA)'s annual report says that between 1982 (granted, near the trough of a deep recession) and 1987 jobs grew 2.7 percent a year, and substantially better than that for blacks (4.7), Hispanics (6.8) and black teenagers (8.2). The unemployment rate fell 5 percentage points for all civilians and even more for Hispanics (7.1), blacks (8) and black teenagers (16.1).

But, Democrats say, the new jobs are low-pay, low-status, dead-end "hamburger-flipping" jobs. Now, disregarding the unpleasant Democratic disdain for certain jobs and the Democratic condescension toward those who fill them (many retirees who are tired of their rocking chairs are flipping hamburgers—have you noticed the "graying" of McDonalds?—and more power to them), the facts according to the CEA are:

Half the new jobs pay more than $20,000. Management and administrative jobs grew especially fast—21 percent—in this period. The slowest growth was in unskilled jobs such as retail sales, janitorial services and—you want lettuce and tomato on your burger, Governor Dukakis?—food processing.

Well, say determined critics, many of the new jobs are not real—meaning full-time—jobs. Actually, 90 percent are full-time, and 80 percent of all part-time workers do not want to work full-time.

Why then, ask skeptics, are living standards falling? They are not. The real median family income rose 9 percent between 1981 and 1986, with blacks doing better (15.5) than other groups.

But surely America's manufacturing muscle has atrophied? Wrong again. Over the last two decades the share of manufacturing in the GNP has been stable, and manufacturing has risen faster than GNP in recent years. Manufacturing output rose 4.2 percent in 1987, twice the 1986 rate.

And things were never as grim as they often were painted. Between 1970 and 1984, manufacturing output rose 53 percent, not far behind the growth of the services sector (62 percent). Employment rose faster in services, but that is partly because of more good news: Productivity per worker rose much faster in manufacturing than services.

(There are dark spots. Dukakis's Massachusetts has lost 11.4 percent of its manufacturing jobs since 1984, 41 percent of all the manufacturing jobs lost nationally.)

Granted, the gap between rich and poor has widened a bit. Granted, one reason median family income rose 20 percent from 1970 to 1986 is the huge increase in two-earner families. Still, families are, as the Congressional Budget Office attests, "markedly better off."

So what should Democrats be saying? Less about hamburger-flipping, for starters. Instead, they should say that the good times have been bought at a terrible price that has yet to be paid, that the hyper-Keynesian stimulus of Reagan's deficits amounts to eating our seed corn.

Politically, the problem is that the country enjoys eating that corn. In all but one year of this decade, personal consumption has increased more than production and income. In this decade, the personal savings rate (raising this was the supply-siders' goal) has declined substantially from what was already the worst level in the industrial world.

The logic of all this dictates a tax increase targeted at consumption. That is no fun, so we can expect Democrats to continue talking about hamburger-flipping and "economic brutality," rather than risk telling truths that would, they fear, provoke the electorate to political brutality.

March 24, 1988

Competence Liberalism or Compassion Liberalism: It's Still Liberalism

ATLANTA—Like drunks deciding to go on a last bender before going on the wagon, Democrats here divided their time between praising sobriety and drinking their favorite brand of demon rum, old liberalism. Finally they put themselves in the care of a temperance preacher, Michael Dukakis, who allowed himself to be televised while watching his nomination and sipping champagne as though it were a detergent.

The Democrats have had two conventions. Now the country has the task of deciding which one represented the real Democratic Party: the convention that ended Tuesday, or the one that ended Thursday.

In the convention hall Tuesday night, few of the thousands of eyes were dry as delegates experienced transports of rapture. In millions of living rooms, the reaction may have been markedly different as the Democratic Party devoted Tuesday to presenting on television its two most polarizing personages, Ted Kennedy and Jesse Jackson. Together they pushed all the hot-button issues that have driven away droves of moderate Democrats.

It was a peculiar evening for a party preening about its replacement of ideological self-indulgence by electoral realism. The wallow in the old liberalism obscured, to the detriment of Dukakis, the difference between his liberalism and worn-out Democratic dogmas.

Dukakis Democrats have rummaged in the recesses of their mental closets and have come up with "competence liberalism." "Compassion liberalism," which also can be called "constituency liberalism," has been put on a hanger. This makes the liberalism of Dukakis's Democratic Party more politically potent by making it seem more realistic and less morally overbearing.

"Compassionate liberalism" argues that the purpose of government is ameliorative action. The proof of compassion is programs for particular constituencies. This doctrine rests on the idea that the interests of particular groups—racial, ethnic, religious, sexual, economic—can be properly represented only by members of each group.

This doctrine was used in recent years to justify the proliferation of caucuses representing factions within the Democratic Party. Four years ago, they and other lobbies reduced the Democratic nominee to a verb: "to Mondaleize" is to belabor a politician and put him through so many hoops that he can never seem presidential.

The doctrine of "compassion" or "constituency" liberalism has underwritten a compassion industry. The assumption is that everyone is a member of a group, every group has an organization, every organization has a leader with whom government can deal. People like Jackson are professional brokers of government benefits for the government's client groups. To such people, the change of the Democratic Party away from constituency liberalism to competence liberalism is bad for business.

The change is betokened by the fact that the "F" word—fairness—was infrequently heard here. Dukakis Democrats come close to conceding, grudgingly and obliquely, the essence of the conservative premise. It is that fairness is equality of opportunity, not equality of condition promoted by government actions of distributive justice. Rather, the foundation of fairness is economic dynamism.

Sixteen years ago "compassion liberalism" was illustrated by candidate George McGovern's "Demogrant plan," a less-than-half-baked idea for giving $1,000 to everyone. Today's nominee speaks the political language of the 1980s, a vocabulary of domestic policy not really grating to most Republican ears.

Granted, when Dukakis speaks of growth he envisions growth that is fostered by more government activism than conservatives consider necessary or prudent. Dukakis's belief in "partnership" between government and business is, by the way, an unremarked congruence between his views and those of Lloyd Bentsen, the Texas corporatist.

Four years ago, the crescendo of the Democratic National Convention came early, in Mario Cuomo's keynote philippic. He pleased the hall full of Democrats by intimating that Democrats have cornered the market on morality. On morality, not merely on prudence or imagination or competence. His was the voice of the virtucrat, saying: If you disagree with us you are not merely mistaken, you are morally obtuse and not nice. Dukakis's is the voice of a man frequently faulted for lack of passion, but at least he lacks the passion of moral pride. He may have intellectual hubris, but not the especially insulting vanity of the virtucrat.

McGovern, recollecting in tranquility the turbulence of the Democratic Party 16 years ago, recently said that a mistake of the antiwar movement was in calling the war "immoral," not merely imprudent or disproportionate or otherwise mistaken. This, McGovern now says, told people: If you disagree with us, you are immoral.

The two conventions here, recollected in tranquility, will pose this question: Which one—the one celebrating compassion liberalism or the one anointing the spokesman for competence liberalism—did the Democrats really mean?

July 24, 1988

The Contraction of the Presidency

Republicans have learned from Ronald Reagan to look on the bright side of everything from deficits (growth stimulated by them cures them) to Gorbachev (good liberals come from Moscow, not Boston). So Republicans, preaching what Reagan practices, can say their presidential campaign will recover from its rocky start.

Reagan himself had an awful August in 1980 when he said, among other interesting things, that trees cause pollution, then arrived at a rally and found a tree decorated with this sign: "Chop me down before I kill again."

But this year, both parties' campaigns are likely to produce an anemic President and therefore produce congressional government. Such government will be the result of a second consecutive vacuous election.

In 1984, there barely was an election. There was an Olympics and Bruce Springsteen's "Born in the USA" tour, and in that celebratory atmosphere Reagan elevated contentment to a political platform: "Morning in America. . . . Back and standing tall." The result was a landslide without a mandate and the reassertion of the national norm: congressional government.

If in 1988 the winner wins principally because he is not the other guy, then by 1992 the nation will have gone 12 years without a clarifying, energizing choice. With either Dukakis or Bush we're apt to enter an era of unheroic politics. It will be an era more typical of American experience than either the Reagan era or the Kennedy era that Dukakis invokes so insistently.

Under either Dukakis or Bush, few Americans are apt to regard the presidency heroically, as many did under, say, Teddy Roosevelt and Franklin Roosevelt and John Kennedy. Few will regard it as a tone-setting institution imparting fundamental direction to national life. Conservatives, with their Jeffersonian impulses, may say: Splendid. That role is not for government, let alone the central government.

But Hamilton, a source of a more sensible conservatism, warned that energy in the executive is a prerequisite of good government.

A weak presidency does not produce sweet passivity in Washington and the blooming of 100 flowers of local control. Rather, it produces congressional ascendancy. That means the enervation of foreign policy and, in domestic affairs, the primacy of parochial interests at the expense of national aspirations. Try to imagine either Dukakis or Bush going over the heads of Congress to appeal directly to the people.

Conservatives, forgetting their enjoyment of Reagan's success doing that, may say: Fine. We oppose plebiscitary use of the presidency. But, again, they should consider the real alternative. It has been increasingly visible since Reagan's 1986 failure to hold Republican control of the Senate. The alternative is government by a fractious committee of 535.

Reagan's presidency has demonstrated the perishable nature of even a real mandate. Reagan's mandate was worn out by September 1981 and only a series of unplanned events made it last that long. He was gallant when shot. A Supreme Court vacancy enabled him to nominate a woman. Two Libyan fighter planes let him act like Teddy Roosevelt. The striking air-traffic controllers let him act like Truman. Even so, his tax and spending cuts, the crux of his agenda, barely passed that summer. How evanescent would Dukakis's or Bush's sway over Congress be?

The presidency is so prominent in national life, and the tendency is so strong to confuse prominence with power, Americans forget that the presidency is an inherently (meaning constitutionally) weak office. There is little a president can do on his own. What he can do is move the country by the force of his words or the pull of his personality and, by doing so, move, or at least inhibit, Congress.

The power of the presidency varies greatly (more than that of, say, the power of the British prime minister) with the personal attributes of the occupant of the office. The power of Congress to initiate and block action, a power increasingly radiated in new laws, only expands. It expands most rapidly when presidential influence contracts.

The 1988 election looks like a recipe for a sharp contraction. We have two low-voltage candidates. One of them, Dukakis, talks with lawyerly wariness about his plans. Bush praises the Pledge of Allegiance and promises not to furlough killers. So even more people than usual are melancholy about the choice. They may see congressional government coming.

Perhaps they should reason as did Sam Weller, Mr. Pickwick's servant: "Well, it's no use talking about it now. It's over, and can't be helped, and that's one consolation, as they always says in Turkey, when they cuts the wrong man's head off."

August 28, 1988

Dan Quayle's Ideological Lint

Since that memorable August moment on the New Orleans riverboat, when George Bush made of Dan Quayle a gift to the country and Quayle overflowed with gratitude, the question has been: Can Quayle, who seems so energetic in body and so indolent in mind, temper his enthusiasm with lucidity? The answer came when Quayle clambered onto the Omaha stage with a cutlass clenched between his teeth, eager to shed blood and vindicate Bush's nomination of him, in defiance of the maxim "Ne Puero Gladium" (never give a child a sword).

Did he prove himself presidential? No, he stayed in step with the top of the ticket. From Boston Harbor to Belgian endive, Quayle touched on—no, tromped on—the themes the Bush campaign considers neat-o. Quayle was so overprogrammed it seemed that someone backstage, armed with a remote-control wand, was operating a compact disc—a very compact disc—in Quayle's skull. His handlers, who doubtless fancy themselves clever fellows because they work so well with papier-maché, tamped into Quayle lots of itsy-bitsy slivers of ideas—notions, really; ideological lint.

Having had the audacity to begin his most curdled stuff (about how Dukakisites despise the common sense of Midwestern grandmothers and sneer at the idea that America is the envy of the world), it is a wonder that Quayle had the sense to stop. Stop he did, but not before confirming the suspicion that his conservatism is less a creed than an absorbed climate of opinion, absorbed in a golf cart.

Back in the backward 19th century, when, unlike today, democracy was imperfectly understood and inelegantly practiced, it was considered unseemly for national candidates to campaign. As late as 1896, McKinley spent the autumn on his front porch, refusing to campaign because speaking involved an unpleasant undertaking: "I have to think when I speak." Most of today's candidates recognize no such requirement, and are emancipated by public tolerance from any such expectations.

It was not surprising that Quayle was not smooth as silk, or even as polyester. And Bentsen was unusually awkward when recurring unnecessarily to his "breakfast club" fund-raising, and when lamely defending it as "legal."

Then Bentsen, with the syrup of his voice seasoned with vinegar, said Quayle is no John Kennedy. (Quayle had said that he has as much experience in Congress as Kennedy had when he ran for president.) Then a questioner (ABC's Brit Hume) made a point that Quayle was perhaps too stunned to make: Quayle is running for vice president with more experience than Bentsen had when he ran for president in 1976.

Democratic voters who participated in the 1976 nomination process should have been spanked and sent to their rooms without dinner: They spurned two fine presidential candidates, Scoop Jackson and Bentsen. Bentsen's performance in Wednesday's debate was, on balance, sufficient to establish him as the most presidential of the four men on the two tickets.

He gave Dukakis a lesson in how to cope with the Democrats' intractable problem—prosperity. Looking like a 19th-century mural of Integrity Reproving Folly, Bentsen said, in effect: Seventy months of economic expansion? Of course. Any fool can slash taxes, give the Pentagon a blank check, finance it all with $200 billion deficits and wind up with a hyper-Keynesian stimulus. But we are storing up trouble down the road. And meanwhile Reagan's deficits—it took him less than five years to double the national debt—are costing every American man, woman and child $640 a year in interest charges.

Three opportunities were not enough for Quayle to come up with a counterpuncher's answer to the question, What would you do first if you had to replace President Bush? The answer is: I would continue with the Bush policies because I agree with the man at the head of my ticket, which is more than Bentsen can say. What would Bentsen have said if asked a similar question? "The first thing I would do is resume contra aid, which Dukakis considers criminal and I consider vital."

Let's be blunt. If Bush is elected, Quayle will not matter as long as Bush has a heartbeat. Quayle will not be trusted to handle even the more serious foreign funerals. If Dukakis is elected, Bentsen will matter because Dukakis knows next to nothing about Washington, or national security, or about how little he knows. If Dukakis wins, the crucial question will be: How good will he be at changing his mind? If the education of Dukakis becomes necessary, Bentsen had better be nearby.

October 9, 1988

Quayle the Candidate: Not "The Candidate"

MCLEAN, VA.—Why is this man smiling, this man in the Indianapolis Colts V-neck sweater, faded slacks and ancient sneakers? Yes, he has spent a pleasant Sunday with his children. But it is dusk and another week of bear-baiting is about to begin, with him cast as the bear. So why is Dan Quayle sipping 7-Up, not something more fortifying?

He is a human eye of a hurricane, preternaturally tranquil. But elsewhere this has been just another manic Sunday.

The newspapers are full of stories about how Quayle is Dukakis's last, best hope. On a morning interview program he has been compared, not for the first or even just the 101st time, to Bob Forehead, an airhead congressman in a comic strip. On the same program there was comment on a *Vanity Fair* magazine article quoting a former classmate of Quayle remembering Quayle as a law student.

Quayle and he, said the classmate, saw Robert Redford's movie *The Candidate* together. Afterward, over a steak dinner and for 11 hours, they discussed the movie. Quayle, according to the classmate, said he is more handsome than Redford and that with skilled packaging, he, Quayle, could go far in politics.

Quayle says the story, like much written about him, is rubbish. He did not see the movie until years later, a few weeks before he won election to the Senate.

Does the constant drizzle of criticism, to which I have contributed, bother him? "Sure it does, but these people do not know me." But actually what bothers many, like me, who know Quayle, and know him to be better than he has seemed, is that he seems to have passively allowed himself to be putty in the hands of handlers. The Quayle of the campaign trail and the debate with Bentsen is not the Quayle of the Armed Services Committee on the Senate floor during the INF Treaty ratification.

One reason for his chipper Sunday demeanor probably was that he had already decided to do what he in fact did on Tuesday. That day he issued a declaration of independence from his assigned retinue of experts who have helped make his autumn so stimulating. From now on, he said, "I'm the handler."

Regarding direction from the top of the ticket, a running mate's duty is clear: Take direction. But the diminution of Dan Quayle has been accentuated by the operatives in the Bush campaign.

Quayle is weary of the "handwringers" in the Bush campaign and has told his wife, Marilyn, "We're just going to have fun these last four weeks." Too much fun has been wrung from politics by handlers who snuff out a candidate's confidence.

Politics is like a sport in that a politician, like an athlete, needs room for the spontaneous, instinctive action that is a sign of confidence. The Bush campaign, after being terrified in New Orleans, surrounded Quayle with hordes of hired guns, like a piece of glass packed in Styrofoam peanuts. This is a good way to convince the candidate, and the public, that he is fragile.

A vignette: Wednesday evening, New Orleans convention. The press is baying in pursuit of Quayle concerning the National Guard. Jim Baker, Bush's head handler, is in ABC's anchor booth with David Brinkley and Peter Jennings, waiting to be interviewed. ABC's cameras are covering Quayle's arrival at the Superdome. Baker, off camera, tells Brinkley and Jennings that when Quayle walks past the waiting journalists, he will say . . . and Baker recites virtually syllable for syllable what Quayle does say moments later. The pupil on the short leash gets a gold star.

Handlers relish the role of intermediaries between the candidates and reality, meaning the media. Candidates fade into the wallpaper as handlers and journalists feed each other's self-esteem, the handlers handing out bits of inside baseball, the journalists intepreting these nuances which attest the cleverness of the handlers. Journalists have privileged insights into the working of the little motor of history, and the handlers are portrayed as the rubber bands that make the motor whir.

If this is Tuesday, this must be Toledo, and if this is 1988, this must be Quayle's plane. However, four years from now, just as four years ago, the candidates will be different (they are almost dispensable), but the permanent part of the process, the handlers and the media, will be back at the same stand, doing business together.

Quayle anticipates a Bush victory and time for "rehabilitation" (his word). But for now the nagging question is: Did his campaign have to be so diminishing? Could he have done worse if, instead of being handed over to rented handlers who are not inclined to respect the people who rent them, he had been sent out to be more than an echo of Bush's dismal campaign for the office of national sheriff?

When on his own in the Senate (where he does not employ a speechwriter), he has shown more mastery than Bush has of arms control and other national-security matters. But instead of allowing us to hear the best of him, he has been sent baying after Dukakis in the Bush-league manner, "helped" by handlers who have taken too much to heart a famous movie—no, not *The Candidate, The Manchurian Candidate.*

October 14, 1988

So Much Cash, So Few Ideas

That guy in Idaho was joking when he said it would have been less expensive if, instead of strafing the state with television commercials, the two Senate candidates had just taken the undecided voters out to dinner. But the guy was right. About 70 percent of Idaho's 515,000 registered voters were expected to vote this Tuesday. Since Labor Day only about 7 percent of those likely voters have been undecided. The two candidates threw more than $5 million at the 25,000 undecideds, or $200 per voter. That would buy a feast in Boise.

Idaho knows how veal scaloppine feel. Many states have been pounded flat by the merciless attentions of people seeking admission to the Senate. This year the pounding hammers were negative television commercials that rarely rose to the level of lowbrow.

The most expensive race was California's. The two Senate candidates spent $20 million. But on a per-capita basis, that was a bargain-basement campaign. California's race involved $1.55 for each of the 12.8 million registered voters. Next door in Nevada the $3.5 million race involved about $10 for each of the 356,384 registered voters.

What money made possible this autumn was a mass conversion of candidates to the Dick Butkus Doctrine of Political Manners. Butkus, a maiming linebacker for the Chicago Bears, once said, "I wouldn't ever set out to hurt anybody deliberately unless it was, you know, important—like a league game or something." This year "going negative"—doing unto your opponent, before he could do unto you—was the preferred style. So as this is being written—appropriately, on Halloween—the body politic is stiffening its sinews and summoning up its blood and gritting its teeth and holding its nose as it prepares to vote.

There are always excuses for going too far in any contest. When Sugar Ray Robinson landed a punch after the bell had ended a round, the ringside broadcaster explained, "It's hard to hear the bell up there. There's a tremendous amount of smoke here in the Boston Garden." This autumn three excuses have been offered for negative campaigning. "The other guy started it." And: "I'm not being negative, I'm just alerting the electorate to my loathsome opponent's squalid record." And: "Negative campaigning is as American as apple pie—and, by the way, did I mention that my opponent hates apple pie."

True, American politics has always had a bare-knuckle side: "Ma, Ma, where's my Pa?" was a Republican reference to Democrat Grover Cleveland's illegitimate child. Democrats added the defiant line, "Gone to the White House, ha, ha, ha." Cleveland's 1884 opponent was James G. Blaine. "Blaine, Blaine, James G. Blaine, continental liar from the state of Maine." Somewhat negative, that. But television has unique immediacy. Today voters do not venture out to experience negativism at torchlight rallies. Today negativism comes to voters in their living rooms.

Congressman Bob Edgar was criticized for negative ads he used against Pennsylvania's Republican senator, Arlen Specter. Edgar's response was that this year's campaigns were not much, if any, more negative than many campaigns have been. The difference, he said, is that the gusher of political money has made the negativism more audible. That is, candidates have always said beastly things about one another in speeches at union halls or lodge meetings, but now there is so much cash sloshing around in the system, candidates can afford to broadcast their attacks.

There is a lot of money around, and it goes a long way in some states. Horace Busby, a consultant, notes that four of this year's fiercest contests were for Republican-held seats in four of the least populous states: Idaho, Nevada, South Dakota and North Dakota, ranked 41st, 43rd, 45th and 46th respectively. They have a combined population of 2.7 million, about half the population of Cook County, Illinois.

Television time is cheap out where the deer and the antelope outnumber the voters. In Dakota Territory you can buy 30 seconds of time on *The Cosby Show* for just $800.

What is new is not just the amount of negativism, it is the niggling tendentiousness of it. Only a candidate sitting on a large and solid lead feels he can be too principled to run negative ads. (New York's Republican Senator Al D'Amato was always so far ahead he felt no need for negative ads. Too bad. His campaign manager's name is Rick Nasti.) And there is nothing wrong with criticizing the public record of public people. What is tiresome is the reckless use of a candidate's votes to characterize the candidate. A vote for a less-than-maximum funding level for a program for the handicapped or against the most stringent sanctions against South Africa become grounds for 30 seconds of rubbish about the candidate voting "against the handicapped" or "supporting apartheid."

One reason for this year's recourse to negative ads is that in recent years they have worked. Another reason is that this year the "issues" were so unsatisfying. The top 10 issues were: drugs, drugs, drugs, drugs, drugs, drugs, drugs, drugs, drugs, the deficit. Drugs is the conservatives' money-throwing issue: "Don't just stand there, Hoss, throw some money at that problem!" But after Congress has denounced drugs and the deficit, and has made the latter worse by throwing money at the former, the situation remains as follows. No one really knows what the federal government can do effectively against drugs. Everyone knows what it can do about the deficit (cut spending or increase taxes, or do both) and no one wants to do anything.

So grown men with too much money, too few ideas and too little respect for the voters get into slanging matches, such as the one in South Dakota. There the Republican incumbent senator accused his opponent of accepting a contribution from Jane Fonda. And that sin was made scarlet by the fact—so said the senator—that Fonda hates a South Dakota export, red meat. However, the Democrat did not personally get a contribution from Fonda. She attended a fund-raiser for all Democratic Senate candidates. And South Dakotans were assured that on a recent trip she pulled into a McDonald's and devoured two Big Macs. It seems somehow right that this political season should end with a Senate contest, and perhaps control of the Senate and—who knows?—the fate of the free world hinging on voters' reactions to the news that Jane Fonda suffered a Big Mac attack.

November 10, 1986

The Pollution of Politics

In years divisible by two we expect the truth to be trashed and decency to be mugged. These are election years, when politics as currently practiced bares its jagged yellow fangs. But even in 1989 (a year divisible by 663) human nature is nothing to write home about, and there are a few political campaigns to prove it. Today, just a year after Willie Horton showed up in your living room, and just when you thought it was safe to turn the TV back on—*they're back!* Negative ads, the pollution of politics, are nastier than ever, so shoo the kids out of the room while we look over the lip of the abyss, into New Jersey.

The good news for New Jersey is that neither of the congressmen trying to become governor is the contemptible mudslinging, fear-mongering, character-assassinating, truth-shading, tendentious, trivializing demagogue that both seem to be. The bad news for the nation is that New Jersey's campaign illustrates a virulent, contagious sickness spreading through American politics, a plague of preemptive assaults and escalating tawdriness.

The Democrat, James J. Florio, started the negative blitz with an ad suggesting that a couple of drums of heating oil that leaked into land owned by his opponent, Jim Courter, prove that Courter is indifferent to—maybe hostile to—health, beauty and legality. Courter replied that a midnight dumper left the drums there, that the mess had been cleaned up and, speaking of messes, that Florio has ties to the mob. That charge, made in a television ad, was hung on the flimsy fact that Florio had received contributions from a union that later was found to be corrupt. The tone of the campaign has been as follows (from a "debate"). Florio: ". . . you lied when you said you sponsored the Martin Luther King Day holiday bill." Courter: "You love to use the word 'lie.' I guess it suits your demeanor." Each candidate has run an ad showing his opponent with Pinocchio's nose.

Courter's campaign began as a version of the joke about the politician who concluded a rousing stump speech by bellowing, "Those are my views and if you don't like 'em . . . I'll change 'em." Courter came out against abortion and against hiring homosexuals for jobs dealing with children. Then when public opinion surged against him, he said, in effect, "Just kidding—didn't mean it," and used negative ads to change the subject.

Florio is from Camden, where the Democratic machine has been corrupt. A Democratic consultant told *The New York Times*, "He knew he was going to be called a sleaze for what had happened in Camden County. His best strategy was to call Courter a sleaze first, knowing that people would vote for a pro-choice, pro-environment sleaze over a right-wing sleaze. That's what the race is about."

Why is there so much negative advertising? For the same reason there is so much crime: It pays, and most of it goes unpunished. Negative advertising works and because it does it provokes reprisals. An attacked candidate cannot spend a lot of time answering accusations. Play defense, you lose. And negative ads are cost-efficient, especially in New Jersey. It is quicker to gain political ground by mugging the other person than by praising yourself. But a tightening downward gyre has begun: as more politicians campaign negatively, more voters become cynical and increasingly resistant to positive campaigning, ready to believe bad news about everyone. Geography drives New Jersey politicians to seek the biggest bang for their advertising buck. Fifty-eight percent of Jerseyites get their local news from New York City television; most of the rest get it from Philadelphia. Candidates must shell out whopping sums to cover the state with ads broadcast from out of state. New Jersey law limits campaign giving and spending, and negative advertising means maximum impact.

What can be done about attack politics? For starters, we could try talking about serious subjects, such as children and poverty, decaying infrastructure, underinvestment in the future. Political lowlifes prosper when politics loses its intellectual seriousness. (Seriousness is sometimes called "the vision thing.") Also, it would be fun were Congress to pass the bill proposed by two senators, Danforth, a Republican, and Hollings, a Democrat. It would require, among other things, that candidates who want to run ads mentioning (which invariably means attacking) their opponents must do so in person, on camera, instead of relying on the disembodied voice of an announcer faking moral earnestness. If candidates want to sling mud, says Danforth, the voters should be able to see the candidates' dirty hands.

Mud is not always, or even usually, composed of accusations that are flagrantly false. In fact most negative ads are infuriating precisely because they use something technically true (a past vote or statement) in a fundamentally dishonest way. The anonymous voice implies (or the candidate's staff does in defense of the ad) that the tiny truth is a symbolic summation of the opponent's "character." Pious invocation of "the character issue" is part of the John Towerization of public life—anything can be used to assault an opponent because concern about "character" makes everything "relevant."

Now, politics need not be an exercise in politeness, a stately minuet. We want politicians who have serious differences and feel free to say so, vigorously. The Danforth-Hollings bill would not kill all political attacks but it would force the attackers to present themselves in a manner befitting guests in our living rooms. This does not mean they must be so decorous that the doilies do not get wrinkled. On the contrary, Americans should loosen up and welcome real verbal roughhousing from their politicians. We would have better politics if we were more at ease with politicians being a little less polite *in person*.

It is a pity America does not have a contemporary tolerance (we certainly have the tradition) of forthright rhetorical abuse. At the recent conference of Britain's Conservative Party, a senior party official declared that Neil Kinnock, the Labor Party Leader, has "a character in which arrogance, conceit and stupidity are each struggling to take the upper hand." Such muscular invective is to be preferred to the mincing sideswipes and synthetic seriousness of America's negative ads.

November 6, 1989

Honey, We Shrunk the Issues

Let's take a stroll down memory lane because it leads to the present, this summer of strange contentment. One year ago Democrats were marching briskly away from Georgia toward the Potomac, leaving Atlanta smoking from the heat of their rhetoric of derision of George Bush. The go-getters around Michael Dukakis, luxuriating in their man's 17-point lead, were wondering where in the White House West Wing their offices would be. The 17-point lead was an artificially high postconvention bounce, but Dukakis was well ahead and his convention had been suffused with certitude: Victory was a foregone conclusion. Liberals, combining sentimentality and sanctimony, believed they would win because they should win, and that they should because they are so everlastingly good. But as Sam Goldwyn once said, "In two words, im possible."

Dukakis was the first sitting governor since Nelson Rockefeller to mount a serious drive for a presidential nomination, and the first since Adlai Stevenson to win one. (Before Stevenson there was Dewey; before him, Landon. FDR was the last sitting governor to win the White House.) Dukakis's subsequent plummet, first in the campaign and then in Massachusetts (a 70 percent unfavorable rating; 49 percent say he is doing a "very bad" job), suggests a twofold argument against nominating governors.

A governor-as-candidate may be tempted, as Dukakis was, to injure his state with grandiose programs (such as his medical-care plan) and cosmetic solutions to serious problems (such as his budgetary gimmicks) to build a record to run on. Today the "Massachusetts miracle" looks like a Potemkin miracle. He cooked the books and bent the rules to allow himself to say he had balanced 10 consecutive budgets. Now he is begging for new taxes, grudgingly slashing spending (700 line-item vetoes to cut $500 million) and watching his state's bond rating sink to the second-lowest among the states, almost to that of Louisiana, the basket case of the oil patch.

Also, a governor-as-candidate will be vulnerable to negative advertising that today has such serrated edges. Governors, unlike congressmen and senators, do things besides vote and make speeches. They have the vulnerability that comes with perceived responsibility. There always will be some blemishes on a governor's record (a Willie Horton, a Boston Harbor) that negative advertising can magnify to fill TV screens. Those issues (plus the Pledge of Allegiance) were fair for Bush to use against

Dukakis. Horton and the Pledge did epitomize Dukakis's liberalism; the harbor pollution punctured his sanctimony. But all governors are particularly exposed targets for the mendacity that is the common currency of current political discourse.

Of course no one is safe. Last week the National Republican Campaign Committee, a running sore on Mr. Lincoln's party, was back doing business in the manner of its Tom-Foley-is-a-homosexual memorandum. In a mailing aimed at 21 House Democrats who opposed an amendment to require random drug-testing in the State Department, Ed Rollins, co-chairman of the NRCC, accused the 21 of "saying it's OK to do drugs if you work in the State Department." Is the NRCC embarrassed by the fact that the Bush administration also opposed the amendment, as did 31 Republicans, some of them quite conservative? No, some refinement is required before embarrassment is possible.

Such nastiness is the province of small people who flourish when there are no large issues stirring the nation. The miniaturization of political issues in 1989 (the pay-raise quadrille, the counting of John Tower's swizzle sticks, Jim Wright's literary life, rallying 'round the smoldering flag) is a sign of contentment in the country, not least among congressional Democrats. Reagan set the terms of debate. Bush does not. What a difference a year makes? What a difference eight make. On July 27, 1981, Reagan, at daggers drawn with Democrats over his tax and spending cuts, took to TV to generate an unprecedented blizzard of telephone calls, telegrams and mail to Congress. Democrats like Bush for three reasons. He is not frightening, he is likable and he is like them. All three are related to the fact that he represents nothing militant on the march.

According to Peter Hart, the Democratic consultant, Democrats still have a 7-point advantage when the question is which party do you identify with, but they have a 9-point deficit when the question is which party do you most trust to lead the nation. Democrats, says Hart, still need what they have needed while losing five of six and seven of 10 elections, "a strong left hook and a good right jab." That is, they need to be strong on Democratic issues, such as education and child care, and at least all right on Republican issues, such as national security and flag arson.

Last July Dukakis, allowing his hopes to determine his analysis, declared that the election would be about "competence," not ideology. The election was almost purely ideological, but in a peculiar sense. It was about "values"—the flag and all that—which sounds grave but is not even serious. In Europe the "end of ideology" meant the exhaustion of communism and serious socialism (and before that, of fascism) as fighting faiths. European postwar ideologies had been radical critiques of society, and radical programs. Affluence, which ameliorated class antagonisms, dissipated those ideologies of the left. European ideological heat was cooled by contentment.

In America, ideology (of sorts) has risen with contentment. The ideology is deeply frivolous, the stuff of visits to flag factories and constitutional amendments against desecration of the flag. The ideology deals with nothing substantial, no difficult duties, no large undertakings, no divisive questions of distributive justice. It is all fakery and the striking of poses. It can be noisy and even nasty. But the nastiness is a cactus that grows in a desert where no prickly principles live. Washington today really is kinder and gentler than it was when people felt strongly committed to particular courses of action. Where there are no burning convictions about needed changes, there are none of the serious passions occasioned by betrayals and disappointments. As was said of Lloyd George, he had no loyalty and therefore had no rancor.

July 31, 1989

Sound-Bite Debates

The raw excitements of summer are yielding to the yet rawer ones of autumn as the presidential campaign careens lickety-split and right on schedule into a familiar cul-de-sac: a debate of sorts, about debates, of sorts. Is this trip necessary? It is inevitable. It is not beneficial.

There will be only two too many debates this year. That is, there will be only two, as George Bush insisted, rather than the four that Michael Dukakis hankered for. By his hankering, he sent a subliminal message: Watch me, I am the Oakland Athletics of debaters.

Bush, following the rule that you should hang a lantern on your problem rather than try to hide it, has been happy to play the hapless fellow, the Atlanta Braves of debaters. His campaign has speculated it would be best for him if the debates occurred during the Olympics and World Series so they would not have the nation's undivided attention. And the last one should occur well before Election Day so Bush will have time to recover from any rhetorical pratfall, any self-inflicted Pearl Harbor. So now he stands to look surprisingly good if even a few of his sentences parse—by no means a certainty.

This Republic prospered from the presidency of Washington through that of Eisenhower without presidential debates, and there was, mercifully, a 16-year hiatus between the first set (1960) and the second. So why, aside from the fact that television exists, do we have debates?

In a fascinating volume of essays, *Presidential Debates: 1988 and Be-*

yond, the editor, Joel L. Swerdlow, says that neither in democratic theory nor in practice were debates between candidates considered important, until recently. He notes that debates were defined as aspects of legislative deliberations, not as instruments of mass persuasion or electoral campaigning. The Lincoln-Douglas debates in the 1858 senatorial campaign were the first in an election of national significance and they did not inaugurate an era of debates.

It is said in defense of debates that because they last longer than 30 seconds they at least counter the trend toward trivializing compression in political discourse in this age of "sound bites." The trend is deplorable. But so are debates which, being incoherently episodic, are part of the problem.

Kathleen Hall Jamieson, a contributor to the Swerdlow volume, notes that voters have voted with their television dials, emphatically rejecting long—nowadays more than 60 seconds—political events. On September 22, 1964, they gave a landslide victory to *Peyton Place* and *Petticoat Junction* over a conversation between Eisenhower and Goldwater. On November 4, 1979, they chose *Jaws* over Roger Mudd's interview with Ted Kennedy. In 1960, viewership declined sharply for the fourth and final Kennedy-Nixon debate.

Broadcasting, says Jamieson, has brought a steady decrease in the length of political messages. "The 30-minute speeches that reached the nation's Motorolas in the 1940s were standard fare by 1952, the year of America's first telecast presidential campaign. By 1956, the five-minute speech and spot were edging out the longer speech. In 1964, the five-minute speech gave way to the 60-second spot and then the 30-second spot." In a wired nation, the political imperative is "survival of the briefest."

Debates reflect this. They are tossed salads of brevity. Here is a question hurled, like a high, inside fastball, at Mondale's head in the 1984 debate in which the format gave him 150 seconds to answer: "Do you accept the conventional wisdom that Eastern Europe is a Soviet sphere of influence? And if you do, what could a Mondale administration realistically do to help the people of Eastern Europe to achieve the human rights that were guaranteed to them as a result of a Helsinki Accords?" Asking the question takes 15 seconds, equal to 10 percent of the time allotted to an answer.

Because neither side is ever sufficiently confident to relish the thrust and parry of real debates, our debates are, inevitably, parallel press conferences. They test skills unrelated to the real tasks of governance. (Presidential press conferences, wisely deemphasized by Reagan, are similarly overrated as useful events.)

Debates are supposed to test a candidate's ability to "think on his feet." But debates are primarily the regurgitation of market-tested paragraphs. Reflexes, not thinking, are crucial. Anyway, who wants a president thinking on his feet? The presidency is not a solo act. Successful presidents surround themselves with specialized talents and act in concert with them.

This year's debates will be bracketed by sound and fury—the hype before and the spin-doctors after—and will signify the institutionalization of yet another idea that diminishes our politics.

September 11, 1988

The Final Debate (Thank God!)

The winner? Are you kidding? Do we give a trophy for being a millimeter less tiresome than the other guy?

It was a national embarrassment. Michael Dukakis was marginally less embarrassing than George Bush was, if only because his canned thoughts were ladled out in understandable syntax. However, the smallmindedness and tactical overtuning were so oppressive on both sides that Bush may benefit. Boredom and disgust may drive down voter turnout so much that Bush (Republicans are more reliable voters) may benefit from the ennui.

Dukakis wanted to look less than he usually does like an alderman unveiling a bust of himself. He did that, if just barely, by smiling—at least, that probably was a smile—and by a closing statement that (faint praise here) made more sense than Bush's.

Bush wanted to prove that he could perform well, or at least passably, when not scripted, as he was in his convention acceptance speech, by a gifted writer like Peggy Noonan. Bush's Sunday-evening performance raised this thought: Why not elect Noonan and cut out the middleman?

Bush is not famous for his concision, but oh, my. Here he is on housing (we join him in full flight): "And how does that grab you for increasing housing? Housing is up. We are serving a million more families now. But we're not going to do it in that old Democratic liberal way of trying to build more bricks and mortars. Go out and take a look at St. Louis at some of that effort. It is wrong." He was referring to a St. Louis public-housing project so bad it was dynamited. You probably understood that if you also understood his references to the McKinney bill.

Bush and Dukakis witticisms are recognizable by the complete absence of one attribute of true wit: spontaneity. Their attempts at humanizing humor were heavy enough to be weighed on truck scales and obviously had been tamped into each candidate by handlers. Why should the humor be different from the serious stuff?

Tracing a Bush thought back from its manifestation in speech to its origin in his thinking is like seeking the source of the Blue Nile. The problem with Bush sentences that reel drunkenly around a topic is not just aesthetic. Neither is the problem only—only!—that syntactic chaos is a sign of a chaotic mind. The basic and alarming problem is that Bush's chaotic mind seems to be a consequence of a lack of public purpose.

Sure, he has a purpose: He wants to be president. But he seems to want that only because it is the next rung up, and climbing the ladder of public life is his life. This is an old axiom: Some people seek office to be something; others seek office to do something. Bush is one of the former. In this, the contrast with Ronald Reagan is complete.

Dukakis has public purposes. Although Bush called Dukakis an "iceman," Bush was more correct when contradicting himself, saying that Dukakis has passions, but the wrong ones. Indeed the most disagreeable aspect of this campaign is Dukakis's disingenuousness, his disguising of his leftward inclination. Again, the contrast with Reagan is instructive: Reagan hardly hid—if anything, he exaggerated—his rightward leaning.

In politics, one does what one is and becomes what one does. Bush skitters like a waterbug on the surface of things, strewing fragments of thoughts, moving fast lest he linger so long that he is expected to show mastery of, or even real interest in, anything. It is well to dwell on him because he is ahead, the clock is running and every indecisive day, like Sunday, serves him.

It is said that about one-third of the supporters of both candidates are so lightly attached to their candidates that they could be detached. It is unlikely that either candidate's support was substantially solidified Sunday night. So Bush left North Carolina in a position to do what the North Carolina Tarheels basketball team sometimes does when it has a lead. It goes into a four-corner stall to kill the clock.

Dukakis, by speaking about medical care and other traditional Democratic issues, is going to find out if there is a Democratic majority out there. And he also has this hope: In the days before the debate, the campaign's dynamics began to change. The change was driven in part by journalists' impatience with Bush's "flag factory" path to the presidency. Thoughtful television journalists are debating whether they have a duty to put on the air whatever spectacle a candidate decides to make the centerpiece of his campaign day.

But back on the trail, Bush is back on a script. In each of the final 40 days he needs 15 seconds of telegenic thoughtfulness. That totals 10 minutes of mind until the final buzzer. He might just make it.

September 29, 1988

The Political Echo of Ecophobia

Just when you thought it was safe to go home and hide under the bed from all the bad news about the environment, the government warns that a man's house may be a menace because of cancer-causing radon gas. No wonder the mood of the moment is ecophobia, the fear that the planet is increasingly inhospitable.

The radon warning came on a day when the St. Louis weather forecast was for "smoky sunshine," a result of windborne haze from forest fires in the Far West. The fires are partly a result of the drought, which may be related to a general warming of the planet—the greenhouse effect that might result in a disastrous rise of the oceans.

If you go to the beach, while there is a beach, to brood about this, do not sit in the sun. The thinning ozone layer raises the risk of skin cancer. And do not go near the water which, even if it is free of medical waste, may have other pollutants that degrade it even more than acid rain is degrading lakes.

Any widespread anxiety should have a political echo, and ecophobia should serve the Dukakis campaign. In 1976, Pat Moynihan wrote that there are two critical choices affecting the quality of American life: "One is how much growth we want; the second is how much government we want." In the third quarter of the century, Americans had opted consistently for more government and less growth. Moynihan saw a reaction coming.

It came. It was called conservatism. Now anxiety about the environment may push the ideological pendulum in the other direction.

It may do for Michael Dukakis what his attempt to portray today's prosperity as a chimera can not do. It may make the Democrats' specialty—government activism—attractive. It gives him more than a subject, it gives him a theme—stewardship. He can ask: Has growth been purchased at too high a price? The price can be measured in accumulated public debt and the inadequate husbandry of the Earth's resources.

The public's attention on such matters is, however, hard to get—and harder still to hold—for several reasons. The intersection of science and public policy is a dark and bloody ground of contention. Today's saturation journalism pounces on environmental episodes—soil erosion today, oil spills tomorrow—and quickly wrings them dry. So there is a constant media hunger for new crises, each one less convincing than the last.

Some environmental activists have played fast and loose with facts to arouse alarm. Zero-growth was advocated in the 1970s by people who already had acquired a nice portion of prior growth. ("Let's all consume less. Someone tell those Sybarites in Bangladesh to tighten their belts.") And the resiliency of the planet has been consistently misjudged.

That said, so must this be: Most environmental difficulties derive from a virtually universal aspiration—economic dynamism. By such dynamism mankind has made more of a mark on the environment in the last 100 years than in the preceding 3,000. But the dynamism has done more to improve life for more people in the last 100 years than was done by all developments in all history prior to that.

Environmental issues are of limited political utility because they illustrate the universality of costs. George Bush says, "I am an environmentalist." That statement is as vacuous as any statement that can be constructed from four English words. Does Bush's environmentalism dictate a "let burn" policy regarding forest fires? Is he for higher fuel-efficiency standards for automobiles, standards that would mean smaller cars and higher fatality rates in highway accidents?

Dukakis is no different. He will not challenge any popular behavior, regardless of its environmental impact. Instead there will be tough talk about easy choices, such as "cracking down on polluters"—as though the environmental danger comes down to a few bad people putting things where they do not belong.

But do not despair. Draw a deep breath and consider this: In 1900, America's cities contained 3 million horses, the healthiest of them producing up to 25 pounds of manure a day. Manure in the streets attracted swarms of flies until, in hot weather, traffic ground it into a dust that (a memoirist wrote) "flew from the pavement as a sharp, piercing powder, to cover our clothes, ruin our furniture and blow up into our nostrils." Then came a solution—one of today's problems, the internal combustion engine.

Want a new worry? Space junk. *Science* magazine says there are 48,000 man-made objects one centimeter or larger orbiting Earth, with an average relative velocity of 10 kilometers a second. NASA is studying how to armor-plate space vehicles.

Man is messy, but any creature that can create space vehicles can probably cope. That is, mankind's inventiveness has been, so far, more creative than mankind's environmental impact has been damaging. So far. What is still missing is the political ingredient, a sustained summons to stewardship.

September 18, 1988

An Argument About Class, Waiting to Be Made

Pelting Michael Dukakis with unsolicited advice is a low-tech but high-growth industry, so here goes. He should tell the country that the Reagan-Bush administration has miraculously made Karl Marx seem correct—this at a moment when there are no longer any believing Marxists east of the Elbe River.

If Marx had been scribbling away in the Library of Congress (our equivalent of the British Museum, where Marx scribbled), in January 1981, as Reaganites marched into Washington, he would have said: The class struggle is about to intensify. During the Reagan Terror, labor will lose ground to capital.

Today it can be argued that compensation of labor, including wages and salaries and fringe benefits, as a share of personal income is at the lowest level of any peak year (meaning any year at a comparable stage of an economic expansion) since 1947. The difference is not huge, but there it is. And according to a study for the Economic Policy Institute, by Lawrence Mishel and Jacqueline Simon, since 1979 income from property ownership (rents, dividends, interest) has risen three times faster than income from work.

Dukakis could say, in language adapted for mass audiences, that we are witnessing the rise of a rentier society. The political potential for Dukakis is in this fact: Most people are not rentiers. Or, more precisely, most people do not think of themselves as such. That qualification is necessary because anyone who is vested in a pension program is involved through it in the stock and bond markets and thus has a stake in interest and dividends.

Dukakis should stress that to pay the interest component of the 1988 budget will require a sum ($210 billion) equal to approximately half of all the personal income-tax receipts. This represents, as Senator Pat Moynihan has said, a transfer of wealth from labor to capital unprecedented in American history.

Tax revenues are being collected from average Americans (the median income of a family of four is slightly under $30,000) and given to the buyers of U. S. government bonds—buyers in Beverly Hills, Lake Forest, Shaker Heights and Grosse Point, and Tokyo and Riyadh. If a Democrat can't make something of that, what are Democrats for?

But here Dukakis confronts the problem of being a "progressive" in an affluent middle-class country. Only a minority of Americans—a small and shrinking minority—think of themselves as "labor." And the vast majority of that minority is already for Dukakis.

Furthermore, Americans are pleased to think of themselves as living in a "classless" society. That implausible belief is actually the imperfect expression of two other ideas. One is that almost everyone is in the middle class. The other is that social mobility is such that with pluck and luck almost anyone can make it into the middle class. (The exception to this rule is the large semipermanent underclass that seem impervious to social policy.)

But such sentimentalities aside, politics is about who gets what, especially as a result of government action. In the Reagan years, a particular social stratum has gotten a lot. The people who get income from property have benefited, especially from the huge deficits that have put in place a permanent high level of government borrowing that produces high interest rates.

For decades, "deficit spending" has been denounced by conservatives as a Democratic device for redistributing income to the undeserving poor. The Reagan deficits have, with fine impartiality, helped the rich.

Marxists, who believe that history has an inner logic, like to say "it is no accident" that whatever happens happens. In fact, the kindliness of Reaganomics toward the property-owning class (according to Mishel and Simon, the value of the financial assets of more than half of all families in this classless society in 1983 was zero or negative—they had more debts than assets) has been the predictable consequence of a class-based policy. The policy is trickle-down economics.

Republicans can reasonably argue that a beneficial policy for those at the bottom of the social heap is a policy that energizes those at the top—the investing, entrepreneurial class that makes the wheels turn in a free society where government does not run a command economy. However, that is a politically awkward argument to make during a political campaign, even in a democracy as committed to capitalism as this one is. Dukakis might do well by forcing Bush to make that argument.

September 15, 1988

Mike, *What . . . do . . . you . . . mean?*

The Dukakis campaign's unconquerable aversion to common sense is on display in a new television commercial that exacerbates the doubts it is designed to allay. It is supposed to present the new, redesigned, cuddly, warm (or at least room-temperature) candidate. In it, the shirtsleeved Dukakis, turning on the fountains of his vast deep, says:

"Today it seems young parents have less time and a lot more to worry about. If I were a young father today I'd want to know that my government wasn't blind to the changes in my life. I'd want my new president to be in touch with the things that are important to my family. That's not a Democratic concern, it's not a Republican concern. That's a father's concern."

That's it. All of it. Really. It must make many viewers want to scream at the screen, "Can you be more—can you be at all—specific? *What . . . do . . . you . . . mean?*"

When I saw the commercial, it came hard on the heels of a McDonald's commercial that was, compared to the Dukakis commercial, as informative as the *Encyclopaedia Britannica.* It told you what you would get from McDonald's: hamburgers and happiness. Does Dukakis assume that everyone knows (because he assumes that everyone thinks as he does?) what he means about the "things" the president should be "in touch with"?

Or is he reticent because he is wary lest specifics seem liberal? Perhaps the problem is a blend of both intellectual arrogance and despair about the supposed immaturity of an electorate that could prefer conservatives to liberals.

For eight years, during which Reagan carried 93 states in 48 months, Democrats like Dukakis have been wondering: How does he do it? Why do they (the voters) do it? Surely it cannot be that they agree with him, because the truth is self-evident and we self-evidently have custody of it.

Dukakis, it is said, is not communicating well. Wrong. He communicates very well, but "well" is not a synonym for persuasively. With what he has done and said over a long public career, and what he now says and will not say, he communicates the transformation of liberalism from a doctrine of popular collective choices and common provision (Social Security, rural electrification, etc.) into something that dare not speak its name. It is the transformation of liberalism from a supportive friend into a nagging nanny.

At about the time Dukakis entered public life, liberalism was changing. It stopped seeming to be a government hand for those needing help and became the rasping voice of bossy government, dictating to people who presumably could not be trusted to know right from wrong (school busing, racial quotas, judicial fiats about abortion, capital punishment and, yes, the Pledge of Allegiance).

Many political commentators specialize in trivializing explanations of election: Dewey lost to Truman because he would not shave his moustache; Eisenhower won because of his grin, etc. For eight years now it has been insistently said that Reagan has won because he said "There you go again" or because of his smile or because of what has been called his "Aw shucks, I stepped on my sneakers' laces" charm. Democrats will begin to do better the day they decide that, in general, a particular candidate wins because people listen to what he says and prefer it to what the other candidate says.

One healthy aspect of a Dukakis defeat might be this: It might leave Democrats no place to hide, no trivializing alibis to enable them to say that the incompetent public let itself be gulled yet again. If Dukakis loses, no one, surely, will suggest blaming the outcome on Bush's charm or charisma.

After the Los Angeles debate, many commentators said: Dukakis failed to "find his voice" or to "present himself." Oh? What have people been hearing and seeing for 16 months if not the voice and persona of Dukakis? After Los Angeles, people said: Dukakis is having trouble "getting his message through." But perhaps he is losing because his message has gotten through.

By the end of this week, the media probably will be nearly unanimous in denouncing the (there is a sublime irony here) "incompetence" of the Dukakis campaign, a campaign that began with the half-boast, half-prayer that the election would turn not on ideology but on competence. Incompetence will be blamed because the dominant culture in the media flinches from the fact that Dukakis's message has been clearly heard and as clearly rejected.

Already many Democrats who share his culture are preemptively trivializing the election result. They are blaming Dukakis's anticipated defeat on his personal attributes (his inability to smile, his lack of charm) rather than on his, which also is their, message. These Democrats are getting a running start on the road to defeat in 1992.

October 20, 1988

The (Best I Can Do) Case for Dukakis

Because neither candidate has made a convincing case for himself, this column today undertakes to do so for Dukakis. The case for Bush comes in the next column.

Consider the case for Dukakis while you are sitting in a traffic jam or on a plane in coagulated traffic at a congested airport. You are then congealed in a consequence of the Reagan-Bush administration's budget deficits.

Whenever you buy gasoline or an airline ticket, you pay taxes that go into trust funds that can be spent only for highways and airports. But these funds are being hoarded to make the deficit seem to be "only" $155 billion. The deficit is the numerical expression of a cultural tendency and a governmental dereliction of duty. America's tendency is to consume more than it produces. The neglected duty is to husband resources and plan for tomorrow.

Three-quarters of the debt incurred by the U. S. government in 190 years prior to the Reagan-Bush administration was the result of war. The debt was (as Alexander Hamilton said of Revolutionary War debt) "the price of liberty." The Reagan-Bush debt is just the price of profligacy. Would Dukakis do worse? Not likely.

Democrats may have learned restraint. Even during the 1982 recession, the worst contraction since the Depression, they did not mount a serious drive for a jobs program. And having campaigned demogogically in 1982 against Social Security cuts, they collaborated in a cut (by raising the retirement age). Of the 255 Democratic congressmen, 138 have arrived here since 1978, after Carter's turn toward austerity. They have not had a chance to acquire the habit of liberality in domestic spending. The decade has produced pent-up pressure for spending, but perhaps a Democratic president would be best for enforcing discipline.

Dukakis rightly insists that some new spending is needed. As productivity growth slows, we are investing less generously in children than previous generations did. For all his flag-waving, Bush will not summon Americans to the patriotic act of forgoing, through taxation, even a small portion of private consumption. Such forgoing would serve the collective good (which, Bush please note, is what government is for) by reducing the deficit. That would reduce the drain of private savings away from productive investment. And more could be spent by government to reduce the dangerous educational deficit of the rising generation of citizens.

Dukakis, in his come-to-think-about-it-I-just-remembered-I'm-a-liberal mood, has been criticizing some American inequalities. Bush says this is un-American: "You see, I think that's for European democracies or something else—it isn't for the United States of America. We are not going to be divided by class."

Bush, you're something else if you think there are no class divisions that condition access to education, legal services, medical care and other important things. It is a national scandal that one-fifth of all children live in poverty and a national travesty that a presidential candidate denies class realities.

As for that object of universal political worship—the middle (if Bush will pardon the expression) class—consider this: Four-fifths of Americans—all but the top 20 percent—are paying a larger portion of their family income in federal income taxes than before Reagan's presidency.

Dukakis's foreign policy is, of course, improvised incoherence generated by dangerous instincts. For example, he criticizes intervention in the "internal affairs" of Nicaragua, but wants to overthrow the governments of Panama and South Africa. And his campaign conversion to the support of some military modernization is unconvincing. But then Bush blithely endorses SDI, MX, Midgetman, the B-1, Stealth, a 600-ship Navy, improved conventional forces and budget restraint. His calculator needs new batteries. The difference between Dukakis, who may find that some systems are jobs programs with Democratic constituencies, and Bush, who is unwilling to put tax money where his moving lips are when praising defense, might be small.

The next president must restrain American and Western European lenders from unleashing a flood of credit to the Soviet Union, a flood that would reduce the pressure on Gorbachev to choose between militarism and improved living standards. But regarding East-West trade, the Republican Party reveals itself as a party of blinkered businessmen and the crassest commercial values. Democrats might do better.

Under Bush or Dukakis, foreign policy for the next few years will be largely a matter of watching while Gorbachev defines himself. A Dukakis administration would at least speed that process of definition by offering a strong temptation to Gorbachev to continue the Soviet drive for politically decisive military superiority.

That is not much to say for Dukakis, but it is the most I can manage.

November 3, 1988

The 5,000 Reasons for Voting for Bush

The campaign, having promised instruction and barely delivered diversion, now sags to a stop and I herewith complete the task begun in my last column. Then I made the case for electing Michael Dukakis. Today I undertake the comparably Herculean task of arguing George Bush's case.

Is Bush better than he seems? No. This low, dishonest campaign, which squandered the precious commodity of the nation's attention, was the carefully prepared and freely chosen culmination of his public life to date. He seems to have passed through the tumults of the 20th century unmarked by any of its great passions or arguments or aspirations. Paradoxically, that may be the key to putting the best face on his performance.

Perhaps he has campaigned basely because he has, in place of substantive political motives, a single ideal. He is moved entirely by an abstract duty to "serve," not by any idea he wants to be in the service of. In the absence of ideas, mere tactics are everything.

He is at once vaguely admirable and ominously empty. What matters is who will fill him up.

That brings us to 5,000 reasons for electing Bush. They are the appointments, from senior White House and Cabinet officers on down, that a president makes or are made in his name. An important question in any election, and the crucial question when both candidates are so inadequate, is: Which party has the better pool of talent from which to draw? The Republican Party is to be preferred until the Democratic Party regains its political acumen and intellectual vigor.

Three other reasons for preferring Bush also pertain to the presidential power to shape the composition of government. Four days after the election, Harry Blackmun will become the third Supreme Court Justice over 80. The others are William Brennan and Thurgood Marshall. All three are liberals. The next president probably will have at least three nominations to make.

Almost the entire public agenda seems to pass through courts. It is urgent that new justices reverse the tendency to turn what should be legislative decisions into litigation. This is important to the rejuvenation of the Democratic Party. The liberal party's powers of persuasion have atrophied as liberals have increasingly relied on judicial fiat rather than mass persuasion to achieve their aims.

A Bush-directed change in the Court's composition might result in reversal of the 1973 abortion ruling, but that might not result in much change in abortion policy. It would ignite 50 arguments by restoring to states the right to regulate abortion. The arguments are needed, given such biomedical developments as intrauterine medicine. But abortion is, after circumcision, the nation's most common surgical procedure. The culture has moved far in 15 years and there now is a majority in favor of liberal abortion laws.

The careful selection of justices requires an interest in constitutional theories that is as foreign to Bush as Mongolia. Liberals should take comfort from the possibility that he may squander his opportunities. There is precedent. Two of the three liberal octogenarians were appointed by Republicans—Brennan by Eisenhower (who also nominated Warren) and Blackmun by Nixon. The fourth liberal, John Paul Stevens, was Ford's choice.

In foreign policy, Bush will offer warmed-over Reaganism—whatever Reaganism means after eight years of dilution. Reagan's grand passion, the Reagan Doctrine—aid to armed resistance within the Soviet empire (Nicaragua, Afghanistan)—seems to matter little to Bush. Reagan has forcefully licensed détente, and hence the moral disarmament of the West. Thus there is little to do but watch to see if he is right—to see if the Soviet regime really has repudiated its first seven decades of words and deeds.

If not, we are in trouble too big for Bush. As Soviet military spending continues its steady increase, the U. S. defense budget is declining and is under increasing pressure that can not be resisted by Bush, the antitax warrior.

Bush's probable secretary of state, James Baker, is a clever fellow, but he may suffer the diplomatic fidgets that afflict political deal-makers when they become diplomats. They think that deals made are the only meaningful ratifications of their exertions. The arms-control lobby should rejoice. Arms agreements are always popular and Bush's campaign indicates that no consideration will ever weigh more than crude political calculations.

Still, Bush may at least have the instinctive caution of a man without a compass. That is faint praise but about as much as he has earned this fall.

November 6, 1988

Another Muddy Message

And so, given a chance, at long last, to get a word in edgewise, the electorate cleared its collective throat, said, "Read our lips" and made one thing clear: Clarity is not now America's political aim. It has not been for some time. The voters' message may be muddy, but it is familiar. By voting again to have the legislative and executive branches controlled by different parties Americans have said that they still are "ideologically conservative" and "operationally liberal." Voting for president is an ideo-logical, expressive act, a national affirmation of what we are and want to be tomorrow. The vote for Congress is operational in that it says what we want right now.

In our expressive lives we are Jeffersonians, with a strong bias against largeness and centralization. This hurts the Democratic Party, which is identified with the large central government. Indeed, its two solidest blocs—actually, its only solid blocs—are blacks, who are disproportion-ately clients of government, and public employee unions, who are gov-ernment as an interest group. In their operational lives Americans are Hamiltonians, comfortable with—indeed, determined to preserve against any conservative attack—a strong national "social insurance state." They hold it responsible for generating prosperity and ameliorat-ing the discomforts of economic dynamism.

This election has produced a hardening of America's division of polit-ical labor at the national level, with Republicans dominating the presi-dency and Democrats looking like a merely legislative party. Some important Democrats in Congress probably do not much mind this. Presidents come and go but the Democratic majority in Congress abid-eth forever. A chairman of a House or Senate committee presides com-fortably over a satrapy, and his position can be especially comfortable when no party loyalty requires deference to the president.

But this division of political labor is profoundly bad for both parties, and the nation. It cannot last because there is an inherent disequilibrium between executive and legislative dominance. A party impotent at the highest—the presidential—level of political competition will come to seem unserious at all levels. A continuing decline of the Democratic Party—world's cldest party; the principal shaper of modern America, hence of the modern world—would be dangerous. It would deprive America of a strong opposition when the nature of the new president demands just that. Bush is politically formless. What Macaulay said of the U. S. Constitution can be said of Bush—"all sail and no anchor." He needs to be watched.

Bush's election means that for at least 32 years, from 1961 through 1992, and perhaps for 36 years through 1996, the nation will have been governed by presidents drawn from a single generation, men born in the 14 years between 1911 (Reagan) and 1924 (Bush). In this the nation has been fortunate. Those men came of age politically in a heroic age of American governance, when the nation stiffened its sinews and summoned up its blood and mastered great challenges—the Depression, the dictators. That generation of politicians had—has—a sturdy confidence in the country's capacity for great exertions.

For Democrats one lesson of 1988 is: Beware of liberals who came of age politically, as Dukakis did, in the 1950s. Their liberalism is apt to reflect three wrong lessons learned from three phenomena—the Korean War, McCarthyism and Eisenhower's presidency. From Korea they acquired skepticism—deepened by Vietnam, another exercise in military incrementalism—about the utility of military power. In reaction to McCarthyism they acquired this bit of cultural chic: anti-anticommunism. And by defining their liberalism in disdain for Eisenhower (and by being "madly for Adlai" Stevenson) they infected liberalism with intellectual vanity and contempt for the electorate.

Remember the liberals' self-flattering joke as they left power in 1953? "The New Dealers are being replaced by the car dealers." It was easy to sniff the snobbery. Soon liberalism was characterized by condescension toward the objects of its solicitousness. Liberals came to think like the Trollope character who said that when doing good to people "one has no right to expect that they should understand it. It is like baptizing little infants."

But conservative complacency about the 1988 election will be short-lived. Campaigning is an expressive activity. Governing is operational. Bush, having won an ideologically conservative campaign, now gets to govern in tandem—and in tension—with a Congress firmly controlled by the forces of operational liberalism. Bush will come to terms with them. Reagan did—that is as clear as arithmetic.

For six years now, ever since the arithmetic of the budget became acutely embarrassing, the Republican chant has been: "Don't blame the president for the deficits—only Congress can spend money." This chant is an example of a falsehood manufactured from a banality. Yes, yes, of course Congress appropriates. But Congress, while tinkering with the allocation, has appropriated approximately the sums Reagan requested. The six fiscal years 1982–87 (the 1981 budget was Carter's; the 1988–89 budgets are products of the Reagan-Congress "summit") produced deficits totaling $1.1 trillion. In those six years Congress voted to spend only about $90 billion more than Reagan's budgets proposed to spend. So Reagan proposed 13/14ths of those deficits. Reagan never sought and, naturally, never got a mandate to cut the entitlement programs that are the essence of today's "social insurance state."

Almost 6,000 Americans turn 65 every day. Americans are living longer, partly because of scientific progress against degenerative diseases, partly because of a government success—the dissemination of health information that moves millions of people to modify their behavior. They are smoking and drinking less, eating and exercising more sensibly. That is nice. It also is a problem. The elderly receive a disproportionate share of entitlement spending which drives the deficit. The only entitlement Bush has recently thought about is Willie Horton's. Now, at long last, Bush must do two things that he showed no inclination to do during the campaign. He must think. And he must tell people things they do not want to hear.

November 21, 1988

The Democrats Get Started on Losing the 1992 Election

Ego is the fuel of politics, and some Democratic politicians, their egos smarting and their prudence telling them to put distance between themselves and the debris, are offering this piquant explanation of Dukakis's downfall: His campaign did not return our telephone calls.

There they go again, those Democrats.

People tend to be diligent about doing what they do well and Democrats are diligently working on losing the next election by ignoring the lesson of this one. They are abetted by the media, unwitting helpers of unappreciative Republicans. The close relationship between political journalists and political operators produces postelection analyses that encourage in Democrats the soothing belief that their party's problems are in the nuts and bolts of the machinery and not in the party's mind.

Granted, had wiser Democrats been heeded, Dukakis would have campaigned better—gone here rather than there, run this rather than that ad—and would have done marginally better. But losing 40 states and 426 electoral votes is not a marginal loss. However, postmortems are preoccupied with marginalia. This preoccupation is encouraged by the media, which have a microview of politics because of the day-by-dayness of journalism.

Journalists talk to political tacticians and, lo and behold, learn from them that tactics are all, and that the tactics would have been dazzling if the tacticians' calls had been returned. It is time for a decade-by-decade view.

Dukakis was the second-strongest Democratic candidate in 24 years. Bush's victory margin of under 8 points in the popular vote was well below the Republicans' 13-point average in their first six victories since midcentury. In those victories, Republicans averaged 455 electoral votes, better than Bush's 426. So? So Dukakis was decapitated, but not drawn and quartered. Some consolation for the deceased.

Yes, Dukakis came close in a number of states. But as politicians say, close only counts in horseshoes and hand grenades. The 1927 Yankees won a lot of one-run games, which made them more, not less, impressive.

"Blame voters first." Democrats say that voters were gulled by trivialities (the Pledge of Allegiance, ACLU, etc.) that better Dukakis tactics could have countered. Actually, Dukakis was lucky. Trivialities worked so well that Bush never needed to use the lethal stuff, like Dukakis's endorsement, when pandering to Iowa's "peace" lobby, of a ban on flight-testing missiles. Such a commitment to unilateral disarmament makes Willie Horton look like Winnie-the-Pooh.

"Rodney Dangerfield Democrats" say Dukakis's achievement—23 out of every 50 votes—was "respectable." Is the goal respect or power? Some Democrats say: 46 percent isn't chopped liver. But Bush gets 100 percent of the presidency.

Here are 49 million reasons for looking beyond the minutiae of Dukakis's tactics: In the last 36 years, 49 million more votes have been cast for Republican presidential candidates than for Democrats. Maybe seven losses in 10 tries says something about the Democrats' message. If Democrats had won 70 percent of the elections and piled up a 49-million-vote surplus, perhaps the media would say the message mattered more than tactics.

Two years ago, a Democrat said: "If we can't beat Bush, we have to pick another country." They should pick the good ol' C. S. A.: Dukakis lost all 11 states of the Confederate States of America. He started 138 electoral votes in the hole—155 adding the border states of Kentucky and Oklahoma.

Democrats devised Super Tuesday to force their candidates to court the South early in the nomination process. They held their convention in the South. They plucked their vice-presidential nominee from the South. They lost the South and the border, 155–0.

Conventions and running mates are marginalia. Voters think the message is more important. Super Tuesday was a failure because so many moderate Democrats, weary of the party's national message, no longer vote in Democratic primaries. In Florida's primary, the two most liberal Democrats, Dukakis and Jackson, got 60.9 percent combined. In November, a conservative demolished Dukakis in Florida.

Look at Tuesday's result and ask: How many states that Dukakis won would Sam Nunn have lost? How many that Dukakis lost would Nunn have won? The answers: None and many.

Then there is a third question: How many times does the electorate have to hit the Democratic Party across the bridge of the nose with a crowbar before the party gets the point? Remarkable beast, that party. Its nose wears out crowbars.

November 13, 1988

PART 5

Rights . . . and Wrongs

"Informative and Persuasive" Panhandling

Just when you think no new folly can make city life more menacing, some moral exhibitionist, wielding judicial power and reeking of liberal self-approval, makes matters worse. Meet Judge Leonard Sand.

He recently ruled that New York City's ban on panhandling in subway stations violates the First Amendment because begging is "informative and persuasive speech." This latest trauma to the First Amendment suggests that any peaceful (although intrusive, annoying and even coercive) conduct that is accompanied by speech is constitutionally protected. This is especially so, says Sand with a flourish of sentimentality, if the speaker is among the (literally) unwashed.

"A true test of one's commitment to constitutional principles," says Sand in one of those self-flattering formulations of which judicial activists are fond, "is the extent to which recognition is given to the rights of those in our midst who are the least affluent, least powerful and least welcome." That advertisement for himself ("what a swell sensitive fellow I am") is nonsense as law or morality.

First Amendment rights do not vary inversely with the affluence of individuals. There is nothing novel about "time, place and manner" restrictions on speech (e.g., no sound trucks near hospitals). Yet the city's attempt to limit one of the unpleasant, even alarming, experiences of subway travel is deemed unconstitutional. Indeed, Sand says that the "unsettling" nature of beggars and their "message" is what turns their "conduct" into constitutionally "protected expression."

The question of what society owes in compassionate help to street people is, surely, severable from the question of what right the community has to protect a minimally civilized ambience in public spaces. However, that second question is rarely even reached because all today's controversies are cast as conflicts between individual rights and a cold, alien government. This is the mentality of severely individualistic liberalism. But conservatives, with their mindless execrations of government, also are blameworthy.

The community, dismissed (when thought of at all) as a fiction without standing, deteriorates through the "broken window" dynamic. James Q. Wilson of UCLA says that if a broken window in a building goes unrepaired, the remaining windows will be broken, because an unrepaired window sends a message that no one cares. Disorder and crime are linked in a developmental sequence. Disorder atomizes communities, dissolving the sense of mutual regard and obligations of civility.

Nathan Glazer of Harvard says that even nonobscene graffiti on New York subway cars tell riders they are entering an uncontrolled environment. Anxiety, wariness, avoidance and truculence increase.

John Leo, a columnist who lives in New York, has described the process, by which street people begin the destabilization process, that ends in "dead parks": "Sandboxes become urinals. Swings are broken. Every park bench seems to be owned by a permanently curled-up dozing alcoholic or perhaps a street schizophrenic. When the cycle is complete, the community withdraws, serious druggies and criminals move in. . . ."

Beggars—many of them deranged by alcohol or other drugs or mental illness, and dangerous in fact or appearance—are human "broken windows." But in the social analysis spawned by liberalism, the individual is the only reality and the community is an abstraction without claims. This leads to the decriminalization of so-called "victimless behavior." Next comes some community-wrecking judge to discover that some of that behavior is a fundamental constitutional right. As Wilson says, such behavior (panhandling, public drunkenness, prostitution, pornographic displays) can destroy a community faster than a gang of professional burglars.

Judge Sand was recently in the news when the Supreme Court reversed his imposition of heavy fines on Yonkers city councilmen. His purpose was to coerce the councilmen into voting to place public housing where he wants it. The Court objected to Sand forcing officials to act with reference to their personal financial interests rather than the desires of constituents. In the Yonkers and subway cases, Sand's jurisprudence says: Representative government—the voice of the community—does not matter; what matters is judicial imperialism on behalf of whatever individual rights strike the fancy of any judge.

Judges like Sand are dangerous—physically dangerous—because their actions feed the anarchic impulse toward violent self-help. Harried, frightened citizens have begun assaulting, in one instance killing, beggars who, in an atmosphere of pervasive menace, are, or appear to nervous people as, dangerous.

Dangerous maybe. Litigious certainly. A news report reads: "Lawyers for the two homeless men who had challenged the no begging policy said. . . ."

Not every American has a home but—first things first—everyone has a lawyer.

February 1, 1990

The "Right" to Live on Sidewalks

NEW YORK—Johannes Miquel, a fervent 19th-century socialist, was with a friend when approached by a beggar. The friend reached into his pocket, but Miquel stopped him, exclaiming: "Don't delay the Revolution!" That seemed humane if you believed that destitution is caused by capitalism, can only be cured by revolution, and that revolution is delayed by charity or reforms.

Today, there are radically different proposals for responding to solitary homeless persons who live on city streets. Most are mentally ill. Many are the sort who, a few generations ago, were in institutions.

One reason deranged homeless persons are today so conspicuous in cities like New York is that three decades ago a new pharmacology and a new ideology intersected. The ideology, "deinstitutionalization," rejected not only the deplorable practices in many institutions, but even the principle of institutions. The pharmacological development was in psychotropic drugs that supposedly made it possible to act on the ideology.

New antipsychotic drugs made possible the control of psychotic episodes. But although the drugs eliminated deranged behavior, that elimination did not itself necessarily transform the patient into someone certain to function competently in society.

For some, whose psychotic episodes are rare, the drugs are sufficient to make them socially competent. But for many people, the drugs do not stop the deterioration of personality. As they suffer the pathologies and victimization of dereliction, they lose even the discipline to take the drugs.

Today the homeless are again making headlines because New York City recently adopted the policy of removing the "severely disturbed" homeless from streets for involuntary hospitalization. State law permits that—when there is substantial risk of physical harm to the person or to others. The first person removed was a woman who had lived nearly a year in front of a hot-air vent on Second Avenue near 65th Street.

There ensued a typically American argument, one impossible to caricature.

A judge ordered her released, in the grand progressive tradition (as with Miquel) of using the poor for large political ends. He said that society, not she, is sick ("the blame and shame must attach to us . . .") and, anyway, the sight of her may improve us. By being "an offense to aesthetic senses" she may spur the community to "action." Her four sisters, who learned about her on television, said it was "racist" and "sexist" for him to say "the streets are good enough for her." But the New York Civil Liberties Union rhapsodized that the ruling was "eloquent, sensible."

The judge was unimpressed by the fact that the woman had a history of drug abuse and psychiatric hospitalization, defecated on herself, destroyed paper money during delusions, ran into traffic, shouted obscenities, was inadequately clothed for winter sleeping outdoors, and was found by city psychiatrists to suffer from paranoid schizophrenia and to be delusional and suicidal. The Civil Liberties Union psychiatrists found her rational, dealt with her practice of running into traffic by noting that many New Yorkers jaywalk, and diagnosed her destruction of money as an assertion of autonomy.

The judge praised her humor, pride, independence and spirit, said she has shown an aptitude for survival on the streets. Besides, he said, freedom is a constitutional right "no less for those who are mentally ill."

A higher, perhaps saner, court has barred the immediate release of the woman, giving New Yorkers time to think this: We are approaching the problem characteristically, which is to say backward. We are focusing exclusively on the individual, and in terms of his or her rights. But the community, too, has rights, needs and responsibilities which, if attended to, will leave the homeless better off.

The judge made much of the fact that psychiatrists disagree and that psychiatry does not attain the precision of mathematics. That does not mean that psychiatry can not come to defensible conclusions, but let us delay the entry of such experts into this process.

Let us pretend that all people sleeping in filth and foul weather are as sane as sages. That is beside the point, which is: There can be no reasonable right to live on sidewalks.

Society needs order, and hence has a right to a minimally civilized ambience in public spaces. Regarding the homeless, this is not merely for aesthetic reasons because the unaesthetic is not merely unappealing. It presents a spectacle of disorder and decay that becomes a contagion.

The community has a responsibility to provide shelter, in exchange for which it can require, as appropriate, work or treatment. The community also has a responsibility to remove judges who express such thoughts as: "To the passerby seeing her lying on the street or defecating publicly, she may seem deranged," but "she may indeed be a professional in her life-style."

November 19, 1987

Theocracy in Pittsburgh

Card-carrying members of the American Civil Liberties Union (ACLU) have rescued Pittsburgh from a seasonal menace that must be slain annually. The menace is theocracy, the "establishment" of religion.

True, there were not hordes of Savonarolas creeping in cassocks and sandals along the banks of the Allegheny, or ayatollahs floating in flat-bottomed riverboats down the Monogahela to stamp out heterodoxy in western Pennsylvania. But there were these displays. A crèche. A menorah.

Last week the Supreme Court churned out 105 pages of opinion, concurrences and dissents (and two photographs) about the constitutionally problematic crèche and menorah. The menorah was legal, the crèche not. So said the Court, 6–3 concerning the menorah, 5–4 concerning the crèche.

Justice Blackmun, wielding the majority's theological micrometer, said the 18-foot-tall Hanukkah menorah on the steps of Pittsburgh's city hall did not violate the First Amendment guarantee against "establishment" of religion because it was smack next to a Christmas tree. That mixture of symbols constituted the constitutionally required clutter. It prevented Pittsburghers from exclaiming, "Yo! City Hall has endorsed Judaism!" (Remember Pawtucket's crèche? It was constitutional because it was surrounded by enough tacky reindeer, Santa's house, snowmen and other secular stuff.)

However, down the block in a Pittsburgh courthouse, a nativity scene was not near any other symbols, so it amounted to endorsement of Christian doctrine. So say five justices. Congratulations to the ACLU on bagging another crèche.

This is the sort of howitzer-against-gnat nonsense that consumes a society that is convinced that every grievance should be cast as a conflict of individual rights and every such conflict should be adjudicated. What is the ACLU's grievance? Heterodoxy.

The ACLU acted not to protect its members from injury. Rather, it acted to force the community into behaving the way the ACLU likes.

The ACLU is a haven for liberals who like to make courts the coercive instruments of truculent people like themselves. They want to compel the community into cleansing public spaces of symbols offensive to them but not in the least harmful to them. They delight in using law, which should be a unifying fabric, divisively, to trample traditions enjoyed by their neighbors.

Justice Kennedy, in a tart dissent joined by Rehnquist, White and Scalia, said, rightly, that the Court had adopted a function "antithetical to the First Amendment": "Obsessive, implacable resistance to all but the most carefully scripted and secularized form of accommodation requires this Court to act as a censor, issuing national decrees as to what is orthodox and what is not. What is orthodox, in this context, means what is secular; the only Christmas the state can acknowledge is one in which references to religion have been held to a minimum."

So litigious liberalism, ACLU-style, has pushed the Court into sitting (in Kennedy's words) as "a national theology board," performing "the inappropriate task of saying what every religious symbol means." And for no reason. There is no danger—none—that religious zealots will turn Pittsburgh or any other community into Calvin's Geneva.

Relations between church and state were often tense and vexing earlier in American history because relations between religious sects were marked by suspicion or hostility. Many early Americans were early Americans because they were too conscientious or scrupulous or stiff-necked or turbulent or intolerant to stomach (or be stomached by) the Old World.

But for goodness' sake, Supreme Court, that was then, this is now. Today the agents of intolerance carry ACLU cards.

At a big banquet in Washington a few years ago, a Washington Redskins running-back, in his cups and overflowing with advice, said to a Supreme Court Justice, "Lighten up, Sandra baby." His manners were bad, but his advice was good for all five justices who kicked over Pittsburgh's crèche.

If they took that advice, they also could take Will's Generic Opinion. It is a one-sentence wonder that is sufficient to dispose of almost all constitutional questions arising from the December decoration of public spaces. The opinion is: "The practice does not do what the Establishment Clause was intended to prevent—impose an official creed, or significantly enhance or hinder a sect—so the practice is constitutional and the complaining parties should buzz off and go knock off enough eggnog to get in the holiday mood."

The justices spend their spare time lamenting the caseload that leaves them with so little spare time. They would have more of it if they wasted less time helping the ACLU turn America into a nation of irritable individualists throwing elbows and deriving malicious pleasure from censoring the community's ceremonies that give the community pleasure and injure no one.

July 9, 1989

Chemistry and Punishment

When Debra Forster was 11, she was raped. At about that time she began drug abuse that has included cocaine and LSD. She was married at 15; by 17 she was the mother of two boys. Not surprisingly, she was a terrible mother. Today she is 18 and the focus of a legal controversy.

A year ago in Mesa, Arizona, she left her infant sons, ages 18 months and six months, alone for three days in a sweltering apartment without air-conditioning. She was on a binge because motherhood was, she says, too much for her. The boys were dehydrated nearly to death. She was arrested and, while in jail, gave birth to a girl.

She could have been sentenced to 30 years. Instead she was put on probation, with an especially troubling wrinkle. Her sentence of life probation not only forbids her to reestablish contact with her children, but also requires her "to remain on some method of birth control." That is for life.

One sympathizes with the sentencing judge, a woman exasperated with "babies having babies." However, this sentence is a step down a dangerous path.

Presumably, Forster will be required to furnish written evidence that she is using birth-control pills. To compel the use of a drug is an intrusive act. To compel the use of a drug that controls an important human capability, as a birth-control pill does, is especially intrusive.

When government tampers, surgically or chemically, with sexuality, it is touching personal identity. In light of the recent elaboration of a woman's privacy right, as defined in constitutional law concerning abortion, it is hard to imagine Forster's sentence withstanding the scrutiny of an appeals court.

But regardless of its constitutional standing (Forster is a Catholic, so the sentence may violate not only the privacy right but the guarantee of free exercise of religion), the sentence is morally repellent.

Compelling Forster to use birth-control pills is not as intrusive as, say, compulsory sterilization would be, not least because what the pill does can be reversed if the compulsion is removed. But intrusiveness is not made acceptable by being reversible.

The seriousness of such an intrusion is suggested by this sensible intuition: It is less troubling for government to remove a child from incompetent or abusive parents than for government to stipulate who shall not have permission to procreate.

Forster's sentence can not be considered mandatory preventive medicine. What is to be prevented—pregnancy—is not an illness. And for a court to mandate medicine for punitive purposes conflicts with the fundamental moral imperative of medicine: "Do no harm."

What the sentencing judge is trying to prevent is not a disease but bad behavior—irresponsible procreation.

But the practice of administering drugs for behavior modification has enormous potential for mischief. Compulsory medication for persons incapacitated by psychosis is not uncommon. But such involuntary medication is undertaken only when the will of the patient is presumed not to exist, or to be so attenuated that only chemical intervention can even partially restore it.

This is utterly unlike the mandating of a drug in Forster's case. There, the purpose of the drug is to incapacitate her body so that society will not have to count on her will to make her behavior better.

There are many potential uses of "chemical penology," all of them subversive of individual autonomy. Rapists could be sentenced to "chemical castration," drug treatments that reduce the body's production of testosterone. Violent recidivists could be sentenced to perpetual sedation. Perhaps drunk drivers could be sentenced to remain on a drug that would make them painfully ill if they consumed any alcohol.

Clearly many such punishments would be crueler, in the sense of more demeaning, than the normal punishment of imprisonment for serious offenses. Forster's offense was serious. She should have been sent to jail. The law should try to regulate behavior by the traditional mixture of influences: The law should appeal to conscience by stigmatizing certain behavior, and should pose a threat to be feared.

Forster's sentence is a step toward treating an offender as a creature devoid of the essence of humanity: the status of moral agent. It is a step toward reducing convicts to raw material for those people that C. S. Lewis called "official straighteners," people armed with modern technologies and a modern disregard for the free will of individuals.

It may seem perverse to say that a convict has a right to normal punishment. But alternatives to such punishment can be worse. Alternatives can dehumanize the convict by chemically nullifying the need for him or her to make moral choices.

June 26, 1988

Capital Punishment: Cruel and Unusual Because Infrequent?

On January 22, 1983, William Thompson was 15 and, as a matter of Oklahoma law, a child. He also was busy.

With three older accomplices, he murdered his former brother-in-law. The victim was beaten severely and shot twice, and his throat, chest and stomach were cut "so the fish could eat his body," Thompson said. Thompson was tried as an adult and sentenced to death.

Now the Supreme Court has ruled 5–3 (Justice Kennedy not participating) to overturn his sentence. Four justices said it is unconstitutional to impose capital punishment on anyone who is even a day younger than 16, no matter how careful the consideration of his circumstances, no matter how much evidence is gathered to overcome the presumption against trying a 15-year-old as an adult.

Because the fifth justice, O'Connor, concurred only in the result, not the plurality opinion, it remains unclear whether such executions would be constitutional if a state specifically adopted, after careful consideration, capital punishment for 15-year-olds. The argument is about how to construe evidence of societal consensus.

In 1972, the Court ruled 5–4 that Georgia's capital-punishment law was unconstitutional. Two of the five majority justices, Brennan and Marshall, said simply that society's "evolving standards of decency" have made capital punishment "cruel and unusual" and therefore unconstitutional. (That claim was promptly refuted—but not abandoned—when 37 states reenacted capital-punishment statutes in conformity with the Court's 1972 criteria.)

The other three justices in the 1972 majority argued only that capital punishment was cruel and unusual when administered capriciously. In 1976, the Court upheld Georgia's revised statute and it seemed that capital-punishment opponents had confounded themselves, causing reforms that immunized capital-punishment statutes from constitutional challenge.

But the Thompson case reveals a new wrinkle.

Justice Stevens, speaking for Brennan, Marshall and Blackmun, erected a rickety statistical scaffolding to support the conclusion that there exists an evolved American "standard of decency" opposed, categorically, to executions of anyone under 16. Stevens noted that all 18 of the states that have adopted a minimum age for capital punishment have adopted age 16.

However, Justice O'Connor, who concurs in the judgment but not Stevens's statistical reasoning, noted that more states (19), and the federal government, have authorized capital punishment without stipulating a minimum age. And Justice Scalia, joined in dissent by Rehnquist and White, noted that in the comprehensive crime legislation of 1984, Congress addressed the question of youth and the imposition of punishment. Congress changed the law, lowering from 16 to 15 the age at which a juvenile can be tried and punished as an adult, as Oklahoma did with Thompson.

Oklahoma law permits that only after a careful finding that the young defendant appreciated the wrongness of his conduct, and that there are no reasonable prospects for rehabilitation within the juvenile-justice system. By the time Thompson committed murder, he had been arrested three times for assault and battery (once with a knife), another time for assault with a deadly weapon, once for burglary.

Stevens argued that many laws (restricting voting, use of alcohol, etc.) recognize that juveniles are apt to be impulsive. Thus juveniles are often not as culpable for their acts, or as easily deterred by fear of severe punishment. But Scalia noted that two hours before the butchery began, Thompson announced his premeditation: "We're going to kill Charles."

Stevens stated that the likelihood of a 15-year-old weighing the probability of execution, when calculating the risk of a crime, "is so remote as to be virtually nonexistent." But a clinical psychologist testified that Thompson believed that his age would protect him from severe punishment. (Many people familiar with the epidemic of gang murders of juveniles by juveniles in Los Angeles say that the killers regard their punishment—if any—as a relatively mild rite of passage through prison. A few executions might get their attention.)

Stevens noted that very few executions in this century (no more than 20; none since 1948) have involved killers under 16. But Scalia noted that the statistic demonstrates only a long-standing consensus that such executions should be rare. And if the relative rarity of an act is construed as conclusive evidence of a consensus that the act is cruel and unusual, then the execution of women could forthwith be declared unconstitutional.

Note the new wrinkle.

A state, complying with the Court's elaborate criteria, gives fastidious attention to the individual circumstances of defendants in criminal cases. That attention makes executions of certain categories of criminals (e.g., those under 16) rare. By a non sequitur (the rareness of a phenomenon demonstrates a societal consensus against the phenomenon generally), this rareness is turned into a constitutional prohibition. So complying with the Court's criteria for constitutional action produces a statistical argument for branding the action unconstitutional.

It is an intellectually elegant wrinkle. It also may be a bit cynical.

July 3, 1988

The Abortion Issue: Back From Litigation to Legislation

As time ticks toward the close of the Supreme Court's term, 7,461 politicians are on tenterhooks. They are America's state legislators. Any day now, they may have handed to them something most of them dread: abortion as a legislative issue.

The ink probably is already drying on the justices' opinions about the Missouri law that has been the focus of contention. The case could, but probably will not, produce a substantial revision of the status of abortion as a fundamental privacy right. That was the result of a Court ruling 16 years ago. However, even a modest revision could make abortion open to increased regulation, and thus to political strife.

So in this short calm before what may be a prolonged storm, consider the history of America's abortion controversy. One survey of that history is in an amicus curiae brief filed by 281 historians opposed to revising the 1973 ruling. The brief is not scholarship; it is partisanship. Still, it does demonstrate the complicated pedigree and path of the abortion argument.

The historians argue that for much of American history, abortion was not illegal; that most 19th-century restrictions applied only after "quickening" (detectable fetal movement); that codified opposition to abortion evolved late and from ideological, cultural and professional interests; that concern for the moral value of the fetus was largely an afterthought invoked when other arguments against abortion became culturally anachronistic or constitutionally impermissible.

The historians overreach when they cite, as evidence that abortion was common in colonial times, the fact that abortion was "rarely the subject for moralizing." (There was also little colonial moralizing about cannibalism.) And the fact, if such it really is, that in the late 18th century one-third of all New England brides were pregnant at the time of marriage suggests that abortion was not common.

However, some studies suggest that in the mid-19th century, there was one abortion for every four live births. In 1871, in New York City, with a population of less than 1 million, there were 200 full-time abortionists, and some doctors performed abortions. In 1898, the Michigan Board of Health said one in three pregnancies in the state ended in abortion.

Between 1850 and 1880, the new American Medical Association became a strong force for severely limiting abortion, for medical and professional reasons. Abortion was more dangerous than childbirth. And medical practitioners, just becoming professionalized, wanted to bring childbirth into hospitals and establish professional supremacy over less professional practitioners, including herbalists, midwives and abortionists.

By the late 19th century, facets of urbanization, including poverty and crowding, were stimulating abortion. In an urban setting, men's work patterns deviated more from women's than they did on farms, and women were increasingly seen as wives and mothers in the service of the "cult of the home."

Also there was a nasty 19th-century worry about demographics. Nativist, and especially anti-Catholic, feeling resulted in restrictions on abortion. The fear was that the reproduction rates of the socially ascendant Protestant stock would not match the rates of immigrants from Eastern and Southern Europe. The result would be "race suicide." When, in 1912, 173 Chicagoans were arrested for disseminating information about contraception and abortion, in violation of the Comstock Act, the *Chicago Tribune* headline was: TAKE CHICAGOANS IN FEDERAL WAR ON RACE SUICIDE.

The historians' brief concludes with a whiff of paranoia, hinting darkly that "protection of unborn life has become a surrogate for other social objectives that are no longer tolerated." Racism, sexism, imperialism? More overreaching by the historians. It would be fairer to say that concern for the value of fetal life, like increased concern for the rights of minorities, represents admirable evolution of society's standards.

The brief does not, and no historical survey of attitudes and practices could, answer what is properly at issue in the Supreme Court: how abortion stands in relation to the logic of constitutional construction. However, the brief demonstrates, unwittingly, that the abortion controversy, at its molton core, does not primarily involve the Court's proper concern—constitutional law.

Abortion is, as the brief illustrates, a highly charged political issue touching large social topics, such as family, the relations of the sexes and correlative social values. Thus the brief makes a powerful case against itself, a case for returning to the status quo ante—ante 1973.

It makes the case for turning the issue back to the 7,461 legislators. They, not judges, should make law after robust political argument.

June 18, 1989

Abortion: There Are Splittable Differences

American politics is a profession for amiable people eager to please and dedicated to the proposition that man's best friend is the compromise. Thus their abhorrence of the abortion issue. It is hard to split the difference between those who consider abortion the killing of a person and those who consider it a morally insignificant private matter. But differences should be split between those who defend the intellectually indefensible Supreme Court formulation of abortion policy and those who, like George Bush, would constitutionalize the issue in a radically different but also problematic way.

The Supreme Court is hearing a case that could result in reversal of *Roe* v. *Wade*, the 1973 ruling that established, in effect, a virtually unrestricted right to abortion. Bush, who favors reversal, could rue the day. Support for *Roe* is collapsing, perhaps in the Court and certainly among thoughtful people. It is collapsing beneath the weight of its incoherence and the accumulating weight of scientific and medical facts. *Roe* rests shakily on this doubly absurd proposition: No one knows when human life begins but the Court knows when "meaningful" life begins. The Court arbitrarily assigned different significance to a fetus in each trimester of gestation—and then nullified its own distinctions. The Court declared a third-trimester fetus "viable" because it can lead a "meaningful" life outside the womb. The Court said states could ban third-trimester abortions—but not when a doctor determines that killing a "viable" fetus is "necessary to preserve the life *or health* [emphasis added] of the mother." (Interesting noun, "mother.") Doctors may make that determination based on psychological and emotional as well as physical factors that might be relevant to the well-being of the patient. And "distress" (which might be caused by denial of an abortion) can constitute a threat to health.

In the Court's formulation a mother has undiluted sovereignty over a fetus that has no more moral claims than a tumor in her abdomen. Yet recently some courts have, in effect, taken custody of fetuses by controlling, even jailing, pregnant women whose behavior (e.g., drug abuse) might jeopardize the health of their fetuses. Neonatal intensive-care units enable hospitals to save the lives of infants that survive abortion procedures. But a right to an abortion is a right to a procedure that produces a dead fetus. When a procedure results in a live birth, the infant may be killed by suffocation or aggressive neglect, lest the abortionist face a malpractice or "wrongful birth" suit.

Prenatal medicine's diagnostic and therapeutic techniques make possible intrauterine treatment of many forms of fetal distress and genetic problems. Ultrasound pictures can show all fingers and heart chambers at 18 weeks. Drugs and blood transfusions can be administered to a fetus, excess fluids can be drained from their skulls and lungs. Mothers may kill fetuses that doctors (remember Hippocrates: "Do no harm") can treat as patients. Medicine, the most humane science, can heal fetuses that the law says lack an attribute of humanity—rights. Science and society are radically and increasingly out of sync.

Roe declares, ludicrously, that a fetus is "potential life." The indisputable fact is that a fetus is alive and biologically human. Pregnancy is a continuum: What begins at conception will, if there is no natural misfortune or deliberate attack, become a child. Abortion kills an organic system distinct from a woman's system. Biology does not allow the abortion argument to be about when human life begins. The argument, in which thoughtful people differ, is about the moral significance and hence the proper legal status of life in its early stages.

Bush says he came to his current convictions "after years of somber and serious reflection." He certainly has come a ways. As recently as mid-1980 he supported only a "states' rights" constitutional amendment that is agnostic about abortion policy. It would simply say that nothing in the Constitution guarantees a right to abortion. That would restore to states the right to regulate abortion. When Bush became Reagan's running mate he joined Reagan in supporting an amendment that says life begins at conception and is thenceforth a "person" protected by the guarantees of "due process" and "equal protection of the laws." (Bush favors exceptions concerning rape, incest and saving the mother's life.) That position has helped Republicans; it could yet hurt them.

The abortion issue has helped Republicans by energizing a conservative constituency. Many millions of voters who would recoil from enactment of the policy embraced by Bush and the GOP platform vote Republican anyway because for 16 years abortion has been largely a subject of litigation rather than legislation. But if *Roe* is reversed, bringing the issue to an instant boil in 50 state legislatures, what does Bush then say from his bully pulpit? "Hey, I was just kidding"? Not after "years of somber and serious reflection." Bush would have a choice. Either he would speak forcefully and often for laws sharply at odds with the culture—laws protecting life from conception on—or he would look like a hypocrite whose convictions were dictated by political calculation.

The culture was moving before the Court moved. Before 1973, abortion laws were liberalized in 16 states with 41 percent of the nation's population. In California, Governor Reagan signed a very liberal law. Since 1973, abortion (1.5 million last year) has become one of the most common surgical procedures. If *Roe* is reversed, either the Republican Party must retreat from its nearly categorical opposition to abortion or it will suffer severe reverses in state legislative contests—and hence in its party-building efforts and its hope of someday capturing the House of Representatives.

However, millions of Americans are, and many more can be persuaded to be, troubled by late abortions of fetuses that can be treated as patients and delivered as infants. *Roe* is bad constitutional reasoning (really anticonstitutional nonreasoning) that has resulted in dismaying practices. *Roe* should be reversed. This democratic nation needs vigorous argument, not judicial fiat, about abortion. Politicians will hate it. Still, they can split some differences if the argument is not about when in pregnancy life begins but when in pregnancy abortions should stop.

February 13, 1989

Abolition and Abortion: Reasoning Lincoln's Way

Jack Rains, running for the Republican gubernatorial nomination in Texas, recently told a right-to-life group he stood "shoulder-to-shoulder" with it. But time (two weeks) passed, and perhaps polls were consulted, and then he announced that, come to think about it, he was an abortion-rights candidate. "My mind has not changed," he explained. "My thinking has crystallized."

Rains may be "right" with the electorate if it is looking for Plasticman, an infinitely malleable creature. But if Lincoln's party is to get off the hook it has impaled itself on regarding abortion, it must look to Lincoln's example.

Here is what the hook looks like. When Republicans convene in 1992, the ticket probably will be long settled and 15,000 bored journalists will have but one big story to make bigger by being a megaphone for both sides. The story will be the floor fight over the platform language— whatever it is—on abortion.

The 1980 platform said: "Abortion, despite the complex nature of its various issues, is ultimately concerned with equality of rights under the law. While we recognize differing views on this question among Americans in general—and in our own party—we affirm our support of a constitutional amendment to restore protection of the right to life for unborn children."

By 1984 and again in 1988, the platform said: "The unborn child has a fundamental right to life which cannot be infringed. We therefore reaffirm our support for a human-life amendment to the Constitution, and we endorse legislation to make clear that the Fourteenth Amendment's protections apply to unborn children." (That means, among other things, that a pregnant woman who abuses alcohol or other drugs is committing child abuse.)

The right-to-life movement will seek to hold, in the platform committee, this maximalist position. The party dare not stand on that plank again. But how can it adapt to political realities without appearing unprincipled? It can begin by looking to Lincoln.

The 1850s arguments that drew Lincoln to greatness concerned not whether slavery should be abolished forthwith or even in the foreseeable future, but rather two other questions, one general, one specific. The general question was: Would national policy stigmatize slavery as a tragic legacy and a moral wrong? The specific question was: Would policy confine slavery to its historic dominion by banning it from the territories, thereby, Lincoln hoped, putting it on a path to ultimate extinction?

Republicans, said Lincoln, should "insist that [slavery] should, as far as may be, be treated as wrong, and one of the methods of treating it as a wrong is to make provision that it shall grow no larger."

Opponents of abortion argue that the abortion issue is akin to the slavery issue because it concerns the scope of the concept of personhood, and because the issue was inflamed by judicial fiat (*Dred Scott; Roe* v. *Wade*). But there is a third similarity Republicans should note: The logic of Lincoln's response to the reality of slavery as a rooted institution is a model for dealing with the reality of abortion as a prevalent practice and a right currently enjoying broad if uneasy support.

In 1860, advocates of immediate, outright abolition of slavery were morally earnest but not politically serious. As with advocacy of abolition of abortion in 1990, the abolitionist position regarding slavery was emotionally satisfying but politically impracticable.

However, the Republicans' first successful presidential candidate knew that to do good you must hold office, and to get to the core of a controversy you should begin by nudging in its borders. The right-to-life movement and its Republican allies should begin at the borders.

Most Americans may favor substantial abortion rights but also are uneasy about the promiscuous creation and destruction of life, often for frivolous reasons of negligence and convenience. There is, I believe, a vague but broad and plausible intuition that the moral status, and hence the protection appropriate for, a fetus changes with its developmental stages. (Hence the power of, and fury from, pro-abortion people concerning photographs of aborted fetuses sufficiently developed to resemble infants.)

Opponents of abortion can aspire to piecemeal abortion, endorsing government policy that treats abortion as (as ownership of slaves was) a contractable right. The first contraction should place severe restrictions on all abortions after, say, the eighth week of gestation. This point can be set with reference to neurological and other fetal developments. It probably would not eliminate even 90 percent of abortions, and if pro-abortion advocates opposed it, they would seem extreme.

Getting an abortion should not be treated as less serious than, say, getting a driver's license or a drink. Therefore, when a minor is involved, policy should require at least parental notification and perhaps parental consent.

Furthermore, long-run abolitionists can insist on stigmatizing the right as a bitter legacy of bad practices and confused thinking. The stigmatizing policy shall be that the exercise of the right shall not be subsidized by public funds.

But such funds shall be used to provide alternatives to it—birth control, adoption, child care, other supports for unwed mothers—just as there were proposals for using public funds to purchase emancipation (a lot cheaper than war, Lincoln said).

Republican thinking must crystallize along some such lines or many Republicans now in office will look unprincipled or will be unemployed.

January 4, 1990

Baby M in the Legal Thicket

Legal reasoning has an admirable parsimony. It reduces controversies to manageable components. But it can sharpen society's mind by narrowing it, and may be doing so in the New Jersey contest for possession of Baby M.

A New Jersey couple wanted a child. For medical reasons, the wife deemed pregnancy too risky. So her husband's sperm was used to inseminate a woman who signed a contract to gestate the fetus in exchange for $10,000. But when the time came for the "surrogate mother" to surrender the infant, she exclaimed, "Oh God, what have I done." What indeed.

But first, what is she? She is not a "surrogate" mother, she is the mother, the "natural mother." The court may treat this case as one concerning contracts or custody (the best interests of the child), but what is at issue is our understanding of the "the natural," meaning the right conduct for creatures of our nature.

This argument about the mother's right to retain the child is logically severable from but conditioned by the Supreme Court's 1973 decision that declared abortion to be a woman's "privacy right." The father's wishes are not legally germane and the fetus has no more legal status than a tumor in the woman.

The 1973 decision gave rise to the legal locution that a fetus is "potential life." The biological absurdity of that is today underscored by the development of fetal medicine. A fetus is a living creature on which medicine can work diagnostic and therapeutic marvels. The imperative of the medical ethic is to help where help is possible. Yet moral vertigo results from attempting to reconcile that imperative with the Court's decision that a fetus is akin to an appendix--a thing of no moral significance.

And now there is emerging a problematic concept of "fetal rights." Civil authorities have intervened to protect fetuses from acts and omissions by pregnant women; they have ordered unwilling women to undergo cesarean sections; a woman is being prosecuted for the death of her fetus as a result of her disregard of doctors' orders.

The idea of fetal rights is inherently problematic and is, like the application of the medical ethic to fetuses, flatly incompatible with the 1973 ruling. That ruling teaches society to consider a fetus as a mere lump of matter that acquires moral significance only when removed from the womb. And if the womb is a rented fetal container, the personhood of the woman renting it is of no significance.

So if suddenly the fetal container (a.k.a., mother) starts acting like a person—"Oh God, what have I done"—she is acting incongruously.

Thus the natural bonding between mother and child is made to seem like the mother's caprice, and seems irresponsible in light of her contract. The very idea of what is "natural" comes to seem a gossamer superstition, a concept entailing no reasonable restraint on appetites.

The New Jersey couple wanted a child but not a "child of their own," as that phrase is used to mean a couple's child of their flesh made one. If we conclude that the mere desire for a child legitimizes such improvisations as womb rental, we establish a new entitlement, the right of couples to suffer no legal impediment to partial (one spouse's involvement) biological parenthood. And there will be no grounds for denying the entitlement to unmarried people of whatever character, or to poor women who may allow their bodies to be exploited to satisfy other people's desires.

The desire for children is strong and wholesome, but life offers no guarantees and good things can have prohibitive costs. To prevent such costs, in the New Jersey case, the contract should be treated as an unenforceable statement of mutual intentions that no longer obtain. The mother must not be deprived of her baby, to which she is now bonded in the natural way.

To try to make womb rental harmless merely by expanding the mother's options for consent—by allowing a grace period after birth during which she can decide to keep the child—makes matters worse. It further subordinates responsibility to willfulness, and further encourages thinking of children as material goods.

All such contracts should be forbidden as a formalization of commerce in babies, and even voluntary donation of wombs for gestation should be forbidden as dehumanizing.

The concept of "dehumanization" is meaningless to people who deny, as the culture increasingly does, the idea of the distinctively human. That concept seems under assault from biochemists, molecular biologists, psychiatrists and others who locate the essence of man in raw material subject to manipulation, unconstrained by any notion of a constant "human good."

The blind assertion of the untrammeled sovereignty of willfulness, served by science, over nature drains all substance from moral philosophy. Philosophy, including political philosophy, which concerns right conduct, must assert sovereignty over manipulative techniques before we learn, too late, this lesson: In some conquests of nature, the conqueror is the defeated.

January 22, 1987

Censorship the Liberals' Way

Two years ago, Professor Charles Lawrence of Stanford Law School produced a scholarly essay of 31 pages, 62 footnotes and one weird idea. It was that the real purport and proper effect of the Supreme Court's 1954 school-desegregation decision is to permit, and perhaps require, sweeping censorship of speech.

Lawrence argued that the Court found segregated schools inherently unequal and unconstitutional because of "the message" of inferiority that segregation conveys. Therefore it is constitutional to suppress speech with a racist message.

It is but a short step—via the manufacture of yet another right (the right to respect)—to the notion that the Constitution sanctions suppression of all speech offensive to any of America's "traditionally subjugated groups" or "victims." Only one group is ineligible for the privileged status of victim: There can be no limits on speech about white males. Speech that liberals disapprove should be suppressed because it expresses ideas that are "culturally engendered" by America's sick society.

Were Lawrence's argument merely one man's eccentricity, it would not matter. However, it exemplifies the ongoing attempt to give intellectual respectability to the spreading movement of censorship by liberals on campuses.

Many colleges and universities have adopted stringent codes stipulating impermissible speech. Such codes often come in a package with mandatory "awareness" classes. These are inflicted by sensitivity-tutors and other official consciousness-raisers. Their task is to make students "aware" of officially approved thinking about race, "sexual preference" and other items of liberal orthodoxy.

The proliferating rules proscribe speech that "slurs" or "stereotypes" or "stigmatizes" or "victimizes." The rules forbid giving offense to any group enjoying the coveted status of victim. The University of Michigan's rule (which a judge laughed out of court) forbade all speech giving offense "on the basis of race, ethnicity, religion, national origin, sex, sexual orientation, creed, ancestry, age, marital status, handicap or Vietnam-era veteran status."

Many such codes strikingly resemble something that recently enraged liberals: Senator Jesse Helms's amendment to prohibit federal funding of art that "denigrates, debases or reviles a person, group or class of citizens on the basis of race, creed, sex, handicap, age or national origin." "Tyranny!" exclaimed some liberals who, pausing over their lengthening lists of forbidden forms of speech, declared that denial of a subsidy constitutes censorship.

Professor Alan Kors of the University of Pennsylvania shrewdly notes that in the 1960s, when most students seemed to the left of faculty and administrations, liberals said: It is illegitimate for universities to assert moral authority over students. But today, most students seem to be to the right of the academic establishment, so liberalism encourages that establishment to control ("raise") the consciousness of retrograde students caught deviating from liberal orthodoxy.

More than at any time in memory, there are many subjects "too sensitive" to talk about freely on campuses that are patrolled by prowling sensitivity-police. Courses on, for example, the history or sociology of race can be considered too problematic to undertake. This is a broader threat to freedom than the liberal mobs that howled down speakers supporting the U. S. commitment to Vietnam. It has more of a "chilling effect" than McCarthyism did because today the forces of censorship arise from within the academic culture.

The censorship that liberals like might seem especially odd in an era of permissiveness regarding curricula. But the permissiveness is itself a ploy in the liberals' struggle to politicize the curricula by ending the "domination" by DWEMs—dead white European males.

Liberals have been First Amendment fanatics (all forms of expression are of equal value—who is to say otherwise?) for a long time. Therefore, only conservatives can make the case for the kernel of truth in what the liberals are saying.

Conservatives can say: An academic community is not a haphazard aggregation of individuals. Rather, it is a community, a complex, fragile organism with distinctive purposes. Fulfillment of those purposes requires a particular atmosphere of civility that can be incompatible with unrestricted expression.

Liberals, however, have long preached universal disdain for all authority, intellectual as well as political. Having asserted that tolerance is the only obvious value, they are singularly unsuited to digging their heels into the academic soil that liberalism has made marshy.

In attempting to temper individualism with communitarian concerns, academic liberals are asserting a right they ferociously deny to every other community—local, state or national: the right to defend community values by circumscribing individual rights.

Among today's academic list-makers, listing all the forms of forbidden speech, are there any who defend the right of the national community to nurture its values by limiting the "symbolic speech" of flag desecration? Any who defend a community's right to defend its standards against pornography? Imagine the incredulity, quickly becoming outrage, if anyone suggested campus restrictions on speech slandering the United States?

The grim administrators of moral uplift at the University of Connecticut are empowered to punish students for "inappropriately directed laughter." Derisive laughter directed at the liberal censors is appropriate.

November 5, 1989

The Liberals' Racism

SAN FRANCISCO—The University of California at Berkeley says it is sorry. About time, you may say, remembering the 1960s. But the Chancellor's grudging apology pertains to something recent, something that looks like racism practiced by a bastion of liberalism.

In a statement in which circumspection competed with contrition, the Chancellor said that "decisions made in the admissions process indisputably had a disproportionate impact on" Asian-Americans. He blamed "insensitivity." But the real reason may be resentment of people who are "different" and have the temerity to be excellent.

One group sensitive to that is the unfortunately named Chinese for Affirmative Action (CAA), located in Chinatown in, appropriately, a building on the site of San Francisco's first bookstore. CAA knows that Asian-Americans are facing what Jews once faced: the resentment reserved for "outsiders" pressing for a fair share of the status conferred by elite institutions. Like American Jews before them, Asian-Americans have an intense desire to achieve social mobility by means of education, respect for which is inculcated by cohesive families.

Generally, "race-conscious" policies are advertised as "remedial." They supposedly place floors beneath particular groups, guaranteeing a certain level of social participation to disadvantaged people. But race-conscious policies toward Asian-Americans may place ceilings through which they are not allowed to rise.

Recently, Berkeley revised the formula by which applicants are evaluated. The new weighting—less weight for high-school grades, more for verbal tests—disadvantaged Asian-Americans, many of whom have English as a second language but are academic "overachievers."

An interesting term, "overachievers." "Over" what? Over their quota of excellence? Of America's rewards? Who sets these quotas?

About 9 percent of California's high-school graduates are Asian-Americans. Today, 26 percent of Berkeley's undergraduates are Asian-Americans. There probably would be more were it not for race-conscious social engineering in the name of the latest theory of distributive justice.

Evaluating the aptitudes of young people for higher education is difficult. Academic freedom requires granting universities discretion in devising admissions policies. However, universities must be monitored because they have proven themselves susceptible to intellectual fads and politicization. California, particularly, is a polyglot state sunk deep in the dangerous business of racial discrimination on behalf of government-approved minorities deemed "underrepresented" in this or that.

The name Chinese for Affirmative Action reflects a felt need to participate in an ethnic spoils system. However, affirmative action discriminated against Asian-Americans by restricting the social rewards open to competition on the basis of merit. We may want a modified meritocracy, but it should not be modified by racism and the resentment of excellence. An egalitarian democracy is prone to such resentment.

Coinciding with rising academic attainments by Asian-Americans has been a suspiciously sudden tendency by colleges across the country to deemphasize high-school academic performance of applicants. Admissions offices place more emphasis on, for example, extracurricular activities. Henry Der, executive director of CAA, says Asian-Americans are "developing a paranoia that they are not well-rounded." They are, he says, sometimes too academically driven, too focused on math and science. Now, in self-defense, they are "attacking extracurricular activities the way they attack calculus."

Der cites a white student who said, "If I walk into a classroom and see five or more Asian-Americans, I'm not going to enroll because they will drive up the grade curve." Lowell High School here is 60 percent Asian-American, and some parents say, "I don't want my child to go there because he will not have leadership opportunities." That, says Der, is just flinching from competition. There even is talk of making whites an affirmative-action group to protect them against Asian-American competition.

Yes, the "Yellow Peril" is back, this time dressed in the language of liberalism. We have been here before, with "the Jewish question."

Earlier in this century, quotas restricting Jews in universities were defended as liberal measures to prevent anti-Semitism. Thus Harvard's president in 1922: "If every college in the country would take a limited proportion of Jews, we would go a long way toward eliminating race feeling. . . ."

Universities are incubators of future elites and some Americans resent Asian-Americans storming the citadels of status. However, Asian-Americans lead all other ethnic groups, including WASPs, in educational attainments. America needs more university students like Asian-Americans.

At a time of high anxiety about declining educational standards and rising competition from abroad, and especially from the Pacific Rim, it is lunatic to punish Asian-Americans, the nation's model minority, for their passion to excel.

April 16, 1989

Rolling Back the Racial Spoils System

Like a pebble dropped into a pond, a presidency radiates lingering ripples. Last week's Supreme Court decision sharply limiting reverse discrimination by governments is a ripple from the Reagan administration, which advocated such a ruling. It does much to roll back the racial spoils system that exists for certain government-favored minorities.

Unfortunately, the ruling only inhibits, not proscribes, reverse discrimination. Government may still allocate shares of wealth to groups—groups, not just individuals—to which government awards the lucrative status of victim.

A Richmond, Virginia, statute, which resembles hundreds of others nationwide, required prime contractors on city construction projects to subcontract at least 30 percent of the dollar amount of each contract to businesses owned and controlled by these groups (the list was taken from a similar federal statute): blacks, Spanish-speaking, Oriental, Indian, Eskimo or Aleut citizens anywhere in America. This statute, passed by a Richmond city council with a black majority, would enable, say, a Hispanic firm in Houston to receive preference in Richmond, ostensibly to remedy past discrimination in Richmond.

Justice O'Connor, writing for the majority, said, among many other things, that such "set-aside" programs, to be valid, must remedy "identified discrimination," not just respond to "societal" discrimination. Although the ruling will go far toward stopping reverse discrimination, the Court flinched from the correct course. It should have retreated all the way to the high ground of this unassailable principle: Government may allocate benefits on the basis of race only to compensate identified individual victims of the government's own past system of racial classification.

Only Justice Scalia affirms that principle. However, Justice Kennedy, who occupies what some of us think of as the Bork seat, strongly sympathizes with Scalia's position.

Some parts of the Reagan administration came comfortably to terms with set-aside programs. However, the Justice Department and many judicial nominees seem to understand this: The 14th Amendment's guarantee of "equal protection of the laws" expresses the constituting doctrine of all open societies. Rights belong to individuals, not groups, and least of all races.

The Court is gingerly backing out of a swamp. It waded waist-deep into this in 1980 when Chief Justice Burger, writing for the Court, upheld a 1977 set-aside law. It was the first law by which Congress legislated a classification for entitlement to benefits based solely on race.

Using conservative language to rationalize a profoundly anticonservative position, Burger said that "appropriate deference" toward Congress's power to provide for the "general welfare" required a ruling that reverse discrimination is compatible with the 14th Amendment's equal-protection guarantee. Besides, Burger said, interfering with "experimentation in things social and economic is a grave responsibility."

But surely some areas are now off-limits to what Burger antiseptically called "experimentation." Justice Stewart, dissenting in 1980, noted that only twice before had the Court upheld government programs that inflicted injury (as reverse discrimination does to those not on the list of government-favored minorities) on the basis of race. These were the Japanese-American curfew and exclusion cases during the Second World War.

The 1954 desegregation ruling seemed to say that governments cannot classify students racially. But soon, many school districts were under court orders to do precisely that for the purpose of forced busing to achieve "racial balance." Hubert Humphrey, the prime mover of the 1964 Civil Rights Act, denied that quotas or other preferential treatment of any group was required by that law. But "race-conscious" actions soon came.

Perhaps we are slowly zigzagging our way back to Justice John Marshall Harlan's principle, enunciated in a noble dissent from a ruling that segregation was constitutional. He said, "Our Constitution is colorblind."

But what is the caliber of thinking on this subject in George Bush's Washington? Here is a sample.

Lee Atwater, Bush's chairman of the Republican National Committee, says he is optimistic about attracting black voters because: "Affirmative action has worked and there's now a much larger black middle class." His words imply something unsubstantiated, almost certainly false, and surprising coming from a Republican. The implication is that government programs of racial preference are primarily responsible for black progress.

Atwater slights not only the working of a free economy but also, and more importantly, the self-reliance and other virtues of rising blacks. Atwater's unconscious disparagement of black achievement is a predictable residue of reverse discrimination. That residue may one day be washed away by actions like last week's ripple from the Reagan era.

January 29, 1989

The Supreme Court Defers to Democracy

While Americans are marveling at the vitality of democratic ideas abroad, the consequences of democracy are appearing in the Supreme Court. These consequences are making many liberals cross.

Consider a recent case: An Alaskan salmon cannery has two categories of jobs, skilled and unskilled. The former are filled mostly by whites, the latter by Filipinos and Alaskan natives.

A suit filed on behalf of nonwhite employees said, and a lower court agreed, that this statistical disparity, even without evidence of intent to discriminate, placed on the employer the burden of proving that the hiring practices that produced it do not violate the 1964 Civil Rights Act banning discrimination in employment.

The nonwhite employees relied on a 1971 ruling by the unanimous Burger Court that a mere statistical showing of "disparate impact" would be virtually sufficient to invalidate "practices that are fair in form but discriminatory in practice."

In the cannery case, the Court, abandoning the 1971 reasoning, ruled 5–4 that mere statistical evidence that nonwhites are "underrepresented" in particular jobs does not do much to advance a discrimination complaint. Disparities must be shown to be caused by particular hiring practices, and employers can validate those practices by showing a legitimate business reason for them. The Court says plaintiffs have the heavy burden of showing a causal connection between a disparity and a particular hiring practice, and demonstrating an alternative practice that would achieve the same business end with less racial impact.

This ruling will undermine reverse discrimination (affirmative action). The fact that mere statistical disparities have often been considered sufficient to demonstrate illegal discrimination has led, in turn, to statistical remedies: racial quotas. These have been imposed by public authorities or adopted preemptively by employers seeking to defend themselves against litigation.

Liberalism has developed the bad habit of invoking principles it does not believe. Today many liberals are saying that the "retreat" from the 1971 ruling is inherently disreputable. Their point ostensibly is that an 18-year life puts a precedent beyond challenge. But liberals know that a 58-year-old precedent was reasonably overthrown in 1954 in the school-desegregation ruling that repudiated the "separate-but-equal" doctrine. That repudiation was called a correction, not a retreat.

The liberals' actual principle, which they are too decorous to assert, is respect for the liberal ratchet: All irreversible change is in their direction. But the ratchet has been repealed.

The majority decision in the cannery case was written by Justice White, a John F. Kennedy appointee (who participated in the 1971 decision). He was joined by Chief Justice (by Reagan's nomination) Rehnquist and three Reagan appointees: O'Connor, Scalia and the newest justice, Anthony Kennedy.

One week later, in another civil-rights case decided 5–4, the same majority further impeded the "race-conscious" policies of affirmative action. It was a case brought by a group of white firemen in Birmingham, Alabama. They charged that under a 1974 agreement between some employees and the city, less-qualified blacks have been promoted ahead of them. The Court (Rehnquist writing for the majority) affirmed the right of whites to sue. The Court held that a voluntary agreement between two groups is not immune from challenge by a third group, in this instance firemen who were not employees in 1974. Rehnquist's reasonable principle is that "a person cannot be deprived of his legal rights in a proceeding to which he is not a party."

This decision may mean an explosion of conservative legal challenges. Litigious liberals are not happy.

Both these decisions are deeply satisfying as ratifications of the sovereignty of the political process. The majority in these cases was completed by the addition of Justice Kennedy. He was nominated when Robert Bork was blocked by forces now fiercely unhappy about both decisions.

The country has said emphatically that it wants at least 12 years of conservative Republican presidents who will appoint justices who are kindred spirits. The attempt by some liberals to nullify that mandate, using the Senate confirmation process, has failed.

The anemia of liberalism as a political movement is part cause and part effect of liberals attempting end runs around the political process. Too often they have resorted to litigation rather than legislation—judicial fiat rather than democratic persuasion—to achieve their agenda. Now liberals have lost (at least on some important issues) even the Supreme Court.

And now Senator Howard Metzenbaum (D–Ohio), a high-octane liberal, has an idea. He is so out of sorts about the Court's ruling in the cannery case that he is contemplating an attempt to amend the Civil Rights Act to codify the position the Court took in 1971. Imagine: a liberal resorting to legislation to change the law. What will they think of next?

June 15, 1989

Punishing Deviation: The Case of an Uppity Black

Another colored boy (the language suits the moment) is acting uppity in Washington, but there are enough liberals left to lead a lynching. The intended victim is William Lucas, President Bush's choice to be assistant attorney general for civil rights.

Last week Chairman Joseph Biden (D–Del.) and some colleagues on the Senate Judiciary Committee were reportedly "stunned" by Lucas's testimony. Lucas's congressman, John Conyers, Jr. (D–Mich.), who warmly praised Lucas when introducing him to the committee, rushed back to recant his endorsement, so shocked was he by Lucas's testimony.

What Lucas said was that he considered two recent Supreme Court rulings "sound." Can't have that, can we, in the Justice Department, people agreeing with the Court?

Let there be no doubting of the white liberal senators' sincerity. Of course they were "stunned." Blacks are supposed to think what white liberals tell them to think. If insubordination like Lucas's is not nipped in the bud, no telling where it might lead among blacks, the last bloc Democrats can take for granted.

One of the Court rulings Lucas considers sound is that a statistical disparity between the racial composition of the community and that of a firm's work force is not sufficient to demonstrate discrimination. Discrimination must be proved, not assumed. The other Court ruling is that whites injured by reverse-discrimination arrangements that they were not involved in formulating can challenge them in court. Are you "stunned"? Grab a rope, tie a noose, find a branch.

Lucas, son of immigrants from the Caribbean, orphaned at 14, grew up in Harlem and put himself through Fordham Law School while working as a New York City policeman. In Wayne County, Michigan, which surrounds Detroit, he ran successfully as a Democrat for sheriff four times and then was elected county executive. He administered a county with a population four times that of Biden's Delaware. In 1986, he changed parties and won the Republican nomination for governor, but lost to the incumbent.

Some opposition to Lucas relates to Michigan politics and his change of parties. Benjamin Hooks, head of the NAACP, has no stomach for resisting his largest dues-paying chapter, in Detroit. Conyers may run for mayor of Detroit. Jesse Jackson, who never stops running (and never runs for an office he might win), endorsed Lucas and then recanted after saying that the Supreme Court rulings were similar to positions taken by China's regime toward the protesters in Tiananmen Square.

The professional civil-rights lobbyists, who sit in Washington acknowledging one another as "leaders" of the civil-rights "movement," began, as usual, by feigning "concern" about flyspecks on Lucas's record. Then they professed themselves shocked that Lucas has little experience practicing law—this from people who revere Robert Kennedy, who became attorney general with zero experience as a litigator.

Such is the cynicism surrounding these Judiciary Committee spectacles, no one feels any need to tell the truth, which is that Lucas's scarlet sin is deviationism. The civil-rights movement and its poodles on the committee are whip-cracking overseers of the last plantation. They enforce the principle that blacks must be kept in their place, which place is trudging along in lockstep with the orthodoxy defined by liberal thought-police.

Lucas is skeptical of reverse discrimination and quotas, the apparatus of the racial spoils system. Let such blacks get away with independent thinking, who will the "leaders" lead? Let the likes of Lucas advance the idea that America is not irredeemably racist, and that blacks should not be wards of the state, what then becomes of the civil-rights lobby that makes its living mediating between the state and its wards?

The Judicial Committee's role is, as usual, sensitivity-mongering. We have seen this before, in the Bork hearings. Then, Committee liberals had the brass to say their concern was "balance" on the Court—no one here but us pluralists. But the Lucas case reveals the real spirit of contemporary liberalism: The choice is orthodoxy or lynching.

So there they sit, a row of white liberal senators, soggy with self-approval, Lucas's moral tutors and sensitivity-trainers, instructing him about sensitivity to black experiences and needs. Senatorial power-grabbing and political cowardice is once again dressed up as intellectual and moral scrupulousness.

What will they do when they have had their fill of the fun of trashing Lucas? They will turn their unspent indignation toward Clarence Thomas, the black Yale law graduate who is President Bush's choice to fill the seat vacated by Bork on the District of Columbia Court of Appeals. Thomas is conservative. More deviationism. A liberal's work is never done.

July 27, 1989

Race As an Intellectual Credential

Robert Clark, dean of Harvard's law school, says the school is trying "to achieve greater diversity." Does that mean hiring conservatives? Hardly. At Harvard, the diversity that counts concerns biological, not intellectual, differences.

Derrick Bell, a tenured professor at the law school, says he will go on unpaid leave until a black woman becomes a tenured professor. (The school's 60 tenured professors include five white women and three black men.) Bell's act is another of the "diversity demands" that drive today's academic spoils system. Hispanics, Asians, homosexuals, the handicapped—all are heard from.

Jesse Jackson has, of course, been heard from, saying that blacks resent "the gross insult" conveyed by the idea that "there is no African-American woman qualified for appointment to Harvard Law School." Actually, no one is saying that. However, Jackson is saying that prevailing standards of qualification are "archaic": "We cannot define who is qualified in the most narrow, vertical academic terms. Most people in the world are yellow, brown, black, poor, non-Christian. . . ." Therefore? Need you ask? The ugly truth is in the adjective "vertical."

The planted axiom is that a meritocracy is racist. But the rationales for racially based hiring are racist, and insulting to blacks, and subversive of the idea of a university.

One rationale is that Harvard's black students need black role models. Now, black students at Harvard are demonstrably privileged, well-launched on upward mobility. The last thing they (or any black youths) need is a role model whose hiring communicates the message that they are participants in a group entitlement to professional advancement. This entitlement mentality causes blacks to cultivate the attitudes of victims, triggers in whites the instinct of condescension, and leads both to discount black achievements.

Such hirings cause "entitled" blacks to regard even benevolent institutions as enemies because victimhood seems to be, for privileged "victims," an unassuageable grievance. Hence the protests and sit-ins at Harvard, a lagoon of liberalism where in the last 10 years almost half the new law faculty hired have been women or minorities.

Within the "role model" rationale for racial hiring lurks a degrading postulate: Black youths are disadvantaged unless taught by blacks because blacks are supposed to have derivative identities, derived from membership in a victimized group.

This postulate leads to the second racist rationale for racial hiring. It is intimated when Bell stresses that the "philosophies" of black academics are shaped by "life experiences" unknown to whites. The corollary postulate, not merely intimated but proclaimed, is that such philosophies are self-ratifying and impervious to criticism from nonblacks.

This theory of racially distinctive and automatically validated scholarship is a particularly slipshod and patently political exercise in the "sociology of knowledge." It argues—no, merely asserts—that all black scholars have had "experiences" that give them unique "perspectives" that whites are not qualified to question. Thus race is an intellectual credential. Bell says: "Race can create as legitimate a presumption as a judicial clerkship in filling a teaching position" regarding civil-rights law.

This is intellectual gerrymandering, carving out for blacks an exemption from competition. It is an academic set-aside program (a construction industry mistake comes to campus), where race confers an entitlement to scholarly authority about judicial review, jurisdiction and other jurisprudential questions. (The set-asides proliferate, for "the women's voice" and "the gay perspective," etc., in literature, history, etc.)

One charm of this theory for its proponents is that they can be highly paid professors without forfeiting the coveted, lucrative status of victims. It rests on racial stereotyping—reactionary means for liberal ends. Black scholars represent "the" black experience. In this "progressive" version of segregation, blacks are supposed to be—indeed, are told to be— homogenized and conscripted into intellectual conformity, apart from the mainstream of American culture.

In a scalpel-like discussion of these intellectual errors, Randall Kennedy, writing in the *Harvard Law Review*, notes that some blacks, such as Bell, are asserting a "proprietary claim over the study of race relations" and other matters. This is, says Kennedy, subversive of the ideal of a cosmopolitan intellectual community in which intellectual merit is an "*achieved* distinction." Kennedy says that by exaggerating white racism, and making ideas and scholarly craftsmanship subordinate to racial status, Bell and others threaten "cultural fluidity, intellectual freedom and individual autonomy."

Kennedy was urged, by the supposed guardians of civil liberties, not to publish his 74 pages of temperate arguments against the Balkanizing of the academic mind. It is discouraging that, in the current militarized climate of academic discourse, it is journalistically necessary to note here that Kennedy, a professor at Harvard Law School, is black.

May 17, 1990

Rights . . . and Wrongs

The Bork Controversy

The Groups Jerk Joe Biden's Leash

If Senator Joseph Biden (D-Del.) had a reputation for seriousness, he forfeited it in the 24 hours after Justice Lewis Powell announced his departure from the Supreme Court. Biden did much to achieve the opposite of his two goals: He strengthened the President's case for nominating Judge Robert Bork and strengthened the Democrats' case for not nominating Biden as president.

Six months ago, Biden, whose mood swings carry him from Hamlet to hysteria, was given chairmanship of the Judiciary Committee, an example of history handing a man sufficient rope with which to hang himself. Now Biden, the incredible shrinking presidential candidate, has somersaulted over his flamboyantly advertised principles.

Hitherto, Biden has said Bork is the sort of qualified conservative he could support. Biden has said: "Say the administration sends up Bork and, after our investigations, he looks a lot like [Justice] Scalia. I'd have to vote for him, and if the [special-interest] groups tear me apart, that's the medicine I'll have to take."

That was before Biden heard from liberal groups like the Federation of Women Lawyers, whose director decreed concerning Biden's endorsement of Bork: "He should retract his endorsement." Suddenly Biden was allergic to medicine, and began to position himself to do as bidden. Either Biden changed his tune because groups were jerking his leash or, worse, to prepare for an act of preemptive capitulation.

He said that "in light of Powell's special role" as a swing vote (that often swung toward Biden's policy preferences) he, Biden, wants someone with "an open mind." Proof of openness would be, of course, opinions that coincide with Biden's preferences. Biden says he does not want "someone who has a predisposition on every one of the major issues." Imagine a Justice with no predisposition on major issues. And try to imagine Biden objecting to a nominee whose predispositions coincide with Biden's.

Senators who oppose Bork will be breaking fresh ground in the field of partisanship. Opposition to Bork (former professor at Yale Law School, former U.S. solicitor general; judge on the U.S. Court of Appeals) must be naked on political grounds. Opposition must assert the principle that senators owe presidents no deference in the selection of judicial nominees, that jurisprudential differences are always sufficient grounds for opposition, that result-oriented senators need have no compunctions about rejecting nominees whose reasoning might not lead to results the senators desire.

If Biden does oppose Bork, his behavior, and that of any senators who follow him, will mark a new stage in the descent of liberalism into cynicism, an attempt to fill a void of principle with a raw assertion of power. Professor Laurence Tribe of Harvard offers a patina of principle for such an assertion, arguing that the proper focus of confirmation hearings on an individual "is not fitness as an individual, but balance of the Court as a whole."

This new theory of "balance" holds not merely that once the Court has achieved a series of liberal results, its disposition should be preserved. Rather, the real theory is that there should never again be a balance to the right of whatever balance exists. Perhaps that expresses Harvard's understanding of history: There is a leftward-working ratchet, so social movement is to the left and is irreversible.

Continuity is a value that has its claims. But many of the Court rulings that liberals revere (e.g., school desegregation) were judicial discontinuities, reversing earlier decisions. Even if putting Bork on the bench produces a majority for flat reversal of the 14-year-old abortion ruling, restoring to the states their traditional rights to regulate abortion would reestablish the continuity of an American practice that has a history of more than 14 years.

Besides, that restoration would result in only slight changes in the status of abortion. The consensus on that subject has moved. Some states might ban third-trimester abortions, or restore rights that the Court in its extremism has trampled, such as the right of a parent of a minor to be notified when the child seeks an abortion. But the basic right to an abortion probably would be affirmed by state laws.

Powell's resignation and Biden's performance as president manqué have given Reagan two timely benefits. He has an occasion for showing that he still has the will to act on convictions, and that he has an opponent he can beat.

Biden says there should not be "six or seven or eight or even five Borks." The good news for Biden is that there is only one Bork. The bad news for Biden is that the one will be more than a match for Biden in a confirmation process that is going to be easy.

July 2, 1987

The Whale and the Anchovies

Judge Robert Bork, with his reddish beard and ample girth, is Falstaffian in appearance. In argument, he has an intellectual's exuberance: He argues for the fun of it. Alas, his adversaries are too distraught to argue. Here, for example, is Ted Kennedy's voice raised in defense of moderation against Bork's "extremism": "Robert Bork's America is a land in which women would be forced into back-alley abortions, blacks would sit at segregated lunch counters, rogue police could break down citizens' doors in midnight raids, schoolchildren could not be taught about evolution, writers and artists could be censored at the whim of government . . ."

Gracious. It is amazing that the Senate confirmed Bork, without a single objection, for an appellate court. Kennedy says America is "better" than Bork thinks. No, America is better than liberals like Kennedy think. They think Yahoos make up a majority which, unless restrained by liberal judges, will tolerate or legislate the tyrannical America Kennedy describes.

Senator Patrick Leahy, a Vermont Democrat, says if *Roe* v. *Wade*, the 1973 abortion case, "came up today, [Bork's] vote would determine that we would not have abortions, legal abortions." Leahy assumes, probably wrongly, that the Senate already has confirmed four justices who are ready to reverse the 1973 ruling. Leahy assumes, certainly wrongly that if it were reversed, restoring to states the traditional right to regulate abortions, legislatures would ban abortions. Opinion polls refute Leahy. There is a broad consensus supporting liberal abortion policies.

Senator Joe Biden, who has used Bork to establish himself firmly as the flimsiest presidential candidate, is courting liberal interest groups by saying: "I will resist any efforts by this administration to do indirectly what it has failed to do directly in the Congress—and that is to impose an ideological agenda upon our jurisprudence." It is unclear what thought is struggling to get out of Biden's murky sentence. If nominating Bork is "indirect," what is "direct"? The adjective "ideological" is today's all-purpose epithet, a substitute for argument, by which intellectually lazy or insecure people stigmatize rather than refute people with whom they disagree. What Biden is try to do is preserve liberalism's ability to do in the Court what it has failed to do in elections. As liberalism has become politically anemic, it has resorted to end runs around democratic processes, pursuing change through litigation rather than legislation.

The Democratic Party advertises itself as the tribune of "the people," but the party expresses distrust of the people when it opposes Bork, who favors broader discretion for the popular (legislative) branch. Regarding Bork, Democratic presidential aspirants resemble "a herd of independent minds." The party resembles a boxer rising wobbly-kneed from the canvas, his back covered with resin. It has been battered by the public's belief that the party is servile toward imperious interest groups. Now, because of Bork, the party is about to land a left hook on its own glass chin. When Senator Pat Moynihan (D-N.Y.), who is up in 1988, hesitated to commit against Bork, Hazel Dukes, Democratic national committeewoman from New York, spoke of Moynihan disdainfully: "I have the votes in New York to defeat him. When I get with his staff in New York, I'll get what I want."

Liberalism has embraced Thurmondism. Liberals who claim the Senate is the president's equal in forming the Court, and who claim a right to reject a nominee purely on political grounds, cite as justifying precedent the behavior of Strom Thurmond in opposing LBJ's 1968 nomination of Abe Fortas to be chief justice. Were the Senate an equal participant, it would be empowered to nominate its own judicial candidates. (When advising and consenting to treaties, it cannot negotiate its own version of treaties.) With judicial nominees, the proper Senate role is to address threshold questions about moral character, legal skills and judicial temperament. The logic of the liberals' position—the idea that the confirmation process is a straight political power struggle turning on the nominee's anticipated consequences—is that we should cut out the middleman (the Senate) and elect justices after watching them campaign.

Biden, chairman of the Judiciary Committee, is stalling, so hearings will not even begin for two months. Nevertheless, Democratic senator and presidential candidate Paul Simon of Illinois says his mind is all but closed against Bork. Why? Because Bork, although "mentally qualified," is "close-minded." Senator Bob Packwood (R-Ore.),who can be as sanctimonious as the next saint when deploring single-issue politics, is threatening to filibuster against Bork unless satisfied that Bork will affirm all the pro-abortion rulings that Packwood favors.

Forty-one senators can block cloture (a forced end to a filibuster). There are 55 Senate Democrats. A significant number of Democrats will not join Biden's grovel before the interest groups, but Biden may have a few Republican collaborators. Suppose liberals block Bork and then block any similar jurist whom Reagan would nominate next. That would leave the court short-handed through the 1988 election—and through two court terms. That would be politically risky. So, having blocked Bork, they might have to confirm Reagan's next choice, who might be a conservative judicial activist.

Bork, believing in judicial restraint, is conservative about the process. A conservative activist would use judicial power the way liberal activists have, in a result-oriented way. Such an activist might hold that abortion is incompatible with the 14th Amendment's protection of the lives of "persons." An activist might favor striking down zoning laws because they violate the Fifth Amendment by taking property without just compensation. An activist might think minimum-wage laws unconstitutionally impair the obligation of contracts (Article I, Section 10). An activist might decide that the progressive income tax violates the equal-protection component of the Fifth Amendment's due-process clause. He even might reject the "incorporation doctrine" that makes the states, as well as Congress, bound by the Bill of Rights. That is something for Bork's critics to think about when they start to think. Until they do, Bork resembles a blue whale being attacked by anchovies—loud ones, but even loud ones are little.

July 20, 1987

No Due Process in the Confirmation Process

Samuel Goldwyn ("oral agreements aren't worth the paper they're printed on") committed one of his famous locutions in the quadrangle of Brasenose College, Oxford. Puzzled by something high on the wall of that ancient institution, he was told it was a sundial. When its working was explained to him, he exclaimed, "What'll they think of next!"

What'll they think of next, those battalions contending over the nomination of Robert Bork to the Supreme Court? Bob Dole has thought that Reagan might, as the Constitution permits, make Bork a "recess appointment." Dole says the idea is "food for thought" for Bork's most inflamed opponent, Senator Joe Biden, chairman of the Judiciary Committee.

Biden is malnourished regarding thoughtful approaches to the confirmation process. He is stalling the process to benefit his flagging presidential campaign. But a recess appointment would forfeit the moral high ground that Biden, by his rush to judgment, has handed to Bork's supporters. Republicans should not contemplate a shortcut around a process that Biden is short-circuiting.

Dole says he mentioned the recess-appointment possibility only to pressure Biden, but the threat is not believable. True, Reagan could appointment Bork in December to counter an unbreakable filibuster. But Bork's tenure would extend only through this Congress, expiring as Reagan leaves office. The new president could renominate Bork, or nominate someone else. A recess appointment would mean an immediate opportunity for a Democratic president.

Eisenhower made three recess appointments (Earl Warren, Potter Stewart, William Brennan). All were subsequently confirmed, but the Senate passed a nonbinding resolution deploring the procedure. The Senate was right then for the reason Biden is irresponsible today. Biden's exploration of the process for political profit involves treating coarsely the most elegant branch of government. The judiciary is the intellectual branch. The executive and legislative branches legitimately can act on motives that are validated by simple power calculations—by the pressure of a majority or a salient faction. The judiciary must ground its actions in reasonings about principles.

Bork is the most intellectually distinguished nominee since Felix Frankfurter (who was nominated by FDR 48 years ago). His Republican and Democratic supporters should be as eager for an intellectually serious confirmation process as Biden is eager for something quite different. The purpose of Biden's stall is to give interest groups time to marshal enough force to turn the confirmation process into a sweaty struggle of political power and intimidation.

How else explain the 71 days that will have passed between Bork's nomination and the beginning of hearings on September 15? For the last 16 nominees, hearings began, on average, 18 days after the nominee's name was sent to the Senate. The longest delay was 42 days. If Biden wanted an intellectually serious process, one turning on a searching examination of the great themes as constitutional law, he could have begun hearings two weeks ago.

He could have, unless the chairman of the Judiciary Committee is not prepared to discuss those themes. If not, how was he prepared to prejudge Bork within hours after Bork was nominated?

Bork will have Democratic supporters. Two Judiciary Committee Democrats—Alabama's Howell Heflin, a former judge, and Arizona's Dennis DeConcini, who has said he does not believe in ideological tests for nominees—seem likely to resist being roped into Biden's herd. Majority Leader Robert Byrd, while reserving judgment on Bork, has deplored attempts to make the Bork vote "a litmus test of party affiliation and loyalty."

However, pounding from the right may hammer Democrats into something like a solid bloc. Some conservative organizations not famous for delicacy are portraying the entire Democratic Party as Bork's opposition. That is dangerous to Bork, who will need Democratic votes to stop a filibuster, if it comes to that. If it does, his supporters can then adopt scorched-earth tactics.

The Senate runs on rules that presuppose mutual civility. Biden, the Oliver North of the confirmation process, is shredding that civility by treating the Bork nomination as a national emergency that licenses his extremism. If the enlists enough Northlings to sustain a filibuster and block cloture, Bork's supporters can tie the Senate in knots, making it impossible for anything debatable (which almost everything is) to be acted upon.

Until then, Bork's supporters should resist being Bidenized, meaning radicalized. In *Animal Crackers*, Groucho Marx asks the musically minded Chico, "How much do you charge not to play?" That is the question Bork's wisest supporters should ask some of his other supporters.

August 2, 1987

Could Justices Black, Harlan and Frankfurter Be Confirmed Today?

Senator Joseph Biden and others who believe that Robert Bork's opinions cause cavities also believe, with nice impartiality, contradictory ideas.

To justify judicial policymaking that pleases them, they say the Constitution is "organic" and must "evolve" with the times. But when Bork suggests reconsidering some Supreme Court rulings, they say that the settled, indeed inviolable, Constitution is under attack.

Furthermore, they locate Bork outside the "mainstream" of constitutional thought, saying his addition to the Court would result in radical decisions. But that means four radicals must already be on the bench. And that suggests that Biden's "mainstream" may be a minority persuasion.

To understand who really are the extremists in this argument, consider this: If Hugo Black and John Harlan, two of the most revered modern justices, were nominated today, they could not pass through the needle's eye that Biden and others want the confirmation inquisition to be.

The tenures of Justices Black (1937–71) and Harlan (1955–71) included the Warren years. Liberals especially admired Black, particularly for his libertarian First Amendment opinions. Conservatives praised Harlan's judicial restraint, meaning deference toward the representative branches of government.

Bork's critics concentrate on his opinions concerning civil rights. But on these issues, the opinions of Black and Harlan are closer to Bork's than Biden's.

Concerning civil rights, Bork's critics emphasize his criticism of the one-man, one-vote reapportionment rulings, his criticism of the Court's 1966 overturning of Virginia's $1.50 poll tax and his criticism of reverse discrimination as sanctioned by the Court's 1978 Bakke ruling.

Regarding reapportionment (the Court's decision that legislative districts must be drawn with strict population equality), Bork says the ruling injects a political preference into the equal-protection clause without "a single respectable supporting argument." Harlan thought likewise.

Dissenting, Harlan said the Court relied on the "frail tautology" that equal protection means no deviation from numerical equality. He noted that the 14th Amendment (containing the equal-protection clause) would not have been ratified were it not for the understanding that it did not restrict the power of states to apportion as they pleased.

Bork's criticism of the overturning of Virginia's poll tax is frequently represented as insensitivity to racial discrimination. Actually, there was no claim or evidence of race discrimination. The Court spoke of wealth discrimination. Bork says evidence of race discrimination would have justified the Court's decision.

In the poll-tax case, Black took Bork's position, charging that the Court, disregarding its two prior decisions affirming the constitutionality of the tax, used the 14th Amendment as a "blank check to alter the Constitution's meaning" in order to "save the country from the original Constitution." Black thought the Court was jeopardizing "the concept of a written constitution."

Harlan, too, dissented, saying the majority used "fiat" to decree that the equal protection clause required "unrestrained egalitarianism," just as an earlier Court had decreed that the clause imposed laissez-faire economic policy. In the Court's two prior rulings sustaining poll taxes, the Bork position was taken by, among other giants of American jurisprudence: Black, Harlan, Felix Frankfurter, Robert Jackson, Charles Evans Hughes, Louis Brandeis, Harlan Fiske Stone and Benjamin Cardozo. All these men are, presumably, banished from Biden's "mainstream."

Regarding Bakke (reverse discrimination in university admissions), Bork said that the Court's ruling that "some, but not too much, reverse discrimination" is constitutional rests on no discernible principle. Such criticism is hardly eccentric. Justice William Douglas had said, "Any state-sponsored preference to one race over another" (in access to professions) is unconstitutional. Professor (now Justice—Biden supported him) Scalia saw in Bakke a "trivialization of the Constitution."

Regarding privacy, Bork criticized the Court's 1965 ruling declaring unconstitutional, as a violation of the "privacy right," a Connecticut law proscribing contraceptives. The Court said that although the Constitution makes no mention of a privacy right, it is a "penumbra" formed by "emanations" from other rights. Bork detested Connecticut's law, but considered the Court's ruling a mere reflection of the Court's detestation rather than the application of a constitutional principle.

Black, dissenting in that case, took the same position. He said the Court was acting as "a day-to-day constitutional convention," as it did when it struck down legislation regulating commerce early in the century.

Bork criticizes the 1973 abortion ruling (based on the "privacy right") not because he opposes legalized abortion (he does not), but because it is an "unjustifiable usurpation of legislative authority." Justice White, President Kennedy's only appointee, agrees. He dissented against the "improvident and extravagant exercise" of "raw judicial power" justified by "nothing" in the Constitution's "language or history."

In 1976, Archibald Cox wrote that such jurists as Frankfurter and Learned Hand would have taken the Bork-White position. Cox says the Court's abortion ruling lacks the "legitimacy" that flows from a constitutional principle.

I could fill the newspaper with other illustrations of the long, noble pedigree of Bork's constitutional thinking. Suffice it to say that Biden's doctrine—the doctrine that Bork's thinking is not merely disputable but disreputable and disqualifying—is intemperate. Biden excludes Bork from the "mainstream." Bork has the considerable consolation of being banished in distinguished company—Black, Harlan, Frankfurter, among many others.

September 13, 1987

Extremism in Pursuit of Bork Is, Apparently, No Vice

Historian Richard Hofstadter should be living at this hour to savor the new flavors of what he called "the paranoid style of American politics." Last Sunday, several newspapers carried ads by the National Abortion Rights Action League, which began its assault on Robert Bork like this:

"You wouldn't vote for a politician who threatened to wipe out every advance women have made in the 20th century. Yet your senators are poised to cast a vote that could do just that."

Auto-intoxication is an occupational hazard of those who work at manufacturing hysteria, and paranoiacs are not easily embarrassed, but really: ". . . every advance women have made . . ."?

That sentiment should be preserved in amber and sent to the Smithsonian. It is a perfect caricature of the liberal notion that all goods issue from government. Indeed, it implies that all progress for women has come from, and can be undone by, the judiciary. According to this reading of history, neither economic growth nor technological advances nor the pill nor changed cultural attitudes have contributed to the advance of women.

Odd, is it not, that organizations purporting to speak for women insist that all women's advances have been bestowed by men in judicial robes? Carla Hills, former assistant U.S. attorney general and former secretary of Housing and Urban Development, has a better grasp of history, noting that women's greatest gains from public policy have come from legislative, not judicial, bodies.

Professor Mary Ann Glendon of the Harvard Law School notes that not a single one of the more than 100 majority opinions Judge Bork has written on the Court of Appeals has been reversed in the Supreme Court. He has joined more than 400 opinions, yet has written only nine dissents and seven partial dissents. Glendon wonders why so much hysteria has attended the nomination of "a judge whose career on the bench has been as uneventful and conventional" as Bork's.

Part of the answer, she suggests, is the uncritical political echo of "the assessments of some of his law-review articles by a few academics who are in the mainstream neither of American life nor American legal thought." She notes that Bork has been critical of what he calls "the professoriate," which she defines as "a small but influential corps of constitutional law professors at leading schools who deeply mistrust popular government.

"As Judge Bork has pointed out many times with gentle humor in his law-review articles, there is no group in America whose political and social attitudes are so faithfully mirrored in the Supreme Court's more controversial decisions than this professorial elite."

It has been 19 years since Chief Justice Warren retired, and not a single landmark ruling of the Warren Court has been reversed. Yet the liberal lobbies practicing today's paranoid style of politics insist that Bork threatens all American liberties. The evident presumption is that he would join four other tyrannical misogynists (is Sandra Day O'Connor one?) already on the Court.

Last Sunday, Planned Parenthood's full-page advertisement began: "If your senators vote to confirm the administration's latest Supreme Court nominee, you'll need more than a prescription to get birth control. It might take a constitutional amendment." Is there even a scintilla of sincerity in such rhetoric? Is it militant cynicism or ignorance?

Could Planned Parenthood name a single state that would proscribe contraceptives if (this, too, is wildly improbable) the Court received a case that provided an opportunity for reversing the 1965 decision overturning Connecticut's law against contraceptives? (Bork considered the law ludicrous but criticized the Court's reasoning in overturning it.)

Planned Parenthood says that, so far, "our democratic system" has blocked the "extremists" who think as Bork does. But Planned Parenthood clearly distrusts democracy. Its position is that Bork "could radically change the way Americans live" because he favors enlarged deference toward representative institutions such as state legislatures—61 percent of whose members are Democrats. Planned Parenthood clearly suggests that those institutions are straining to slip the short leash liberal courts have them on, and if they get off the leash they will legislate an end to (among other things) contraception.

Among the flops that Planned Parenthood says are not "farfetched" are government-imposed childbearing quotas for families. Such nonsense has not been heard in American politics since the John Birch Society was saying Eisenhower was a communist agent.

Birchers, like some of Bork's critics, despise Americans as manipulable fools. But at least Birchers did not have the effrontery to advertise themselves as models of moderation. And there were no senators at that time willing to use such paranoia as fuel for presidential campaigns.

September 17, 1987

The Compassion Industry Against Bork

Senator Bob Packwood, an Oregon Republican, is an evenhanded moralist who, with fine impartiality, apportions his fervor on several sides of some issues. Today he is among those who are pioneering a constitutional wrinkle the framers neglected to provide—popular election of Supreme Court justices.

Robert Bork's opponents are of three sorts: those who say he is dangerous because he is an "inflexible ideologue" (flexible ideologues are, presumably, preferred), those who say he is too changeable, and those who, suffering cognitive dissonance in the service of their country, say both. Packwood, who will filibuster if necessary, says Bork is intolerable regarding "privacy," meaning abortion.

Now, no one expects Packwood or any other politician to be a martyr on the altar of consistency, but this is a bit thick coming from the man who, when opposed in an election by an antiabortion candidate, was operatic in his denunciation of single-issue politics. Jack Minor, a reader of the *Portland Oregonian*, writes in a letter to the editor: "Is this the senator who said that the voters should not oppose him last election solely because of his pro-abortion stance because it should not be a one-issue campaign? Do I smell a hypocrite?"

Not really. Packwood's opposition to single-issue politics certainly does vary too much with the issue. But he also is showing fidelity.

He has sincerely supported and has received generous financial support from feminists. What is, however, dismaying about Packwood's current politics is the disappearance of an important inhibiting distinction. It is the distinction between fighting for friendly and worthy interests in purely political controversy, as Packwood did for Oregon's timber industry regarding tax reform, and putting one's political power at the service of constituents and others eager to guarantee certain results from judicial processes.

Reasonable people can disagree about the propriety of Bork's beliefs and the proper role of the Senate in confirmations. But surely some things—for starters, the ability to debate reasonable distinctions—are lost when the ethic of routine political competition and transactions is extended to the solemn task of constituting a court.

Today, fund-raising campaigns are financing media blitzes to share opinion-pole results that will, the interest groups hope, reduce enough senators to the status of passive electors in an Electoral College sitting in the Senate chamber. Bork's supporters are now driven, against their correct sense of decorum, to arm themselves with television ads and other paraphernalia of a campaign, or else concede defeat. Such is the dialectic of the degradation of judicial institutions.

The scale and intensity of the anti-Bork campaign refutes the premise that is supposed to legitimize the campaign. The premise is that there is nothing new going on, that the Senate has always "considered a nominee's judicial philosophy," as though that is what is going on.

This process has had its moments of unintended hilarity, as when the painter Robert Rauschenberg testified (by Lord knows what authority) on the fears and tremblings of America's artists—every paint-smeared one of them. In a statement that used words the way Rauschenberg uses paint (it was the rhetoric of random splatter), Rauschenberg announced that America's artists, who once cultivated an aura of Bohemian nonconformity, are remarkably "unanimous" in opposition to Bork. (Talk about a herd of independent minds.)

The anti-Bork army, which sometimes has attributes of a mob, has been swollen with organizations such as the Epilepsy Foundation of America, the United Cerebral Palsy Associations, the Retarded Citizens Association, among many others. Many Americans would be surprised to learn that their charitable support has been conscripted for the liberal onslaught on Bork.

The ease with which such groups have been swept together for the first time in such a campaign reflects, in part, the common political culture of the people who run the headquarters of the compassion industry.

Today's attempt to break the Supreme Court to the saddle of manufactured or (as in the Rauschenberg case) fictitious opinion is a more fundamentally radical attack on the Court than FDR's attempt to pack the Court by enlarging it. Packing was to be a one-time tactic that could not have been repeated regularly unless the Court's bench was going to be replaced by bleachers.

The transformation of the confirmation process into a contest between massed battalions is a perverse achievement of people who, like Packwood, claim to be acting to protect the Court from Bork's jurisprudence, which they say would leave all our liberties to be blown about by gusts of opinion.

October 1, 1987

The Bork Nomination

The following editorial appeared in *The Washington Post* on October 5, 1987.

The uncharacteristic silence in this space over the past couple of weeks on a hot, controversial topic has been the silence of second thoughts. When Judge Robert H. Bork was nominated to the Supreme Court, we hoped and expected to be able to support his confirmation—comfortably and unequivocally—even though his political inclinations are far from our own. Those many aspects of the campaign against him that did not resemble an argument so much as a lynching only reinforced our original instinct. But we find, at the end of a period of total immersion in the subject—the written record, the testimony for and against Judge Bork and, most tellingly, the testimony by him—that we cannot.

By now the question may of course be academic; the Bork nomination appears to be gone. The reason for this, we suspect, is not the one being offered by President Reagan's perennially disappointed conservative constituency—i.e., that the White House failed to campaign for Judge Bork as a Great Avenger of the Right, a law-and-order man who would roll back the detested tide of permissiveness. Rather it was that Judge Bork's natural and expectable support never materialized in the political middle. There was almost no real or serious resistance in this quarter to the assault from the left against him; there was instead *a lot* of uncharacteristic silence.

Why? The commonest explanations have been political—conservative southern Democrats afraid to offend the blacks who have, ironically, become the decisive constituency in the party in that region, moderate northern Republicans likewise fearful for their reelection. But behind these political weak spots has been an abscess of a different kind. On a careful reading of the evidence, a preponderance of powerful reasons to support Judge Bork was fatally undermined by a couple of even more powerful and critical reservations that finally, for us and, we suspect, for many others disposed to support him, could not be overcome.

We are not being playful when we say that much of the anti effort was almost enough to make you pro. It's not just that there has been an intellectual vulgarization and personal savagery to elements of the attack, profoundly distorting the record and the nature of the man. It is also, more important, that the dismal political and programmatic content of some of the argument against him, as heard day after day in the committee hearings, could only confirm a suspicion that the time is ripe for a rigorous challenge to the lazy and dangerous clichés that often pass for policy wisdom and juridical profundity among liberals these days. There was also something disquieting in the idea that intellectual audacity and a challenge to prevailing legal orthodoxy were automatically to be punished or at least put down.

A second factor in Judge Bork's favor was the conventional view to which we continue to subscribe and which has now fallen into such disrepute, namely that a president has a large claim to support in nominating a judge of proven competence and distinction to the court; we think there is something to currently expressed anxieties that the Bork events pave the way to a demagogic, highly politicized future where confirmation proceedings are concerned.

And finally there is the intelligence and professional achievement of the man. On the opposite page today we print a piece by Judge Bork's journalist son, expressing fury and frustration that his father has been so cruelly characterized by those fighting his appointment. Robert Bork, Jr. is surely right in protesting that his father is neither a "neanderthal" nor a "racist," nor the rest of that litany, and that the man is far from being the caricature presented. Judge Bork is also, on the evidence, one of the most thoroughly schooled and knowledgeable students of constitutional law ever nominated.

What, then, is enough to overcome all this? The impression, never disturbed throughout the hearing and never refuted by the nominee no matter how many questions just *begged* for such refutation, that he did *not* change in the one respect that matters most: Judge Bork has retained from his academic days an almost frightening detachment from, not to say indifference toward, the real-world consequences of his views; he plays with ideas, seeks tidiness, and in the process does not seem to care who is crushed.

What people like ourselves needed when confronted with this impression was modest, but critical. It was not evidence that Robert Bork is a political liberal or in fact a political anything, and it was not evidence that he would have approved of everything the Supreme Court has done on matters of race, other forms of discrimination, privacy, free speech or other such issues in recent years, or that he would be swayed by emotion. Rather it was a simple assurance that, in addition to the forensic brilliance, the personal integrity and the care for the law, Robert Bork's moral sensibility could be engaged with the questions on which he had pronounced so forcefully, that in these great cases that were to have so profound and intimate an effect on people's lives, he had a feeling for justice, not just for the law. They are not always the same.

This was an assurance of which we could find only the palest traces in the copious written record, and one Judge Bork either could not or would not provide in the course of his prolonged interrogation. He had a hundred opportunities, and he never did it. Instead all the talk was in the opposite direction.

Judge Bork is driven by the idea that the judiciary in recent years has substituted values—inevitably its own—for the law, and in the process is dissipating its authority, threatening its legitimacy. And the excruciating thing about his nomination is that, to some considerable extent, he is right in this. He has been pilloried in part of having had the effrontery to raise questions that ought to be raised and that are difficult to answer, about the nature of the constitutional provisions and the statutes the courts are called upon to construe, and about the proper role of the courts in doing so. It is not as clear as advocates would wish—often as we would wish—that the Constitution bars all forms of sex discrimination; requires one-man, one-vote; bars any form of state aid to sectarian schools; creates a clear shield of privacy. And so to some extent Judge Bork is being skewered for having rightly said so.

His saying these things is not our objection to his nomination, however. We go the next step, to what he has not said. The genius that has allowed the Constitution to survive for 200 years lies partly in its elasticity. Many of the nation's clearest and ugliest inequities—racial discrimination and chronic malapportionment among them—have been mitigated only because judges used that elasticity to deal with issues that, for various reasons, the other branches would not. Judge Bork, it seems to us, is much more likely to note injustice but refuse to use the full powers of the Supreme Court to remedy it. He does not read the Constitution generously.

If the answers to the most important judicial questions were easy, if judges did not, in answering them, have enormous discretion, there would be no problem here. But they do have great discretion; they *must* apply values, because they are confronted daily with the need to make value judgments at points where the written law provides no absolute guide. Judge Bork in his zeal to move away from values does not take us to a value-free zone, much as he might like to. He takes us to a place where the courts too often say no. Those results are expressions of value, too. He may go in a healthy direction, but he goes too far.

©*The Washington Post*

The *Post* and Moral Exhibitionism

In announcing itself editorially opposed to Robert Bork, the *Washington Post* expressed embarrassment about the company it was keeping. The *Post* should be embarrassed, but about more than the "intellectual vulgarity and personal savagery" (the *Post*'s description) of the big battalions opposing Bork. The *Post* should blush about its role in reducing liberalism to the politics of flaunted feelings.

The editorial denounces demagoguery (". . . profoundly distorting the record and nature of the man . . . lazy and dangerous clichés") that has succeeded against Bork (and has not prevented the *Post* from piling on). The *Post*'s behavior calls to mind those Republicans who said Joe McCarthy was appalling but that "the cause" was somehow independent of, and superior to, its methods.

However, what worthy cause comes enveloped in smarminess? Are not the tactics used against Bork, like those used in McCarthyites, entailed by the nature of the people and arguments that depend on the tactics?

The *Post* says Bork would not "read the Constitution generously" to exploit its "elasticity" for desirable results:

"Many of the nation's clearest and ugliest inequities—racial discrimination and chronic malapportionment, among them—have been mitigated only because judges used the Constitution's elasticity to deal with issues that, for various reasons, the other branches would not. Judge Bork . . . is much more likely to note injustice but refuse to use the full powers of the Supreme Court to remedy it."

The liberal political agenda is packed into the antiseptic phrase "deal with." And the phrase "full powers" is not synonymous with "properly used powers." Most important, the *Post*'s anxiety is conspicuously abstract. The *Post* does not mention a single social problem, or a single "discrete and insular minority," that only judicial institutions can "deal with."

Since the civil-rights revolution and reapportionment, what group falls helplessly between the cracks of representative government? Certainly not blacks or women, given the responsiveness (the politest possible term) of the political process to anti-Bork pressure applied in their names.

Perhaps the *Post* is worried about students. A judge in Kansas City, annoyed about the electorate's rejection of bond issues and tax increases that would bring city spending on schools closer to suburban levels, has ordered several tax increases. In severing the links between taxation and representation, he said: "A majority has no right to deny others the constitutional guarantees to which they are entitled." How is that, *Post* editors, for a generous reading of the Constitution? Is that not the use of a court's "full powers" to "deal with" problems?

The judge said he had to do what other branches of government would not do because "students are helpless without the aid of this court." His moral megalomania is (to use the *Post*'s vocabulary) the "real-world" result of the *Post*'s ideology. Self-aggrandizement and self-indulgence are easy to disguise as merely "generous" readings of the Constitution.

The *Post* rightly says justice and law "are not the same." But the *Post* seems to license judges to supply justice, according to their lights, when law is (by the *Post*'s lights) inadequate. The *Post* intimates that the patience required by democracy is evidence of callousness. Thus is conservatism diagnosed as a character flaw.

Having lauded Bork's intelligence, integrity and professional attainments, the *Post* locates his disqualifying defect—lack of compassion: "Judge Bork has retained from his academic days an almost frightening detachment from, not to say indifference toward, the real-world consequences of his views; he plays with ideas, seeks tidiness, and in the process does not seem to care who is crushed."

"Tidiness" is disparaged when logic is inconvenient, and "play" is a loaded verb to disparage Bork's moral seriousness. The words "frightening" and "crushed" are absurdly hyperbolic and suggest the *Post* is trying to talk itself into a pitch of passion that the *Post* knows is disproportionate. The *Post* gives no hint of who might be crushed because Bork is frighteningly indifferent. Again there is a notable abstractness to the *Post*'s indictment of Bork's (the *Post* believes) excessively abstract approach to judging.

The *Post* says it is particularly distressed by what Bork "has not said." He has not said whatever the Post requires for "assurance" that his "moral sensitivities would be engaged." Here is the heart of the matter.

The moral obligations of judicial restraint that Bork derives from democratic values do not count to the *Post* as moral sensitivities. What counts is "caring" or, more precisely, "seeming" to care. When "seeming" is the only valid sign of sensitivity, ethics acquire an anti-institutional aroma and a high content of histrionics. Judges can only pass the *Post*'s test of "moral sensitivity" by maximum "generosity" in reading "elasticity" into the Constitution as they "deal with" this and that (by implementing the *Post*'s agenda, which has not been faring well in elections).

The Bork battle has efficiently sorted people out, and the *Post* has come home to liberalism. But liberalism is now little but sensitivity

snobbery. The categorical imperative is to allow no institutional obligations to interfere with the moral exhibitionism of "seeming to care."
October 8, 1987

Dear George . . .

The following editorial appeared in the *Washington Post* on October 8, 1987.

Our beloved columnist George Will has finally met the enemy, and it is
us. In a steamy piece on the opposite page today, Mr. Will takes on our
editorial opposing the elevation of Judge Robert Bork to the Supreme
Court. He attacks us without mercy. This is, of course, as it should be,
mercy being yet another of those wobbly concepts—like compassion,
caring and God knows what all else—that liberals will run on about.

Our sin in Mr. Will's eyes is the same one we committed in the eyes
of Judge Bork's most committed opponents: a failure of wholehearted-
ness. We denounced the opponents—or some of them—for what we
continue to believe was one of the ugliest campaigns on record to block
a nomination, a campaign based in part on deliberate distortion and
reeking of a kind of intellectual fear and intolerance that both mocked
and stripped away its claims to virtue—but then we joined in opposing
Judge Bork's confirmation. We found great merit in much of what Judge
Bork has written and said over his career, above all some of the very
critiques of revered decisions for which he paid most dearly in the confirmation process, and his view that too often modern judges have let
their preferences rather than the law guide their decisions. Yet in the
end we backed away from the nomination because it was not clear to us
that Judge Bork would ever let broader considerations of justice guide
him as he handed down opinions, because of a belief, of which he never
chose to disabuse the inquiring committee, that even on the great occasions he would dole out justice about as a pharmacist dispenses pills.

So Mr. Will, who himself seems to favor this pharmaceutical school of
judging, has indeed found us out. We are ambivalent. Nor do we hang
our heads for that. It seems to us that no one of independent mind could
have watched Judge Bork's long week of absorbing testimony and not be.
Only lobbyists could do that, the tin tongues of the right and left. The
great virtue of conservatives—indeed of Mr. Will when he is not so
disappointed and is at his best—is their comfort with ambiguity, which
they recognize as part of truth. Here Mr. Will opts for doctrine instead.

We do not "license judges to supply justice, according to their lights,
when law is" by our standards "inadequate." But neither do we believe,

nor does anyone with even minimal knowledge in these affairs, that the answers to the difficult questions that rise to the highest courts leap off the printed page. We say again: a judge is not a pharmacist filling a prescription. He judges; he brings value to bear.

That's why we did need a sign, just as our columnist has charged, that on some of the great questions concerning race, free speech, fair representation and privacy, Judge Bork seemed to care—that is, that somewhere along the line in his extended and highly articulate legal career he had given evidence that he thought the outcome of his reasoning at least mattered. He didn't give it. Mr. Will—a little priggishly, we thought— was pleased to call this standard one of "moral exhibitionism." That, too, is fine with us. We do indeed believe that there are issues and occasions on which a judge should show a little leg.

©*The Washington Post*

Senators Say the Darndest Things

In the present unsatisfactory state of the law we are not permitted to horsewhip lawmakers, for which fact some senators should give thanks. They deserve thrashing for their behavior concerning Judge Robert Bork—their behavior since the vote. They are giving constituents odd and sometimes dishonest explanations of why they opposed him for a seat on the U.S. Supreme Court.

Obviously, some senators are not proud of what they did or why they did it. A wise man once said, in defense of wartime deceptions, that sometimes the truth needs a bodyguard of lies. Today some senators do, too, when dealing with their constituents.

Alabama's Howell Heflin (D) should listen to his conscience, understood (by H. L. Mencken) as the inner voice that warns us that someone may be watching. Heflin is a large, loud man who seems to think the lungs are reservoirs of learning. In his newsletter to constituents (your tax dollars at work) and in letters, such as one to some constituents in Mobile, Heflin charged that "the history of his [Bork's] life and his present lifestyle indicated a fondness for the unusual, the unconventional and the strange."

Regarding Bork's present life, Heflin says not a syllable to substantiate his smear. It just hangs there, reeking of innuendo and its author.

Concerning Bork's past, Heflin says Bork once considered himself a socialist. Heflin does not say that Bork committed that crime when he was a teenager. Then, Heflin says, "he nearly became a communist—he recruited friends to attend Communist Party meetings."

That is another lie. As Bork has cheerfully recounted his adolescent intellectual life, when he was 16 he and a friend attended one—count with us, Heflin: one—communist meeting.

In his role as God's servant, Heflin told an Alabama radio station that he was "disturbed by his [Bork's] refusal to discuss his belief in God—or the lack thereof." To this Heflinism, three responses are required.

First, there was no "refusal." Second, in the hearings Heflin himself eschewed such questioning, noting that the Constitution says "no religious test shall ever be required as a qualification to any office." Third, with Heflin now implying such a test, there is a noticeable silence from the self-appointed guardians of "the American way." The liberal lobbyists are too tuckered out from Bork-bashing to rise to the challenge.

Heflin is not just disagreeable, he is ammunition for disagreeableness in others. Senator John Warner (R-Va.) has quoted to constituents Heflin's smear about Bork's "fondness" for the "strange."

A Warner constituent wrote to Bork to report that Warner said he had looked Bork "right in the eye" after questioning Bork, and that Warner had told Bork he would opposed him. The constituent also sent to Bork a news story from the *Richmond News Leader*. It reported Warner saying that he did not "get satisfactory answers" to questions he put to Bork. It reported that Warner concluded from his questioning that Bork lacked a philosophic "center of gravity."

Well now.

Responding to Warner's constituent, Bork says he was available to Warner for more than three months and Warner did not ask to see him until the day of the Senate vote. Then Warner called. Warner said he had not studied the hearings. They met for approximately 10 minutes. Warner reminisced about a judge, then asked Bork about a Heflin remark about Bork's intellectual history. Bork answered. Warner did not respond. To Warner's constituent, Bork writes:

"I said I hoped he would vote for me and he simply did not answer. Nor did he look me in the eye. Our entire conversation was brief, devoid of content, and wholly unsatisfactory. When Warner had left, one of my clerks expressed surprise that the conversation was over so quickly. The absence of any real discussion made me think that Warner had merely wanted to be able to say he talked to me. After reading the account of his misrepresentations in the newspaper, I am convinced of it."

Some senators have said silly things to inquiring constituents. Florida's Bob Graham (D) wrote to a Daytona Beach Shores man that Bork did not understand that "the Supreme Court is the living instrument of the will and yearnings of the American people." How, then, does the judicial branch differ from a political branch of government?

Tennessee's Jim Sasser (D) wrote to a Signal Mountain, Tennessee, voter that because Bork is not a Southerner, his nomination jeopardized the Court's "regional balance." And in refreshing departure from a pretense of high principles, Sasser said "scientifically conducted polls" showed that Bork was unpopular.

Ohio's irrepressible Howard Metzenbaum (D) wrote to a priest in Cuyahoga Falls, Ohio, that Bork "would support reinterpreting the antitrust laws to eliminate the right of retailers to give consumers a discount." This is an exquisitely misleading way of saying that Bork (perhaps the nations's leading authority on antitrust laws) favors allowing resale price maintenance for manufacturers. But Metzenbaum may be explaining things as well as he can.

January 21, 1988

The Tempting of America

As Justice Oliver Wendell Holmes drove off after lunch with Justice Learned Hand, the latter exclaimed, "Do justice, sir, do justice." Holmes halted his carriage and reproved Hand: "That is not my job. It is my job to apply the law." That story involving two of America's finest legal minds is told by a third such, Robert Bork, in his elegant and entertaining new book, *The Tempting of America.* The story encapsulates the philosophic stance that brought down upon Bork unprecedented furies. His book is a ringing defense of what his most fanatical opponents feared: democracy.

In politics, virulence is often inversely proportional to sincerity. As Bork's readers will be reminded, many senators and others opposing him lied promiscuously, which did them a kind of credit: They were ashamed of their real motives and had no confidence in their arguments. Many of the politician's motives were cowardice and opportunism. The motives of interest groups and their intellectual justifiers were more interesting. They involved a systematic assault on constitutionalism, and hence on democratic practice. The "temptation" to which Bork's title refers is the seductive notion that nothing—not democratic due process, certainly not the text and structure of the Constitution—should prevent courts from imposing desired social results.

Paradoxically, this subversion of constitutionalism—government of delegated, enumerated and limited powers—arises, in part, from confused reverence for the Constitution. Many Americans revere the Constitution so much they assume it must mandate good government and must proscribe all bad and foolish laws and even neglect of social problems. This naive, sentimental source of judicial overreaching is less sinister than the theoretical justifications formulated by sophisticates who prefer judicial authoritarianism they agree with to democratic results they do not.

The Constitution's fundamental distinction is between what is public and what is private—between the spheres where majorities may and may not rule. Judging, properly understood, rests on a great renunciation, a refusal to infuse the law with any content other than that of the framers of the Constitution or legislators. "In law," says Bork, "the moment of temptation is the moment of choice, when a judge realizes that in the case before him his strongly held view of justice, his political and moral imperative, is not embodied in a statute or in any provision of the Constitution. He must then choose between his version of justice and abiding by the American form of government."

The rhythms of American politics have been such that, periodically, people whose agendas are not faring well in elections—for example, conservatives in the Progressive and early New Deal eras, liberals in recent decades—have used activist courts to displace democratic choice. The Bork confirmation battle, in which moral assault drove away discourse, exemplified the style of political minorities that are morally self-righteous but electorally impotent. A minority with an agenda that is neither mandated by the Constitution nor given a mandate by the electorate has a choice. It can try to persuade the electorate. Or it can try to capture the judiciary, stocking it with people taught to think that constitutional language is so open-textured, or so obscure in the framers' usage, that judges can, indeed must, read it into their own preferences.

Bork dissects the politicized teachings (most from the left but some from the right) of many law schools where tomorrow's law clerks and the day-after-tomorrow's judges are learning not just that the Constitution does not mean what it says, but that it does not mean much of anything at all. The theories justifying disregard of original intent are often recondite—the more abstruse the better, from the theorists' point of view. Then constitutional construing becomes the business of a clerisy, a mandarinate speaking a private language inaccessible to outsiders.

Bork asks: If the framers' and ratifiers' original understanding of the Constitution is no longer controlling, what is? Judges are—judges rampant, unrestricted by anything but their own principles or prejudices. Those might be noble; enforcing them might serve some public good. But when judges are in a legislative mode, the doctrine of the separation of powers is shredded and, in the long run, so is a great public good—popular sovereignty. When constitutional construing is severed from the anchor of original intent, judges cannot avoid exercising illegitimate discretion. So severed, judges' reasoning is no longer *constituted*, no longer rests on the foundation of fundamental law. Judges' reasoning becomes a personal choice followed by a rationalization—"results first, premises to follow." Bork says such reasoning is like free verse as defined by Robert Frost—"tennis with the net down." The discipline of rules is missing.

Courts are the last redoubt for people unable to win by the rules of democratic persuasion. Given the conduct of Congress, it is understandable that many Americans are tempted to trade self-government for rule by appointed judges. Congress is invariably untidy and frequently vulgar, irrational, venal, cowardly, mendacious and pandering—as in the Bork battle. But judges who usurp power corrupt the public mind. They are disingenuous about their authority and tendentious in their rationalizations. Besides, the argument for democracy is moral and prudential, not aesthetic. It is that in the long run, democratic regimes are best at taming power and giving people what they deserve, which includes the elevating experience of exercising sovereignty. Bork's book, which belongs among the few masterpieces of American political reflection, reminds readers that nothing guarantees that democracy shall have a long run.

Will Bork's book reopen old wounds? I hope so. The alternative to waging the cultural war is acquiescence in the advancing atrophy of democratic processes, which is the inevitable result of allowing the judiciary to become a second, and supreme, legislative branch. Writing well is the best revenge and Bork brings Falstaffian zest to the cheerful fun of making his adversaries look foolish. (Hilarious, but not really funny, are pages 301 to 305, containing portions of his hearing transcript, in which he tried to explain a simple point to an even simpler senator.) He loves a fair fight and readers will understand why his opponents did not dare to give him one.

December 4, 1989

PART 6

Coda

Why Are We Here? Accidents Do Happen

All is quiet along the Potomac just now, the federal community having given itself over to seasonal indolence and indulgence. Such enjoyment came to this city surprisingly late in its history. President Grover Cleveland in 1894, for the first time, gave civil servants Christmas Day off.

Among the many treats that leaven our civilization, those associated with Christmas sometimes test one's capacity for taking life philosophically. The task of eating a pfeffernuss cookie without coating yourself with powdered sugar is as difficult as spelling "pfeffernuss," but it is easier than eating fruitcake, which is the worst feature of this season.

Christmas, which—let us be fair—should not be judged by fruitcakes, is, of course, a lot older than almost all the rituals that now encrust it. But, then, Christmas, like mankind, is a late arrival, as reckoned by Harvard's Stephen Jay Gould, who takes the long view, as paleontologists are wont to do.

The human species, he says, has been around for about 250,000 years, approximately .0015 percent of the history of all earthly life, "the last inch of the cosmic mile." The planet, indeed the universe, got along swimmingly without us until, as it were, just the other day. This makes our arrival look awfully like a cosmic afterthought, an accident rather than the culmination of a plan.

Furthermore, says Gould, the many evolutionary factors that produced us are "quirky, improbable, unrepeatable and utterly unpredictable." However, unpredictable does not mean random. "It makes sense and can be explained after the fact. But wind back life's tape to the dawn of time and let it play again—and you will never get humans a second time."

Well, "never" is a tad, if only a tad, too strong. What Gould means is that getting human beings on a second run through the evolution of life would be a statistical long shot with the odds approaching infinity-to-one. If, that is, it were possible to "approach" infinity, which it isn't—but never mind, you know what I mean.

So how come we humans are here? "Because," says Gould, "one odd group of fishes had a peculiar fin anatomy that could transform into legs for terrestrial creatures; because the earth never froze entirely during an ice age; because a small and tenuous species [he means us], arising in

Africa a quarter-of-a-million years ago, has managed, so far, to survive by hook and by crook."

Actually, we are not as tenuous as all that. Gould's "hook and crook" means mind, which is a formidable thing. True, mind has produced, among other things, fruitcake and modern physics, both potentially lethal to the species. Still, "tenuous" does not do us justice.

Actually, Gould gives us generous justice by noting the exhilarating aspect of the lowly and improbable (fins and all that) explanation of us. The explanation may be superficially deflating, but it is ultimately liberating: "We cannot read the meaning of life passively in the facts of nature. We must construct these answers ourselves—from our own wisdom and ethical sense."

Gould may be right, but for many people the meaning of Christmas is that there is a "higher" answer, a providential purpose to the evolutionary outcome. For some people, the origin of religious sentiment—awe— is in this thought: The stunning improbability that produced us is itself an intimation of some special intention.

Tom Stoppard said that it may be slightly less improbable that a deity intended us, and planned our wayward path to existence, than that green slime began to change and give rise, in time, to Shakespeare's sonnets. Stoppard is a playwright, so perhaps he is sympathetic to an explanation that features a playwright who purposely causes characters to come and go on the cosmic stage.

Anyway, no matter where life came from, or why, the fact is it beats the alternative and makes things interesting. Alice Walker put philosophy in its place and gave consolation for a universe afflicted with fruitcakes when she wrote in one sentence almost all that needs to be said on the subject of life: "Life is better than death, I believe, if only because it is less boring, and because it has fresh peaches in it."

December 25, 1988

Science and Sensibility

Your response to science news depends on your sensibility. I, for one, am delighted by the discovery of 1989FC, a cosmic jaywalker. That asteroid may or may not smash lots of us to smithereens. However, it certainly teaches an always timely, because chastening, lesson about the irreducible disorderliness of everything.

1989FC (why do we give better names to Buicks—Electra, Riviera— than to really important things?) was recently discovered from a Mount

Palomar Observatory photograph after the asteroid made one of its annual passes near Earth.

It is big—perhaps more than half a mile in diameter—and fast (46,000 mph). When two objects are in overlapping orbits, the bigger one inevitably pulls the smaller into its path. So a scientist says, "Sooner or later it should collide with the Earth, the moon or Mars."

It would be nice to know which one and how soon. Should we paint the house or are we going to get smooshed? 1989FC would bump with the force of 20,000 one-megaton hydrogen bombs.

The cosmos is not crowded. If there were just three bees in America, the air would be more congested with bees than space is with stars. But there is a lot of stuff besides stars whizzing around.

Earth is constantly pelted by small bits of matter, and some not so small: In 1908, passengers on the trans-Siberian express were startled by a bright blue ball of fire as a small comet leveled a 70-mile strip of Siberian forest. A hotly disputed hypothesis is that the evolution of life on Earth has been marked by radical disjunctions because of collisions with extraterrestrial material. Some scientists say one such collision occurred 65 million years ago and caused climatic changes that led to the rapid extinction of dinosaurs.

It is estimated that asteroids of more than half a mile in diameter hit Earth once every 40 million years or so. A few weeks ago 1989FC came within half a million miles of (let's look on the bright side) Congress. That counts as a near-miss. (Why do we say "near-miss" when what we are describing, with an airplane or an asteroid, is a near-hit?)

If 1989FC hits Earth, the odds are it will hit an ocean, raising (depending on its angle of entry) waves several hundred yards high, inundating coastal areas. (New York City? Every cloud has its . . .) Striking land, it would dig a crater a mile deep and five to 10 miles across. There goes the neighborhood.

The Lisbon earthquake of 1755 was enough to cause people to question the idea of progress and to doubt a divinely ordained orderliness of the universe. That earthquake was an intellectually improving event. Imagine what a collision with a big asteroid could do for the moral and intellectual climate.

In 1610, Galileo discovered moons around Jupiter. The discovery convulsed Europe's religious and (hence) political passions. It proved something deflating about the nature of our solar system: Earth is not the center of the universe.

Ever since we were evicted from where we think we belong, science has delivered a series of affronts to our sense of dignity and autonomy. Darwin, by saying mankind is continuous with the slime from which mankind has only recently crept, imbedded mankind in the mud of the planet that has itself been revealed to be peripheral. Then Freud said there are within us uncharted depths with their own turbulences.

Early astronomy may have displaced our planet from the place of honor in the cosmos, but at least Newton said the universe was intelligible, even decorous. He was the great orderer. His clockwork theory of the universe gave rise, through the seepage of science into the wider culture, to an arid deism in theology: God was envisioned as the winder of the clocklike mechanism of the cosmos. There even was the clockwork political theory, the clearest expression of which is the U.S. Constitution with its tidy (on paper) system of checks and balances—politics as physics.

Neither Newton's universe nor our Constitution works as clocklike as we had hoped. And now we have 1989FC to worry about.

Before Darwin, many people believed that no living thing could become extinct because extinction would suggest that there had been imperfection in God's original plan. What will people think if one of 1989FC's big brothers comes crashing along and makes everything extinct all at once?

If 1989FC itself hits Earth, causing localized catastrophe, one result will probably be a religious revival. The catastrophe will be construed as evidence that a caring God exists and is not amused.

April 27, 1989

In Defense of the Messy Desk

The Divinity (a.k.a. Victoria Will) will soon be seven, which philosophers call the age of reason. Fat lot philosophers know about young girls. I have shared a small desk with one for several years and now am sharing a huge desk, and she and I are wrestling with the intellectual problem of desktop tidiness.

For the Prodigy (a.k.a. the Divinity) and me this is a problem, because some afternoons after school we now sit across from each other at an old (new to me) "partners' desk," one of those enormous constructions with drawers on each side. The top, on which an F-15 could land, can hold a lot of clutter.

Father favors tidiness. Daughter finds clutter congenial. And it turns out she is correct: Science proves that it is rational to have a messy desk.

In *Discover* magazine Hugh Kenner, professor of English at Johns Hopkins and a confirmed advocate of chaos, last year wrote a spirited defense of the messy desk. Kenner considers tidiness not only evidence of an unattractive character ("clean-deskers measure their vermouth with an eyedropper, walk their dogs by the clock, succor their spouses by the calendar"), but also a practice invalidated by the 80-20 rule, a.k.a. Zipf's Law.

Kenner says: Consider my desk. I take a reference book from a shelf and, knowing I will refer to it again soon, I leave it on my desk for now. And this letter inviting me to a conference. I'll leave it next to the book for now because I'll be referring to it when I make travel arrangements. These notes for the essay I'm writing—I turn to them frequently so I'll leave them here for now. The "for nows" accumulate and so does the stuff.

For Kenner, a messy desk is a matter of principle, not sloth. The principle is: What you need now you're apt to need again, and again. That is why the paring knife is left on the kitchen counter, and the nutmeg grater is not.

The principle pops up all over the place, as in our use of words. Kenner says we make more than 50 percent of our normal talk by recycling about 100 words. Feel inarticulate? Cheer up.

Shakespeare's works contain 29,066 different words, but 40 words make up 40 percent of the texts of his plays. James Joyce's *Ulysses* contains almost the same number of different words—29,899—but just 135 words (*the, of, and, to,* etc.) make up half the text. Such words are the utility infielders of discourse. We keep them handy on our desktops, so to speak. They illustrate this principle: Most of every activity uses only a small fraction of available resources.

The common words are like paring knives: They perform many functions. The rarely used words (Kenner's example: "colubriform," meaning snake-shaped) can be defined in a few lines. But in the large *Oxford English Dictionary*, an all-purpose word like "set" (get set to set the table with the dining set, then set the alarm so we can set out . . ., etc.) requires an *OED* entry two-thirds the length of *Paradise Lost*.

Like the clutter on a cluttered desk, such words are the ones we reach for frequently. The clutter on our desks is the stuff we strew there in accordance with (whether we know it or not) "the principle of least effort."

That was expounded in 1950 by George Zipf, a Harvard philologist who became the ideologist of clutter. He established the rationality of the messy desk with this law: Frequency of use draws near to us the things that are frequently used, so some messes accumulate for good reasons.

Kenner says that intelligent secretaries have long known that files in heavy use should not be refiled—that 80 percent of the action involves 20 percent of the files. But the 80-20 rule actually inconveniences clutterologists such as Kenner because, as noted in the 1963 *IBM Systems Journal*, the 80-20 rule applies, in turn, to the active 20 percent.

That is, if you keep 1,000 files, of which 200 bear most duty, then 20 percent of the 200—just 40 files—get most of the use, as do eight of those 40, and two of those eight. Two files make for a tidy desk.

Victoria gets her way because her father thinks she is perfect in every way and is becoming more so day by day. Unfortunately, Victoria consents only to one application of the 80-20 rule to her 175,000 Crayolas, stencils and other instruments of the serious business of being seven.

September 20, 1987

The Rolling Stones: A Revolt Turned Into a Style

When in blasting overdrive (and he never is not), Mick Jagger looks alarmingly invertebrate, like an eel being electrocuted. William James wrote about a man who could read while juggling four balls, a feat not much more remarkable than Jagger singing while hurling himself around a huge stage in the rain at R. F. K. Stadium. Jagger is an acquired taste, one acquired by several generations.

His time spent at the London School of Economics honed his business instincts, which are considerable, as a record-industry executive attests: "In his head he figured out what the French royalty would be on a record, doing the conversion and taking off the VAT tax." The addictive hold of rock music's hypnotic pleasures on those who grow up with it has caused rock to be called the perfect capitalist product: It intensifies demand by the process of serving it. And it is increasingly the vernacular of decreasingly verbal people.

Poetry has been defined as music subdued and transformed by reason. Jagger, a Byronic figure for generations unschooled in poetry, excited young people 25 years ago as someone mad, bad and dangerous to know. Today he and three of the other four Stones are older than Dan Quayle and by now they are evidence of our commercial civilization's power to tame radical forces, turning them into consumer goods.

A rock critic has said that rock 'n' roll produced "an unprecedented contradiction in terms, mass Bohemianism." Mass means middle-class. Middle-class Bohemianism of the 1960s, like the associated political radicalism, was recreational. Since the mid-1950s, rock music has been the signature of the baby boomers. They comprise a generation large enough and with enough leisure time and discretionary wealth to be a market for its own expressive culture.

In the fall of 1954, Davy Crockett coonskin caps became one of the early manifestations of baby boomers as a mass market. The Stones are the boomers' longest-lived cultural artifact. But they had, as it were, some memorable opening acts: Elvis Presley, James Dean, Holden Caulfield.

Presley, who exploded rock into the lives of white middle-class adolescents, saw the movie *Rebel Without a Cause* (1955) over and over, and could recite most of the lines of James Dean. Dean was the prototype of the mildly, vaguely alienated middle-class youth whose self-dramatization was problematic because all he had to feel alienated from was . . . parents.

A rock historian has formulated "Little Richard's First Law of Youth Culture": Please kids by horrifying parents. In 1956, on *The Ed Sullivan Show*, the cameras were focused chastely above Presley's pelvis. On the same show 11 years later, Jagger avoided network censorship by mumbling (his description) the title line of the song "Let's Spend the Night Together." Here, dear parents, comes your 19th nervous breakdown.

Jagger was adolescent insouciance with a dash of menace, an electrified, amplified Marlon Brando from *The Wild One* (1954). The Stones were packaged and marketed as the wicked siblings of those four winsome moppets (as they then seemed, thanks to good marketing): Paul, John, George and Ringo.

It has been well said that rock "turns revolt into a style," making revolt transitory and unserious, merely a swan song of childhood naughtiness. But there are those who take it seriously, even some who are deranged as the pose takes over their personalities.

The first clear sign of the baby boomers' distinctive self-awareness was the huge audience for (how anachronistic this now seems) a book. It was J. D. Salinger's *The Catcher in the Rye* (1951), the protagonist of which, Holden Caulfield, was a nonstop pouter defined by his concentrated, comprehensive dislike of adults. The young men (born in 1955) who in 1980 murdered the middle-aged John Lennon was clutching a gun—and a copy of *The Catcher in the Rye*.

Rock is the trigger and substance of the nostalgia of people who came of age with it. And this nostalgia is narcissism, fascination with episodes (songs, bands, "Woodstock Nation") important only because those people and those episodes were contemporaries. The thinker was right who said that such nostalgia is modern man's worship of himself through veneration of things associated with his development.

Not much development. Less and less. A, say, Bruce Springsteen concert is a literature seminar compared with a Stones concert. The Stones are nothing if not shrewd and they obviously know how hard it is for music, even rock music, to hold the light, thin, attenuated attentions of their audiences (which, judging by the Washington concerts, have an average age of thirtysomething). So the deafening music is—what shall we say? "leavened"?—leavened by explosions, blinding flashing lights, clouds of smoke, inflated women 55 feet tall.

It is a sensory blitzkrieg: "I am bombarded, therefore I am." It is, strictly speaking, infantile: pre-(post-?)verbal stimulation.

But the Stones, binding the generations, linger in the air, the incense in the children's private church. It is an interesting experience driving down broad suburban streets, listening to two eight-year-old girls in the backseat singing along with the radio—it is tuned to one of the "classic rock" stations—their clear, birdlike voices, as sweet as swallows, singing, "I can't get no satisfaction."

September 28, 1989

Stephen King: The Horror, the Horror

If you relish having your blood curdled and millions of Americans do, dim the lights and think about this: Stephen King's new novel, *The Dark Half*, had a first printing of 1.5 million hardbacks. Laid end-to-end they would reach from Chicago to Cincinnati, about 300 miles.

A nation's recreational tastes are important for their effects and as symptoms, and anything that so many people choose to do is fascinating, especially when what they choose is so unpleasant (". . . the man's face almost seemed to be boiled. . . . Sticky, unthinkable fluid ran down hillocks of proud flesh . . ."—you get the flavor). Unpleasant, but strangely pleasurable, surely, to be worth $21.95.

The plot skids along a sheet of blood and bursts of the bizarre. Thad Beaumont, King's protagonist, has a headache. Not surprising, that. He has a brain tumor and the surgeon removing it also removes from Beaumont's brain an eye (and three fingernails, two teeth and a nostril—no partridge in a pear tree, however). They are remainders of what would have been a twin had the fetal Beaumont not absorbed it in utero. This is somehow (a little suspension of belief is required and King, who recently published four novels in 15 months, does not tarry for fine points) related to Beaumont's real problem, which is George Stark.

Under that pseudonym, Beaumont, a serious novelist, writes schlock crime novels of extreme violence. When Beaumont stops writing them, Stark comes to life and is not happy. He carves his way toward Beaumont wielding a razor and a blowtorch with which to torture Beaumont's babies, if that is necessary to get Beaumont to start writing as Stark again.

Savagery erupts with metronomic regularity. Why do millions read it? Well, why do drivers slow down to gaze at highway carnage? There is a pornography of violence, and especially of sadism. Something in us is drawn toward what we are ashamed of being drawn toward. Call that something our darker half.

The fiction of horror and the supernatural has a distinguished pedigree, stretching from Homer (*Odyssey*) through Poe and Henry James. Beneath an arresting headline (KILL! BURN! EVISCERATE! BLUDGEON! IT'S LITERARY AGAIN TO BE HORRIBLE), Michiko Kakutani of *The New York Times* explains today's increase of hideous episodes even in serious fiction as, in part, a postmodernist return to traditional storytelling that yields accessible morals.

Kakutani notes that fiction dealing with heightened emotions and bizarre events was mass entertainment in the Victorian era when, as today, journalism supplied stories of lurid real-life episodes. Then as now there was anxiety about dissolving social values and evolving science and technology (industrialism).

Today's popularity of horror fiction and films has occasioned much heavy theorizing, such as that by the thinker who says (with special reference to movies in which folks get eaten), "We don't seem to have gotten used to being at the top of our food chain." The King phenomenon has loosed a torrent of sociology, including one fellow's notion that King is the sort of catharsis required by capitalism: "We are meant to feel always aroused, always unsatisfied. But even in the most advanced states of capitalism, no consumer is so heady with acquisitive power as to avoid the need to seek respite and expiation from living vicariously." Eastern Europe, be warned: First comes capitalism, then comes Stephen King with razor murderers to make it all bearable.

Two academics have studied horror films and concluded that teenage boys who watch the films stoically are—yep—attractive to girls, who are attractive to the boys when they shudder. That is social science doing what it so often does, stumbling upon the obvious with a sense of discovery.

However, a not-at-all-trivial datum is this: 60 percent of the audience for the "slash" and other horror films are black and Hispanic teenagers. People whose lives are menaced by everyday violence tend to feel helpless. They combat that feeling by identifying with violent aggressors.

The eyes of those audiences are glued to movie screens, not King's pages, but many young people do read him. There is nothing new about young people being attracted to things that "gross out" adult society. And it is perhaps nice that they are reading something other than cartoon books (the favorite nonrequired reading sold in college bookstores) and T-shirts. King's books (he compares them to fast food) may whet some appetites for gourmet reading.

But they may also be symptoms and, to some extent, causes of a desensitization of the mass audience. In the 19th century, that audience devoured serializations of Dickens's novels. Today's mass audience, shaped by graphic violence, may not be able to respond to anything subtler than a slashing razor.

December 10, 1989

Nubile Feet? Yes, and It Was a Dark and Stormy Night

(Drum roll) . . . and the envelope, please. *(Pregnant pause.)* A winner in the annual Bulwer-Lytton Fiction Contest is:

"The sun rose slowly, like a fiery furball coughed up uneasily onto a sky-blue carpet by a giant unseen cat."

It is heartening to see that standards are being maintained—standards of awfulness, that is. The coughing-cat sentence compares favorably with the following recent winner in the contest that challenges writers to compose the worst opening sentences for the worst novels never written:

"The camel died quite suddenly on the second day, and Selene fretted sulkily and, buffing her already impeccable nails—not for the first time since the journey began—pondered snidely if this would dissolve into a vignette of minor inconveniences like all the other holidays spent with Basil."

The contest is named after the writer who in 1830 published a novel that began, "It was a dark and stormy night. . . ." Bulwer-Lytton's sentence churned on until it coagulated in a description of the wind "fiercely agitating the scanty flame of the lamps."

The contest is linguistic vandalism with an academic rationale, literary delinquency with a legitimate purpose. Some sentences submitted are disconcertingly familiar. I have the awful feeling I have read a detective novel that began with this Bulwer-Lytton winner:

"There are things a good detective can feel in his bones, and Dillon Shane knew Jasmine Kimberly Collingsworth did not drown in her sleep on New Year's Eve." And every spy novel I read loses me in a hairpin-turn first sentence like:

"It came to him in a cocaine rush as he took the Langley exit that if Alrich had told Filipov about Hancock only Tulfengian could have known that the photograph which Wagner had shown to Maximov on the jolting S-bahn was not the photograph of Kessler that Bradford had found at the dark, sinister house in the Schillerstrasse the day that Straub told Percival that the man on the bridge had not been Aksakov Paustovksy, which meant that it was not Kliest but Kruger that Cherensky had met in. . . ." (That is about half the sentence that recently won the Bulwer-Lytton spy-fiction category.)

"During an exuberant rainfall, a languid bottle of salad dressing sat passively on a Formica countertop." Bulwer-Lytton sentences, polished to perfect imperfection, are works of antiart. They are clogged with metaphors, similes, adjectives and adverbs. The word pile into and crumble onto one another like (stop me before I overdose . . . the disease is catching) cars tailgating at high speed on a foggy freeway. Modifiers multiply madly, as in a "garden redolent of burgeoning tropical paradise."

Run for shelter, gentle reader: Rain is "splattering like raisins dropped by uncaring gods." But do not jostle the elderly woman whose lined face is "like a patchwork of meandering rivers strung together over a bed of waffles." Thrill to adventure: "The lovely woman-child Kaa was mercilessly chained to the cruel post of the warrior-chief Beast, with his barbarian tribe now stacking wood at her nubile feet. . . ." Admit it: You get guilty pleasure from the phrase "nubile feet."

The impressario of the Bulwer-Lytton contest is Scott Rice, professor of English at San Jose State. Because the contest demands only one sentence, it is, he says, perfect for persons "with short-winded muses." Obviously he is having fun, as are the authors of the 10,000 entries. But he has a serious point.

He believes that before you can write badly enough to win his contest, you must be a good writer. You must have a feel for how language misfires, how clumsy syntax can swallow thought. His contest is word-play with a pedagogic purpose. If you can figure out what makes things (sentences, painting, foreign policies) awful, perhaps you can reason back to rules of excellence.

"Clad in a light summer frock, the mauve print which James gave her when James was still interested in frocks and she in James, Vera sits brooding at the tea table and stirs a cup of what she expects is execrable Irish Breakfast, wondering why it is that when one's lovers become one's friends the resulting social discomfiture is impalpably but inescapably less intriguing than the sequestered malaise which results from the reverse."

As my blushing pen reproduces that sentence, a congressman is asking Admiral Pointdexter if a particular person had been asked to do something in connection with the Iran-contra debacle. The congressman asks if the person had been "tasked with the effort." A Bulwer-Lytton dishonorable mention to the congressman who treats "task" as a verb.

July 23, 1987

The Enjoyment of Joseph Alsop

Joseph Wright Alsop, the columnist, was, first and always, a fine writer: "The U.S. Army of the late 1920s and most of the 1930s was not only tiny and almost wholly without modern equipment, it was also almost completely dominated by an antiquated elite of cavalrymen, whose boots (always from Peel in London) shone splendidly, in contrast to their intellects, which did not." There, in one sentence, you have him—syntactically complex yet elegant, with an eye for the telling detail, and the sting of dry wit.

Administrations come and go but amid Washington's shifting sands there are grand outcroppings of rock. Alsop was an eruption of flint among less solid material. However, not even rock is immune to wearing down by time, and last week Alsop died of cancer at 78. When last I saw him, in July, he felt so sick he could not do justice to the lunch that came from his fabled kitchen. Yet such was his unquenchable curiosity, his unslaked appetite for learning, he was that day engrossed in Donald Keene's book *Travelers of a Hundred Ages: The Japanese as Revealed Through 1,000 Years of Diaries*. His body was dying but his mind still voyaged.

Washington is a city where action is valued more than, and often is disconnected from, thought. Here the life of the mind often has a narrow utilitarian cast. Alsop preached, and practiced, the usefulness of anything high, fine, noble. Journalists live tethered to events. Their occupational hazard is depletion of intellectual capital. Their challenge, to which none has arisen as well as Alsop did, is to irrigate their judgment and imagination with clear, cold waters from springs—history, literature, art—that flow far from the deadening everydayness of public life.

To Alsop's table came the leading public personages of five decades. Today such conviviality causes pursed lips among some self-appointed custodians of "journalistic ethics." Some journalists are too fastidious to be friends and confidants of leaders. Often these journalists are spurning choices not really open to them. They say a journalist cannot be friendly with, and also independent of, people of power. They say a journalist cannot be both congenial and, when necessary, adversarial. However, they speak only for, and of, themselves. One reason Alsop was a wise commentator is that he knew, with an empathy born of intimacy, the texture of life as political people live it.

Alsop had wonderful powers of invective, as with the Watergate culprit he described as a "bottom-dwelling slug." Alsop could dislike heartily. He disliked Walter Lippmann, who he thought had bad judgment and a weak character. On May 19, 1933, Lippmann, having heard a Hitler speech, pronounced it "genuinely statesmanlike" and "evidence of good faith," adding: "We have heard once more, through the fog and the din . . . the authentic voice of a genuinely civilized people." The anti-Semitism? Lippmann, a Jew, said that by "satisfying" the Nazi yearning to "conquer somebody" the persecution of Jews was "a kind of lightning rod which protects Europe." Lippmann, who was at best ambivalent about his Jewishness, was disgracefully silent about the Holocaust, and earned Alsop's disdain.

Reverence for Lippmann is reflexive among journalists who remember not much more about him than that he, like them, opposed the Vietnam War. Lippmann turned against the war at about the time the intelligentsia—that herd of independent minds—whose approval Lippmann valued, also turned. Alsop was a hawk to the end. But considering the political culture of the journalistic community in which Alsop worked, Meg Greenfield is right to say that "the term 'Vietnam dissenter' could most properly have been applied to one holding the position he did."

One evening in Oxford in the early 1950s Alsop, Isaiah Berlin, Stuart Hampshire and one other person, whose name is now forgotten, were discussing whom they would most like to see thrown off Magdalen College Tower. One person said Stalin, another said Joe McCarthy, a third mentioned another lurid villain. Alsop said: Adlai Stevenson. Alsop could not abide the side of Stevenson that caused Stevenson to say, when accepting the 1952 nomination, that he, like Christ in Gethsemane, had "asked the merciful Father, the Father of us all to let this cup pass from me." Alsop's political judgments were never just aesthetic. An Alsopian adjective—an encomium dispensed sparingly—was "long-headed." It denotes a compound of prudence and patience, the ability to wait for the ripeness of events and the toughness to pay the price of decisive, timely action. Stevenson was not, Alsop thought, long-headed. Alsop thought FDR was.

When leaving Alsop's house for what proved to be the last time, I paused by a portrait of Teddy Roosevelt and ventured the opinion that TR was the century's greatest president. "No," said Alsop. Not, "well, in my opinion" or "some would argue that . . ." Alsop just said: No, FDR was. In 1982, on the centenary of FDR's birth, Alsop wrote a lapidary "remembrance" which illuminated both subject and author. Alsop noted that Teddy Roosevelt at 21 wrote a serious book of sea power, whereas at about that age FDR was writing puerile editorials about the Harvard football team's deficient spirit. FDR's intellectual limitations, wrote Alsop, came to matter greatly when his world view mattered greatly. "For want of wide-ranging historical reading . . . his world view always retained something of the provincialism of the very provincial though very privileged American group he came from."

Alsop knew that group. His grandmother was TR's sister. Eleanor Roosevelt's father was TR's brother and Alsop's mother's cousin. His mother was a distant cousin of FDR. Alsop knew what Washington never learns, that everyone is provincial until educated to broader, deeper understanding. He valued intellect a lot but—and here is FDR's hold on his affections—he valued kindness more. Alsop considered FDR's greatest achievement "the inclusion of the excluded." FDR broke the virtual monopoly of his (and Alsop's) class on public power. And FDR had, said Alsop, "a capacity for enjoyment and for communicating enjoyment." In this there was, between Alsop and his distinguished relative, a strong family resemblance.

September 11, 1989

Sidney Hook, an Honest Man

Sidney Hook, the political philosopher whose exemplary life ended last week in its 87th year, was a combative man who died knowing that his side had won. It is wonderful to lead a life such that your autobiography is a survey of the intellectual vitality of your time.

Such is Hook's *Out of Step: An Unquiet Life in the Twentieth Century*. Hook liked to say that passions make for keen observations but defective conclusions. His is the story of a reasonable man's passions and a passionate man's reasonableness.

Born in Brooklyn and educated at City College when New York was intellectually vibrant, he was young when the Russian Revolution was, and like many intellectuals of his generation he read in that Revolution an ethical imperative. However, he was too good a philosopher not to soon reject Marxism, and too honest a man not to be energized against the mendacity required of those who support a false philosophy for political purposes. From the mid-1930s on, his life had the golden thread of antitotalitarianism.

In the 1930s he was a leader, with John Dewey, in exposing Stalin's show trials that preceded the assassination of Leon Trotsky. One of Hook's students, who occasionally visited Trotsky in Mexico, was one day in New York given a ticket to Paris by another leftist who claimed to be unable to use the ticket. In Paris, there was a "chance" meeting with a dashing "Belgian" who charmed her. Actually, he was a Spaniard, Ramon Mercader, who used Hook's student to insinuate himself into Trotsky's household, then murdered him.

In the 1940s, with Raymond Aron and others, Hook combated the communist and fellow travelers' hegemony in cultural institutions. In the 1950s, he was fiercely anticommunist and anti-McCarthyite. He paid a price in personal relations for being prematurely correct about so many things. It would have been nice, but uncharacteristic, for his critics to denounce Stalin before Khrushchev did.

Once in the 1960s—like the 1930s, a low, dishonest decade—Hook was in an audience for a lecture by Herbert Marcuse, a bad philosopher and darling of the New Left. It was Marcuse's usual harangue against the "repressive tolerance" of American culture and the "embourgeoisement" of American workers.

Hook asked: Did not the Voting Rights Act and other improvements in the civic standing of blacks indicate America's capacity for improvement? Marcuse answered that such improvements were useless because blacks were choosing the tawdry middle-class values of American civilization. Hook asked: "Which would you prefer, a situation in which the blacks had no freedom to vote or one in which they had the freedom to vote but chose wrongly?" Marcuse replied: "Since I have gone so far out on the limb, I may as well go all the way. I would prefer that they did not have the freedom to vote if they are going to make the wrong use of their freedom."

Using logic to saw off such limbs was Hook's life work. In the 1970s, he was a critic of the détente that preceded the surge of Soviet expansionism. In the 1980s, he was a critic of reverse discrimination, saying his opposition "goes back to the days and words of Hubert Humphrey." Hook, like Humphrey, was a liberal whom liberalism left by turning left.

Engagement in political controversies has often been fatal to the quality of intellectuals' work and to intellectual integrity. Hook showed that it need not be so. Most of the participants in his controversies are gone and it is hard to recollect the intensity of the arguments. If many of the controversies seem far removed from the way we live, thank Hook and others like him. Their efforts at intellectual hygiene helped make many mendacities into mere museum pieces of intellectual history, rather than the orthodoxies of regimes.

Marx's grave in London's Highgate Cemetery bears Marx's words: "The philosophers have only interpreted the world, in various ways; the point, however, is to change it." Marx, having misinterpreted reality, changed the world for the worse. Hook helped better it by understanding that the great argument is not between capitalism and socialism (an avalanche of evidence settled that) or between religion and secularism (Hook was a secularist), but between friends and foes of freedom.

"The older I become," he wrote at 85, "the more impressed I am with the role of luck or chance in life." The biggest intrusion of chance is the earliest. It decides when and where one is born. America and Hook were mutually lucky 86 years ago in Brooklyn. At the end, the author of *Out of Step* found himself in step with his century—or it with him. That satisfaction, not accorded many, was hard-earned by Sidney Hook.

July 20, 1989

Washington Unrefined

A tall, stately, elegant Washington monument, David Brinkley, has written a book, *Washington Goes to War*. Trees do not grow fast enough to produce the paper that will be needed to print copies of it when readers start spreading the word about his hilarious and instructive tour through the alphabet soup of wartime Washington's proliferating agencies such as PWPGSJSISIACWPB (it had something to do with plumbers).

It was a Washington of patriotic slogans ("An idle typewriter is a help to Hitler"); a Washington in which a gas mask once hung from the President's wheelchair and the second most powerful person was the Speaker of the House, a Texan whose office wall was adorned with five portraits of Robert E. Lee, all facing south, and who did not socialize because "these Washington society women never serve chili"; a Washington to which the Soviet foreign minister came carrying a suitcase filled with sausages, brown bread and a pistol; a Washington with 15,000 outdoor privies and a cleaning establishment that dealt with white flannel suits by taking each one completely apart at the seams, hand-washing each piece, drying each in the sun, then reassembling the suit in a process that took at least a week (longer when skies were cloudy) and cost $10.

Brinkley has written an impressionist history, comparable to a pointillist painting composed of small points of color which, seen whole, comprise a remarkably truthful record of reality. Impressionism was a style of painting especially accessible to the growing middle-class public of the late 19th century. Brinkley's book is history rescued from the sterility of the academic clerisy and made accessible to the general reader.

Since Napoleon, war has been an increasingly collective and collectivizing enterprise. It has been the great intensifier of forces and accelerator of history. The Second World War lit the long fuse of liberation for women and blacks. (At NBC, as elsewhere, women were not allowed to broadcast news because the company considered them "biologically incapable of total objectivity.")

There were many wartime drives for scarce materials such as rubber. (Interior Secretary Ickes scooped up the White House doormat, and a service-station sign announced, WE ACCEPT ANYTHING MADE OF RUBBER ACCEPT CONDOMS. One of Brinkley's riveting details, inserted in his narrative without fanfare, is that a scrap-metal drive collected an old slave chain from Mississippi. The melting of that chain was a sign of coming times.

Brinkley's book has an understandable undertone of melancholy about the transformation that war wrought on the provincial 19th-century city that Washington was until the 1940s. But the cure needed for what ails Washington today would be more of what has made today's Washington—growth. It needs a growing diversity. What ails Washington is the self-regarding, self-absorbed knowingness of a town with too few competing elites—commercial, financial, religious, academic, literary, artistic.

Much, but not too much, has been made of the recent move of the quarterly journal *The Public Interest* from New York to Washington. The move symbolizes the supplanting of New York by Washington as the intellectually ascendant city. Lawrence Mone of the Manhattan Institute is among those who worry, with reason, about unhealthy aspects of this.

Washingtonians, he says, pride themselves on merely instrumental knowledge, of how things work and the personalities who make them work. This produces a myopic pragmatism altogether too proud of itself and in need of enrichment by abstract speculation. Washington has a "brushfire-fighting mentality" and a blinkered indifference to questions not intensely practical.

The capital came to be in a swampy village because of a deal struck in Manhattan in June, 1790, when the secretary of state (Jefferson), treasury secretary (Hamilton) and a Virginia congressman (Madison) met. The deal was that the national government would move south and would pay the Revolutionary War debts, many of them owed to Northern financiers, many of whom were Hamilton's friends.

This was, as Senator Pat Moynihan says, an essentially "constitutional" settlement establishing "a separation of powers" as important in its way as that between the branches of government. Culture "in the largest sense" was in New York. Government was to be elsewhere. The result has been provincialism in both places.

When read with this in mind, Brinkley's is a cautionary tale about how the nation's capital achieved critical mass. Deprived of New York's diversity, Washington is, in Moynihan's words, "not prepared to be great. The power is unrefined. There are too few filters of sensibility through which ambition must pass toward fulfillment; too few standards that must be set." And too few Brinkleys.

April 14, 1988

The Bouillabaisse of Bookselling

NEW YORK—With its ornate black Beaux Arts facade embellished with gold leaf, 597 Fifth Avenue looks like a building with a furrowed brow, a pleasantly serious place. It looks like a bookstore, which it is, but not for long.

Intellectuals like loitering in bookstores and they like detecting signs of the decline of the West. They can do both simultaneously on January 22 when Scribner's bookstore closes its doors after 75 years. But discerning large cultural portents in small commercial decisions is usually, as in this case, a mistake. Bookselling is still a sphere of robust pluralism, even healthy eccentricity, among the more than 21,000 bookstores.

The 10-story Scribner's building opened in 1913 and until 1984 housed the offices of Scribner's publishing company, which was founded in 1846 and once dominated American publishing as no house has since done. Its authors included Edith Wharton, Edmund Wilson, Ring Lardner and Winston Churchill. In a fifth-floor office the celebrated editor Max Perkins dealt with Fitzgerald, Hemingway and the chaotic manuscripts of Thomas Wolfe. One of the first shoppers downstairs was Teddy Roosevelt.

But all that's beautiful drifts away like the waters, and when has beauty been a match for the iron laws of real-estate values? The basic problem is that Manhattan is made up of just 14,000 acres and those in midtown are so pricey that it is hard for book sales to pay the rent.

It can be done. There are several Fifth Avenue bookstores nearby. But the intractable problem is how to be sufficiently profitable while being interesting. What makes a bookstore worth supporting, or mourning, is a rich selection of a slow- as well as fast-moving titles drawn from back-lists and from the smaller sources of the nearly 56,000 new titles published each year.

Away from the highest-rent districts, bookselling on a small scale, as a haven of quirky individuality, is thriving, or at least surviving. Consider Bridge Street Books in Washington, D.C. It is the pride and joy of Philip Levy, 44, who in his bulky sweaters and unpressed slacks looks like what he is: a '60s radical who has come to terms with commerce.

Levy recalled, with middle-aged bemusement, an early crisis of conscience. He wanted to specialize in literature of the Left. Should he sell Henry Kissinger's memoirs? He did. Booksellers read election returns.

However, Levy's Georgetown store is a small island of individuality where his tastes and hunches are offered to the eclectic whims of bookstore browsers. He has packed about 8,000 titles into a two-story building 12 feet wide and 27 feet deep. He specializes in trade (high-quality) paperbacks and hardbacks, many of which you would not find in the sort of bookstores that sell board games and greeting cards.

His hardback best seller—he sold about 20 copies—during the Christmas season was Richard Posner's *Law and Literature* from the Harvard University Press. His second–best seller was *1791: Mozart's Last Year.* It is highly probable that no other bookstore in the nation had those two books at the top of its list. But other small stores had other odd lists because other proprietors exercised interesting discretion in what they decided to display.

One of the sublime delights of being an author is attending the teeming convention of the American Booksellers Association. There, you are apt to be told by a no-nonsense woman that she is "thinking about" ordering six, maybe even eight, copies of your book for her store, The Bookworm in Jackson, Mississippi. It is of course splendid when one of the large chains orders your book in the thousands, but there is a special pleasure in the personal judgments of these intense individualists who bring their interests to the attention of small portions of the reading public.

Among owners of, and aficionados of, small bookstores there is resentment of the big chains—Waldenbooks, B. Dalton, Barnes & Noble and Crown Books. The chains emphasize mass marketing and thus cater primarily to mass preferences. They enjoy economies of scale that enable them to get from publishers and give to customers discounts which small sellers cannot match.

But the existence of the chains does not mean the extinction of the smaller bookseller, any more than McDonald's has killed the neighborhood restaurant. Price isn't everything. Small bookstores survive because enough readers, like enough diners, will pay a bit more for the pleasures of personality.

So is the West doomed? Sure. So is the East. Everything is. Nothing lasts. Even the continents drift. Why should Scribner's stay there forever? But intellectuals are too easily convinced that commerce is homogenizing America. Bookselling, like the country it reflects, is still a bouillabaisse, not a bland puree.

January 15, 1989

Take Me Out to a Night Game

What is wrong with this picture? Nothing. But bitter controversy swirls around the things that cast the shadow on the grass in the picture. The picture is of Wrigley Field, where the Chicago Cubs have played daytime baseball since 1916. The shadow is cast by light standards. There will be night games at Wrigley. "The horror, the horror," say shocked "tourists." But their position is pure malarkey.

Playing some night games will enhance something that can stand a bushel and a peck of enhancing—the Cubs' competitiveness. The Cubs will play fewer games in the sauna of Midwestern summer afternoons. They will have less difficultly adjusting to the sharp difference between their home and away schedules.

Real baseball purists want to see the game played well. That consideration seems decidedly secondary to many Cub fans who natter on . . . and on . . . and on about the Wrigley Field ambience, gestalt, "experience," etc. While they are waxing poetic and semitheological about the sunshine (which can be found elsewhere) and the democracy of the bleachers (a democracy of, by and for the people privileged enough to skip work in the afternoon), the Cubs are getting waxed by better teams. Too many Cub fans seem to think that, leaving aside the mundane business of batting and pitching, and fielding, the Cubs are, morally, a cut above the other 25 major-league teams. Such fans think of the Cubs as baseball's Williamsburg, a cute, quaint artifact of historic preservation. They say lights are horrid because the Cubs are custodians of sacred tradition.

In 1913, when Churchill was a young First Lord of the Admiralty, some stuffy men accused him of traducing the traditions of the British Navy. "And what are they?" replied Churchill. "They are rum, sodomy and the lash." Wrigley Field's most conspicuous tradition is mediocre baseball. The Cubs have not won a pennant since 1945, the year the Dow Jones high was 195, *Carousel* opened on Broadway and a hit song was "On the Atkinson, Topeka and Santa Fe." The song was about passenger trains. The Cubs have not won a World Series since 1908, two years before Mark Twain died. The Cubs are now in the 80th year of their rebuilding effort. If—when—they fail to win the pennant this year they will break a record previously held by the St. Louis Browns: the longest span (43 years) without winning a league championship. In the seasons 1946 through 1987 the Cubs won 3,033 games and lost 3,567, putting them 534 games below .500 for that period. As this is written, they are below .500 this season. They could go undefeated in the 1989, 1990 and 1991 season and still be below .500 for the postwar era. Real Cub fans should say of tradition, "Enough already."

I will wager dollars against doughnuts that 99 44/100ths percent of all the "baseball purists" who have worked themselves into a tizzy about Wrigley's lights are not even serious fans. They are dime-store aesthetes cultivating a pose of curmudgeonliness, confusing that with a delicate sensibility. As they rhapsodize about Wrigley Field, untroubled by the aesthetic shortcomings of the baseball played there, they sound like those fishermen who say it is not catching fish that matters, it is the lapping of the water against the boat and the murmuring of the breeze in the pines—the ambience, gestalt, experience, etc. Fiddlesticks. People satisfied with fishless fishing will not catch fish and are not real fishermen. People satisfied with the Wrigley Field experience—see them swoon about the ivy on the outfield walls—should be as serious about baseball as they are about botany.

When next you see a Cub fan theatrically suffering the vapors at the mere mention of being deprived of day baseball 18 times a year (that is the night-game limit until the year 2002) ask that person to answer under oath this question: How often do you actually go to Wrigley Field to savor the ambience, gestalt, experience, etc.? Remember, baseball fans, like fishermen, fib. For example, you cannot swing a cat by the tail anywhere in America without conking on the head someone who swears that he or she spent his or her formative years in Brooklyn's Ebbets Field and that the cup of joy was forever dashed from his or her lips when the Dodgers went West. But if all the sentimentalists who say these things had really passed through the Ebbets Field turnstiles a tenth as often as they say, the Dodgers would still be in Brooklyn.

There have been night games in major-league baseball since 1935. Fifty-three years constitutes a considerable tradition in an institution only 112 years old (the National League, "the senior circuit," was founded in 1876. And were it not for Pearl Harbor, the Cubs today would be in their fifth decade of night baseball. Material for light standards had been bought and was donated to the war effort.

There is today too much aestheticization of judgments. Dukakis is "Zorba the clerk." Bush is preppie. But peace and prosperity are at stake. The point of politics is good government, not the display of charm. And the point of a baseball team is good baseball, not inferior play somehow redeemed by a pretty setting. Part of the Cubs' problem may be that too many Cub fans have an attitude problem. They are too devoted to the wrong thing. Let there be lights.

August 15, 1988

Therapeutic Rudeness and Other Signs of Decline

Riiiiiiinnng. Riiiiiiinnng. Riiiiiiinnng. Click. "Hi, it's me, I called to say Miss Manners has just published"—*thock*—"sorry, that's my 'call waiting,' let me put you on hold for just a second."

Pause. More pause. Still more pause.

"I'm back. Now, where was I? Oh, yes. Miss Manners says . . ."

Miss Manners is, yet again, dismayed. Having spent a lifetime writing bulletins from the front lines in the unending etiquette war, she has had so many searing experiences it is well-nigh impossible to flabbergast her, but flabbergasted she is by call-waiting.

That is the latest wrinkle in telephone annoyances. It is a system by which the telephone, while in use, makes a peremptory noise—*thock!*—telling the users that a third party wants the attention of the party who owns the telephone equipped with call-waiting. That misguided person would not have installed it were he or she not prepared to commit the impoliteness of receiving such incoming calls on a "last-come, first-served basis," thereby reversing the sensible order of precedence.

Miss Manners says call-waiting "is like a child screaming for attention while one is on the telephone." It is the second-worst idea, so far, from the world of telephones (It is impossible to write, in language suitable for a family newspaper, about the practice of playing music at people whose calls have been put on hold. Being on hold is tolerable; one can day-dream, write letters, read novels. But being on hold with Barbra Streisand singing about the lucky people who are needy for people? Intolerable.)

These are subjects for Miss Manners' severities in her latest canonical publication, *Miss Manners' Guide for the Turn-of-the-Millennium*. To people who practice the instant intimacy she so rightly deplores ("Nowadays, if someone said, 'Call me Ishmael,' few people would. Strangers would say, 'How y'doing, Ish?' "), Miss Manners is known as Judith Martin, the columnist.

To those of us who sit at her feet for guidance, she is the tutor who alternatively purses her lips and clucks her tongue (she might be able to do both, simultaneously) as she peers, with eyebrows arched and head tilted back sufficiently to elevate her nose for an editorial sniff, through her lorgnette at the stricken field of modern manners. Determined not to let society seek its own level, she fixes upon offenders a glare that would freeze claret or wilt lettuce, and vows not to let up until everyone is behaving.

"Ah," she says, "the adventure of modern living; so many interesting questions." Indeed.

We live in a statistically improbable moment, when divorces seem to outnumber marriages and, as she delicately observes, "Weddings are held at what we shall ever so gently call a later state of courtship." It is an interesting question. How does one properly refer to a person of the opposite sex sharing living quarters? POSSLQ does not have enough vowels to denote anything other than a small railway junction in Wales. How about householdmate? Paraspouse? Pliancé? (Rhymes with fiancé. Derives from "persons living in a noncommitted environment.")

Miss Manners stands at Armageddon and battles against people practicing therapeutic rudeness. She increasingly hears idealism invoked as an excuse for bad manners, as in the all-purpose, self-flattering explanation that "I am too free a spirit to . . ." (You name the social convention: wear socks, write thank-you notes, eat what is put in front of you.)

To all those shouting, "Oh, wow! Freedom," she says, "Nice try. Now get a grip." And she asks, "What about when society is right? That does happen occasionally."

Sincerity (as in, "Don't you think the fur in your coat looked better on the animal?") is no excuse for being offensive and neither is "caring," or even truthfulness. OK, it is true that I should not have ordered the fried mozzarella sticks to go with my steak-and-cheese sub. But be a little less caring, please, about my cholesterol level. As *Miss Manners* says, "Cut out all this helpfulness, right now."

She is almost comprehensive about what we must do, what it would be nice to do, and what it would be unforgivable to do or fail to do. However, the lacuna in her system concerns another device which, like the telephone, is ubiquitous: the automobile.

I know, I know: The basic challenge of manners is to be exposed to the bad manners of others without imitating them. But please, Miss Manners, tell us it is permissible to speak sharply to, if not strafe, drivers who sit in the left-turn lane at a red light and, when the light turns green, edge into the intersection and only then, when we already know, use their turn signals.

November 2, 1989

Enraging News About Anger

A doctor has published evidence that hostility is hard on the heart. I hate that doctor.

In the 1970s, research identified certain personality traits as significant risk factors in heart disease. Specifically, Type A people were said to be especially prone to heart attacks.

Type A people are the kind who do not stop to smell the roses (or even at stop signs). They are list-making, clock-watching workaholics who think about and do several things simultaneously (such as jogging while listening to taped lessons in Japanese). They play to win even against children, measure success quantitatively (sales made, patients seen, cases argued, columns written) and generally charge headlong through long days, from five A.M. aerobic through tutorials with Ted Koppel, then to sleep, perchance to dream, but dream efficiently.

I took such 1970s research to (so to speak) heart. I tried to become an Olympic-class rose-smeller, a disciplined smeller of a complete array of roses: more smelled today than yesterday, more tomorrow than ever. Now Dr. Redford Williams, director of Duke University's Behavioral Medicine Research Center, has published *The Trusting Heart: Great News About Type A Behavior*. What he calls great news is heartbreaking.

It is that "only the hostility and anger associated with Type A behavior actually contribute to heart disease." The problem is not workaholism or competitiveness or even perpetual impatience. Rather it is a quickness to anger that derives from a hostile outlook and cynical mistrust of people.

It is infuriating. They have taken from us dry martinis, marbled steaks, ham-and-eggs and most other pleasures, and now, not content with multiplying our reasons for being angry, they are proscribing anger. However, to be fair (this is especially enraging), Williams's fascinating book is a persuasive account of research regarding the biological consequences—the toxicity—of anger.

Since the 19th-century advancement of the germ theory of disease, medicine has emphasized the search for specific, often single, causes of particular diseases. The "one disease, one cause" approach has, Williams says, often been fruitful, as with the conquest of pneumonia by penicillin and of smallpox and polio by vaccines.

The search for a technological silver bullet is suited to the American spirit. However, it is less successful when the problem is not contagious diseases but the more complex diseases that now account for most of today's staggering health costs.

The search for multiple factors in heart disease has led to scrutiny of what Williams calls "negative mind-body interactions." Research has moved "from anecdote to epidemiology" regarding increased risks of illness as a result of the impact of states of mind on the body. New learning about the physiology of stress (brain activities stimulated, bodily chemicals released) points Williams to old religious teachings about living.

Be more tranquil, less worldly. "If yours is a hostile heart, you need to change it into a more trusting heart," trusting that people are essentially good and generally trying to be fair.

Heart disease is the major cause of death in the United States and other industrial societies. Perhaps that is because such societies place high value on striving, efficiency and other potentially stressful behaviors. Williams believes that especially since the 1960s there has been an evolution of cultural norms that are, strictly speaking, unhealthy: lonely individualism of restless enslavement to appetites.

His moral precepts would be banal were they not backed by interesting science. I have vowed to try to heed them when provoked to hostility by, for example, the outrage of improperly used turn signals.

Imagine this: You are in a hurry to get home to see the evening news. (No, not the network newscasts—SportsCenter on ESPN.) You are driving on a four-lane street, in the left lane. As you approach a red light, drumming your fingers on the steering wheel, you think: Should I get into the right lane—is the car in front of me going to turn left? No, its turn signal is not blinking.

But it should have been blinking. As the light turns green, the incompetent driver, who should be horsewhipped, pulls into the intersection, stops, and only then turns on his turn signal, thereby telling you what you already know. Next to you, in the right lane, the Type B rose-smellers are moving and you are not. Oh, to be driving a tank, for the savage pleasure of squishing the turn-signal criminal in front of you.

You are shouting inside: Move, or I'll kill you. Williams is whispering: Lighten up or you'll kill you.

May 11, 1989

Measuring Out Our Lives in Coffee Spoons

People like Michael Fortino are probably necessary, but is it necessary for him to be so depressing? Probably. He lives in Pittsburgh (which has suffered enough) and runs a consulting firm specializing in "priority time-management training," a new form of efficiency studies. His slogan should be, "You shall know the truth and it shall make you neurotic."

He says he has determined that over a lifetime the average American spends seven years in the bathroom, six years eating, five years waiting in lines, four years cleaning house, three years in meetings, one year searching for things, eight months opening junk mail, six months sitting at red lights. He also says the average married couple spends four minutes a day conversing and the average working parent converses 30 seconds a day with children.

Even if not all of those numbers describe your life, they are nevertheless cumulatively depressing. They underscore the fact that life is cumulative and we do in fact measure out our lives in coffee spoons of small activities.

Think of something, anything, you do for the minor pleasure of it. When you calculate its cumulative cost in time, the pleasure will evaporate. At least it will if you are, as Americans tend to be, determined to streamline your life for enhanced efficiency.

You say that for about 175 days a year you devote 15 minutes a day to reading baseball box scores? You wastrel. Try enjoying the sports pages tomorrow knowing that over 50 years your diversion devours 2,187 hours, or nearly 55 weeks of eight-hour working days.

Much of what we do we cannot avoid doing—shaving, commuting, shopping and all the rest of life's maintenance functions. It is shattering to calculate that you will spend 120 hours in the next decade brushing your teeth (assuming just two minutes a day). A depressing sense of being nibbled to death by ducks comes over you when you think how much time is consumed by demands that are little in themselves but not in their accumulation.

Let it be said of Fortino that he is as American as mass-produced apple pies and his profession has a fascinating pedigree. Its founding father was Frederick Taylor, pioneer of the "science of shoveling" and other applications of scientific management.

As historian Daniel Boorstin writes, it was not until clocks and watches became common that it became possible to analyze work in small units of time. Mass production made such analysis profitable: Assembly lines can move only as fast as the slowest talk can be performed.

This was one of those perceptions that, years later, look banal. But at the time it was a blazing insight. It blazed from Taylor, one of those creatively obsessed persons whose mania for efficiency led him to wear loafers in an era of high-button shoes, thereby saving Lord knows (and Taylor knew) how many minutes a year.

The exertion of becoming a valedictorian of his Exeter class produced in him a physical breakdown, for which a doctor prescribed manual labor. Taylor became a machinist and then a revolutionist, reshaping the concept of work.

His method was to break every factory operation down to its elementary components of workers' movements and then find the most efficient way to perform each. After three years of studying shovels and shovelers at a steel mill, 140 men were doing work previously done by 600 and were being paid 60 percent higher wages.

"Scientific management" became famous in 1910 when Louis Brandeis, representing shippers, convinced the Interstate Commerce to deny some railroads a rate increase because more efficient management of the railroads would produce sufficient profits. The human cost of the passion for efficiency was the reduction of workers from craftsmen to interchangeable parts in a relentless process of the sort Charles Chaplin satirized in *Modern Times*. But this human cost led to a new science.

A long, close study of six women assembling telephones at a Western Electric plant showed that no matter what variable varied, from the organization of the work to the sleep the women got the night before, their productivity improved. Suddenly it dawned on the researchers: Research itself—the show of concern for the workers—was enhancing efficiency. As Boorstin says, the "science of human relations" was born. The quest for efficiency led to a more humane workplace.

Fortino, like Taylor, has a humane vision: efficiency producing time for conversation. Time is money, but the efficiency story has an antimaterialist moral: Use money to buy time, not things. Fortino's cool numbers radiate a chilling intimation of our mortality. Time is the only thing that no one can ever have enough of.

September 1, 1988

Ms. Popcorn Detects Cocooning

NEW YORK—From her office at the foot of the street of dreams, No. 1 Madison Ave., Faith Popcorn can see a few years ahead. That is why BrainReserve, the company she founded 13 years ago, is coining money. She is a trend-detector and today she sees a future full of women with hips, men with martinis, and microwave meatloaf.

If Popcorn is right—she has prospered by being so in the service of corporations eager to anticipate consumers' whims—the heartbeat of America is fluttery. She paints a melancholy picture of the national mood as revealed in consumption.

We are, it seems, nearly neurotic about the supposed fragility of our health, fatigued to the point of making a booming industry of pizza deliveries, starved for self-expression yet so out of practice that wearing denim and cooking with mesquite seems expressive, hungry for tradition but with such an attenuated sense of the traditional that the hunger is satisfied by eating macaroni and cheese, eager to rebel against constrictive circumstances but satisfied to rebel by saying, "I'll not face another piece of fish; give me beef."

Popcorn has unwittingly pioneered the compliant theory of capitalism. By conducting thousands of interviews and scrutinizing hundreds of publications, she helps corporations connect consumer products with people's anxieties and grievances.

In flight from shoddiness, people will spend $2 for a Dove Bar, an upscale ice-cream bar. In flight from sterility, they'll pick products identified with striking personalities (Lee Iacocca, Frank Perdue). A Popcorn sunburst of inspiration is that people express themselves by identifying with such product personalities through consumption, and therefore what the fish industry needs is a "Frank Perdue of fish." A desire to express anger accounts for the popularity of Oprah Winfrey, Phil Donahue, *60 Minutes*, capital punishment and 800 numbers connecting callers to people they can shout at.

A nagging sense that the environment is unsafe and our behavior even more so—first herpes, now AIDS—has produced a grim preoccupation with "wellness," even unto theories connecting particular foods with the well-being of particular organs—broccoli for the respiratory system, brussels sprouts for hearts.

Not even the water is safe, but bottling the stuff can make the mundane an instrument of status: A "water bar" in Beverly Hills sells 200 brands of water. Popcorn says that because AIDS is giving thinness bad associations with a wasting disease, and because working women are eating more to sustain the energy burned up by stress, women increasingly are, if not Rubenesque, at least more ample.

"We've blanded out," says Popcorn, showing a way with verbs that earns her a place with honor on Madison Avenue. Down with white things, be they wines or veal, and up with beef. An oppressive sense of the everydayness of everyday life leads people to seek adventure and a sense of indulgence buying jeeps, shopping at Banana Republic, sipping mixed drinks, even going to Australia to hang out with Crocodile Dundee. Among trend-detectors, Australia-chic is a sure bet.

On the other hand, the harassments of daily life—looming nuclear incineration, rude waiters—have driven people to "cocooning." They have gone to ground in their dens with their VCRs and compact-disc players, snug in their Barcaloungers equipped with stereo headphones, the better to keep at bay the modern world, the discontinuities of which have produced a longing for tradition. That longing is so superficial, it is assuaged by '50s "mom food" like macaroni and cheese, and microwave meatloaf. Even crinolines are coming back.

Popcorn says the pace of modern life and the perpetual exhaustion of couples who have become parents for the first time in their thirties, leads to "grazing"—taking little bites off the surface of life. There is a desire for snippets of experience, hence *People* magazine, *USA Today*, and restaurants serving only hors d'oeuvres. Take-out food is selling well; every kitchen appliance but the microwave is being used less than it was four years ago.

Critics of capitalism have argued that in societies such as ours, all "natural" needs and desires have long since been satisfied, so capitalism will collapse unless manipulative marketing manufactures fresh appetites. The critics say our material progress depends on our moral degradation to manipulated creatures.

But if Popcorn ("We use products to cheer up our little boring lives") is correct, capitalism can be kept cooking by people who regard consumption as therapy for the disappointments and aggravations they suffer in a capitalist society. Given the guidance of trend-detectors, capitalism is not doomed by internal contradictions. It is powered by an internal dynamic of aches assuaged by creative products, such as microwave meatloaf.

June 11, 1987

Ambush Advertising and Other Attention-Getting Ideas

You are flipping, faster and faster, through *Time* magazine, racing to get past the grim stuff (stories about the Iran-Iraq war and Raisa Gorbachev's manners) to the safe haven of the back of the book. Suddenly as you turn a page, a bottle of brandy jumps up and bites you on the nose.

It is only a folded paper pop-up replica of a bottle and it does not really bite, although that is not from lack of trying. Trying too hard is the spirit of contemporary advertising.

Many a reader has been startled out of a year's growth by these advertisements that lurch up from ambush in magazines. They are like the pop-up bunnies of children's books. Pop-ups for grown-ups: *perestroika* on Madison Avenue.

Ordinary advertising is losing its power to get attention and shape appetites. This matters. America is a nation inured to the temptation of thrift, but advertising is nevertheless important in keeping the money moving in consumer spending, which accounts for $3 trillion of our $4.5 trillion economy.

Part of the problem is advertising clutter. The typical American is exposed to approximately 3,000 commercial messages—from newspapers to billboards—a day. It is said the average American spends a year and a half of his life watching television commercials. The number of messages transmitted by broadcast and print media doubled between 1967 and 1982 and may double again by 1997.

The sense of clutter is especially intense on television. Because 30 seconds of prime can cost an advertiser hundreds of thousands of dollars (in the 1950s you could run an epic-length 60-second commercial—the standard length then—for $15,000), there is a shift to 15-second formats.

Add to the regular commercials the five-second network promotions and it is not surprising that viewers feel abused. They can be bombarded by upward of 50 messages in a prime-time hour. But they can fight back.

Half of America's households have VCRs. Viewers can rent entertainment without commercials, or they can tape network entertainment and hit the fast-forward button when the commercials appear. Television sets have remote controls that enable viewers to mute the two-minute commercial "pods."

And now here comes the staccato future: On Japanese and European programs, there are 7.5-second commercials. That is long enough for "reminder" advertisements of products as familiar as, say, Coca-Cola.

To make the most of whatever hold they get on our attention, some advertisers are melding commercials: Coco-Cola, which owns Columbia Pictures, has advertised a movie within a soft-drink commercial. Miller Lite has advertised itself as just the stuff to wash down Frito-Lay product.

Some television commercials are avoiding hummable jingles that hymn the glories of, say, an antacid. Instead, they are using odd noise—droning, panting, buzzing, and other sounds—that psychologists say can trigger emotions and stimulate cognition. And there are zany ads: the bar of soap that foams in a man's pocket, the Isuzu ads that label the pitchman a liar.

Most amazingly, some advertisers have fallen back on language—plain words—to communicate. These less-is-more ads put words on the screen, no pictures.

What will they think of next? New places to put advertising, that's what.

"Alternative media" are getting a growing slice of the nearly $100 billion spent annually by American advertisers. Advertisements are appearing on parking meters, ski-lift towers, bus shelters, supermarket shopping carts, on closed-circuit television in supermarkets, on giant television screens at baseball parks, on mobile billboards towed by trucks through city streets, as lead-in segments on movies rented for home use, on restaurant menus, on the stall doors in restaurant restrooms, in dentists' offices, in hospitals, in doctors' lounges and even doctors' scrub rooms. The advertisements there are for financial services. One does hope that, while scrubbing, the surgeons are thinking of things other than their stock portfolios.

Maybe most of this advertising is audible and visual wallpaper—there, but not noticed. The increasing desperation of the barrage suggests advertisers' anxieties about diminishing impact. One shudders to think about what they will try next.

Perhaps magazines soon will have pop-up contraptions that grab readers by the lapels and hold on for however long it takes for the average reader to recover from the shock and read the text celebrating the brandy. It will be enough to drive you to drink, which is, come to think about it, the idea.

December 17, 1987

Spenser Becomes (Say It Ain't So!) Sensitive

BOSTON—The burly man with the bushy moustache sips his Samuel Adams beer in the Ritz-Carlton bar near Newbury Street, a shopper's paradise, and says to his wife, "Joan, there is somewhere in the middle of the Arabian peninsula you would like to shop. You would like to shop in Iran."

Tough guy, right? Wrong. Robert B. Parker, author of 16 novels featuring the private eye Spenser, is, I regret to report, a gentleman. That may explain why Spenser is becoming that annoying paragon, "The Eighties Man." Spenser is becoming . . . sensitive.

Time was when the fictional private eye was an unreconstructed primitive, not a reproach. He smoked like a chimney, his only exercise (aside from punching people) was bending his elbow, he was decidedly pre-Miranda in his construction of criminals' rights, he read nothing but racetrack tout sheets and ate in greasy spoons. He represented the anarchic impulse that we who wear civilization's bridle can express only by identifying with a fictional private eye.

Now he is being taken from us. The melancholy decline of the detective into good character, Eighties-style, was sealed in 1985, in the 12th Spenser novel when Spenser used the R-word. He said to his lover, Susan Silverman, "I'd be pleased to spend the rest of my life working on this relationship."

That is the new voice of the new ideal, the Vulnerable Man. Can you imagine the word "relationship" issuing from the lips from which Bogart's cigarette drooped?

In a nifty essay in *Harper's*, Charles Nicol notes that today's fictional detectives are becoming domesticated, as the essay's droll title suggests: "The Hard-Boiled Go to Brunch." The hard-boiled are becoming good eggs, have "gone from Mean Street to Easy Street and moved in with Ozzie and Harriet," where they are practicing connoisseurship and aerobics.

The closing of the frontier in the 1890s drove the cowboy to town, where he became a detective. Nowadays in town, Spenser dines in yupped-up restaurants thick with hanging plants that remind him of Rousseau's paintings. Spenser does occasionally drink too many margaritas, but then he goes jogging, lifts weights, does gourmet cooking and soaks up poetry like a sponge who has earned a Ph.D. in English lit. Parker did that, writing a dissertation on "The Violent Hero, Wilderness Heritage and Urban Reality," a study of some fictional detectives.

Nicol recalls D. H. Lawrence's judgment that James Fenimore Cooper's frontiersman, Leatherstocking, was "a saint with a gun . . . an isolate, almost selfless, stoic, enduring man . . . the very intrinsic–most American." Later, Leatherstocking, private eye, opened up a walk-up office in the inner city. And today his gumshoes are Nikes that cushion the concrete.

Parker's novels, which will gross about $5 million for Dell this year, are used in some schools for delinquent children to get the rascals to read. Young readers get a satisfying amount of toughness (especially from Spenser's black sidekick, Hawk—Sancho Panza with a black belt) with some poetry insinuated.

"Hawk and I stood still. No one got out of the car. 'The only sound's the sweep of easy wind and downy flake.' Hawk unsnapped his Red Sox jacket . . ."

"Death is the mother of beauty," Spenser remarks when Susan says that life's hazardousness makes things more precious. Spenser descends steps "with wand'ring steps and slow." When he jokes with Susan about being too tough to get sunburned, she murmurs, "I'd smite the sun if it offended me." He tells a friend that the noblest love exists "only when love and need are one and the work is play for mortal stakes." Recovering from a reverie, he says, "Human voices wake us and we drown." When Susan suggests he propose marriage, he says, "Songs unheard are sweeter far." When feeling amorous, he says to Susan: "Complacencies of the peignoir and late coffee and oranges in a sunny chair, and the green freedom of a cockatoo upon a rug." She, ever sassy, says: "I never heard it called that."

Tough guys of yesteryear were not given to speaking with the tongues of (in the paragraph above) Robert Frost, Wallace Stevens, Milton, Shakespeare, Frost again, Eliot, Keats, Stevens again. (Parker says the passages are sometimes not quite accurate because Spenser calls them up from memory.)

Joan, like Susan, is an employee of the Massachusetts department of education, and has what may be an Eighties Woman's unconcern about the fact that millions of readers think Susan's sex life is hers. Parker growls, "I've toned it down for publication."

Now that's hardboiled, right? No, he still has a soft yolk as he and Joan walk into the misty autumn evening up Newbury Street holding hands.

October 18, 1987

Tom Wolfe's Lasting News

NEW YORK—Literature has been defined as news that stays news. Tom Wolfe's crackling new novel, *The Bonfire of the Vanities*, is being avidly read—actually, gulped—here and in Washington and elsewhere where news is devoured. The best seller reverberates with subjects in today's news. However, it also touches passionately on perennial themes that will give it staying power.

In its fullness, its fascination with a city and social classes and the movements of money and morals, and in its capacity to convey and provoke indignation, the novel is Victorian, even Dickensian. Yet in its themes and characters, it is as contemporary as this autumn's headlines.

Bonfire is Wolfe back where he belongs, in the take-no-prisoners rambunctiousness of his earlier books about abstract art, modern architecture and the "radical chic" politics of limousine liberals. His protagonist is Sherman McCoy, 38, bond-trader supreme and, in his eyes, "Master of the Universe." It is a shattering story of total loss of mastery when McCoy and his mistress get lost in his Mercedes in the moonscape of the South Bronx and, roaring away from a fracas with two young blacks, fatally injure one of them. McCoy becomes what the white elected district attorney of the Bronx desperately desires: the Great White Defendant.

There is, as in Dickens, a cartoon quality to some characters and episodes, such as the dinner given by a "social X-ray" ("an impeccably emaciated woman") who is "this year's hostess of the century." And there is a nouvelle cuisine restaurant serving "veal Boogie Woogie"— rectangles of veal, squares of spiced apples and lines of pureed walnuts arranged like Mondrian's painting *Broadway Boogie Woogie*.

But Wolfe's depiction of the processing of human raw material in the criminal-justice system is hair-curlingly faithful to fact. And there is a ring of truth in the episode when a journalist asks a Bronx high-school teacher if the injured boy is an "outstanding" student and the teacher replies, "We use comparative terms, but 'outstanding' isn't one of them. The range runs from cooperative to life-threatening."

Critics have a partial point when they complain that Wolfe's fascination with clothes and furniture suggests an inability to deal with things beneath surfaces. His strength is not the inner lives of his characters (although he chillingly conveys the emotional vertigo of a "respectable" person suddenly on the receiving end of the criminal law). However,

Wolfe's subject is the inner life of another kind of organism, a seething city.

Besides, one of Wolfe's themes is that too much of the tone of our time is set by people like McCoy who have no stable selves, only a constantly shifting composite of elements acquired from the social environment. The class Wolfe most sparingly describes lacks moral ballast, and Wolfe leaves hovering in the air the implication that this may be both cause and effect of the "immense, new inexplicable wealth," wealth related more to sharp practices than to real productivity.

Wolfe relies much more on his reporter's eye, a gimlet eye, than on any muse to move his pen. So did another novelist who was first a journalist: Dickens. Critics who call the result a "conservative" novel are more correct than perhaps they understand.

Certainly some conservative hobbyhorses get ridden hard. There are withering sketches of trendy Christians making guilt-assuaging contributions to a black clergyman-operator, a self-styled "street socialist" who profits handsomely from the government's racial spoils system, and "journalists peddling mockish compassion."

But Wolfe also expresses an older, deeper, noble conservatism that should discomfit those among today's conservatives whose philosophy is fully expressed by market-worship and getting and gaining. Wolfe casts a cold eye on the ethos of overripe capitalism as exemplified by the frenzies of people swapping paper. You may laugh aloud, then quickly wonder what is really funny, about the episode when McCoy flounders while trying to answer his six-year-old daughter's question: "Daddy, what do you do?"

Wolfe is wickedly amusing about, but not amused by, the sight and sound of "the greed storm" in a Wall Street trading room: "the sounds of well-educated white men baying for money on the bond market." Flocking to Wall Street to do that is, Wolfe suggests, unworthy of "the sons of the great universities, these legacies of Jefferson, Emerson, Thoreau, William James . . . inheritors of the lux and the veritas."

Bonfire is news that will stay news because a century hence readers will find preserved in it the strong flavor of some unfortunately important slices of life in our time.

November 22, 1987

"Play Bail!"

The second pitch Ed Cicotte of the White Sox threw in the first game of the 1919 World Series hit Cincinnati's leadoff man. New York gamblers got the signal: The Series was fixed. Today, in a political season that mocks the idea of progress, a season loud with lamentations about sleaze in Washington and sharp practices on Wall Street, it is well to revisit an era when America was really raw.

The era is accessible through the movie *Eight Men Out*, based on Eliot Asinof's book of that title about the Black Sox scandal. There are two fine novels on that subject, Harry Stein's *Hoopla* and W. P. Kinsella's *Shoeless Joe*, which is being made into a movie. Who, half a century from now, will write novels and make movies about Watergate? As many as today are interested in the Teapot Dome scandal. But when scandal touched baseball, it touched a national nerve.

The Black Sox scandal involved two timeless themes of art: love and regret. In that instance, it was love of vocation and regret about losing it. The most poignant figure was Shoeless Joe Jackson, the illiterate natural who compiled the third-highest batting average in history and who was so reflexively great that even when throwing the Series he could not stop himself from hitting .375 and setting a Series record with 12 hits.

The scandal is a window in a dark basement of American history. In 1919, Americans were feeling morally admirable, if they did say so themselves, and they did. They had been on the winning side in the "war to end wars." The fixed Series occurred three months before the beginning of a misadventure in moralism, Prohibition.

But gambling was as American as the gold rush—the dream of quick riches—and when the government closed racetracks during the war, gamblers turned to baseball, which then was America's biggest entertainment industry. Hotel lobbies where teams stayed teemed with gamblers. "Hippodroming" was the 19th-century word for throwing games, and in postwar America there was a new brazenness by gamblers.

On September 10, 1920, various Wall Street brokerage houses received "flashes" on their news wires: Babe Ruth and some teammates had been injured in an accident en route to Cleveland. Quickly the odds on that game changed, and the gamblers—the source of the lie—cleaned up.

The White Sox conspirators assumed they would get away with it because they assumed, almost certainly correctly, that other major-leaguers had gotten away with fixes. The team owners, frightened about the possible devaluation of their franchises, rushed out and bought some virtue in the person of a federal judge to serve as baseball's first commissioner.

Kenesaw Mountain Landis, with his shock of white hair over craggy features and his mail-slot mouth, looked like Integrity Alerted, just as Harding, elected in 1920, looked like a President. Landis was a tobacco-chewing bourbon drinker who would hand out stiff sentences to people who violated Prohibition. He had a knack for self-dramatizing publicity. He fined Standard Oil of Indiana $29,240,000 in a rebate case (the Supreme Court overturned him) and tried to extradict Kaiser Wilhelm on a murder charge because a Chicagoan died when a German submarine sunk the *Lusitania*.

Landis barred from baseball eight Sox players, including one who merely knew about the conspiracy but did not report it. It was rough justice. Nothing happened to the gamblers, and some of the players were guilty primarily of stupidity and succumbing to peer pressure. Most of them were cheated out of most of the promised money and only one player made much ($35,000). But roughness can make justice effective. Baseball's gambling problems were cured.

The 1920s, the dawn of broadcasting and hence of hoopla, would wash away memories of the scandal. Those years were the Golden Age of American sport—Babe Ruth, Jack Dempsey, Gene Tunney, Red Grange, Knute Rockne, Bobby Jones, Bill Tilden, Man o' War.

From Wall Street to Main Street, and including both ends of Pennsylvania Avenue, America back then—when a U.S. senator appeared in advertisements endorsing Lucky Strike cigarettes—was immeasurably less scrupulous about standards of behavior than it is today. Baseball put its house in order because of the Black Sox. Ten years later the crash ushered in a new age of regulation of financial institutions. And various scandals, before and after Watergate, have produced refinements (and some overrefinements) in rules about comportment in the corridors of power.

Civilization advances by fits and starts, often stimulated by shocked sensibilities. As another baseball season comes to a climax, it is well to consider how far we have come in the 68 years since Chicago children began their sandlot games with the cry "Play bail!"

October 6, 1988

"I Was Raised But I Never Grew Up"

SARASOTA, FLA.—Baseball, sport of the long season and strong oral tradition, tells of the time when the Cincinnati Reds plane hit severe turbulence and Pete Rose said to a teammate: "We're going down. We're going down and I have a .300 lifetime average to take with me. Do you?" The teammate's response, which could reasonably have been homicide, is not recorded.

As this is being written, while teams break camp and head for hard work, Rose's infractions, if any, regarding rules about gambling, have not been revealed. No such infractions are unserious. However, much good news about Rose has been revealed through the seasons.

Rose has baseball in his chromosomes. Tell him Lindbergh flew the Atlantic in 1927 and he responds, "The year Ruth hit 60." To you, 1941 means Pearl Harbor. To Rose, 1941 means DiMaggio hitting in 56 consecutive games and Williams hitting .406. A statistician once tried to stump Rose with this arcane question: What active player has the highest ratio of flyouts to groundouts? Rose replied, "Easy. Gary Redus." Rose was right.

"The trick," said Casey Stengel, "is growing up without growing old."

"I was raised," Rose once said, "but I never grew up."

"All games," says baseball writer Tom Boswell, "offer an alternative reality," and baseball, with its relentless schedule and statistical richness, particularly appeals to the fanatical personality. But Rose the manchild has an adult understanding of the ethic of sport.

He was last the focus of national attention four seasons ago in his quest for his 4,192nd hit to break Ty Cobb's career record. Boswell, in his new collection of baseball essays, *The Heart of the Order*, remembered the Sunday in Chicago that began with Rose two hits shy of Cobb's 4,191. That night the Reds would head home for a soldout series where he would break the record.

Player-manager Rose was not going to play that Sunday because the Cubs had scheduled a left-handed pitcher. But the left-hander got hurt, was replaced by a right-hander, and Rose immediately wrote himself into the lineup. By the fifth inning he had tied Cobb with two hits.

In the ninth inning the score was tied, no outs, Reds runners on first and second, Rose at bat. He could sacrifice the runners over to second and third, saving The Hit for the home folks. But Dave Parker, a slugger, was on deck. If Rose sacrificed, the Cubs would walk Parker with first base open. So Rose calculated, reasonably, that the Reds would have a slightly better chance of winning if he tried for a hit.

He failed. To get a hit, that is. But he succeeded brilliantly at showing, as Boswell says, the meaning of the phrases "integrity of the sport" and "best interest of the game."

Boswell rightly notes that Rose, like Cobb, is not a balanced personality. But Cobb was a hideous caldron competing with ugly ferocity. Rose combined cheerfulness and a competitiveness that burned with a hard, gemlike flame. He competed simultaneously against the other team and his own high standards.

Sport can produce self-absorption, and a moral sense that is sharp only because, like a knife blade, it is very narrow. This leads some stars to a sense of exemption from the restraints relevant to others. Rose may not have resisted that temptation.

But one reason for participating in sports is to become better—better at the sport and in the soul. Acquisition of particular skills leads to appreciation of all skills. To learn a sport is to learn what mastery means, even if you fall short of it. Playing a sport, and appreciating the play of a Rose, is an apprenticeship in craftsmanship.

Becoming better at something is called self-improvement, a term with two meanings. It means improving one's self, one's character, one's core identity. It also means unavoidable loneliness, getting better by oneself, in submission to severe self-judgments, in the aloneness of private determination, under the lash of the necessity to satisfy one's demanding self. Sport can be an exciting and elevating school.

So:

In a restaurant near Wrigley Field there is this sign: ANY EMPLOYEE WISHING TO MISS WORK BECAUSE OF DEATH OR SERIOUS ILLNESS PLEASE NOTIFY THE OFFICE BY 11 A.M. ON THE DAY OF THE GAME. In that spirit, the teachers of Victoria and Jon Will are hereby notified that, because of an annual April emergency, Victoria and Jon must be in Baltimore Monday afternoon. But Geoffrey Will will be in school, drawn by love of learning (that's a joke, son) and baseball practice.

April 2, 1989

Only—Only!—The Pleasure of Words

Your children have been out of school and underfoot for less than a month and already you are counting the days—minutes, you say?—until school regathers them to its bosom in blessed September. For now, enroll them for two hours in Welton Academy. You, too, might as well matriculate for the pleasure of studying poetry with John Keating.

Keating, played with restrained perfection by Robin Williams (there is no "Goooooooooooood Morning Vermont!"), is the intense but deft English teacher whose spirit drives *Dead Poets Society*. This movie may wean a few adolescents away from addiction to the merely visual. It can spark appreciation of the raptures—that is not too strong a word—they can receive from words.

The title itself speaks well of the movie's makers. Notice, no roman numeral. In this summer of sequels (coming soon, *Ghostbusters Go Star Trekking Through a Nightmare on Elm Street with Indiana Jones, Part XIV*) this is an original idea. The title is quirky and probably off-putting to the lowing bovine herd of people who are put off by anything odd. Poets? Today, slam-bang mindless action seems required to arrest the attention of the jaded public with its flickering five-second attention span. This movie promises only—only!—the pleasure of words.

A prep-school teacher as hero? Keating is heroic, but not in the banal manner of the whip-cracking, death-defying archaeologist Jones. Keating's heroism is his discipline, the purity of his devotion to his vocation. It is, for him, literally a *vocatio,* a calling. Language spoken by dead poets calls him. He will summon from some sons of the upper class a sense of the wonderful wildness of life.

Wildness is severely suppressed at staid Welton in rural Vermont in 1959. But Keating enkindles seven students who revive a secret society, the Dead Poets. It meets after midnight, against school rules, in a cave, where poetry is read after an invocation by Thoreau: "I wanted to live deep and suck out all the marrow of life." When they prance through the forest fog toward the cave they resemble druids in duffel coats. Youth usually has its private language. The seven boys experience from poetry a bonding and delight that today's youth derive from rock music and the pathetic verbal slouching of rap.

Robin Williams's favorite poet is e. e. cummings. That figures. Or:

tHa)t fi!Gu s. cummings, whose exuberance was too protean for ortho-

     r

     e

dox typography, said

> the Cambridge ladies who live in furnished souls
> are unbeautiful and have comfortable minds.

Williams's Keating begins refurbishing his pupils' souls by telling them they are mortal, "food for worms, lads! . . . *Carpe diem*, lads." The boys declaim lines from Whitman while kicking soccer bolls. Keating's credo is Whitman's, "the powerful play goes on and you may contribute a verse."

A powerful teacher like Keating may at times teeter on the brink of intellectual bullying, making individuality mandatory. However, Williams rightly describes Keating as a "catalyst" for the boys, and Keating periodically recedes from the story. That is the movie's point. Keating is always there because a good teacher is a benevolent contagion, an infectious spirit, an emulable stance toward life. That is why it is said good teachers enjoy a kind of immortality: Their influence never stops radiating.

The school (actually, St. Andrew's in Delaware) has an N. C. Wyeth mural. On one side, boys surround a figure of Liberty; on the other, industrialists surround a drafting table. The mural serenely suggests the easy compatibility of liberty and practicality, the free man as pragmatist. The movie sees a shadow over life, a tension between the poetic and practical impulses. Both are natural and dignified. What is perennially problematic is accommodating individuality and social ambition.

The story is set on the eve of the 1960s, so it may seem quaint that Keating must toil to overcome student passivity. Actually, few '60s students fit the '60s stereotypes. Furthermore, this story of adolescent awakening is both of the late '50s time, and timeless. Although the 1950s are called years of "conformity," the principal conformity was that of the chorus decrying it. The characterization of the Eisenhower years as "the bland leading the bland" does no justice to the intellectual ferment and literary vigor. David Riesman's *The Lonely Crowd* (1950), C. Wright Mills's *White Collar* (1951), Sloan Wilson's *The Man in the Gray Flannel Suit* (1955) and William Whyte's *The Organization Man* (1956) anticipated a 1960s anxiety, the suffocation of individuality by social structures and pressures. In *Dead Poets Society* these pressures are incarnate in a thin-lipped father practicing parental fascism and hounding his son to Hell and Harvard Medical School.

There was in the '50s an unhealthy concern with producing "well-adjusted" (to what?) adolescents so "well-rounded" they had no edges.

Keating is an admirable sort of '50s figure, an intellectual eager to carve edges or prevent them from being abraded by the rasp of a dull school. However, he is not a harbinger of the 1960s, not a politicized academic. His politics (and, for all I know, Robin Williams's) may be part Nietzsche, part Pogo. The power of his personality is in the purity of his conviction that literature, the high mountain pass leading to passionate understanding, is so large and absorbing it leaves no time for lesser, supposedly more "relevant" (to what?) matters.

Hollywood has an almost unconquerable itch for moral black and white, and this movie has a two-hanky ending that manipulates emotions too mechanically. But at the core of the movie is a flinty, unsentimental message: The wildness of life can be dangerously wild. Creativity can have painful costs that must be paid in the coin of personal, family and social stresses.

Speaking of stress, while waiting for September do note that Keating tells the boys they may address him either as Mr. Keating or O Captain! my Captain! (from Whitman's poem about Lincoln's death). This summer, answer your children only when so addressed. It will work wonders for your morale, the tone of your household and the caliber of the long days until Labor Day.

July 3, 1989

Father and Hot Air

ASPEN, COLO.—By September, when sunshine has bleached all marks previously made by schooling on children, parents seek ways to insinuate edification into entertainment. Thus the three Will children recently found themselves hanging beneath a hot-air balloon in a wicker basket so small they could not dodge a little learning.

Ballooning, like skiing and sailing, involves collaboration between the individual and natural forces. Except for periodic bursts from the propane heater, balloonists experience a silence more pure than that of a meadow. And there is the luxurious dependence on wind. It is luxurious because it removes the burden of decision: You go whither the wind tends. Best of all, ballooning gives dad an opportunity to be didactic to a captive audience.

Ballooning is a booming pasttime, as it should be (say I, as the children's eyes begin to glaze) in the Constitution's bicentennial summer. Ballooning captured the Founders' imagination as an expression of freedom. John Jay, Benjamin Franklin, John Adams and his son John Quincy saw some of the earliest balloonists while negotiating the Treaty of Paris in 1783. George Washington, a better President than meteorologist, anticipated a day when "our friends at Paris will come flying through the air instead of ploughing the ocean."

At first, would-be balloonists believed it was smoke itself, not heat, that pushed ashes up chimneys, so they fueled fires beneath balloons with old shoes and rotten meat. Then when they got their physics straight, they had a moral problem to solve.

In 1783, a balloon made a sheep, a duck and a rooster the planet's first air travelers. Man would not be next, but Louis XVI, who was a bit pre-Miranda in his thinking, wanted to send up a criminal, in case flight proved unhealthy for humans. However, a marquis convinced the king that the honor of succeeding where Icarus had failed belonged to the gently born.

So on November 21, 1783, two gentlemen made mankind's first flight, rising from the Bois de Boulogne in front of Louis, Marie Antoinette and 400,000 others—approximately the population of Paris. Two years later, in a balloon using "flammable air"—hydrogen—one of the two gentlemen became the first person to die in an air crash.

On June 24, 1784, Edward Warren, a 13-year-old Baltimorean, went aloft in a tethered balloon, there by becoming the first American to take flight from the Republic's soil. It is not recorded if he also was the first American air traveler to have his luggage lost.

As the balloon floats over elk herds on the mountain slopes below, the children, fascinated by the physics, enthralled by the history and awed by the beauty, pepper father with questions: When is breakfast? Where is breakfast? What is for breakfast? To the undisguised dismay of the children, their questions elicit yet another freshet of information from father.

He says that it is a tradition to have wine and food at the end of a balloon voyage. The tradition reflects the fact that when early balloons, belching smoke, landed unannounced on farmers' fields, the farmers often concluded, not unreasonably, that the balloons were Satan's devices.

The farmers attacked the balloons, and sometimes the balloonists, with pitchforks. So balloonists carried food and drink with which to appease the farmers.

Such is mankind's inclination to put all inventions at the disposal of Mars, that even the silent, graceful balloon has been pressed into war service. Balloons were used for surveillance of enemy lines during the Civil War. They were used for getting passengers and mail in and out of Paris when the city was besieged by the German army in 1870.

Furthermore (a word that causes the children to flinch in anticipation of still more information), in late 1944 and early 1945 the Japanese launched thousands of bomb-carrying gas balloons high into the jet stream over Japan. Only 285 made the 6,000-mile voyage, scattering along the coast of the United States and Mexico. On May 8, 1945, six Oregonians discovered one and became the only people killed on American soil by enemy action in the Second World War.

Warming to his theme, father is about to explain the cultural importance of the fact that until construction of the Eiffel Tower, balloonists were the only people who had seen a city from higher than the highest rooftop. But father subsides, knowing that all information bounces harmlessly off the invisible shells that surround children in summer, protecting them from mental improvement.

However, if around Labor Day you belabor your children with information, they may regard school as a refuge where teaching is at least not attempted by a parent, who is supposed to be a friend and so should not do that.

September 6, 1987

Modernity Arrived by Bicycle

CHEVY CHASE VILLAGE, MD.—In this constitutional Republic, the weather is free to do what it wants and what it often wants to do in Washington in December is drizzle. But this Christmas Day, drizzle or no, holds in store for me a bicycle ride to Mt. Vernon, a 27-mile journey about which this can be said: It could be worse.

Worse is being home at midday Christmas with children who have unwrapped their presents, broken most of those that were not instantly boring and discarded those that needed the batteries that daddy neglected to purchase.

By midday the children are demanding that daddy assemble the gift given by a sadist. It is a do-it-yourself computer with 4,789,265,974 indispensable parts, one of which was vacuumed up with the pine needles that fell when the tree did, a casualty of the general hysteria. The 12-year-old boy will not even sit in the same room with the—if he will pardon the word—book that he lifted from its wrapping the way you would lift a dead carp, gingerly, with thumb and forefinger, to minimize contaminating contact with learning.

By midday Christmas, the tattered remnants of peace and goodwill are retreating before the onslaught of hyperactive children, whose boiling energies can best be burnt off in the open air, on bicycles.

One reason for the perennial popularity of bicycles as Christmas presents is that they are durable dissipaters of children's energies. One reason for the resurgent popularity of bicycles among adults is the aging baby-boom generation's intermittent passion for physical fitness. (As a wit has observed, Americans are dedicated to fitness, and to parking as close to the stadium as possible.)

But when the bicycle first burst—and that is the right word—upon mankind, it was more than a merely utilitarian device. It was a sign of a beckoning, dazzling future.

In his delightful new book, *France, Fin de Siecle*, Eugen Weber argues that the bicycle was "an emblem of Progress and one of its agents." Weber cites Zola's declaration that bicycle riding is "a continuous apprenticeship of the will" and adds:

"Though intellectuals have always been prone to give ponderous treatment to simple matters of convenience or pleasure, this sort of encomium was neither exceptional nor undeserved. It becomes more comprehensible not only in the context of the contemporary obsession with physical and moral decadence but also in the context of a world where the sort of mobility permitted by the bike was scarce, rare, and exciting.

The three decades 1880–1910 probably saw more technological change than occurred in the preceding three millennia. New instruments for the conquest of time and space—instruments of communication and transportation—were democratizing experience, making elite enjoyments accessible to the masses. Physical, especially technological, changes brought spiritual changes, hence changes in morals, hence in politics.

Modernity meant, among other things, a sense of vastly expanding freedom of choice that would make change, not continuity, the new norm. It suddenly dawned on people that fads and fashions in all things—dress, morals, politics, the arts—could be willed into existence and made to pass away. And what we consider the humble bicycle was a glittering part of the epiphany.

Not everyone was pleased. Renoir loathed bicycles after he broke his arm in a fall from one. Others disliked bikes because, as one anxious gentleman said, "With the bicycle, the last appearance of feminine modesty disappeared." Eminent physicians warned that the bicycle, like the sewing machine, would cause "nymphomania" and "hysteria," "voluptuous sensations" and "lubricious overexcitement" and "accesses of sensual madness."

The bicycle was a cause of an epochal change in fashion: Women began wearing trousers. Furthermore, the corset, "a new Bastille to be demolished," was done in by the bicycle. The need for freedom to pedal fueled a revolt against constricting corsets. They harmed women's breathing, digestion and fertility and even led to alcoholism, a result of drinking to deaden the discomfort.

Corset reform—and hence the bicycle—was an aspect of the emancipation of women because unreformed corsets had, in the words of a contemporary, placed women in "an unjust and illogical state of inferiority." Physical comfort, mobility, independence—no wonder the president of the feminist congress of 1896 gave a banquet toast to the "equalitarian and leveling bicycle."

The bike path to Mt. Vernon follows the Potomac River. From Maryland, the rider goes in the direction of the river's flow, so it must be downhill, at least a bit. It is necessary to think such encouraging thoughts when you are middle-aged and your companions are young and your bike is just a bike, not an exciting harbinger of an exotic future. Still, for the middle-aged, a bike is a reassuring reminder that there are pleasant as well as ominous associations with the idea of going downhill.

December 25, 1986

Winston, the User-Friendly Cat

I announced it and meant it: No cats. I am an austere father, deaf to the entreaties of children chafing beneath parental sovereignty. Well, deaf to the entreaties of male children. But then, there is Victoria, who is nine and perfect and has eyes that express entreaties in the most melting manner. She wanted a cat for Christmas.

Let me tell you about our cat.

Winston is white and, like Victoria, is alternatively sweet and volatile, playful and somber—and lovely to look at. A cat does furnish a room. Like a graceful vase, a cat, even when motionless, seems to flow. But a cat also is a flawlessly designed killer.

It is lost in the mists of history, the moment when cats condescended to adopt people. From this transaction, cats got room and board. People got civilization.

Cats are carnivores that prey on vegetarians. When humans advanced from hunter-gatherers to tillers of soil, they needed cats. Agriculture, and hence everything else, depends upon storage of surpluses, and hence depends on control of mice and rats. Small wonder Egyptians worshiped cats. Later, when Europe was swept by plagues, cats helped control rodents that were disease carriers.

Cats sleep more than other mammals—16 hours a day, a few minutes ("catnaps") at a time—but even in deepest sleep their brains are as active as when they are awake, processing information. The stories of cats bolting from buildings just before earthquakes or volcanic eruptions are true. The myth of a feline "sixth sense" reflects the refinement of the five senses, including the ability to sense minute tremors and changes in air pressure.

Although there are about 500 million domestic cats in the world (and more strays than that), in a sense the phrase "domestic cat" is an oxymoron. The cat-and-mouse "game" of trap-and-release that a cat plays with a prey before killing it is rare in the wild. It is the behavior of cats with too few opportunities to express their instinct to kill.

However, cats kill for natural, ecologically rational reasons. That is more than can be said for mankind, which has made cats the focus of virulent superstitions. For centuries the Christian church encouraged the belief that cats were associated with—even were—witches. Some persons convicted of witchcraft were drowned in sacks full of cats. Among the festivities at the coronation of Queen Elizabeth in 1558 was the burning of an effigy of the Pope—stuffed with live cats. Even in 19th-century France, some Christian festivals included roasting baskets full of live cats, the ashes of which were considered sources of good luck.

J.C. Suares, who has written much about cats and recounts these and other atrocities (such as the celebration of Lent by tossing cats from the tops of cathedrals), wonders what in the nature of cats (dogs have no similar history) taunts humans to fury. The answer may be in the fact that Julius Caesar, Genghis Khan, Napoleon and Mussolini hated cats, surely cats are embodiments of independence. (It is said cats even purr to please themselves.)

But if solitariness and inscrutability arouse against cats the brute that sleeps lightly (when it sleeps) in mankind, those qualities make cats especially suitable companions for creative people, because creativity requires solitude.

Isaac Newton took time off from finding laws of physics to invent the "cat flap" that enables cats to avoid the ultimate cat horror, the closed door. Samuel Johnson took time off from dictionary-writing to shop for oysters for his cat Hodge. One of Charles Dickens's cats used his paw to snuff out Dickens's candle when the cat thought it was time to play. Henry James, he of the feline subtlety of syntax, would sometimes write with a cat on his shoulder. Mark Twain, who, like Hemingway, kept cats (Hemingway as many as 30 at a time), believed that "if man could be crossed with the cat, it would improve man but deteriorate the cat."

As a cat fancier has written, your cat is undoubtedly the cleanest member of your household and the only one who eats no more than necessary. And Winston is a user-friendly cat. In fact, too much so.

He and I need to come to an understanding about this practice of putting his nose on the nose of Victoria's father at four A.M., an act which, the day after Christmas, caused the iron to enter my soul: I now have three children, two dogs and a cat. That's it. No more. That's final. I am an immovable object: No more pets. Unless, of course, The Irresistible Force, a.k.a. Victoria, wants, say, a horse, in which case . . .

It is said that as long as little girls are interested in quadrupeds (horses are another of Victoria's passions) they are not apt to develop strong interests in bipeds of the boy variety. I plan to have cats and other pets for a while.

December 28, 1989

Jon's Friend Angel

This year Jonathan Will, age 15, is getting the greatest gift that can be given: a friend. The fact that this friend, a large dog, does not need to be wrapped is but one of its merits.

Her merits. Angel is a blond Labrador. About her, as about all members of that dignified species, there clings, like banker's worsted, the aura of knowing what is best but being too well-bred to insist on it. So she will improve the tone of the household, as she has done of Christmas.

"We shall soon be having Christmas at our throats," says a P.G. Wodehouse character who should be ashamed of himself. The routs and revels that erupt in connection with Christmas do take their toll on body and soul. Once you have had your fill of eggnog, which is easy to do, you have pretty well drained Christmas of most of what it has to offer in the way of physical pleasures.

Furthermore, Christmas Eve invariably is a Walpurgisnacht of trips to drugstores for batteries that were not included for the toys in the boxes on which were printed those three terrible words: "Some Assembly Required."

Dogs come assembled and need no batteries. Blessed Angel is six and has graduated from finishing school and is ready to do what dogs do. A cynic once said that to his dog, every man is Napoleon, hence the popularity of dogs. Actually, no sensible person wants to feel like a Corsican brigand, so for "Napoleon" substitute, say, "Alan Greenspan." Dogs make us feel lofty but not so forbiddingly grand as to be unapproachable.

A philosophic dog like a Labrador will, if given half a chance, give to us the closest we are apt to come to unconditional love. Pedants may take issue with the ascription of love to an animal. But however we categorize what dogs do for us, it is what it is, and it comes down to this: Our dogs are always glad to see us. They want to step high, wide and plentiful with us, and then doze in the sun in close proximity to us.

These days Jonathan is a boy of the great indoors, having discovered Bon Jovi (a rock group) and the teenage pleasure of sovereignty in one's own room. Angel—who, by the way, is approximately the color of rich Devon cream—presumably will put up with a lot of Bon Jovi. But she also will insist on brisk walks, which will do both of them a world of good.

Jonathan is handicapped (Down's syndrome) and sometimes has trouble making his abundant thoughts and feelings understood by strangers. So at times, with poignant urgency, he has turned for companionship to a neighbor's dog, another blond Lab, named Skylab.

There is a large lesson here about the handicapped. Jon is just like everyone else, only a bit more so, in the following sense.

A shadow of loneliness is inseparable from the fact of individual existence. This shadow is perhaps somewhat darker for people like Jon because their ability to articulate—the ability by which we all cope with the apartness that defines out condition—is, even more than for most of us, not commensurate with their abilities to think and feel.

So Jon has found, as all dog-lovers do, consolation in the company of a four-legged friend. If Skylab could speak—and, come to think about it, he does, with eloquent body language from tongue to tail—he would testify to the fact that Jon's handicap is no impediment to the flow of friendship.

In fact, watching the reciprocated pleasure between Jon and Skylab, I have come to a conclusion suited to this season. It is that some small mitigation of the harshness of life's lottery, some gently compensating thumb on the scale of justice, has given Jon an enlarged talent for friendship, with people and with their best friends.

So this year Jon gets Angel. Or Angel gets Jon, which is much the same thing. The unencumbered mutuality, the free flowing of giving between a dog and a boy, is a lesson in life's goodness, and the lesson is part of the greatest gift.

December 24, 1987

Acknowledgments

For the fifth and, I hope, not the final time it is a pleasure to thank Erwin Glikes of The Free Press, Bill Dickinson and Anna Karavangelos of the Washington Post Writers Group, and Rick Smith and Olga Barbi of *Newsweek* for the attention, always beneficial, they give to my work. Thanks also to Dusa Gyllensvard, Mary Moschler, and Gail Thorin who take much of the work out of working in my office.

Index

Abolitionism, 151
Abortion, 42, 72, 149, 206, 207, 293, 307, 311–318, 336, 339, 340, 343, 346
Acheson, Dean, 117
Adams, John, 133, 253, 402
Adams, John Quincy, 402
Adenauer, Konrad, 101
Advertising, 19–21, 390–391
Affirmative action, 16, 325–329, 342, 375
Afghanistan, 36, 39, 293
Against All Hope (Valladares), 35
Agriculture, 159, 160
AIDS (Acquired Immune Deficiency Syndrome), 19, 20, 30, 35, 37, 39, 199, 201, 203, 244, 388, 389
Albania, 51
Alcohol, 35, 71, 196, 199–201
Alexander the Great, 3
Allen, Fred, 19
Allende, Salvador, 135
All Quiet on the Western Front (Remarque), 125
Alsop, Joseph Wright, 372–374
Alternative media, 391
Amazon rain forest, 39
Ambrose, Stephen, 119
American Booksellers Association, 379
American Civil Liberties Union (ACLU), 305–306
American Graffiti, 260
"Americanization of the left," 113
American Medical Association (AMA), 312
American Revolution, 51, 52, 54, 137
Andreotti, Giulio, 95

Andropov, Yuri, 69
Anger, 384
Anticommunism, 117, 142, 149, 157, 295
Antietam, Battle of, 118
Antipoverty programs, 160
Anti-Semitism, 127, 322, 323, 373
Arafat, Yasir, 261
Arendt, Hannah, 56, 57
Argentina, 108, 109, 129
Aristotle, 36, 149, 215
Armenia, 38, 53
Arms control, 34–35
Aron, Raymond, 375
Arts subsidies, 17–19, 320
Ascherson, Neal, 60
Ash, Timothy Garton, 99
Asian-Americans, 322–323
Asinof, Eliot, 396
Assault rifles, 41, 179–183
Astaire, Fred, 38, 155
Asteroids, 362–364
Atlee, Clement, 112
Atomic bomb, 122–123
Atom smasher, 31–33
Atwater, Lee, 325
Auschwitz, 127
Austria, 35, 45, 82, 91, 124

Babbitt, Bruce, 233, 234
Baby boomers, 259–261
Baby M, 37, 317–319
Baker, Howard, 36
Baker, James, 95, 153, 239–240, 272, 293
Bakke case (1978), 342–343
Bakker, Jim, 37

Bakker, Tammy, 37
Balfour, Arthur, 256
Ballooning, 402
Baltimore Orioles, 10, 23–25, 40
Bangladesh, 38
Barbie, Klaus, 36
Barchas, Isaac, 211
Barnes & Noble Book Store, 379
Barnett, Correlli, 3, 4
Barzini, Luigi, 96, 104, 106
Baseball, 23–25, 37–38, 40, 43, 380–382, 396–399
B. Dalton Bookseller, 379
Beastie Boys, 36
Beatles, the, 367
Beecham, Sir Thomas, 87
Beethoven, Ludwig van, 4, 125
Beggars, 301–303
Behavior modification, drugs and, 307–308
Belgium, 105
Bell, Derrick, 330, 331
Bennett, Alan, 10
Bennett, William, 182, 192, 210, 224
Bensonhurst, New York, 42
Bentsen, Lloyd, 240, 266, 269–271
Berlin, Irving, 40
Berlin, Isaiah, 373
Berlin Wall, 41, 49, 50, 91–94, 99, 101, 116
Berra, Yogi, 38
Bhutto, Benazir, 39
Bias, Len, 35
Bicycling, 404–406
Biden, Joseph, 36, 260, 261, 328, 335–343
Big Chill, The, 260
Bill of Rights, 182, 339
Bipartisanship, 151, 241–242
Bird in Space (Brancusi), 18
Birthrates, 177
Bismarck, Otto von, 96, 98
Black, Hugo, 341–343
Blackmun, Harry, 292, 293, 305, 309
Blacks, 37, 42, 147, 195, 223, 233, 262, 328–331, 348, 375
Black Sox scandal, 396–397
Blaine, James G., 274

Bloom, Allan, 28, 37, 44, 211–215
Boesky, Ivan, 37, 250
Bogdanor, Vernon, 110, 111
Bokassa, Jean-Bédel, 36
Bolivia, 129
Bonapartism, 80
Bonfire of the Vanities, The (Wolfe), 37, 40, 44, 195, 394–395
Bookselling, 378–380
Boorstin, Daniel, 77, 178, 179, 387
Bork, Robert, 37, 155, 327, 329, 335–358
Bork, Robert, Jr., 349
Boswell, Tom, 398–399
Bourgeoisie, 17–19, 44
Boxer, Barbara, 233, 234
Bradley, Omar, 120
BrainReserve, 388
Brancusi, Constantin, 18
Brandeis, Louis, 342, 387
Brando, Marlon, 195, 367
Brawley, Tawana, 40
Brazil, 129
Breathing Lessons (Tyler), 14
Brennan, William, 292, 293, 309, 340
Brett, George, 256
Brezhnev, Leonid, 68
Bridge Street Books, Washington, D.C., 379
Bright Lights, Big City (McInerney), 198
Brinkley, Alan, 254
Brinkley, David, 272, 376–378
Brooke, Rupert, 125
Brooklyn Bridge, 6
Brooklyn Dodgers, 381
Bryan, William Jennings, 130, 162
Bryce, James, 251, 253
Budget, federal, 146, 157–159, 270, 295–296
Bulgaria, 51
Bulge, Battle of the, 120
Bulwer-Lytton, Edward, 370
Bulwer-Lytton Fiction Contest, 370–372
Burger, Warren, 325
Burke, Edmund, 5, 137
Burns, George, 40

Burris, Roland, 233
Busby, Horace, 274
Bush, George, 9, 150, 156, 175, 243, 261, 382
  abortion issue and, 313, 314
  baseball and, 25
  Chinese policy of, 41, 96, 241
  Congress, relations with, 240, 242
  Dukakis, debate with, 282–283
  environmentalism of, 161, 204, 285
  ethics and, 152–154, 161
  fiscal issues and, 152, 157, 162, 242
  flag-burning and, 206, 207
  on German reunification, 95, 97–98
  gun control and, 154, 179–183
  inaugural address of, 151–152, 157, 241
  Panamanian policy of, 41, 132, 133, 218, 241
  presidential campaign and election of 1988, 36, 40, 233, 257–259, 267–269, 278–280, 287, 290–297
  Quayle nomination and, 269–270, 272
  in Republican presidential candidates debate, 255–256
  Soviet–U.S. relations and, 85–86, 293
  style of, 160–162
Business Week, 238
Busing, 325
Butkus, Dick, 273
Byrd, Robert, 340
Byrne, Jane, 223

Cable-equipped television, 44
Caddell, Pat, 260, 261
Caesar, Julius, 407
Calhoun, John C., 172, 173
California, 273, 322–323
Call-waiting, 382
Cameroon, 34
Campanis, Al, 261
Camus, Albert, 194
Capitalism, 77–80, 84, 99, 113, 143, 369, 376, 388, 389
Capital punishment, 309–310, 388
Cardozo, Benjamin, 342

Caro, Robert A., 228–230
Carranza, Venustiano, 130
Carter, Jimmy, 86, 108, 142, 151, 161, 260, 290, 295
Cash register, invention of, 178, 179
Castro, Fidel, 35, 72, 134, 135, 143, 261
Catcher in the Rye, The (Salinger), 367
Cats, 406–408
Censorship on campus, 320–321
Central Intelligence Agency (CIA), 214
Central Park gang rape, 25–27, 42
Chadwick, James, 122
Challenger astronauts, 34
Chamberlain, Neville, 124
Channon, "Chips," 79
Chaplin, Charles, 77, 387
Chapman, Mark David, 367
Cheating, 21–22
Chernobyl accident, 34, 89
Chicago, Illinois, 13–14, 220–224
Chicago Cubs, 36, 40, 43, 380–382, 398
Chicago school of economics, 87
Chicago Tribune, 13, 221
Chicago White Sox, 396–397
Childhood development, 187–189
Chile, 39, 128, 135
China: see People's Republic of China
Chinese for Affirmative Action (CAA), 322, 323
Cholesterol, 39, 42
Chou Teh, 124
Christmas, 361, 362, 404, 408
Chrysler Building, 6
Chrysler Corporation, 77
Churchill, Winston, 57, 96, 111, 113, 119, 124, 143, 149, 160, 378, 380
Cicero, 149
Cicotte, Ed, 396
Cincinnati Reds, 396, 398
Citicorp, 38
Citizens (Schama), 136
Civil rights, 54, 157, 329
Civil Rights Act of 1964, 325–327
Civil War (American), 143
Clark, Robert, 330
Clean-air legislation, 204–205
Cleveland, Grover, 254, 274, 361

Close, Glenn, 38
Closing of the American Mind, The (Bloom), 37, 44, 211–214
Clutter, 364–366
Coal and Steel Community, 106
Cobb, Ty, 398, 399
Cocaine, 35, 185, 192, 194, 196, 197
Cocooning, 389
Cohn-Bendit, Daniel, 54
Cold War, 8, 36, 44, 79, 80, 117–119, 121, 132, 143, 164, 242, 243
College football, 208–210
Colombia, 192
Commentary, 197
Committee on the Present Danger, The, 69
Common Market, 106
Communications technologies, 89
Communism, 41, 49–51, 52, 61, 65–72, 76, 77, 80, 82–88, 96, 97, 99, 101, 135, 279
Communist Manifesto, The (Marx and Engels), 73
Communist Party, 54
Compassion (constituency) liberalism, 265–267
Competence liberalism, 265–267
Compulsory medication, 307–308
Condom commercials, 19–21
Congressional terms, 235–236
Connally, John, 227
Connecticut, 237
Conquest, Robert, 58
Conservatism, 8, 10, 11, 36, 79, 87, 102, 112, 113, 143, 146–149, 158–160, 168, 174–176, 208, 268, 269, 284, 321, 341
Conspicuous compassion, 28
Constitution of the United States, 15, 75, 182, 207, 208, 341–343, 350–352, 356–357, 364
Containment, 85, 142, 233, 240
Contraception, 19–21, 37
Contras, 39, 40, 134
Conyers, John, Jr., 328
Cook, Jamie, 237–238
Coolidge, Calvin, 143, 258
Cooper, James Fenimore, 393

Cooper, Lady Diana, 35
Corporate Community School, Chicago, 220–221
Corsets, 405–406
Council of Economic Advisers (CEA), 263, 264
Courter, Jim, 276
Cox, Archibald, 343
Crack, 184, 185, 192, 194, 198, 203, 244
Craig, Marvin, 41
Crime, 25–27, 35, 42, 179–183, 189–190
Crown Books, 379
Cuba, 72, 131, 135
  missile crisis, 114–115
Cuban-Americans, 135
cummings, e. e., 400–401
Cunard, Lady, 79
Cuomo, Mario, 230–232, 252, 266
Curriculum revision, 15–16, 210–212
Cycles of American History, The (Schlesinger), 253
Czechoslovakia, 41, 51, 53, 99, 100

Daily Telegraph, 116
Daley, Richard J., 222, 252
Daley, Richie, 222–224
D'Amato, Al, 274
Danforth, John C., 277
Danforth-Hollings bill, 277
Daniloff, Nicholas, 35
Dark Half, The (King), 368–369
Darwin, Charles, 363
Dayton, Ohio, 177–179
D-Day, 120
Dead Poets Society, 400–402
Dean, James, 195, 367
Deaver, Michael, 37
Debates
  presidential, 280–283
  senatorial, 255, 281
Declaration of Independence, 75
DeConcini, Dennis, 340
Defense spending, 49, 146
de Gaulle, Charles, 94, 98, 102, 108–109, 143
Deinstitutionalization, 303

Democracy, 64, 85, 128, 129, 356–358
Democratic Party, 8, 115, 130, 131, 142, 155–157, 165, 168, 170, 220, 232–234, 249–250, 254, 263–267, 276, 279, 284, 287–292, 294–298, 338, 340, 348
Dempsey, Jack, 397
Der, Henry, 323
Descartes, René, 4
Detectives, fictional, 392–393
Détente, 17, 44, 70, 119, 149, 293, 375
Deterrence, 256
Deukmejian, George, 176
De Vries, Peter, 10
Dewey, John, 375
Dewey, Thomas, 225, 258, 278, 289
Diamond, Larry, 129
Dickens, Charles, 227, 370, 394, 395, 407
Dickson, Clarence, 186
Diet of Worms, 49
Dillon, Douglas, 142
DiMaggio, Joe, 398
Dinkins, David, 225
Discover magazine, 364
Discrimination in employment, 326
Disraeli, Benjamin, 3, 219
Dobrynin, Anatoly F., 114
Dogs, 408–409
Dole, Robert, 118, 161, 256–259, 339
Dominican Republic, 129, 131
Donahue, Phil, 388
Dos Passos, John, 125
Douglas, Steven, 255, 281
Douglas, William, 342
Dozier, James, 104
Dred Scott v. Sanford (1857), 316
Drug Enforcement Administration, 192
Drug legalization, 196–198
Drug use, 13, 14, 35, 144–145, 183–187, 191–195, 198–199, 201, 274–275
Drunk driving, 71, 200–201
Dukakis, Michael, 42, 130–131, 232, 233, 250, 253, 263–268, 270–272, 278–280, 282–292, 296–298, 382
Duke, James H. (Red), Jr., 202–204
Dukes, Hazel, 338

Dulles, Allen, 119
Dulles, John Foster, 117–119
du Pont, Pete, 256
Durkheim, Émile, 195
Duvalier family, 34

Eagleburger, Lawrence, 153
Earth Day II, 7–8
Earthquakes, 11–12, 38, 41, 363
East Germany, 45, 82, 84, 91–103, 116, 241
Ebbets Field, Brooklyn, 381
Eberstadt, Nick, 70–72
Economic Opportunity Act, 191
Economic Policy Institute, 286
Economist, The, 66–67, 89, 94, 145, 228
Ecuador, 129
Edgar, Bob, 274
Edison, Thomas, 6
Education, 13–14, 47, 212–213
  Asian-Americans and, 322–323
  corporate funding of, 220–222
  curriculum revision, 15–16, 210–212
  history (subject), 216–218
Edwards, Don, 206
Efficiency studies, 386–387
Egan, Jim, 187–189
Eiffel, Gustave, 5
Eiffel Tower, 5–7
Eight Men Out (Asinof), 396
80–20 rule, 365–366
Einstein, Albert, 6
Eisenhower, Dwight D., 24, 117–120, 141, 145, 194, 253, 258, 281, 289, 293, 295, 340, 345
Elderly, 42, 146, 219–220, 252, 296
Eliot, T. S., 393
El Salvador, 129
Emancipation Proclamation, 118
Emerson, Ralph Waldo, 395
Eminent Victorians (Strachey), 29
Enola Gay, 122, 123
Environmentalism, 7–8, 10, 161, 204–206, 284–285
Environmental Protection Agency (EPA), 172
Enzensberger, Hans Magnus, 104–105

Equal Rights Amendment (ERA), 208
Ergonomics, 77, 78
Eroica (Beethoven), 4
Estonia, 53
Ethics, 152–156, 161
Eurocentrism, 16, 17
Eurocommunism, 80, 103, 135
European Community, 95, 105–107
Europe, Europe: Forays into a Continent (Enzensberger), 104
Evans, Timothy, 223
Evil, 26–27
Evolution, 361–363
Exposition Universelle (1889), 5
Extinction, 364

Failure to thrive syndrome, 187–189
Falk, Bibb, 43
Falklands War, 108, 109, 132
Family structure, 190, 191
Farewell to Arms, A (Hemingway), 125
Fechter, Peter, 49
Federal Reserve System, 157
Federation of Women Lawyers, 335
Fetal medicine, 318
Fetal rights, 318
Fifth Amendment to the Constitution, 339
Finland, 124
Finn, Chester, Jr., 216, 217
First Amendment to the Constitution, 207, 242, 301, 305, 306, 341
First World War, 123, 125
Fitzgerald, F. Scott, 177, 378
Flag-burning, 41, 206–208, 218, 242, 280
Flexible response, 121
Florio, James J., 275–276
Foch, Marshal, 4
Foley, Tom, 235, 279
Fonda, Jane, 275
Food hazards, 42
Foot, Michael, 112
Football, 33, 208–210
Forbes, Malcolm, 42
Forbes magazine, 237
Ford, Gerald, 150, 260
Ford, Henry, 6, 77

Foreign Affairs, 89
Forests, 39
Forster, Debra, 307–308
Fortas, Abe, 338
Fortino, Michael, 386
Fourteenth Amendment to the Constitution, 316, 324, 325, 339, 342
France, 43, 95, 98; *see also* French Revolution
France, Fin de Siècle (Weber), 405
Frank, Barney, 218, 233–234
Frankfurter, Felix, 340, 342, 343
Franklin, Benjamin, 402
Frederick the Great, 94
French Revolution of 1789, 5, 41, 51, 53–55, 136–137
Frenzel, Bill, 235–236
Freud, Sigmund, 6, 60, 65, 124, 364
Friedman, Milton, 87, 196–197
Frost, Robert, 358, 393
Fussell, Paul, 125

Gagnon, Paul, 217
Galileo, 363
Gallatin, Albert, 172
Galnoor, Itzhak, 66
Gambling, 237–239
Gandhi, Indira, 129
Gangs, 35, 193–195
Gartner, Michael, 116–117
Gates, Daryl, 180
Genghis Khan, 407
Genocide, 58, 60, 64, 106, 126–127
George III, King of England, 36
George VI, King of England, 107
Gephardt, Richard, 240, 250
Germany, 4, 5, 49–51; *see also* East Germany; West Germany
Gershman, Carl, 128
Giamatti, Bartlett, 22, 40, 43
Giuliani, Rudolph, 224–225
Gladstone, William, 69, 219
Glasnost, 45, 60, 67, 85, 89, 148
Glazer, Nathan, 302
Glemp, Cardinal, 127
Glendon, Mary Ann, 344
Glory and the Dream, The (Manchester), 20–21

GNP (gross national product), 49, 145, 157–159, 173, 174, 264
Goldwater, Barry, 228, 229, 257, 281
Goldwyn, Sam, 278, 339
Good-bye to All That (Graves), 125
Goodman, Benny, 35
Goodman, Paul, 195
Gorbachev, Mikhail, 36, 39, 50, 53, 63, 64, 66–67, 76–77, 85, 92, 249, 267, 291
  at Iceland summit, 34–35
  Lithuania and, 74, 75, 240, 241, 243
  quoted, 16, 51, 52, 72, 88, 97
  Reagan and, 34, 86, 148
  values of, 68–70, 88
Gore, Albert, 249–250
Gorman, Tom, 35
Gottwald, Klement, 41
Gould, Stephen Jay, 361–362
Governmental growth, 159–160, 284
Governmental support for the arts, 17–19, 320
Graham, Bob, 355
Gramm, Phil, 168
Gramm-Rudman deficit-reduction law of 1985, 156, 157, 165, 168, 172
Grand Illusion, 125
Grange, Red, 397
Grant, Cary, 35
Grant, Ulysses S., 253
Graves, Robert, 125
Great Britain, 43, 44, 95, 107–113
Great Depression, 143, 150
Great Terror, The (Conquest), 58
Greece, 129
Greenfield, Meg, 373
Greenglass, David, 122
Greenhouse effect, 284
Greening of America, The (Reich), 117
Greenspan, Alan, 90, 158
Greenspan Commission, 167
Grenada, 72, 108, 129, 131–133, 135, 250
Growing Up Absurd (Goodman), 195
Guatemala, 129
Gun control, 179–183
Gysi, Gregor, 100

Haffner, Sebastian, 102–103
Haig, Al, 256
Haiti, 129, 131
Hall, Arsenio, 42
Hall, Fawn, 36
Halley's comet, 34
Hamilton, Alexander, 268, 290, 377–378
Hampshire, Stuart, 373
Hand, Learned, 343, 356
Harding, Warren, 258, 397
Harlan, John Marshall (1833–1911), 325
Harlan, John Marshall (1899–1971), 341–343
Harper's magazine, 232, 392
Harris, Jean, 231
Harrison, Benjamin, 119, 256
Harrison, George, 259
Hart, Gary, 36, 40, 261
Hart, Peter, 260–261, 279
Harvard Business School, 37
Harvard Law Review, 331
Harvard Law School, 330–331
Harvard University, 336
Harvest of Sorrow, The (Conquest), 58
Hayek, Friedrich von, 87
Hayes, Denis, 7
Health care, 29–31
  in Soviet Union, 71–72
Health insurance, 42
Heart disease, 384–385
Heart of the Order, The (Boswell), 398
Heflin, Howell, 340, 354–355
Heller, Mikhail, 59
Helms, Jesse, 17, 320
Helmsley, Leona, 42
Hemingway, Ernest, 125, 378, 407
Herman, Babe, 38
Heroin, 196, 197
Hess, Rudolph, 36, 59
Hess, Stephen, 251
Hills, Carla, 344
Hiroshima, 122, 123
Historicism, 56
History, study of, 216–218

Hitler, Adolf, 3, 4, 6, 40, 58, 76, 79, 82, 91, 94, 100, 103, 120, 124, 126, 127, 143, 373
Hobbes, Thomas, 13
Hoffer, Eric, 145
Hofstadter, Richard, 344
Hollings, Ernest F., 277
Holmes, Oliver Wendell, 356
Holocaust, 126–127, 373
Holtz, Lou, 208
Homeless, 303–304
Homer, 369
Honduras, 129
Hook, Sidney, 374–376
Hooks, Benjamin, 328
Hoopla (Stein), 396
Hoover, Herbert, 258
Horowitz, Vladimir, 43
Horror fiction and films, 368–370
Horton, Willie, 182, 275, 278, 279, 296, 297
Housing and Urban Development (HUD), Department of, 41, 218, 242
Houston, Sam, 240
Houston, Texas, 226–228
Hoyer, Steny, 27–28
Huerta, Victoriano, 130
Hughes, Charles Evans, 251, 258, 342
Hughes, Robert, 5–7
Hugo, Victor, 37
Human relations, 387
Hume, Brit, 270
Humphrey, Hubert, 252, 325, 375
Hundred Yard Lie, The (Telander), 209
Hungary, 41, 56–57, 74, 82–84, 91, 92, 100, 107
Hunt, Bunker, 227
Hunting, 181–183
Huntington, Samuel, 214–215
Hurricane Gilbert, 38
Hurricane Hugo, 41

Iacocca, Lee, 388
Ibarruri, Dolores, 41
Iceland summit, 34–35
Ickes, Harold, 377
Idaho, 273, 274

Income, 264, 286, 287
India, 129
Individualism, 49, 50, 164, 171, 206–208, 252
Indochina, 129
Industrial Revolution, 5
Infant mortality rates, 244
Inflation, 44, 108, 109, 110, 142, 157, 158, 242, 255, 263
Infrastructure, 171–174
Insider trading, 34, 35, 37
Interest rates, 157, 158
Intermediate Nuclear Forces (INF), 44, 162
Iowa primary, 251–252
IRA (Irish Republican Army), 107
Iran-Contra affair, 34, 141
Iranian hostage crisis, 255
Iraq, 39
Isolationism, 151, 244, 250
Israel, 39, 69, 127
Italy, 80, 103–105

Jack Gance (Just), 223
Jackson, Andrew, 256
Jackson, Bo, 42
Jackson, Henry M. (Scoop), 270
Jackson, Jesse, 40, 42, 223, 233, 249, 261–263, 265, 266, 298, 329, 330
Jackson, Robert, 342
Jackson, Shoeless Joe, 43, 396
Jagger, Mick, 366, 367
James, Henry, 369, 407
James, William, 366, 395
Jamieson, Kathleen Hall, 281
Japanese-Americans, 325
Jaruzelski, Wojciech, 80–83
Jay, John, 402
Jay Treaty, 151
Jefferson, Thomas, 49, 52, 53, 64, 137, 142, 149, 150, 253, 377, 395
Jennings, Peter, 272
Jews, 35, 126–127, 263, 322, 323, 373
Jimmy the Greek, 261, 263
Joel, Lucille, 30, 31
John Birch Society, 345
John Paul II, Pope, 43, 44, 99
Johnson, Ben, 21–22, 40

Johnson, Lyndon B., 117, 191, 228–230, 252–254, 260, 338
Johnson, Paul, 60
Johnson, Samuel, 145, 407
Jones, Bobby, 397
Jordan, Michael, 37, 42, 263
Joyce, James, 365
Juan Carlos, King of Spain, 80–81
Just, Ward, 223

Kakutani, Michiko, 369
Kant, Immanuel, 153
Kates, Don, Jr., 179, 180
Kaye, Danny, 38
Keating, Kenneth, 115
Keats, John, 393
Keegan, John, 120
Keillor, Garrison, 37
Kellman, Joe, 220–222
Kellogg-Briand Pact of 1920, 131
Kemp, Jack, 242, 256
Kennedy, Anthony, 306, 309, 324, 327
Kennedy, Edward M., 34, 265, 281, 337
Kennedy, John F., 117, 142, 147, 191, 202, 252–254, 258, 260, 267, 270, 281
    Cuban missile crisis and, 114–115
    Supreme Court appointments of, 327, 343
Kennedy, Paul, 40
Kennedy, Randall, 331
Kennedy, Robert F., 114, 329
Kenner, Hugh, 364–366
Khomeini, Ayatollah, 43
Khrushchev, Nikita, 59, 60, 68, 375
King, Martin Luther, Jr., 16
King, Stephen, 368–370
Kinnock, Neil, 109, 277
Kinsella, W. P., 396
Kinsey, Alfred, 20
Kirkpatrick, Jeane, 39
Kissinger, Henry, 379
Klaus, Vaclav, 87, 88
Koch, Ed, 225
Kohl, Helmut, 93, 100
Koop, C. Everett, 200–201
Koppel, Ted, 384

Korean War, 295
Kors, Alan, 320
Koryagin, Anatoly, 59–61
Krenz, Egon, 92, 98

Labedz, Leo, 69
Labor Party (Britain), 43, 110, 112
Labor unions, 109, 110
La Follette, Robert, 262
LaGuardia, Fiorello, 224–225
Landis, Kenesaw Mountain, 397
Landon, Alfred M., 258, 278
Lansing, Robert, 119
Lardner, Ring, 378
Lauder, Ronald, 225
Law and Literature (Posner), 379
Lawrence, Charles, 319, 320
Lawrence, David, 252
Lawrence, D. H., 393
Leacock, Stephen, 9
League of Nations, 131
Leahy, Patrick, 337
Lee, Robert E., 118, 376
Lenin, V. I., 51, 52, 58, 64, 72, 73, 84, 101, 148, 169
Lennon, John, 367
Leo, John, 302
Leonard, Sugar Ray, 37
Leonardo da Vinci, 35
Leveraged buyouts, 39
Levy, Philip, 379
Lewis, C. S., 308
Liberalism, 10, 116–117, 143, 147, 168, 207, 208, 228, 230, 265–267, 288–289, 295, 320–322, 326–329, 336–338, 341, 351, 352, 357, 375
Libya, 131, 250
Life magazine, 39
Lincoln, Abraham, 36, 38, 49, 52, 53, 64, 74, 75, 118, 149–151, 173, 174, 228, 253, 255, 281, 315–317, 402
Linguistic vandalism, 370–372
Lippmann, Walter, 373
Lithuania, 74–75, 240, 241, 243
Lloyd George, David, 280
Locke, John, 16
London, Jack, 31–32

Lonely Crowd, The (Riesman), 401
Long, Huey, 84
Los Angeles Basin, 175–177
Los Angeles Times, 261
Lotteries, 237–239
Louis XVI, King of France, 137, 163, 403
Lucas, William, 328–329
Luce, Clare Boothe, 38
Lukacs, John, 106, 124, 125
Lukas, J. Anthony, 114
Lukes, Steven, 66
Lusitania, 397
Luther, Martin, 49–51, 92, 94, 106
Luttwak, Edward, 69

MacArthur, Douglas, 120, 122, 151
Macaulay, Thomas, 294–295
Machiavelli, Niccolò, 123, 215
Mack, John, 27, 28
Macmillan, Harold, 111
Macrae, Norman, 89, 145
Madison, James, 172, 173, 253, 377
Mailer, Norman, 21
Manchester, William, 20–21, 77
Man in the Gray Flannel Suit, The (Wilson), 195, 401
Manley, Dexter, 208–209
Manners, 382–384
Man o' War, 397
Manufacturing output, 264
Mao Tse-tung, 124
Maravich, Pete, 40
Marconi, Guglielmo, 6
Marcos, Imelda, 34, 84
Marcuse, Herbert, 375
Marie Antoinette, 403
Markham, Felix, 137
Marshall, George, 120
Marshall, Thurgood, 292, 309
Marshall Plan, 17, 119, 233, 240
Martin, Billy, 40
Martin, Judith, 382–383
Marx, Karl, 50, 52, 56, 68, 73, 80, 84, 97, 286, 376
Marxism, 52, 71, 73–74, 92, 134
Massachusetts, 237
Mass production, 6, 77, 78

Maternal deprivation syndrome, 187–188
Mather, Cotton, 237
Maupassant, Guy de, 7
McCarthy, Joseph, 351, 373
McCarthyism, 295, 321
McClellan, George B., 118
McGovern, George, 233, 266–267
McGuire, Mark, 37–38
McInerney, Jay, 198
McKinley, William, 269
McPherson, Darryll, 243, 245
McPherson, James, 173
Means of Ascent (Caro), 229
Mecham, Evan, 40
Media, 8, 144, 261–263, 280–283, 289
Medicare, 219
Meese, Edwin, 155
Mencken, H. L., 354
Mercader, Ramon, 375
Mercedes Corporation, 89
Metzenbaum, Howard, 327, 356
Mexican War (1846–1848), 151
Miami, Florida, 183–187
Microwaves, 389
Milken, Michael, 238
Miller, James, 33
Mills, C. Wright, 401
Milton, John, 393
Minor, Jack, 346
Miquel, Johannes, 303
Mirabeau, Honoré-Gabriel, Comte de, 137
Mises, Ludwig von, 87
Mishel, Lawrence, 286
Miss Manners' Guide for the Turn-of-the-Millennium, 382–383
Mitchell, George, 204
Mitterrand, François, 98
Modern Times, 77, 387
Molotov, Mrs. Vyacheslav, 59
Molotov, Vyacheslav, 35, 57–59
Mondale, Walter, 252, 281
Mone, Lawrence, 377
Monroe Doctrine, 115
Montesquieu, Baron de La Brède et de, 16
Mootry, Primus, 221

Moro, Aldo, 104
Morris, Jan, 226, 227
Mosley, Elaine, 220
Moynihan, Daniel Patrick, 17, 146, 147, 158, 286, 338, 378
  on governmental growth, 159–160, 284
  on social problems, 190, 191
  Social Security tax proposal of, 167–170, 242
  on Wilson, 131
MTV, 8, 10
Mudd, Roger, 281
Mussolini, Benito, 143, 407

Nagasaki, 123
Naked and the Dead, The (Mailer), 21
Napoleon, Louis, 80
Napoleon I, Emperor, 3–6, 51, 64, 80, 136, 137, 407
Nasti, Rick, 274
National Abortion Rights Action League, 344
National Academy of Sciences, 214–216
National Aeronautics and Space Administration (NASA), 38
National Association for the Advancement of Colored People (NAACP), 328
National Association of Manufacturers (NAM), 169–170
National Broadcasting Company (NBC), 43, 377
National Cash Register Company (NCR), 178
National Coalition to Ban Handguns, 180
National Endowment for Democracy, 128–130
National Endowment for the Arts (NEA), 17–19
National Firearms Act, 180
Nationalism, 43, 44, 53, 72–74, 94, 234, 244, 245
National Journal, 171
National Republican Campaign Committee, 279
National Research Council, 215–216

National Review, 83
National Rifle Association (NRA), 181
Nature, 38–39
Nazi-Soviet pact of 1939, 59, 60, 73, 75, 98
Negative campaigning, 273–277
Nekrich, Aleksandr, 59
Nelson, Ricky, 35
Nevada, 237, 238, 273, 274
New Jersey, 275–276
New Republic, The, 162, 232, 249, 250, 254
Newton, Isaac, 364, 407
New York City, 224–226, 301–304
New Yorker, The, 117
New York Review of Books, 60
New York State, 237
New York Times, The, 21, 26, 40, 116, 162, 182, 239, 276, 369
New York Times Magazine, 114
Nicaragua, 72, 115, 134–135, 291, 293
Nicol, Charles, 392, 393
Nigeria, 129
Nightingale, Florence, 29, 31
Nimitz, Chester W., 122
1989FC, 362–364
Nixon, Richard M., 161, 191, 240, 258, 260, 281, 293
No Laughing Matter (Lukes and Galnoor), 66
Noonan, Peggy, 282
Noriega, Manuel, 39–41, 54–55, 132–133, 135
North, Oliver, 36, 155
North Atlantic Treaty Organization (NATO), 44, 93, 97, 98, 101, 102, 107, 119
North Dakota, 274
Nunn, Sam, 298
Nursing, 29–31
Nurturing, 14

Oat bran, 39
Obolensky, Aleksandr, 63–65
O'Connor, Cardinal, 27, 28
O'Connor, Sandra Day, 309, 310, 324, 327, 345
Ogarkov, Marshal, 69

Oil, 90, 227–228
Oil spills, 42
Okinawa, 125
Olivier, Laurence, 43
Oppenheimer, Robert, 122
Organization Man, The (Whyte), 401
Organization of Petroleum Exporting
    Countries (OPEC), 108
Organ transplants, 205
Origins of Totalitarianism, The
    (Arendt), 56, 57
Ortega, Daniel, 134
Orwell, George, 55, 65
Oswald, Lee Harvey, 135
*Out of Step: An Unquiet Life in the
    Twentieth Century* (Hook), 374,
    376
Ozone layer, 39

Packard, David, 39
Packwood, Robert, 338, 346, 347
Panama, 39, 41, 54–55, 132–133, 135,
    218, 241, 291
Parenting, 14, 187–189
Parker, Dave, 398
Parker, Robert B., 392–393
Pasteur, Louis, 6
Patterson, John Henry, 178
Penn, William, 237, 239
Pennsylvania, 237
People magazine, 389
People's Republic of China, 41, 53–55,
    57, 65, 96, 135, 241, 329
Perdue, Frank, 388
Perestroika, 44–45, 67, 69, 85, 148
Perkins, Max, 378
Perle, Richard, 87
Peru, 129
Peter the Great, 88
Philby, Kim, 40
Philippines, 129
Physician–nurse relations, 30
Pinochet, Augusto, 128
Pittsburgh, Pennsylvania, 305, 306
Planned Parenthood, 20, 37, 345
Plato, 56
Pledge of Allegiance, 268, 278, 279,
    289, 297

Poe, Edgar Allan, 369
Poland, 78–83, 99, 124–128
Political science, 214–216
Poll tax, 342
Pollution, 175–176
Popcorn, Faith, 388–389
Portugal, 81, 98, 129, 135
Posner, Richard, 379
Poverty, 14, 34, 188, 190, 191, 219,
    221, 222
Powell, Lewis, 335, 336
Presidential campaigns and elections
    1980, 267
    1984, 162, 257–258, 267
    1988, 36, 40, 233, 257–259, 263–272,
        278–298
Presidential Debates: 1988 and Beyond
    (ed. Swerdlow), 280–281
Presidential press conferences, de-
    emphasis on, 281
Presley, Elvis, 367
Presumed Innocent (Turow), 37
Privacy right, 343
Prohibition, 396
Proposition, 13, 44, 260
Proust, Marcel, 124
Psychiatry, 59–61
Public housing, 13
Public Interest, The (journal), 377
Public Interest, The (Wright and
    Wildavsky), 157

Quantum theory, 33
Quayle, Dan, 40, 269–272
Quayle, Marilyn, 272
Quirk, Jamie, 23, 24

Rain forest, 39
Rains, Jack, 315
Rapallo, Treaty of, 98
Ratushinskaya, Irina, 61–63
Rauschenberg, Robert, 18, 347
Reagan, Nancy, 36, 144
Reagan, Ronald, 9, 117, 131, 160, 231,
    259–260, 263, 268, 279
    abortion and, 149, 314, 315
    Bork nomination and, 336, 338, 339
    budgets of, 146, 157, 270, 295–296

Bush and Dukakis, contrasted with, 283

Cold War and, 36, 44, 119, 143

drug problem and, 192

on freedom, 148

Gorbachev and, 34, 86, 148

governmental growth and, 159

inflation and, 108, 142, 158, 242

Medicare, expansion of, 219

Nancy and, 144

Nicaraguan policy of, 134

personality and temperament of, 144–146

political career of, 142–143, 149–150

popularity of, 141

presidential campaigns of, 162, 257–258, 267, 289

press conferences, deemphasis on, 281

rhetoric and, 149

Soviet Union and, 130, 135, 293

Strategic Defense Initiative and, 44, 146, 256

Superconducting Super Collider, endorsement of, 31–33

Supreme Court appointments and nominations of, 327, 336, 338, 339

taxation and, 146, 147, 167

Thatcher and, 108–111

Reapportionment, 342

Rebel Without a Cause, 367

Rector, Lucinda, 116, 117

Red and the Black, The (Stendhal), 136

Redford, Robert, 271

Redus, Gary, 398

Reflections (Burke), 5

Reformation, 49–51

Regan, Donald, 34, 36

Rehnquist, William, 34, 306, 310, 327

Relativism, 212, 213

Relativity, 33

Renoir, Jean, 405

Repeated-trauma disorders, 77, 78

Reports on Roads and Canals (Gallatin), 172

Republican Party, 119, 143, 155–158, 165, 168, 220, 255–259, 287, 291, 292, 294, 297, 314–317

Reverse discrimination, 324–329, 342, 375

Rhetoric, 149

Ribbentrop, Joachim von, 59

Rice, Scott, 371

Riesman, David, 401

Right-to-life movement, 316

Ripken, Cal, 24

Rise and Fall of the Great Powers, The (Kennedy), 40

Ritty, James, 178

Rivera, Geraldo, 40

RJR Nabisco, 39

Roberts, Oral, 37

Robertson, Pat, 255

Robespierre, Maximilien, 52, 54, 137

Robinson, Frank, 24

Robinson, Jackie, 37

Robinson, Sugar Ray, 43, 273

Rockefeller, Nelson, 253, 258, 278

Rockefeller Center, 42

Rock music, 366–368

Rockne, Knute, 397

Roe v. Wade (1973), 313–316, 318, 337, 343

Rogers, Don, 35

Rogers, Harold, 239

Rohatyn, Felix, 170

Rolling Stones, 366–368

Rollins, Ed, 279

Romania, 51, 107

Roosevelt, Eleanor, 70, 253, 374

Roosevelt, Franklin D., 143, 150, 151, 158, 191, 230, 253, 258, 260, 267, 278, 340, 347, 373, 374

Roosevelt, Theodore, 149, 150, 161–162, 174, 191, 251, 253, 267, 268, 374, 378

Root, Elihu, 164

Rose, Pete, 40, 43, 398–399

Rousseau, Jean-Jacques, 137

Rudman, Warren, 166

Rushdie, Salman, 42–43

Rusk, Dean, 114, 117

Russian Revolution of 1917, 51, 374

Ruth, Babe, 396–398

Ryan, Elaine, 231

Sadat, Anwar El-, 44
Safety belts, 205
St. Louis Browns, 381
Salinger, J. D., 367
Samuel, Juan, 226
Sand, Leonard, 301, 302
Sandinistas, 39, 40, 134, 135
San Francisco earthquake, 11–12
Sasser, Jim, 355–356
Saturation journalism, 8
Savings-and-loan scandal, 240, 241
Sawyer, Eugene, 223–224
Scalia, Anthony, 306, 310, 324, 335, 343
Schama, Simon, 136
Schell, Jonathan, 117
Schlesinger, Arthur, Jr., 115, 253–255
Schmidt, Helmut, 93, 94
School desegregation, 319, 325–327, 336
School prayer, 149
Schroeder, Patricia, 36
Schwitters, Roy, 33
Science, 31–33
Scientific management, 386, 387
Scowcroft, Brent, 151, 152
Scribner's Bookstore, New York, 378, 380
Sears, John, 254–255
Secession, 74–75
Second World War, 120, 122–127, 377
Seismology, 11
1791: Mozart's Last Year (Landon), 379
Shakespeare, William, 365, 393
Sharpton, Al, 40
Shcharansky, Anatoly, 35
Shields, Mark, 257
Shmelve, Nikolai, 88
Shoeless Joe (Kinsella), 396
Sikorski, Radek, 83
Simon, Herbert, 214
Simon, Jacqueline, 286
Simon, Paul, 250, 255, 257, 338
Simple, Peter, 116
Single-parent households, 190, 191
Six Armies in Normandy (Keegan), 120
60 Minutes, 388
Skinner, Samuel, 173

Slavery, 316
Sledge, Eugene, 125
Smoking, 199–201, 205–206
SMU (Southern Methodist University), 37
Social class, 286–287, 291
Socialism, 43, 50, 66, 73, 75, 78, 80, 84, 86, 99, 110, 112–113, 279, 376
Social Security, 165–170, 219, 242, 290
Solidarity, 78–80, 82
Somme, Battle of the, 123
Sorensen, Ted, 114–115
Sosa, Juan, 54–55
South Africa, 34, 291
South Coast Air Quality Management District (SCAQMD), 175
South Dakota, 274
South Korea, 129
Soviet Union, 36, 39, 44–45, 49–53, 57–77, 82, 84, 85–88, 95, 98–101, 114–115, 119, 121, 124, 130, 131, 134, 135, 148, 149, 243, 244, 291, 293, 375
Spain, 43, 80–81, 98, 129
Spanish-American War (1898), 151
Specter, Arlen, 274
Sport, 21–25, 33, 37–38, 40, 43, 208–210, 380–382, 396–399
Springsteen, Bruce, 368
Stabler, Ken, 32
Stalin, Joseph, 3, 57–59, 73, 79, 148, 373, 375
Stanford University, 210–212
Stanley, Alessandra, 162
State lotteries, 237–239
Stein, Harry, 396
Stein, Herbert, 158
Stendhal, 136
Stengel, Casey, 398
Stern, Fritz, 16
Steroids, 21–23
Stevens, John Paul, 293, 309, 310
Stevens, Wallace, 393
Stevenson, Adlai, 278, 373
Stevenson, Coke, 229
Stewart, Potter, 325, 340
Stigler, George, 87
Stockman, David, 167

Stock market (October, 1987), 146
Stone, Harlan Fiske, 342
Stone, Norman, 94
Stoppard, Tom, 362
Strachey, Lytton, 29
Strategic Defense Initiative (SDI), 44, 69, 146, 256
Strauss, Bob, 255
Street people, 301–304
Suares, J. C., 407
Sudan, 39
Suez crisis of 1956, 111
Sukhov, Leonid, 63–65
Sullivan Law of 1911, 179
Sununu, John, 161
Superconducting Super Collider (SSC), 31–33
Supreme Court of the United States, 9, 42, 206, 207, 292–293, 305–306, 309–314, 318, 324–329, 335–358
Surrogate motherhood, 317–319
Swaggart, Jimmy, 40
Swerdlow, Joel L., 281
Swords and Plowshares (Taylor), 121

Taft, Robert, 258
Taft, William Howard, 119, 251, 253, 258
Taiwan, 129
Tammany Hall, 252
Taxation, 146, 147, 152, 157, 162–170, 179, 203, 204, 225, 286
Taylor, A. J. P., 124
Taylor, Frederick, 386, 387
Taylor, Maxwell, 120–121
Taylor, Ralph Waldo, 38
Tebbit, Norman, 107–109
Technology, 89–90
Teenage contraception, 19, 20
Telander, Rick, 209
Television commercials, 19–21, 390–391
Tempting of America, The (Bork), 356–358
Terrorism, 56, 104
Thailand, 129
Thatcher, Margaret, 36, 94, 102, 107–113, 148

Thatcherism, 110
Theocracy, 305
Thomas, Clarence, 329
Thomas, Norman, 262
Thompson, Jim, 252–253
Thompson, William, 309
Thoreau, Henry David, 53, 395, 400
Thornburgh, Richard, 181
Three Soldiers (Dos Passos), 125
Thurmond, Strom, 262, 338
Thurmondism, 338
Tiananmen Square, 41, 53–55, 57, 65, 329
Tibet, 135
Tidiness, 364–366
Tilden, Bill, 397
Time magazine, 99
Titanic, 34
Tocqueville, Alexis de, 137
To Kill a Mockingbird (Lee), 141
Tomlin, Lily, 72
Totalitarianism, 50, 55–57, 67, 85, 91, 129, 131
Tower, John, 41, 155, 218, 242, 279
Transplants, organ, 205
Trauma care, 202–204
Treblinka, Poland, 126–127
Trend-detectors, 388–389
Tribe, Laurence, 336
Trollope, Anthony, 170, 295
Trotsky, Leon, 57, 375
Truman, Harry S, 117, 119, 191, 233, 234, 240, 253, 268, 289
Trump, Donald, 36, 39
Trusting Heart, The: Great News About Type A Behavior (Williams), 384
Tunney, Gene, 397
Turgot, Anne-Robert-Jacques, 163
Twain, Mark, 407
Tyler, Anne, 14
Type A behavior, 384

Ukraine, 73
Ulysses (Joyce), 365
Unemployment, 157, 158, 263–264
United Auto Workers (UAW), 77
United Nations Charter, 119

University of California at Berkeley, 322
University of Connecticut, 321
University of Michigan, 320
Uruguay, 129
USA Today, 389
USS Stark, 36
Utopia in Power (Heller and Nekrich), 59

Valéry, Paul, 53
Valladares, Armando, 35
Vance, Cyrus, 68
Varkonyi, Peter, 83
VCRs (videocassette recorders), 43, 44, 390
Veeck, Bill, 35–36
Verdun, Battle of, 123
Versailles Conference, 131
Victimology, 26
Vienna school of economics, 87
Vietnam War, 121, 135, 214, 254, 373
Villa, Pancho, 130
Voltaire, 137
Voyager 2, 41
Vrdolyak, Edward "Fast Eddie," 223

Walden, George, 98
Waldenbooks, 379
Waldheim, Kurt, 35
Walesa, Lech, 50, 79, 81, 96
Walker, Alice, 362
Walker, Jimmy "Gentleman Jim," 226
Wallace, George, 249, 262
Wallace, Henry, 262
Wall Street Journal, 116
War and Remembrance (Wouk), 123
Warhol, Andy, 38
Warner, John, 355
War of 1812, 151
Warren, Earl, 293, 340, 345
Warren, Edward, 403
Warsaw Pact, 101, 102, 107
Wartime (Fussell), 125
Washington, D.C., 189–190, 376–378
Washington, George, 64, 137, 150, 253, 403
Washington, Harold, 223

Washington Goes to War (Brinkley), 376–378
Washington Monument, 5
Washington Post, 27, 124–125, 198, 351–352
Washington Quarterly, The, 129
Watergate, 240, 254
Watson, George, 113
Weber, Eugen, 405
Wedtech, 40
Welfare state, 110, 149, 164, 252
Wells, H. G., 63
Wesley, John, 149
West Germany, 45, 92–103
West Side Story, 194, 195
West Virginia primary, 252
Whales, 39
Wharton, Edith, 378
Wheatcroft, Geoffrey, 45, 96
White, Byron, 306, 310, 327, 343
White Collar (Mills), 401
Whitman, Walt, 401, 402
Whitmire, Kathryn, 227
Whitten, Jamie, 236
Whyte, William, 401
Wildavsky, Aaron, 157
Wilding, 25–27, 42
Wild One, The, 195, 367
Wilhelm, Kaiser, 397
Will, Geoffrey, 9, 10, 399, 402
Will, Jonathan, 9, 10, 399, 402, 408–409
Will, Victoria, 9, 10, 364, 366, 399, 402, 406, 408
Williams, Redford, 384–385
Williams, Robin, 400–402
Williams, Ted, 398
Williamsburg Bridge, New York, 171
Willkie, Wendell, 258
Wilson, Edmund, 378
Wilson, James Q., 27, 144, 196–199, 301, 302
Wilson, Sloan, 401
Wilson, Woodrow, 76, 119, 130–131, 150, 251, 253, 254
Windsor, Duchess of, 35
Winfrey, Oprah, 42, 388
Wisconsin primary, 252

Wodehouse, P. G., 408
Wolfe, Thomas, 378
Wolfe, Tom, 40, 44, 195, 394–395
Woolf, Virginia, 10
Wordsworth, William, 55
Wouk, Herman, 123
Wright, Jim, 27, 41, 155, 156, 161,
    218, 279
Wright, Joseph, 157
Wrigley Field, Chicago, 380–382
Wriston, Walter, 89–90

Yalta Conference, 79
Yardley, Jonathan, 25
Yellowstone National Park, 39
Yeltsin, Boris, 84
Ypres, third battle of, 4
Yugoslavia, 53, 74

Zakaria, Fareed, 107
Zipf, George, 365
Zita, Empress, 41
Zola, Émile, 405